Baseball's
Fallen Angel

A Major Leaguer's life story of high
expectations, hidden pitfalls and
his ongoing fight in recovery

with Douglas Williams

Eli Grba

Copyright © 2016 by Jon Douglas Williams and Eli Grba

Editor: Susan Pongratz
Cover design: Mike O'Reilly
Photo editor: Mike O'Reilly
Endorsements by: Bobby Richardson
Bob "Buck" Rodgers
Dean Chance

Photographs: Used with permission from the Eli Grba family collection
and the Douglas Williams collection

Trademarks, logos and other photographs used with permission from The Topps Company, Inc. and the Los Angeles Angels of Anaheim American League Baseball Club

ISBN 978-1-4958-0667-4

Published April 2016

INFINITY PUBLISHING
1094 New DeHaven Street, Suite 100
West Conshohocken, PA 19428-2713
Toll-free (877) BUY BOOK
Local Phone (610) 941-9999
Fax (610) 941-9959
Info@buybooksontheweb.com
www.buybooksontheweb.com

ACKNOWLEDGMENTS

I am alive and sober, only by the grace of God and only God. On August 1, 1981, He took the demons of alcohol from me and set my life on a different course. He replaced those demons with blessings of love, freedom and hope: love which I can pass on to my family and friends; freedom from my addiction, and hope that I may help someone avoid the same dreadful disease which stole so much from both me and my family. But long before God miraculously salvaged my life and placed me on the road to recovery, He blessed me by putting so many exceptional people in my life who supported, protected, nurtured and loved me, even when I did not deserve it. It is to these individuals that I own my utmost gratitude for the roles they played in my life, helping me to find my way and helping me make it to the place in life where I am today.

Also, please understand that the individuals who I name specifically in the following paragraphs are by no means an all-inclusive list of everyone I wish to thank. Inasmuch, to those I have failed to mention, and I am sure there are many, I offer my sincere apologies. And be assured that I am grateful for your help and support as well.

First among all is my mother, who sacrificed and worked so hard to make sure I had everything a young boy would need to succeed in life. To provide for me, she worked long hours on jobs which were physically demanding, while in an abusive marriage to my father. I am forever thankful to her for her unwavering love. I am also grateful for the spiritual transformation she experienced, which in a single moment, changed her life, for I am certain that it was that miraculous revelation which pulled her back from the brink of despair and gave her the assurance she needed to persevere in life. The choices she made were all based on what she thought was best for me, and for this, she gave up many of her own dreams, and any hopes she may have had for a social life for herself. At a time when I was ready to quit baseball to make more money working full time in the steel mills, she wouldn't hear of it. She insisted that I pursue my dreams instead of a bigger paycheck. Mom, you were the wind beneath my wings.

I also thank my father, who, in spite of being terribly abusive, was the source of my natural athletic talent. And though I may have inherited his bad, often violent temperament, I am thankful to have rid myself of this trait as part of my recovery from alcohol abuse. Moreover, I credit my mother for giving me a calmer, more gentle demeanor, which is the side of my personality that finally surfaced in my later years and the one I hope to continue to project.

When I was young, I was also blessed to have experienced the love of family, and for that I am grateful to my mother's parents, whom I acknowledge in Serbian, as my grandfather, Deda and my grandmother, Baba. Together, they provided me with love and guidance as well as an occasional dose of discipline when Mom wasn't home. It was Deda, whose name was Nikola, who took me on a trip across town to Wrigley Field, when I was a young boy, to see my first ballgame. He knew very little English, but he knew everything about being a grandfather.

There were my mother's sisters, Mila, Sophie, Mary and Vietta, who spent countless hours babysitting me. These ladies, along with Aunts Seya and Helen, have given me such wonderful memories of my child-hood. I also had my mother's brothers, Adam, Teddy, Marco, Pete and Eli who lovingly gave me their time and attention, playing with me and teaching me how to be a boy. But it was my namesake, Uncle Eli, who as a decorated army veteran and CIA agent, I idolized. There was never an adult in my life whom I admired more.

I was also blessed to have had aunts and uncles from my father's side of the family who were involved in my upbringing, and to those I will be forever thankful. I could never forget Uncle Mike and the encourage-ment and support he gave me. I could always count on him to be in my corner. And my dear Aunt Millie, who married my dad's brother, Mike, recently turned 100 years young! She is one of the most precious ladies I have ever known. May God continue to bless her.

Having to leave home at a young age to attend the Glenwood School for Boys was a frightening experience for me. After getting into trouble at home, I went there lacking discipline and having very little respect for authority. However, I left there a different boy. The staff at Glenwood instilled respect in me and taught me to say "yes, sir" and "no, sir." Above all others at the school, I wish to acknowledge George "Jeep" Pieretti for the example he set for me to follow. He may have never known it, but he inspired me to set my sights high and work hard.

My teenage years were difficult ones. Thankfully, I had men such as Harry Pritikin, my high school coach, who pushed me to play sports. It was Coach Pritikin who would not take "no" for an answer and insisted that I try out for the basketball team, and because of him, I enjoyed playing basketball more than any other sport during my school years.

Another man who did so much to promote sports in our community was Jim Fitzgibbons. Throughout his life, he worked tirelessly to organize athletic programs in our area. Yet it is unfortunate that he received much of the credit and recognition he deserved posthumously. As baseball coach for both the American Legion and semi-pro Sun Dodgers, he instilled confidence in me and worked patiently with me to become a pitcher. Thank you, Coach Fitzgibbons, for all you did for me and our community. May you rest in peace.

Again, as I run the risk of overlooking any individuals who have played a vital part in my life, I will list a few guys who were my closest friends back in the day as I was growing up. There are far too many for me to mention each by name, and to those I have omitted, I ask for your forgiveness.

Ray Aleman has been the best friend a guy could ask for. We had many great times playing sports together and I hope we will get together and relive some of them in the near future. Jack Massucci is another lifelong pal and confidant who was part of our community band of brothers. As youngsters, he and I were inseparable and I am blessed to still count him among my good friends. Nonetheless, I am deeply saddened by the loss of my dear friend, Ron Moreland. Ron, who was one of our gang from the old neighborhood, battled cancer for more than 20 years and was the epitome of strength and determination. With excruciating pain throughout his body, he suffered quietly to the very end. Ron, you were a great guy, who showed tremendous courage in the face of a horrible disease.

The scout who signed me to my first contract in professional baseball was Chuck Koney of the Boston Red Sox. A native of the Chicago area, Mr. Koney had my respect and admiration from the very beginning of our relationship. He was a man of strong moral character who, in spite of suffering a traumatic injury in an explosion which ended his promising career as a player, went on to become one of the more respected scouts in all of baseball. I would learn for myself that Chuck's honesty and integrity weres indicative of the type of organization he represented. I am forever grateful to Chuck for the confidence he showed in me and to everyone involved with the Red Sox system at that time.

I owe the late Harry Dorish, Boston's roving pitching coach, a debt of gratitude for helping to refine me as a pitcher. He stressed the importance of making the baseball move, and in just one quick lesson, he taught me the mechanics of throwing an effective sinker, which became my bread and butter pitch throughout the remainder of my career.

Sheriff Robinson, who was my manager during my early seasons with the Red Sox, was like a father to me. He always had my best interest at heart, but unfortunately I ignored much of the advice he offered. Like so many others, he did his best to steer me clear of trouble, but even Sheriff Robinson had his limitations. He was an extraordinary man who contributed a lot to baseball.

From team owner, Tom Yawkey, down to the clubhouse attendant in the lowest minor league, all employees of the Boston Red Sox were treated with dignity and respect. They were considered the elite organization in all of professional baseball. And today, I am still proud to have been part of the Red Sox family.

I also thank Iron Workers Local 395 in Hammond, Indiana, for providing me with off-season employment for several years while I was in the minor leagues, especially business agent, Pete Parker. Pete saw to it that I was paid very well as I went through the process of learning the value of hard work. And considering that the steel mills paid me two to three times as much as my minor league salary, the job was hard to turn down. But it was Mom who pushed me to go back to training camp each spring. She knew that my heart was with baseball, and insisted that I follow my dreams.

Things were not going the way I had planned when Uncle Sam called me for duty in the spring of 1957. At the time, serving in the United States Army seemed like nothing more than a demoralizing interruption to my career. However, I am fortunate that my time of service fell in between the Korean and Vietnam wars and I was not called into combat. And today I look back at my military service as a rewarding experience, wherein

I learned many valuable lessons about life, played a lot of baseball and encountered an assortment of unforgettable individuals. Among them was my platoon officer, Sergeant Watts, who never called me by name, always referred to me as "Marble Player," and following numerous misadventures on the firing range, eventually taught me how to shoot straight.

There are also many people who were part of the New York Yankees' organization who earned my sincere gratitude. First, among them is the immortal Casey Stengel, who in spite of not allowing me to pitch in the World Series, gave me my first chance in the major leagues. He was another who never called me by my name, but only as "the pitcher with the funny name." Casey, you were one of a kind, and I will never forget you.

There were other managers and coaches in the Yankee system who helped me progress in baseball, including Ralph Houk, a true gentleman, whose trust and support meant so much. Another was Ed Lopat, my pitching coach at Richmond, who was one of the great Yankee pitchers of his era. Ed was an outstanding teacher, who willingly passed on his knowledge and expertise to many young minor league pitchers who went on to have successful careers in the big leagues.

Also, while with the Richmond Virginians, I became close friends with several of my teammates who would prove to be friends for life. Ken Hunt, who was with me with both the Yankees and Angels, would become the brother I never had. He was there for me and my family when the bottom fell out. Thanks also for helping me get back into baseball, recommending me for a job as a minor league pitching coach with the Milwaukee Brewers. Kenny, I miss you terribly.

Deron Johnson, the big man from San Diego, was another great friend. Deron sure knew how to have a good time, but he left us much too soon. Our manager at Richmond was Steve Souchock, a highly decorated veteran of World War II and ex-major leaguer with the Yankees and Detroit Tigers. To Steve, who passed away years ago, I say "Thanks for your help."

Through the years, Johnny James has proven to me what being a good friend is all about. At just five feet, ten inches tall, the tiny right-handed pitcher has been with me through thick and thin. We were first together at Richmond and later teammates in the major leagues with the Yankees and Angels. He was my best man at my wedding and is still among my best friends today. Johnny has established himself as a successful business man and I am blessed too know that he is only a phone call away. Thanks, John for all you've done.

I am fortunate to have had some of the greatest Yankee players of all time as my teammates, but also to have had them as friends. Yogi Berra, Mickey Mantle, Bobby Richardson, Whitey Ford, Gil McDougald, Clete Boyer, Bob Turley, Jim Coates, Johnny Blanchard and Tony Kubek were all great players who knew how to play winning baseball. And I must mention my Yankee roommates, Roger Maris and Bob Cerv, who persuaded me to shop for good clothes, and together, taught me to dress appropriately whenever we went out on the town.

Mr. Gene Autry, the legendary owner of the Los Angeles Angels, was much more than just our boss, he was like a father to each of his players. He had genuine interest and concern for all of his employees and I am honored to have known this great man. To Fred Haney, I say "Thank you. I sincerely regret any troubles I may have caused."

Of major significance in my life was Bill Rigney, the longtime Angels' manager, who in contrast to the many others who helped me, tried every-thing within his power to ruin me. Yet, as I go about life from day to day, I am thankful to the Higher Power of the Universe for giving me the chance to make peace with Bill prior to his death in 2001. Mahatma Gandhi once said, "Forgiveness is the attribute of the strong." Inasmuch, I am eternally thankful to God for the brief opportunity wherein I encountered Billy again, after so many years, and I thank Him for the strength it took to shake his hand. May you rest in peace, Rig.

Other expressions of appreciation go to Ernie Serfas, another wonderful friend and fraternal brother. Ernie was another of my best men as well as my mentor and coach, many years ago when I first embarked on my journey in Freemasonry.

For my dear aunt, Mila, I have the utmost respect and admiration for having the gumption to kick me, her drunken nephew, out of her house. After numerous warnings, she and her husband, Manny were forced to put me out. Thank you, first of all, for caring enough to take me in, and also for having the courage to do what was right when I failed you.

To my first wife, Bonnie, I am forever thankful to you for our two wonderful children. When we were first together, many people saw us as the picture-perfect couple, the real-life version of *Ken and Barbie*. But back then, I had no idea about how a marriage should work or how to be a husband. Through the years I have often thought about the turbulent times in our marriage and asked myself, "Why did we?" But whenever I see our daughter, Stacy, and our son, Nick, I receive my answer.

I am extremely proud of Stacy, who served seven and a half years overseas with the United States Air Force, and her husband, Rich Draves, a retiree of the City of Tucson, Arizona Fire Department. The two of you have done quite well for yourselves and I look forward to your next visit.

Also, an Air Force veteran, Nick served for 27 years. He and his wife, Stacia, have given me two exceptional grandsons, Devin who is 20 years old and Landon who is 15. In The Book of Proverbs we read, "Children's children are a crown to the aged." And for both of you, I will always want the best that life has to offer.

I am tremendously saddened by the passing of my dear friend, Dean Chance, who only weeks ago helped me by endorsing the writing of this book. Yet unfortunately, he will not be around to join me in celebrating its upcoming release. Dean, you were one hell of a pitcher and an even better friend.

Each day I offer a word of thanks for my wife, Reggie, who has given me her undying love and support throughout the 24 years we have been together. She is my best friend and soul mate. I admire her for always being the lady she is, and for all she has done in her life.

I am also forever indebted to the writer of this book, Doug Williams, a kind, soft-feeling person who was willing to take on the difficult task of writing my story. Thanks, pal for your patience and hard work.

My gratitude is also extended to our editor, Susan Pongratz, a gem of a lady, who worked tirelessly to make corrections and keep things in order. Thanks Susan, for inserting a tender female tone in the places where it was needed. Also, I give a big "thank you" to Mike O'Reilly, our photo editor and graphics designer. Good job, Mike! The front and back covers are fantastic and the images inside look great.

Even if I could go on, there could never be enough pages to acknowledge all of my friends, in and outside of baseball and everyone in my family. I have tried my best, but I am sure there are still some who have been overlooked. Please accept this as my best effort at an impossible task.

I feel bad for the doubters, may God bless you all. This project has been a most rewarding undertaking and I am very blessed to see it through to its completion. Most importantly, thanks be to the Higher Power, whom I call God. I know it was He who has been watching me from the very beginning. I thank Him for giving me this privilege and may this writing be used for the good of many.

Eli Grba,
Florence, Alabama
November, 2015

TABLE OF CONTENTS

FOREWORD

It was the 1960s. I was plundering through my collection of old baseball cards, pointing out a few selected favorites to my nephew, Alden. Being almost 15 years old, I felt the time had come for me to explain the birds and bees of card-collecting to my willing seven-year-old relative, if he were to ever assume his rightful place among the who's who of bubblegum card collectors. For this rite of passage to be properly executed, it was my responsibility to see that he could readily interpret the statistics on the back of each one: the player's height and weight, innings pitched, batting average, E.R.A. and so forth.

As a caring and concerned uncle, it was also my job to make sure Alden was briefed on some of the more advanced points associated with baseball trading cards, such as that both Mets and Yankees had a "NY" on their caps; that a "P" could be either Pirates or Phillies; and even though it could not be detected in most photographs, the Los Angeles Angels had a peculiar-looking halo which encircled the tops of their caps, an odd but innovative feature, picked up by only the most astute collectors.

Proper pronunciation of player names was another facet of baseball card-collecting we were required to cover. Names like Ernie Banks, Jimmie Hall and Wally Moon were never a problem. However, there were some ballplayers with unusual ethnic surnames which even caused problems for an articulate high school freshman like me. Hank Aguirre, Jim Pagliaroni and Jim Lefebvre were always tough. And had the Minnesota Twins not made it on TV for the 1965 World Series, I wouldn't have known where to start with a name like Zoilo Versalles. Yet, the big quandary for that particular day did not occur until Alden and I reached even deeper into that old green picnic basket full of cards and pulled out a 1963 Topps card, number 231, Eli Grba.

"Who's this guy?" my nephew asked, handing me the card. Slowly and carefully I examined the front, took a quick glance at the picture and then began to study the text, trying to come up with verbal sounds that would fit the vowel-deficient arrangement of letters which was the player's last name. Next, I turned the card over and began to read from the reverse side, as if that would help solve the problem.

"I don't know," I finally confessed. "He's a pitcher for the Angels. He's right-handed, and he's a pretty big guy. It says here that he weighs 212 pounds!" Alden stared upward in disbelief. It wasn't often that his all-knowing uncle couldn't provide a proper answer. I began to stall, while I struggled to come up with a response sensible enough to satisfy a second-grader. "It looks like Ellie Grabber to me," I offered, trying to sound confident. "Yeah, that's it," I assured him, "Ellie Grabber. I think I've heard it said that way before." Alden nodded with approval. He seemed perfectly comfortable with the butchered pronunciation. If the answer came from his Uncle Doug, then it was good enough for him. At almost 15-years-old, his Uncle Doug knew just about everything!

Now the years have slowly passed, almost 50 of them to be precise, and Alden and I are still as close as an uncle and nephew can be. But there can be no comparing our separate stockpiles of accomplishments, as he goes to work each day, teaching at an affluent four-year university, applying the attributes of his PhD, while I continue to cling to my collection of aged and tattered baseball cards. Nevertheless, over time I have made considerable progress in pronouncing the names of some of my boyhood baseball heroes which had me stumped years ago, Eli's being among them. However, should I need help today with any big word or any sort of unusual name, it is reassuring to know that the help and guidance of Dr. B. Alden Starnes is only a phone call away, confirming that some writers have more resources than others.

On a hot afternoon in August 2012, I received an unexpected email from Byron Robar, a baseball fan and friend of Eli Grba, who lives in West Kelowna, British Columbia. Byron, a retired officer of the Royal Canadian Mounted Police, was familiar with some of the baseball biographies I had written and explained how Eli, who was interested in publishing his own memoirs, had been unsuccessful in his search to find a compatible co-author to help with the project. "Eli has a great story to share," he pointed out. "He had all the makings for a great baseball career, pitching for the Yankees, and being the first player selected by the Los

Angeles Angels in the 1960 expansion draft. He was destined to be the star player of the franchise, but then alcohol addiction took it all from him. It should make a great book," he insisted. "And I believe the two of you would work well together."

American author and philosopher, Henry David Thoreau said, "If one advances confidently in the direction of his dreams, and endeavors to live the life he has imagined, he will meet with a success unexpected in common hours." Inasmuch, I believe that each of us has been placed on this earth with specific missions to perform. However, for most of us, discovering our own unique divine purpose and then recognizing it as such can be difficult. To assist us, there are several points we should assess when seeking our special calling, including our passions and talents, our willingness to disregard the expectations of others, and our conclusions about who will benefit from our work.

We should also expect to see signs of assurance, which will tell us that we are pursuing our intended path. Among the most telling is the realization of how amazingly fast the elements for success will fall into place, once we get on the right track. When we are fulfilling the purpose for which God placed us on earth, the things we need to reach our goal will be provided. The time, place and tools needed to do the work will show up on cue. Individuals with the necessary experience and skills will suddenly appear, willing to help, ready with advice and prepared with answers to all of your questions. This is one of God's fundamental laws of the Universe. It is the basis for how an ex-mountie in British Columbia can bring together a virtually unknown baseball author in Virginia and an ex-major league pitcher in Alabama. It is how prayers are answered and how, through God's power, dreams are turned into reality.

It has been a pleasure to work with Eli Grba for the past three years. It has been rewarding to find that he is much more than a former athlete who wants to share his life story. He is a big man who never claimed to be perfect. He is strong man, secure enough to own up to his mistakes and compassionate enough to want others to benefit from them. He loves his wife and family, his country and he still finds a way to love baseball, the game that turned sour on him many years ago. Eli Grba is one of the fortunate ones among us who has identified his own unique divine purpose, which is to continue to give back to this Universe as much as he can for as long as he can. He has given me his trust and friendship, for which I am forever grateful.

I am also grateful to Byron Robar for suggesting that Eli and I would be a good fit. That was a great call. It's too bad that Byron is not an umpire!

And last, but certainly not least, I owe a great deal of thanks to my loving wife, Mary Lou, for being considerate and turning down the volume on the TV whenever I tried to write. When we were married in September 2014, Mary Lou was not very interested in keeping up with baseball. But, slowly and surely she is starting to come around. I figure that maybe, just maybe, in another year or two she will be a die-hard fan of the Cleveland Indians just like me!

CHAPTER 1
ARE YOU SURE YOU'VE GOT THE RIGHT GUY?

T he lazy Tennessee River stretches southward across the state line and down into Alabama before it abruptly breaks to the northwest. The river is one of the beautiful wonders of nature as it widens and then narrows again, several times, winding its way toward my home in Florence. I've been told that it's the huge volume of clean water that makes the Tennessee the perfect river for catching some of the finest smallmouth bass and blue catfish in the world. The river is a fisherman's paradise and I feel as if I've entered my own little corner of heaven every time I grab my bait and fishing rod and spend a few hours fishing along her northern banks.

Sure, the fishing is fantastic and I've even managed to hook a few citation-size beauties over the years, but the perfection runs even deeper. Along with the crystal blue water, there is that beautiful Dixie sky which often matches the river with both clarity and color. Then there's the mesmerizing peace and calmness that is broken only by an occasional bird's call or a distant motorboat.

For me, fishing is therapeutic; it's what I do; it's what I enjoy. My time at the river's edge is the pleasure of my life. And with a handful of my local fishing buddies, I'm there year-round, experiencing the changes of the weather and the seasonal moods of the catfish and bass. It lies somewhere between a pastime and a passion, yet fishing is something that I stumbled upon almost by accident just a few years ago. And for that very reason, I find myself relishing every minute I have a rod in my hands. I should have slowed my life down and allowed myself time to discover it long before I did.

While cruising along the highway, I gripped the steering wheel, and my hands began to warm up a little as I drove back to the house. It had been a bright but cold January afternoon of fishing and the heat inside my car was a welcome relief. It had been the sort of day that looked inviting while you were indoors, looking out through a window. However, the cold temperatures and brisk winds were well disguised by the brilliant sunshine. I had enjoyed spending the afternoon outside, fishing and chatting with a few friends on the marina dock, but it was the pleasure of catching a couple of good-sized bass that had turned a nice day into a very rewarding day. As I got closer to my neighborhood, I thought about getting one of those popular bumper stickers that say, *"The worst day of fishing is better than the best day at work!"*

I stopped the car at the end of my driveway to check the mailbox. After driving so long in my warm car, I was in no rush to get out. I could see that my wife Reggie hadn't made it home from work, but I knew I would still get an enthusiastic welcome once I got inside. I collected the mail, parked the car, and wasted little time unlocking the front door. Inside, I was greeted by two energetic Shih Tzus who couldn't wait to show me how much I had been missed.

I paused in the kitchen and tossed the car keys onto the counter top. I started to thumb thoughtlessly through the mail. *Just once it would be nice to get more checks than bills,* I wished, trying to think positively. *But I'll never see it happen.*

Suddenly, there in the stack of letters was an envelope that caught my eye, one with a colorful logo and a return address in the upper left corner:

Los Angeles Angels of Anaheim
2000 East Gene Autry Way
Anaheim, Ca. 92806

What could they possibly want with me? I asked myself. *It has been almost five decades since I played baseball for them, and even then, we did not part ways on the best of terms.*

I opened and read the letter intently, completely ignoring the dogs clamoring for my attention. It seemed that the Angels were about to enter a special season, one where they would commemorate the 50th anniversary of their franchise. *Could it really have been that long?* I wondered. After all, I was with them in the beginning when they started in 1961 and remained an Angel until '63.

The letter was from Tim Mead, one of the team's VPs, who carefully described how the Angels were looking forward to the upcoming 2011 season and how they planned to celebrate their "Golden Anniversary." "Throughout the season, we hope to bring in as many members of the original Angels as we can, along with other former Angel luminaries who have left a mark on our team's history." He went on to say, "We are inviting you and your family to be with us in Anaheim and ask that you will join us in our celebration activities."

I'll confess that Mead's letter did not come as a total surprise to me after receiving a phone call a couple of weeks earlier from an old friend Scottie Keene, who phoned me from his home in Southern California. Scottie worked as an Angels' batboy many years ago when I was with the club. Yet, he continues to keep abreast of the Angels' affairs and somehow always gets the latest dope on what's going on in the business. He called to give me a heads-up about the plans the Angels were making for their anniversary season. He also mentioned that I would likely be asked to take part. But still, I felt a little disappointed by what Scottie reported, telling me that they planned to have an ex-Angel throw out the ceremonial first pitch at each of the 82 home games during the year.

Now, please, don't misunderstand. I saw this plan as a grand idea and I would be honored to participate whenever my turn came up. Yet, I still carried hopes of seeing my old friends, the fellows I had played with. I still preferred an arrangement that would reunite as many of my old teammates from the original 1961 team as possible, while there is still time to organize such a gathering. I wanted to catch up with those guys who were close to me during a time that was special and exciting for all of us. I was longing to see old friends like Ken McBride, Dean Chance, Jerry Casale, and our team's own "Boy Wonder," Jim Fregosi. Yet, Tim Mead's letter did nothing to suggest that it would happen.

I looked up from the page and stared out through the window and into the backyard. Suddenly, my thoughts came back down to earth. *I'd better let these dogs go outside,* I reminded myself. *Reggie will be home soon and we will need to make plans for dinner.*

Over the following weeks, the fishing was good, but the weather was showing no signs of yielding to spring. That's about the time I received an unexpected phone call from Tim Mead in early February.

"We would like for you to be with us for our home opener," he offered. "The team will start the season on the road, but will arrive home to play the Toronto Blue Jays on Friday, April 8th, and we would like you to throw out the first pitch that night. We feel that you should be here with us," he urged. "We want you there for the ceremonies we have planned to kick off our anniversary season."

"Wait just a minute, Tim," I countered. "I don't get it. You want to fly me and my family out there to Anaheim for the first home game?" I pried. "Why me? Are you sure you've got the right guy?"

"Sure, I've got the right guy!" he confirmed. "You'll be the first of our former players to be honored this season. You're the first we want to recognize for playing a significant role in our history."

"That's just wonderful!" I responded, as I scrambled for my next words. "And who have you chosen to catch me? Have you tried calling one of my old catchers like Bob Rodgers or Earl Averill?"

"Not yet, Eli," he confessed. "That's one of the details we haven't addressed. But trust us. We're going to line up someone who deserves the honor, someone who'll do a good job. Right now, we've only made our choice for pitcher, and that's you!

"But why me?" I asked. "Why don't you folks pick one of the all-time great players with the club? Why not choose someone like Nolan Ryan, the greatest pitcher to ever wear an Angel uniform?"

"Well, let me give you a little insight on this," Tim proposed. "It was unanimous, Eli. At our last staff meeting, we took into account every name we could think of, and of all the possibilities. We all agreed that you would be our best choice. You were the Angels' first pick in the first ever expansion draft back in 1960, which made you the first player listed on our first roster. You were our starting pitcher in the first game for our franchise, and you won that game on opening day back in '61. You're the guy who got this team started, Eli. That's why our staff was in full agreement. You were the first Angel!"

There was a short pause in our conversation as I struggled to come up with a response. Tim could sense my emotions were building and waited politely for my reaction. I noticed a crack in my voice when I finally spoke.

"I really don't know what to say to you, Tim," I blurted. "I am flattered by all of this and I am completely overwhelmed by your offer. I'll be there, my friend! That's for sure. Reggie and I will be there!"

My eyes started to glisten with tears the very instant I placed the receiver back on the hook. I couldn't seem to trust my own thoughts enough to believe that Tim's call had really taken place. Without knowing what was in store, I would soon find that this moment would be just the first of many surreal moments I'd find waiting for me just around the corner.

Thoughts swirled in my head. *Maybe it's all just a dream. Surely, there is a whole new generation of folks in charge of operations for the Los Angeles Angels. Maybe they never heard the full story about why I left the team so abruptly in August of 1963. Did they bother to research the circumstances? Did any of them know that my relationship with the Angels had soured to the point that I was benched and saw no action over the final two months of the season? Maybe it's all forgotten. If not, I'd like to believe it's all forgiven.* So many questions ran through my mind.

Regardless, it's all water under the bridge. Now, it's a half century later and so much has changed. The world has changed and so has the game of baseball. But even more, I'm still here to recognize and appreciate the many changes in me.

It was obvious from the very start that Tim Mead and his staff are among the best when it comes to scheduling, securing accommodations and setting an itinerary for their guests. The Angels welcomed us as if we were royalty. The flight into Santa Ana's John Wayne Airport, our transportation from the airport, and our hotel rooms were all first class. For the big event, Reggie and I had tried to gather our family and some of our closest friends, but as is often the case, everyone was busy with their own families, jobs and personal commitments.

Naturally, my son, Nick, who is currently a 26-year Air Force veteran living in Yukon, Oklahoma, had too much on his schedule to break away for the trip. We would have loved to have had him, his wife, Stacia, and their boys, Devin and Landon, with us in California, but Nick's boss Uncle Sam, had too many other things for Nick to do. On the other hand, we did have a little better luck with my daughter, Stacy, who lives in Arizona, not far from Tucson. While her husband Rich couldn't be with us, Stacy, another veteran of the U.S. Air Force, caught a flight to L.A. and arrived in town in plenty of time for the start of the game.

It was back in the summer of 1997 that one of my most enduring friendships came to a sudden end with the unexpected passing of my former teammate Kenny Hunt. Kenny and I had played together in the minor leagues and again in the majors with the Yankees and Angels. With less than a month's difference in our ages, we had grown up together in baseball and his death was a huge loss for me personally. *If only he could see this,* I mused. *He would be as happy and proud as anyone.*

Taking matters into my own hands, I telephoned Ken's widow Sherry at her home just south of Los Angeles. A lovely lady with a congenial personality, there was no doubt that she would enjoy herself and in our own way, we could remember Kenny together on that special night.

"Come on out to the ballgame and you'll be part of our family," I urged her. "It's not far from your house and I'll make sure to have tickets waiting for you at the stadium."

After just a brief pause to think it over, Sherry accepted the invitation and also agreed to bring her daughter along for the fun.

To go along with the Angels' home-opener hype, we arrived in Anaheim a day early, allowing time for any interviews and photo shoots they had scheduled. We hardly had time to get settled in our room before I got a call from *USA Today* photographer Robert Hanashiro. A personable fellow who truly enjoyed his work, Robert offered to drive to our hotel and take me out for a short photography session just outside of the stadium. I took this as an opportunity to hook up with my longtime friend, Scott Keene. The two of us had done a good job of staying in touch, yet in spite of the phone calls, it had been years since we had seen each other. He lived nearby, so I called him from the hotel and invited him to come along.

Throughout the short drive over to the ballpark, the reality of the times had yet to take hold of me. At the time I was still a bit apprehensive, not quite sure just how much of a "special guest" I really was. *Was there a place for me in all of this?* I wondered. *Were they really expecting me to show up?*

Robert coasted his car to a stop in front of the park's main entrance. Scottie and his mom were already there waiting for us. Before I could step out onto the sidewalk, Robert was looking skyward as if he had spotted a spaceship and was squawking to catch my attention.

"Check it out, Mr. Grba," he yelled from across his parked car, pointing toward the exterior of the stadium. "There's your answer!" he declared. "Now there should be no doubt about whether or not they are expecting you! You're the guest of honor!"

I looked upward toward the outside wall of the ballpark, at the massive structure that encircles the entire stadium. There, high above ground level and fastened to the masonry work at each of its four corners was a huge banner-like sign. It must have measured at least 20 feet square and it was a giant portrait of me! "Eli Grba" it read below my picture, "1961 - 1963."

"Holy smokes!" I gasped, stunned by the giant-sized likeness of myself. I was suddenly struck by the magnitude of the moment. So much to see, so much to feel, and I've yet to go inside!

It was Jenny Price, the Angels' Director of Special Events who literally kept the wheels rolling during the entire visit. It was Jenny who greeted us at the airport and gave us a lift over to our hotel. And it was Jenny, knowing the streets around Anaheim like the back of her hand, who scooted me over to the ballpark for the big game in the team's colorful Los Angeles Angels of Anaheim van on the following afternoon.

The California sun was sinking fast as we drove into the restricted parking area and Jenny pulled the van into her reserved space. "This place will be packed tonight," she warned, "and it's as chilly as we've ever had for our first game."

As I closed the van door and stepped out into the cool dry air, I instantly caught a whiff of that unmistakable ballpark smell. It was a combination of freshly mowed grass, smoking charcoal, roasting peanuts and other aromas that I had missed in recent years. It was a familiar smell

I had known for much of my life and I hadn't been mindful of its gaping absence until this moment.

I followed Jenny through one corridor and then another. Then, into an elevator and further on, into an area far removed from the grandstand. We were well away from the public and on our way to the team's press room. Jenny was constantly talking as we walked, but there were so many straying thoughts buzzing through my head, that I'll admit, I had no clue about what she was telling me. We stopped in a foyer outside the press room, located close to several team offices. The central reception area was bustling with activity. Team personnel were rushing past us, each on a mission, hurrying to take care of some last minute detail. Some were on cell phones, others were jabbering into walkie-talkies as they went by. Tonight was opening night, an event that had been months in the making, and there was no room for mix-ups or miscommunications.

Inside the press room, Jenny and I were met by Tim Mead, who no doubt had prepared himself for cold weather. Not only was he wearing a stylish windbreaker, zipped the top, but he was also clutching a bright red Angels' team jacket by the collar, letting it drape across his shoulder.

"Welcome back to the Angels, Eli," he offered with a big smile and a hearty handshake. He immediately asked about my flight and our room and was intent on seeing that our every need was met. "Are you by yourself?" he asked.

"Yes, I'm alone for now. Reggie is still back at the hotel," I reminded him. "She and my daughter, Stacy, will be out here later in time for the game."

"That's right, and we are also expecting Mrs. Ken Hunt and her daughter," Tim recalled. "It's all been taken care of, Eli," he assured me. "We have tickets for some great box seats waiting downstairs at the ticket office, and we'll see that everyone is comfortable and enjoys the game. We also hope that you will have time to watch some of the game after you get finished with all you have to do. We want you to know right up front, Eli," he quipped, "this is not just a big night for you, it's also a very special night for us, and we are so pleased to have you and your family with us."

A handsome, well-groomed gentleman who looked to be in his early sixties approached just as there was a break in our conversation. With him was a lovely dark-haired lady, who seemed completely at ease in spite of all of the commotion around us. It became clear that Tim had been expecting the couple and was ready to make introductions.

"Eli Grba, I would like for you to meet Mr. and Mrs. Arte Moreno. Arte is our club's owner and CEO."

"Eli Grba," Arte said with an anxious tone. "It's an honor to have you with us tonight and it's great to finally meet you. I know that we don't have much time right now," he continued, "but we'll be sure to get together a little later on."

"I guess we better be heading downstairs," Jenny interrupted, after taking a quick glimpse at her watch. "There's a golf cart waiting for us at the field level gate and from there, I'll give you a ride over to the dugout."

"Oh, there's one other thing before you go," Tim remembered, as he started to step away. "This Angels' jacket is for you, Eli," he offered, holding it open for me to slip it on. It's a little gift we thought you would appreciate. And you should know better than anyone how valuable a good jacket can be to a pitcher on a chilly night like this!"

We scurried through a long hallway that stretched under the grandstand. Jenny's hurried pace indicated that there wasn't much time to waste. We walked on to a huge open area illuminated by dozens of high-powered flood lights, each housed in a protective steel cage. A hefty fellow in an Angels' uniform was leaning over, picking up baseballs from the floor and tossing them into a large canvas bag. "Hi Mickey" Jenny snapped. "It's time to get another season underway!"

"That's right, Jenny," the man replied, looking up. "And we're ready. It's gonna be a great year for us."

Jenny stepped away and gave the guy a friendly pat on the back. "Eli, this our hitting coach, Mickey Hatcher," she said, turning to me. "He's one of my favorites."

"And you must be Eli Grba," the coach deduced, offering his hand. "I heard that you're here to toss out the first pitch tonight."

"That's what they tell me, Mickey. I'm here to do whatever these folks ask of me. But I still haven't been told who my catcher will be. Do you guys have any ideas about that?" I asked.

"Not a clue," Mickey admitted, as both he and Jenny shrugged. "But if you have a minute or two, I'm going to suggest that you take some time to warm up that arm while you're down here. You'll get only one pitch and you'll want to make it count."

I accepted Mickey's offer and threw several baseballs against a large net located off to the side of the batting cage. "That ought to do it, Coach," I concluded after spotting my last couple of pitches in the strike zone. "I don't want to keep Jenny waiting. She's a very busy lady, ya' know!"

We sped along the stadium wall and headed for the home team dugout. But it wasn't until Jenny brought the golf cart to a stop that I felt the butterflies in my stomach swarming like never before. *Holy crap! Is this really happening to me? What am I doing here?* I looked up into the stands and suddenly realized that I was surrounded by thousands upon thousands of fans, all there to observe the start of a special season, a season that marked 50 years of Los Angeles Angels' baseball. So many years had gone by, some good and some not so good, since I last walked onto the field at a major league ballpark. My nervous uncertainty was as real as it was back in July of 1959, when I made my pitching debut in Yankee Stadium. And this was only the start of the evening.

A chilling gust of wind blew past just as I stepped down into the dugout. I was fastening another snap on the front of my new jacket when I spotted Tim Mead, not far away, doling out some last minute instructions to some of his staff. I was tempted to just walk up to him and ask him who my catcher would be, but then I reminded myself to be a grateful guest instead of a pest.

A handful of the Angels players were chatting and milling around near the bench and I couldn't help but be impressed by their size and muscular physiques. They seemed oblivious to who I was or the fact that I was a special guest. I began to doubt if any of those young athletes even noted my very presence. For a moment, I sensed that time had passed me by. Maybe to them, I was nothing more than an extinct creature from a bygone era. *They don't know who I am,* I reasoned, *and don't care who I used to be.* In my inner silence I felt a quick flash of self pity, which was halted suddenly by a friendly voice coming from behind me.

"Hi, Eli, my name is Torii Hunter." I turned around to find a muscle-bound hulk of a young man smiling and reaching out to shake my hand. "I just want to take a minute of your time to introduce myself and to say thank you for what you did to get this franchise started."

Naturally, I knew all about Torii, the Angels all-star outfielder. I had kept tabs on his career ever since he joined the Halos three seasons earlier. I knew from the start that he would pan out to be a great acquisition for the team and his numbers over the past two seasons had proven me to be on the mark.

"I want to wish you good luck, Eli, and say thanks again for joining us tonight," he continued, shaking my hand vigorously. He spun around and hurried to rejoin some of his teammates at a spot farther down the bench.

"Thanks, Torii, I'm gonna need it!" I replied. "I'm going to need all the luck I can get tonight, just to get the ball over the plate!"

Beside the impression he made on me with his tremendous baseball skills, this super-star athlete impressed me as a young man with class and integrity. He will never know how much his kind words did to restore my faith in the young high-salaried ballplayers of today. *At least there's one of them who recognizes what the old guys did for this game, so many years ago. Hopefully, there are more out there like him.*

In a futile attempt to work some of the tension out of my body, I stretched my arms outward and then over my head. After years of chronic rotator cuff issues and countless injections to stave off the pain, my aching shoulders were telling on me. Still I wasn't about to let a little discomfort and stiffness get in the way on what was going to be one of the most monumental nights in my life.

The "Big A" appeared to be filled to capacity, yet there were still many fans up on the concourse and in the aisles scurrying to get their food and find their seats. *What a difference time can make,* I pondered, recalling how small our home game crowds were in tiny Wrigley Field in South L.A. back in the early '60s. During those same years, it was only a few miles across town that the Dodgers packed their house on a regular basis. We knew that our organization was in its infancy and accepted the fact that we were the new kids on the block.

I trudged back up the steps and joined Tim and Arte on the grass in front of the Angels' bench. Near the coach's box stood a large gathering of media folks standing around with cameras and microphones ready, poised like a band of mounted hunters waiting for the fox to be released.

Suddenly, I got the answer I had been waiting for. I finally took notice of Mr. Moreno's left hand and realized that he was wearing a black baseball glove! He caught me staring at the mitt and admitted that the cat was out of the bag. He pounded his fist into the pocket a few times and gave me a sheepish look.

"I'm going to be your catcher tonight, Eli," he confessed. "And I hope you'll make this easy for me. I'm going to be mighty nervous out there in front of this big crowd, and I sure hope I don't miss the ball."

"What about me?" I chuckled, but still genuinely concerned. "I just hope and pray that I can get the ball to you and don't skip it in the dirt!"

He gave me a smile and an encouraging pat on the back. "We'll do all right," he said with assurance.

To a fellow with such confidence, I wasn't about to reveal anything about my trips to the local batting cage back home in Florence, where I threw countless baseballs against a net, just to prepare myself for tonight's special pitch. I was conscious of what the years had done to my creaking shoulders, and I still wasn't sure how much I could trust my tired old pitching arm on such a cold night, not considering the added restrictions of a bulky jacket.

Suddenly, like a voice from heaven, the sound of the public address announcer cut through the chill and asked for everyone's attention.

"LADIES AND GENTLEMEN, MAY I HAVE YOUR ATTENTION, PLEASE?
IT IS TIME TO INTRODUCE YOUR 2011 LOS ANGELES ANGELS OF ANAHEIM!

"Okay, Eli. It's time for you guys to get ready," Tim advised. "After the player introductions and the National Anthem, you and Arte will need to take your places on the field."

The visiting Blue Jays were introduced first and within a few short minutes the starting line-ups and team introductions were complete, leaving the baselines full of managers, coaches and baseball players standing shoulder to shoulder. During the final notes of the National Anthem, my heart began to pound like a jackhammer. I started to make my way to a spot just in front of the pitcher's mound and wondered if my shaky knees were up for the challenge. All the while there was black and white action footage of me streaming on the *Diamond Vision* screen beyond the centerfield wall. I heard bits and pieces of what seemed like a lengthy introduction, blaring over the P.A., yet it sounded as if it were coming from hundreds of miles away. I recall hearing indistinct phrases, such as "Let's welcome back the first Angel, Eli Grba" and "Angels' owner and CEO, Arte Moreno, will be doing the catching."

I knew that my pitching had suffered from diminishing velocity over the years, so I reminded myself to take it slow and easy as I started into my motion. With less than mediocre speed, this letter-high "fastball" was as straight as an arrow, showing absolutely no trace of movement. It was a pitch that a slugger like Torii Hunter could have belted over the wall and into the next county. Yet to a thunderous ovation, it hit its target and landed squarely in the pocket of Arte's glove! I breathed a sigh of relief and waved to the crowd as Arte and I left the infield. He plopped the commemorative anniversary baseball with its colorful logo into my hands and gave me a final pat on the shoulder. "Hang on to this," he barked, above the noise of the crowd. "It's yours to keep."

"It's over!" I mumbled under my breath. "Now I'll breathe a little easier."

I continued to wave my cap to the crowd and purposely savored the applause until it began to fade. Suddenly I thought about how few ever get a chance to feel the roar of 44,000 happy baseball fans as it cascades down onto the playing field and how grateful I am to be one of them.

I had been asked to appear at an hour-long autograph session after the ceremony on the stadium concourse. The response was a warm one and the waiting line of fans and collectors was longer than I could have ever imagined. I signed my name countless times on a wide array of items, many of which were linked to the old days and my career as an Angel. There were folks who brought bubblegum cards, old photos, newspaper clippings, even a few old-styled Angels caps. It was wonderful to chat with so many fans, both young and old, many who remembered me as a player and some who had only heard of me through their parents or grandparents.

Later in the evening I was asked to spend a little time in the Angels' broadcast booth with Terry Smith and former all-star pitcher, Mark Gubicza, a couple of true professionals. We had a fun time doing an on-air interview while the game was in progress. For almost two innings, we discussed the early days of Angels' baseball, back when hopes were high and attendance was low. We sang the praises of the club's late owner, Gene Autry, who was not only one of the true cowboy movie idols of the past, but was also a daring pioneer in the world of major league baseball. The three of us concurred that it is due to the resolve and vision of Mr. Autry that an American League franchise ever found a home in Southern California.

It was the late innings of the game before I could join Reggie, Stacy, and the others in our box seats behind the Angels' dugout. Instead of a hero's welcome, I got there only to find that the curtain was quickly coming down on my short-lived ego trip. "Did you gals save me a seat?" I asked, standing patiently in the aisle.

"Sure we did, Dad!" Stacy piped up, preoccupied by the action on the field.

"Absolutely, Honey! Reggie confessed in a half-hearted tone. "Where have you been and what have you been doing? You've been missing a great ballgame!"

The Halos fell to the Blue Jays that night in a close one, 3-2. Yet personally, it was so much more than a game that was won or lost. It was a personal victory of grand proportions. It was an event that embodied a personal triumph within my life. It closed the door on doubts that I had been carrying for years. That night I found answers for myself and answered questions that others may have had about me. Earlier, I had been hesitant to face the truth about how the game of baseball and its fans would remember me. I had given years of thought wondering if my brief career had been misplaced or simply forgotten by some who may have chosen to do so. Would I be remembered as someone who didn't appreciate the chance he had been given? Was I thought of as a promising young pitcher with lots of potential who carelessly tossed it all away? Or would I be remembered as a player who, in spite of his shortcomings, gave the game of baseball the best he had for as long as he could?

We were both physically and emotionally drained by the time Reggie and I returned to our hotel. It had been an incredible experience, truly a night to remember. From the recognition and accolades of the evening, I had discovered that I was well remembered and still alive in the hearts of a lot of good people, baseball fans who appreciate the insignificant things

I accomplished on the ball field many years ago. It's truly the best I could have hoped for.

I had just witnessed firsthand how time can heal. I had just seen how, at times the universe can be forgiving. I had experienced what it was like to be welcomed, vindicated and forgiven, by some I may have disappointed or offended in the distant past. I also learned that I, too, am able to forgive. Forgiveness is a powerful word!

Here I am with the special commemorative anniversary baseball. Mr. Moreno said it was mine to keep.

CHAPTER 2
HOME IS WHERE YOUR JOURNEY BEGINS

I t was in his late nineteenth century novel, *The Time Machine*, that science fiction author H. G. Wells wrote, "For after the battle comes the quiet." And so it was for me in the days that followed my "triumphant" return to Los Angeles. It was a time for personal reflection and a time for me to digest the emotional impact which had caught me by surprise once the applause and fanfare had ended. It was time to return to Alabama and for my life to get back to normal.

We flew directly into the sun on our return flight, passing high above the dark, jagged Rocky Mountains. Moments later I found myself staring out of the tiny window again, this time peering down at the beige flatlands of Arizona and then New Mexico. Rather than pull out the tattered magazine stashed in the seat pocket in front of me and wasting time looking at senseless ads for overpriced items, I decided to take advantage of the peace and quiet and entertain myself with my thoughts. I had many to choose from, but my most prevalent thoughts were of the special people in my life who were unable to be with me at such a special time.

While it meant so much to have Reggie and Stacy and the others with me, my mind kept drifting back to family members, my parents, my aunts and uncles, my grandchildren and others who could not be there. In particular, I thought about my dear mother, who had passed away tragically almost 40 years earlier in an early morning commuter train disaster. I assured myself that even if she could not have been there physically, I have no doubt that she had been there with me in spirit. I felt her presence and sensed her pride. And then there was my Aunt Sophie, my mother's sister, who had practically raised me as a child. I had phoned her from my home back in February to tell her about my part in the big celebration, knowing all along that she would never make the effort to come. Nevertheless, I was confident that her thoughts were with me.

My mother had passed away tragically almost 40 years earlier, but I know she was there with me in spirit.

Then there was my "other family," my Angel teammates from the early 1960s. They were a special bunch of guys who, even as young men, recognized the value of camaraderie and how important it was to our ballclub. Throughout the entire anniversary celebration, I felt the void left by them, especially those who had passed on. We had been like a band of brothers who had shared so many of life's ups and downs together.

I couldn't help but be mindful of a time when we were on the road, playing a weekend series against the Orioles in Baltimore. There was a group of 16 of us who went out to dinner together. There were Dean Chance, Bo Belinsky, Lee Thomas and Jim Fregosi, so many great guys-- pitchers, catchers, position players-- all of us seated together, enjoying our food, our drinks and our own company. I'd dare say that you'll ever find something like that happening on any of today's high-salaried ballclubs. We were a close-knit group who played together as a team. We traveled together, roomed together and partied together. However, what some of us failed to see as a warning sign of a looming problem was the bill for our night on the town in Baltimore. We hardly gave it a thought when our bar tab came to almost twice as much as our total dinner bill!

It is still painful to look back over the years and realize the large number of teammates who left this life much too early. Fritz Brickell, the club's original shortstop, was the first Angel to leave us. The personable pint-sized, tobacco-chewing infielder from Kansas was barely 30 years old when he lost his battle with jaw and mouth cancer. Still, there were other fellows from that expansion club like ex-Yankee pitcher Tom Morgan, and our pair of power-hitting first basemen, Steve Bilko and Ted Kluszewski, who sadly went on to their rewards just as they passed into the years of middle age.

Thoughts of Kenny Hunt, Joe Koppe, Art Fowler, Leon Wagner, Del Rice and others shot through my mind in no particular order. And who could ever forget the team's owner, Mr. Gene Autry, the original Singing Cowboy, a marvelous man whom I had idolized since my boyhood. Memories of the good times we shared and the certainty of how each of them would have shared my joy at this time of celebration weighed heavily on my mind.

The recent years had also been cruel to the club. Ronnie Kline, Eddie Sadowski and Belinsky, the team's playboy and renowned anti-hero, all had left us only a few months earlier, or so it seemed.

In addition to the ballplayers, there were a few others on the club who made it a point to maintain our friendships long after the cheering had stopped and our careers in baseball were over. One such fellow was Billy Malone, an employee of the Angels, who for several seasons worked as a clubhouse manager. However, because he was assigned to work the clubhouse of the visiting teams, I didn't get to know Billy as well as I would have liked. Of course, we were friends who exchanged greetings and small talk whenever we saw each other at the ballpark, but it wasn't until many years and many telephone conversations later that

I became a close friend of his and discovered what a special individual he really was.

After leaving baseball, Billy joined the Los Angeles Sheriff's Department in time to find himself involved in one of the ugliest social uprisings in the city's history. He had served on the force for little more than a year when the racially motivated Watts Riots erupted in the late summer of 1965. For seven days the streets in this L. A. neighborhood became a combat zone with police in riot gear clashing with gangs of angry Blacks. Several city blocks were burned and more than 30 people were killed in the violence. While a steady barrage of rocks and bottles continued to sail through the air, Billy and many other officers were subjected to brutal physical scuffles with the rioters in the streets and on sidewalks. Somehow in the fury, Billy suffered serious spinal injuries which would leave him crippled and disabled for the rest of his life.

However, that was not the end for Billy Malone. Incredibly, his injuries only seem to mark a turning point in his life. Throughout his remaining years, Billy was dedicated to various efforts that served others. He found ways to send love to areas of hate and peace to regions wherever he saw conflict. In spite of the agony and constant pain throughout his body, he worked tirelessly in support of benevolent and charitable causes across the country. In his late years, he focused his energy toward the Wounded Warrior Project, a wonderful program which helps severely injured troops cope with their transitions to civilian life. At his own expense, Billy wrote letters and mailed out hundreds of official Major League baseballs to prominent entertainers and athletes and requested their autographs. As responses rolled in, he saw to it that each signed ball was either presented as a gift to one of our wounded war veterans or put up for auction to raise funds for the project.

I was delighted to have Billy's widow, Nancy, and his sister come out for the night of celebration in Anaheim. But amid the excitement of the event, we were still burdened with the sadness of Billy's death which had occurred only a few weeks earlier. It had been my intention to have him with us at the stadium, and in some way, have him recognized for the wonderful work he had been doing. I had gone as far as to present my idea to Tim Mead and suggest that the Angels honor Billy for his hard work and for the incredible way he had lived his life. I wanted Billy to be honored for his service to others. But like so many other things in our lives, it was too late. It just didn't work out.

I will never forget the night Nancy phoned us to say that Billy had passed away. The call left me in total shock. "Why would he be taken?" I asked prayerfully. "He committed his life to helping others." His passing was a tragic loss for so many, yet I will always remember Billy Malone as an angel who truly deserves his halo.

Holy smokes! The list goes on and on!

I snapped out of my trance and glanced over at Reggie, sitting close beside me. In spite of the snug seatbelt and the lack of leg room, she was obviously comfortable and totally engrossed in her magazine. The hypnotic hum of the jet engines had helped lull me into this somber mood, but still I wasn't finished. With hundreds of miles left to go and little else to do with my time, I had lots of thinking still ahead of me.

"What am I doing here?" I asked myself. "Am I here to serve some special purpose?" After sinking to some of the darkest depths imaginable, why was I left to survive? It certainly wasn't because I had led a model life. And it wasn't because I had taken good care of myself physically and safeguarded my health. I wasn't one who passed through life as a doer of good deeds and heaven knows I didn't always project the image of a positive role model. Truly, I was no angel.

So why me? Is there a reason? Is there something left for me to do? Maybe I'm to live the remainder of my life helping others avoid the pitfalls that almost destroyed me. Of course, that's it! It makes perfect sense. But how? How could I do that?

Maybe I should write a book!

The Chicago White Sox of 1934 were a dismal bunch. They ended the baseball season at the bottom of the American League standings, finishing a distant 47 games behind the front-running Detroit Tigers. To add to the team's peculiarities, their roster was stocked with equal parts of rookies and veteran underachievers with an unusual pitching staff, composed of 14 different hurlers, all of whom were right-handed. And with the exception of aging George Earnshaw, who had just been acquired during the off-season from the Philadelphia Athletics, there was no other pitcher on the club who finished the '34 campaign with a winning record.

I had the dubious blessing of growing up a White Sox fan, although I actually had no choice in the matter, considering that I was born just south of their home stadium, Comiskey Park, in our family's house on Houston Avenue. Without question, they were our hometown team. And with the squad's losing record notwithstanding, I find it uncanny that the baseball record book shows that the Sox of '34 were mired in another lengthy losing streak at the time of my birth. Yet they celebrated my arrival into the world by inadvertently avoiding a loss on the blessed afternoon of Thursday, August 9th. Luckily, the league schedule gave them a much needed day off, a welcomed break coming at a time when the entire city of Chicago needed to catch its breath and collect its thoughts. It had only been two weeks since Public Enemy #1 John Dillinger had been mortally wounded by FBI agents on our downtown streets in front of the Biograph Theater, not to mention the sobering news that Adolf Hitler had become Fuhrer of Germany earlier that same month.

Going back as far as early childhood, I can always remember having a strong burning desire to play sports. I would have been hard-pressed to choose a favorite since I always seemed to find myself totally absorbed in whatever game was in season. At that time, there was no presence of organized activities and sports for kids like you see today. While groups like Little League Baseball and Pee Wee Football were still years away, my buddies and I put our imagination and ingenuity to good use and found ways to have our own athletic games. Even then, space was a rare commodity in a big city like Chicago, even in the schoolyard of James L. Marsh Elementary School over on Exchange Avenue. Yet we managed to get by with what was available. Along with my friends Chucky Harnisch, Alfred Brokop, Roger Kristovich, Sam Poznanovich, Wally Bolden, Jerry Wesson and another kid known simply as "Beer-Beer," we found enough space between the sidewalks at the school to punt our football. There was no grass for us to play on, only a small open yard covered with sand and pebbles, and still we spent hours upon hours there, kicking the pigskin back and forth, contemplating our future careers as star players for the Chicago Bears.

Although football was our sport of choice from the beginning of autumn until the frigid winds of winter chased us inside, it was baseball that kept us active and outdoors, from the first warm days of spring and all the way to the end of summer vacation. However, since we could never get enough boys together to make full teams, we conjured up our own variations of baseball. There was one game in particular that had us play the roles of our favorite big league stars, a game we called "Strikeout."

To play, we each got a turn at bat while the other boys grabbed their mitts and took positions on the field. The batter could choose to be any big league team he wanted, but he was required to announce the name of a player of that team as he stepped up to bat. When hitting, he had to emulate that player and as best he could, he had to copy the player's batting style and his trademark mannerisms. For instance, I always chose the Boston Red Sox. So, whenever I stepped up to the plate to bat as Ted Williams, I batted left-handed with my feet spread wide, keeping my hands back. I gripped the bat near the end of the handle with my hands close together. To imitate Ted's teammate Bobby Doerr, I moved around to the other side of home plate and batted right-handed. I kept my hands high with the bat cocked and angled behind my head. I gripped the bat about an inch above the knob.

Quite often arguments erupted at the start of our games over who got the next turn to be the hometown White Sox. In spite of the club's low ranking in the A.L. standings, these boys were a loyal bunch who would come close to the edge of trading blows just for a turn to mimic their favorite players. Regardless of who got the honor of being the White Sox for the day, that boy was responsible for giving us a flawless rendition of the Sox's star shortstop, Luke Appling. If he knew what was best for him, the batter went up to the plate and batted right-handed, keeping his hands out and away from his body and choked up a little on the handle. As a final ritual before the first pitch, it was imperative that the Appling imitator use the fingers on his right hand like a whisk broom and sweep his finger tips across the imaginary SOX logo on the left breast of his make-believe uniform. That's exactly how "Old Aches and Pains" would have done it. Luke Appling was our hometown favorite and was truly one of the greatest to ever play the game.

At this point there must be some question concerning my affection for those out-of-town Boston Red Sox. And I may have had what some would say was a legitimate reason, even if many White Sox fans found it hard to swallow.

My father was a serious baseball fan. As a young man he had played briefly as farmhand in the St. Louis Cardinal's minor league system. The story was told that prior to signing a contract with the Cardinals he was known as the finest player in any of the industrial leagues in the steel mill region of the city. Because of his batting heroics, he was known as the "Babe Ruth" of South Deering. But his drinking and his temper quickly put an end to his career as a pro. According to the story that was passed around in the family, his exit from professional baseball had nothing to do with a shortage of talent. It seems that while he was in the minor leagues, my father got into a fight with the catcher on his own team. It was a vicious brawl that resulted in serious back injuries for the young catcher and walking papers for my dad. As bad luck would have it, the manager for the team was also the father of the injured player. Given his unconditional release on the spot, my dad never made it back to professional baseball.

My father Joe Grba was the son of first generation Serbian immigrants, who as a society were known to be industrious and hard-working, but they were also reputed for their penchant for strong drink. My grandparents arrived here in the United States seeking a fresh new start in life, one with steady work in a new and freer environment for themselves as well as their children. On the other hand, to go along with these newly discovered advantages and opportunities, my grandfather passed on a curse that would prove to be as binding as ropes and chains, the curse of hard and heavy drinking. And while this vile imprecation never seemed to keep either my dad or grandfather from holding down a job and earning a good wage, the cost it placed on our family was immeasurable. This demon of alcohol, which my grandfather brought with him from across the Atlantic Ocean, would continue to thrive in America and wreak havoc in our lives for two more generations.

However, I must give the devil his due. It was my father who first introduced me to baseball. He took me with him several times to see the White Sox play at Comiskey Park and while I can't recall many specifics, I remember that he took time to point out a few of the prominent players and tried to explain to me some of the finer points of the game.

I was not quite two years old when I tasted
alcohol for the first time.

It was a simpler time back then at old Comiskey Park. It was back
during a time when fans would often walk out onto the playing field after
the game and have a quick word with a player who wasn't in a big rush to
get into the clubhouse. After one particular game, while the players were
leaving the field, Dad yelled and got the attention of one of the visiting
St. Louis Browns. It was a fellow who years earlier had been a minor
league teammate of Dad's and it was time for the two of them to get
reacquainted. The player was Mike Kreevich, a journeyman outfielder,
who recognized Dad and paused on the infield grass for some friendly
conversation. That moment made quite an impression on me, taking my
first steps on a major league baseball field. The grass was so green and
plush while the bright red clay along the baselines seemed as hallowed as
the surface of the moon. I can still recall how that brief encounter led to
my first handshake with a real big league ball player.

Oddly enough, the baseball influence I received in my formative
years was not simply limited to what came to me through my father. In

her own way, my mother also did her part to see that appreciation and enjoyment of the game would be an integral part of my upbringing. Of course, she was never one to discuss the techniques of batting or base running with me like my dad, but she followed the local sports quite well for a working lady with a very limited amount of free time. One of my favorite baseball memories is of a special day when I was in my early teens and I got to spend an unforgettable day at the ballpark with my mother.

The White Sox were at home for a Sunday doubleheader; the weather was beautiful and the stands were overflowing. Getting the best tickets she could afford, Momma and I found our places out in right field which weren't bad seats for a weekend sellout against the Cleveland Indians. We had just settled in for a long day of baseball when suddenly, in the early innings of the opening game Larry Doby, the hard-hitting slugger for Cleveland smashed a long line drive in our direction. I hardly had time to notice the futile effort of the right fielder as he turned and headed toward the wall. The baseball sailed high through the bright summer sky, closer and closer to us, before it appeared to slow down on its path of approach. Finally, as if in slow motion, it began to descend, losing altitude until it fell perfectly into my open hands. The catch stung my palms, but I wasn't about to let it show as I spun the ball over and over with my fingers, examining it just long enough to get a quick glimpse of the official stamp of *William Harridge, American League President.* Responding to the cheers of everyone seated in our section, I gripped the baseball tightly and raised it into the air. Disregarding the fact that the wallop added on another score for the visiting Tribe, the applause continued with shouts of "Way to go, kid!" and "Great catch, sonny!"

Catching a prized ball such as this one struck by Larry Doby brought on offers from several envious fans. Proposals for five and even ten dollars were mine for the taking, but I refused them all. Instead, I decided that it would be to my advantage to hang on to the coveted baseball and take it home as a keepsake, as it would make the perfect souvenir for display in my bedroom. After all, any high demand item that could attract pricey offers of five to ten bucks should be kept in a safe place.

For about two weeks the ball was safely hidden in my dresser drawer, nestled among my clean socks and underwear. It saw the light of day on only a few occasions, and then only long enough for me to hold it in my hands and feel its magic as I replayed in my mind the majestic homerun that Doby hit with that very sphere. *This ball is not for playing*, I had convinced myself. *It's for keeps!*

Unfortunately, it was just a few days later when we were about to play another game of "Strikeout" over at the schoolyard that we realized that we had everything we needed to get started except a baseball; we had a bat, some bases, a couple of mitts, but no baseball.

"No problem, I have one at home we can use," I offered. "I'll run back home and get mine."

That was the last time I recall seeing that baseball. I'm not sure if we lost it in the weeds, split the cover open with our bats or if one of the guys claimed it as his own took it home. Today, I can only imagine how special it would be to own an authentic Larry Doby homerun baseball, especially the one I caught in the right field stands at Comiskey Park. That was a special ball from a special day, one I'll never forget.

But I have one other memorable ballpark moment that still stands head and shoulders above all others. It was the sort of incredible experience that can thrill a young boy and give memories that last a lifetime.

Baseball was showing signs of returning to normal. The war was over and White Sox fans were happy to have some of their regulars back in the line up. Guys like Don Kolloway, Thurman Tucker and Taffy Wright were again in their rightful positions on the diamond. That also meant that other teams around the league were celebrating the return of some of their best players. Bob Feller was back on the hill for Cleveland and Detroit's first-sacker, Hank Greenberg, was batting clean-up once again for the Tigers. However, it was Boston's Ted Williams, who had returned home as a military hero and was going full speed once again in a Red Sox uniform.

And it was Ted Williams whom my dad had in mind when he hurried home from work one afternoon, rushed through an early dinner and took me along with him for a night game at the ballpark. It was Ted Williams, "The Splendid Splinter," that he talked about on our way to the stadium. And even after we got inside and were watching the pre-game warm-ups, Dad pointed out that it was number nine in right field that we had come to see. "Keep your eyes on that guy, Eli," he instructed me. "You'll be seeing one of the best to ever play this game!"

Batting practice had ended, and the Red Sox were leaving the field when suddenly my father was struck by a grand idea. It was a rare occurrence, but for a brief moment I saw him show the joy and excitement of a young boy. "Come on, Eli! Let's go!" he barked, heading down the steps toward the wall along the right field foul line. "Let's get his autograph!"

I rushed to follow behind him, thinking that whatever we were about to do must be extremely important. "Let's get Ted before he goes inside," he shouted, pushing his way through the fans that had congregated along the wall. He snatched the stub of a pencil and a crumpled piece of paper from his jacket pocket and placed them in my hands. "Now be ready," he warned. "He's coming this way."

Ted trudged slowly closer. Aware that he needed to keep his distance, he stopped a couple of feet away from the base of the wall. Without saying a word, he accepted balls, game programs and autograph books from his worshipers and scribbled his name on each of them. He stood tall and lean with the handle of his bat resting against his thigh. Every few seconds he looked up only long enough to pass a signed item back to its rightful owner. I leaned forward over the wall offering my scrap of paper and holding my breath as if I were about to receive the Pope's blessing. For a brief moment I was in the presence of greatness and I knew it. For a young boy, it was the chance of a lifetime. For a man in his seventies, it's a wonderful memory.

For nine innings that day I did exactly as my father told me to do. I followed Ted's every move. I watched how he changed his defensive spot in the outfield to suit the White Sox batters. I noticed how on each of his swings, his bat wrapped around his body, like the stripes on a barber's pole. That was the day that Ted Williams became my baseball idol.

This all happened before the days of baseball on TV, which made the chances we had of seeing our favorite players in game action few and far between. To feed our baseball appetites, we put our imaginations to work and used the miracle of radio to stay connected. It was the artful descriptions of Bob Elson and Jack Brickhouse that brought vivid accounts of White Sox games into our homes over the airwaves of WGN Radio and it was through their on-air descriptions that we saw every swing of the bat, every hit and every catch of the game in our mind's eye.

Besides radio, there were articles and photos in the sports section of the Chicago Sun-Times to go along with any tidbits that we overheard while talking baseball with the other fellows in the neighborhood. Yet with such primitive communications, we were still able to follow our favorite baseball players closely enough that we could copy even their most subtle mannerisms with startling perfection.

However, beneath the cover of neighborhood football games, sandlot baseball and a few scattered afternoons at Comiskey Park, the ugly demons that my father inadvertently inherited from his father were still very much alive during my early childhood. My time at school and my involvement in sports were only temporary escapes from some of the unforgettable horrors that occurred at home.

From my earliest memories I recall living in a number of different apartments, all of them close to my father's work. There was one particular place on Torrence Avenue, across from the Wisconsin Steel Plant where Dad worked, that stands out in my mind more than the others. For the few short years that we were there, I saw harrowing displays of my father's temper but nothing that would prepare me for the volatile conditions that awaited us at our next address.

Even without my mother employed outside of the home, we were finally able to buy our own house and relocate a few miles to the north, to the Hill District neighborhood. The move landed me in a totally new environment with a completely different culture. I was enrolled at a new school with kids I didn't know. I was forced to make new friends and struggle through a lot of tough adjustments. I was the new kid in school at Joseph Warren Elementary who sorely missed his old buddies from the old neighborhood. Yet having to adjust socially to different people and new surroundings was nothing compared to the increasing number of violent explosions of abuse that took place behind closed doors at our house at 1815 East 93rd Street. Those were horrors that no wife or son should ever be forced to endure.

A man with an evil temper fueled by alcohol can cause as much pain as a man with a machete and can inflict as much damage as an earthquake. In such cases the memories and pain can last a lifetime and the wrongs of abuse can never be righted. It was a different time then and divorce was not as widespread or as easily accepted by our society as it is today. In those days divorce was considered a last resort for a failed marriage and often viewed as a disgrace. Perhaps that's why my mother, Eva, tried so desperately to hold on to her marriage. With nothing more than a broken spirit and her little boy, this angel of a lady struggled to keep her values and fought to keep her family together. Nevertheless, there was only so much she could do on her own and only so much abuse that she could stand. I was still quite young when my parents' divorce was finalized.

Today, I am still haunted by vivid images of my father pulling my mother down the stairs by her hair. These horrible memories, the hurting and the screams have never left me. They are etched in my mind forever and are as painful today as they were almost 70 years ago.

Is forgiveness the answer? I believe so, but I continue to ask myself if I have enough strength to do that fully and completely. I've also been told that time heals all wounds, but I often question that as well.

CHAPTER 3
A NATURAL

It was German-American philosopher Paul Tillich who pointed out how our language gives us the word "solitude" to describe the *glory of being alone*, while it also provides us with the word "loneliness" to express the *pain of being alone*. Personally, I find it fascinating how two words can describe the same physical condition, yet imply two entirely different feelings or emotions. I suppose it is all determined by whether or not an individual has a choice in the matter.

As children, we have very few decisions to make for ourselves and even then, the choices we are allowed to make are insignificant and have very little effect on our lives. Many conditions of childhood are determined by our parents, particularly the decisions they make concerning the ways and to what degree they become involved in the lives of their sons and daughters. Children are heavily impacted, not only by parents who are present and choose to participate in their lives, but also by the parent who is absent and no longer part of the family. Over the years I came to discover that it was the void created by the absence of my father that I spent so much of my life trying to fill.

There is no doubt that fathers have a powerful influence on their sons and that it starts at the moment of birth. I believe that since the beginning of time, young boys have always sought a strong male role model to come into their lives, even though they are normally unaware of it. There is so much evidence on how male influence can easily set a negative or positive example for a young boy and be such an important factor in determining the path he will follow. Perhaps that's the reason I was so excited when a man named Bill Yeoman spent some time with me and provided me with some much needed encouragement and approval.

We had moved into our new house up in the Hill District, but things were far from settled. My mother stood no chance of making the type of home life she had always wanted for us. My father's hard drinking and his vicious temper made it a virtual impossibility. As I recall the times he came staggering home, drunk, angry and vomiting in a metal wash basin, I imagined I endured all of the emotions that a small boy could handle. My reactive feelings were a mixture of fear, anger, disappointment and pity. Those were times when it felt like I had nowhere to turn and no one to turn to.

As a small boy, I was unaware of the widespread changes that our country faced once we entered World War II. Being so young, I accepted it all in stride, having had very little time to get to know what a peacetime America was all about it. War bonds, ration tickets and paper drives were all part of my early life. So were baseball and football. But oddly enough, it was the game of golf that caught me by surprise.

Like all forms of entertainment and recreation during the war, the game of golf was reeling from the hard times. Private clubs and public courses across the country were forced to deal with the drop-off of paying customers as well as the problems of operating a business with a smaller staff. Grounds keepers, caddies and golfers themselves were in short supply, as so much of our male population was shipped overseas to fight. And this was likely the situation for Mr. Yeoman, the man who operated the driving range across the street from our house. This probably had a lot to do with why he was willing to put me to work, even before I had reached my tenth birthday.

Even with some of the most famous players in the game's history making headlines, golf still wasn't the type of sport that caught the attention of many young boys in Chicago during the 1940s. Byron Nelson, Ben Hogan and Sam Snead were all in their heyday, yet none of them seemed to garner the appeal of our local baseball heroes, such as Luke Appling, Wally Moses or Ted Lyons. For most kids, golf just wasn't as exciting.

Still, there was something that fascinated me about watching the golfers over at the driving range. For hours on end, I would watch, observing them closely, noting the different stances as they addressed the ball, the concentration, the varying swings and their follow–throughs. But it was the long distance tee-shots that caused my mouth to drop open in awe. There was nothing like standing outside the range, peering through the fence and spotting a proficient golfer as he smacked the ball off the tee, driving it high into the air, outward beyond the 200-yard marker. I recall looking into a bright summer sky and having to squint as I followed the paths of these balls sailing out of sight. Yet, I was just a small boy, standing alone, on the outside looking in.

I continued to miss my pals from the old neighborhood, and getting adjusted to the new area, the new school and the kids in this unfamiliar part of town wasn't working out as well as I had wanted. That's why I was hanging around the driving range, trying to enjoy my own company when Mr. Yeoman walked over to the fence and out of the clear-blue, yelled to get my attention.

"Hey kid," he called to me. "You look like you're looking for something to do. Would you like a job?"

Surprised at the attention, I forced my hands deeper into my empty pockets. He didn't sound angry, and I wasn't doing anything wrong, so I stepped a little closer to the fence.

"Well, what about it, son?" he asked again. "You could use an extra buck or two, couldn't you?" He stooped over to pick up a couple of empty wire baskets from the ground while he waited for an answer. "I've seen you out a lot and I could use some help, if you're willing to work." He could see that I was slow to come up with an answer, so he took matters into his own hands. "Come on around here to the gate, and I'll let you in so we can talk this over." Moments later, I had accepted his offer. I had my first job and I was excited to know that I would be earning my own money!

The job he gave me wasn't an easy one. It was hard work, but I soon found that it was a lot better than sitting in a boring classroom or being alone at home. Now keep in mind that this was long before the days when motorized lawn mowers with protective steel cages were used to scoop up the range balls and the common method for retrieving them was not only a lot more primitive, but it was also a lot more dangerous.

While the paying customers were whacking golf balls in every direction, it was my job to be out in front of them, picking up the balls, one by one, with nothing more than a hand-held protective shield made of expanded metal and a five-gallon bucket.

On the other hand, Mr. Yeoman and I got along fine. I showed up for work on time and did whatever he asked of me. I worked hard enough to keep him happy and smart enough to keep from getting hurt. He was a pleasant, easy-going fellow to work for and I went out of my way to see that he stayed that way. After just a day or two on the job, I began to sense that he trusted me because he allowed me to work on my own with a minimal amount of supervision. This bit of independence did wonders for my confidence. On occasions, he even gave me a pat on the back and let me know that he was pleased with the job I was doing. For a nine year old, getting that kind of approval was just as important as getting paid.

Mr. Yeoman was also perceptive enough to see just how anxious I was to get my hands on one of those golf clubs and try taking a few swings for myself. Watching the paying customers swinging away, going through bucket after bucket of balls, stirred my curiosity. Some of those golfers drove their balls for long distances with impressive accuracy, while others hit them no farther than they could spit. I had confidence in my own abilities and knew I could do a lot better than some of those high-dollar hackers who were much older and a lot bigger than I was. Mr. Yeoman must have felt the same way.

One particular morning had all of the signs of being another hot sultry day in Chicago. I had been on the job only a few minutes, retrieving as many balls as I could from the wet grass in front of the tee mats, before any of the usual early-bird customers started to show up. Suddenly I heard Mr. Yeoman call for me. He was standing outside the door to his tiny office, holding some sort of golf club in his hands.

"Eli!" he shouted. "How about taking a break for a few minutes? I have something here for you."

I grabbed the handle of my half-filled bucket and sprinted in his direction. In a matter of seconds I screeched to a halt in front of him, wondering just what in the world he would have to offer me. "Yes, sir. What is it?" I asked, my heart racing beneath my damp T-shirt.

"This is for you, son," he replied, offering the handle of the club. "Try it out and see if you like it. It's one of the old drivers that I've been keeping in the office. I shortened the shaft and had it re-gripped, so it would be closer to your size. Why don't we walk over there to the mats and have you tee up a few balls and try it out?" I didn't answer, but he knew I couldn't wait to get started.

He stood closely behind me as I took my stance at the tee. With his long arms extended around mine, he leaned forward and demonstrated how to properly grip the club. He spoke over my shoulder, correcting the position of my feet and instructing me to keep my left arm straight and my head down throughout my swing. "Okay, let's see what you can do," he said with a positive tone. Stepping back as I started into my backswing, he offered one final bit of instruction, "Keep your eye on the ball, Eli, and you'll do fine."

Mr. Yeoman smacked his hands in disbelief as I whacked one ball and then another, making solid contact with each swing. To my own surprise, the balls seemed to be jumping off the tee, each one sailing higher into the air and carrying for a longer distance than the one before. "That's great, son!" he shouted with approval. "I'll bet those balls are going out there at least 75 yards and some a hundred or more! You're a natural! Keep it up and you'll be turning pro in no time!"

I continued until there were no golf balls left in my bucket. Then realizing that it must be time for me to get back to work, I turned and noticed that Mr. Yeoman was standing a few feet away, slowly nodding, obviously very pleased with my performance. Pleased with myself, I could do nothing but stare back at him and smile with a wide grin.

The brief time I spent hitting those balls with Mr. Yeoman brought me a lot of happiness. Surely, the feel of driving those golf balls with my very own customized driver was a real thrill for me, as it would have been for any sports-minded little boy. But the joy extended much further than that.

Like any other boy at that age, I had been searching for male influence. Without knowing it, I had been longing for the kind of positive reinforcement and approval that I received from Mr. Bill Yeoman. He offered me my first job, taught me about the virtues and responsibilities of earning my own money and in his own special way, he encouraged me to pursue athletics at a time when I really needed it. I never got to tell him how he bolstered my sense of self-worth and how he helped me gain enough pride and self-esteem to make my life a little easier for a while. But for what it's worth now, thanks Mr. Yeoman, you were a good man.

It's hard to describe how great you feel when someone calls you a natural.

I seemed to be a natural in almost all sports,
even when I was very young.

CHAPTER 4
RUNNING WITH THE WRONG CROWD

With the strife and hardships of war impacting our country every day, one would think that there was no need for Americans to go looking for more trouble than we already had. But in some ways, that's precisely what we did. During the 1940s, Americans consumed whiskey and beer at an unprecedented rate, while the percentage of Americans who smoked cigarettes was at the highest level ever. The 1940s was a decade highlighted by catchy billboard ads and radio jingles which were very effective in hitting their marketing targets. As public concern about smoking-related health problems was beginning to surface, big tobacco companies with huge advertising budgets were quick to discredit any of those findings. They put out lavish ad campaigns which made claims about how more doctors smoked Camels than any other cigarette and how there wasn't a single cough in a whole carload of Old Gold cigarettes. So much of our adult population went about their lives in a trusting way, having little regard for the consequences of their habits. During the war when cigarettes were in short supply, Americans went to great lengths to get their weekly allotments. My dad often had to wait in line to buy his smokes at the local tobacco store down at the corner of 92nd Street and Commercial Avenue. And though it was an imposition, I'm sure that for him as well as all the others, the pleasure was worth the wait. Yet, I always found it ironic that his brand of choice was Homerun Cigarettes, the ones with the intricate drawing of an old style baseball scene on every pack. *Would this brand help a fellow become a better ballplayer?* I wondered.

Of course, many Americans were misled, but in some ways it seems like a big portion of this generation had a self-destructive penchant for trouble. Now, as I look back at my life, growing up in the 40s, I can see how, at a young age, I started taking a path for trouble and didn't have a clue about how to change my course.

Before I had even reached my teens, I began to see that I had developed quite a knack for finding trouble or in other cases, made it easy for trouble to find me. I was no more than 11 or 12 years old when life was becoming more difficult and confusing and things were quickly getting to the point where even I wasn't pleased with my behavior. I felt like I was swimming against the tide as I tried to fit in with the boys in the neighborhood and struggled to make a place for myself in a makeshift family comprising my grandfather and several aunts. Naturally, I was angry and upset that my father had left us, but like any young boy, I wanted him to remain a hero. I didn't want to see the truth, and I didn't want to blame Dad for anything I was going through. Sure, I knew the difference between right and wrong. These were things my family taught me at an early age. But how much attention would I get if I didn't get into trouble?

Once Mom and Dad separated, I did my best to get ready for the drastic changes that I knew would come my way. I tried to prepare myself for life as a boy who would grow up without a father. I knew he was moving out, and I didn't know how frequently I would get to see him. What I wasn't prepared for was the little time I would get to spend with my mother.

As a result of the separation, we lost our house in the Hill District and Mom soon got an apartment less than a block from the home of her parents. To keep us afloat financially, she went to work, taking jobs with long hours and hectic schedules. These were demanding jobs that left her tired and exhausted with little room for me in her life. She had no other choice but to go forward with her life, which was a far cry from anything she had ever wanted or imagined. I know she wanted me, but living with her was just simply out of the question.

Although her ground floor apartment was nothing fancy, it was affordable and close to the rest of the family. It was located about four doors down from the home of my grandfather, Nikola. "Deda," as he was known in the family, is a Serbian word for grandfather. He lived with my Mom's younger sisters, Sophie, Mary and Mila. My grandmother, Baba, had passed away a couple of years earlier, leaving my three aunts to care for him. This unusual family arrangement became even more unconventional when I moved in as the only child.

My grandparents, Deda and Baba

With the house at full occupancy and then some, I was relegated to sleeping on a daybed in the dining room next to a huge window. In addition to the usual amount of creepy night noises that could only be heard by a wide-eyed kid with a vivid imagination, I seemed to have been tuned in to more than my share of things that go bump in the night. In the late hours, before drifting off to sleep, I often heard the eerie sounds of footsteps or whispering voices or sometimes the sounds of someone tampering with the lock on the front door. Still, the scariest of times came on sultry summer nights whenever a thunderstorm rolled through the area on the heels of a hot day. Horrendous bolts of brilliant lightning would flash through the window by my bed and illuminate the entire room. Within seconds, a sudden clap of thunder would shake the house from footing to roof, followed by the frightening sound of electrical current sizzling above my head! There in the center of the dining room, suspended from the ceiling was an old-fashioned ornate chandelier with its brass chains and dangling glass crystals. It was the type that would have fit well with the décor of Collinwood Mansion on the set of the popular horror movie, "Dark Shadows." But what was so scary and mysterious about this old electric light fixture? After each bolt of lightning, its wiring connections buzzed with energy. It crackled and snapped as if it were about to short-circuit. I was so frightened by that startling sound I could've jumped out of my skin!

Could it be a ghost or had the devil himself come to get me? Did I really smell smoke? Was the house on fire? Should I get out of bed and wake everyone up? There's just no limit to the imagination of a frightened young boy.

My mother had been raised in a large family, with five brothers and four sisters. Yet, after her failed marriage, she found herself living alone and struggling to make ends meet, at a time when jobs were scarce. She was fortunate to land a job at the cereal plant of General Mills, which was within walking distance of her apartment. Being able to walk to and from work helped cut her expenses and saved time, but the drawbacks of the situation outweighed the advantages. While her job there was strenuous, she was required to work a schedule of rotating shifts which constantly moved workers from day shift to night shift and back again. For hours during each shift, she monitored a conveyor belt as tons of Wheaties whole wheat flakes moved past, on their way to the next machine that filled the waiting empty boxes. It was a hard-working life for my mother, but she had no choice other than to keep working as the burden of monthly rent always kept her strapped for money.

Eventually, Mom was able to escape the rigors of shiftwork at the cereal plant and go into an entirely different line of work. She became a waitress and stepped into a whole new world. I'm not so sure that the money was better, but she gained the benefit of working the same hours each day and being at home each night. She put in many long days working as a waitress, getting up at 4:00 a.m. to ride the Illinois Central morning train and then catching a bus to finish her commute. While the change brought on new complications, such as the daily travel and her sore aching feet, her new job did a lot to broaden her social horizons. The people she met while serving tables at The Peter Pan Restaurant, a popular dining spot on 72nd Street, helped her to extend herself intellectually beyond the limits of our neighborhood and our close-knit family. Mom was able to exceed even her own expectations and go beyond the ordinary. She was exposed to new topics that had never been discussed at home and acquired new ideas about diet, nutrition and new methods of cooking and preparing food. By working each day in this more affluent part of town, Mom became acquainted with people who helped point her in the direction of work she found more specialized and more rewarding. She took a job as a proof reader, working for two prominent publishing firms in the area, The R. R. Donnelley Company and Pool Brothers Publishing. It was her restaurant customers who saw my mother's potential and visualized a life for her that would surpass the realm of her education. She went on to work extensively on many highly regarded medical reference manuals and was graciously humbled when she learned that one of those publications had been dedicated to her in recognition of her hard work.

I was still in grammar school and looking for approval from the boys in my new neighborhood when I first started running into real trouble. Already banking on the fact that breaking the rules would go a lot further in becoming one of the boys than simply conforming and behaving, I wanted to test the system to see what I could get away with. I was having a tough time doing everything by myself and I was desperate to make friends, whether good or bad. When I decided to pull one of my first stunts of mischief, I quickly found out that living four doors away from Momma was not far enough to keep her from finding out where I was and what I was up to.

Just west of Marsh Elementary School was a vacant, not-then-developed area, which was referred to as "The Swamp." It was a low-lying spot with a narrow, normally-stagnant stream stretching through its center. The sloping banks near the water were covered with an assortment of ferns and weeds which seemed to thrive in the muddy soil. During the months of spring and summer, any number of young boys could be seen hanging out near The Swamp, playing among the tall leafy weeds, puffing on stolen cigarettes or pussy willow stalks or perhaps wading in the murky water with a can attached to the end of a string, trying to catch guppies. Each winter the fire department flooded the area and allowed it to freeze, making a perfect skating rink for our hockey games.

Yet in spite of all of the unsupervised rascality the local kids could stir up, The Swamp was primarily infamous for being the setting for so many ghost stories and grizzly horror tales that were passed on through generations in that part of South Chicago. All of us kids had heard the gruesome details of mysterious creature sightings and how innocent, unsuspecting children who had wandered into The Swamp were never seen or heard from again. I had been known to play in that area often with the other boys, catching everything from spiders to guppies to poison ivy. Even then, I was only allowed to go there after getting permission from Mom or Aunt Sophie along with one of their typical last minute reminders to play safely and be careful.

One of the worst things I could think of doing was to be sneaky and venture into The Swamp during school hours. But one day I felt lucky and gave it a try. That's when I learned that doing something behind Mom's back was a very serious offense, serious enough to warrant my first and most severe whipping.

She had already heard the news. Along with a buddy of mine, I had been seen cutting school and trying my hand at catching guppies down at The Swamp. The other kid had been sent home to his parents who would deal with his own painful fate. But for me, the justice system was a little more complicated. First, I had to undergo a round of questioning from Deda and Aunt Sophie and only after that would I be turned over to face the wrath and ire of my mother.

Even with my mother coming from four doors down the block, I still didn't have enough time to run for safety. "Come here to me, Eli!" she ordered angrily. Her voice was like nothing I had ever heard from her. At the start, there may have been 50 yards between us, but she closed in on me fast. I could see in her hand the switch that she had snapped off from a nearby shrub, as she swung it back and forth at her side. With nowhere to run, I stood helplessly in that one spot, as motionless as Lot's wife. I started to cry before she was even close enough to reach out for my wrist. She started immediately to flail away on the backs of my calves. The switch stung more with each lash and burned the backs of my legs like a swarm of angry bees! The switching continued as she yanked my arm, pulling me along as we headed in the direction of her place. With her fingers still firmly locked around my wrist, there was no possible way I could get out of striking distance of the long slender stick. My yelping and wailing were enough to draw the attention of all of the other mothers and children on the block and the noise only served to infuriate Mom a little more. Without slowing down or missing a beat, she kept me in tow, pulling me through the front door of her apartment building and up the stairwell. I found no relief or refuge inside as the punishment only intensified. "I'll teach you not to cut school!" she shrieked. "This will be the last time for you, my young man!"

I continued to fight and resist, jumping and pulling away to avoid the pain of Mom's switch striking my legs. Yet, at the same time, I felt another unavoidable pain, one which caused me to feel sick and hurt on the inside. Even at such a young age, I knew that I had hurt the only person who loved me more than life itself. I had hurt Momma deeply. I had disappointed her and tried to deceive her. The feeling of shame that came from hurting her was an unforgettable pain I never wanted to experience again. I promised myself that I would never again hurt this "angel of a lady."

It was the first and only whipping my mother ever gave me, and it was the only time I was ever seen in The Swamp during school hours. As for as the punishment in this case, I have no misgivings. I got exactly what I deserved. But as the years went by, I came to see how during her time on earth, Mom never got to know the rewards of the good life that she so richly deserved.

My mother, an angel of a lady.

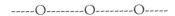

For a short time following the separation of my parents, my father lived in town, but the times I got to see him were few and far between. He got himself a room at the local YMCA, which was not the type of environment he would have preferred to have his young son visit him. He was also aware of the danger he would put himself in if he were to drop by the house at a time when Deda and some of my mother's brothers were there. What had been an abusive marriage had now led to an ugly divorce, and my grandfather and uncles weren't about to forget the horrors he had put Mom through. The very fact that my uncles didn't go after Dad and give him the lickin' he deserved is reason enough for him to have considered himself a lucky man.

His search for greener pastures led him to St. Louis, where he landed another job and leased a modest apartment. While this arrangement signaled a new start for Dad, it put a gap of about 300 miles between us. Though it wasn't the ideal situation for visiting, a day trip out of Chicago by train was all it took for me to see him on a couple of occasions. I once stayed with him for a two-week summer vacation, which gave me more time and attention from my father than I had ever known. It was a short stay as the time passed quickly. We talked a lot, went places together and even took in another big league baseball game. There aren't too many things more beneficial to a young boy than spending time with his dad.

Deda was getting up in age, and after 44 years with Youngstown Sheet & Tube, he retired and lived comfortably with three of his daughters. In addition to him, these three ladies deserve a lot of credit for the care and nurturing I received over a significant part of my formative years. But that's not to say that my mother's brothers weren't close by and attentive. They each devoted their share of time and energy to me, their energetic and all-too-often mischievous nephew. I was always happy whenever any of my uncles stopped by the house. They all had a special affection for me and were always willing to talk with me about sports or school or any of a wide range of other topics. And because they were all hard-working young men holding down full-time jobs, each of them would slip me a buck or two from time to time, just for being a good kid.

There were Uncle Adam, Uncle Ted, Uncle Mike, Uncle Pete and finally, Uncle Eli, the oldest of the bunch. But like in so many American families during the war, our able-bodied male relatives answered the call to duty and left home to serve in the military. In our case, it was my uncles Pete, Mike and Eli who joined the armed forces and served honorably. However, Uncle Eli saw the most action and returned home highly decorated for his gallantry in combat. He never wanted to share his war stories with any of us or talk about his battlefield heroics, so any specifics concerning his involvement in the fighting remained a mystery. Then, for many years following the war, his work and his whereabouts continued to be a mystery for us. We were told only that he worked for the Central Intelligence Agency, that his assignments were dangerous and critical to our country's defense, and that we never knew when to expect him home. Needless to say, having these five upstanding men as my uncles gave me and our whole family a lot to be proud of.

Still, it was Uncle Mike who made such a lasting impression on me. He was handsome and athletic, yet forceful in his part to instill high personal values and principles in me. I was always happy to see him and I treasured every moment we were together. Whenever he dropped by to visit the family, he always had time to spare a few minutes with me outside kicking the football. In my father's absence, he was what I was searching for. He was a positive male influence for me, but we were never together often enough or long enough for him to see that I stayed on the right path. And while he was never aware of how much I looked up to him, it was his image and character I always wanted to emulate.

Being raised by my three aunts, however, brought issues into my life that were often hard for me to deal with, like the clothes they bought for me to wear. While all of the other boys at school were wearing long pants, I was an easy target for their teasing and ridicule whenever I came walking down the sidewalk sporting a pair of knickers! Now there's no argument that these trendy, calf-length trousers weren't the latest style of the time. They were in all of the popular catalogs and in the display windows of the finest department stores. But while I was trying my best to fit in with the guys in my new neighborhood, they were the last thing I needed. I'm sure my aunts felt that they were doing me a good turn whenever they brought home a new pair for me to try on. But these ladies obviously had no idea what it was like to be called a sissy!

I thought long and hard for a way to turn my situation around and find favor with the guys. Meanwhile, the barrage of teasing and name-calling continued, and I was tagged with every name in the book, from "Spanky" to "Little Lord Fauntleroy." I soon deducted that if I were to go from being an outcast to being one of the gang, I would need to take some drastic measures.

Any of the boys who had worked his way into a place of prominence within the neighborhood gang had not attained his position without first earning the reputation of being a shrewd and daring shoplifter. It was a practice that required ingenuity and nerves of steel, a couple of qualities that could go a long way in helping a kid make a name for himself. Although it wasn't so much the value of the item that got attention, it was the frequency of the crime that was essential in building a reputation.

Being raised by my three aunts brought issues into my life that were often hard to deal with, like the clothes they bought for me.

Not far from our house were a couple of retailers who fell victim to our thievery a lot more often than they ever realized. It was the local F.

W. Woolworth Company and S.S. Kresge Store which were located next to each other. Just the fact that they were so close together made them easy targets whenever the boys decided to go on a stealing spree. The preferred method of shoplifting was a simple matter of making sure that a certain area in the store was not adequately monitored by the clerks and floorwalkers and then quickly moving in for the take. We were careful to wear clothes that would easily hide our stash, and we worked as quickly and quietly as possible to avoid being noticed. After we had cased the area and slipped a few items in our pockets, we only had to move our operation next door to the other store to pull off a similar job. While toys and games would make for the best pickings, we often found that it was those sections of the store that were watched the closest once a bunch of us kids came through the door. It really made no difference what items we lifted, but it was essential that we prove to the other boys that we would defy authority and could execute under pressure.

Those silly-looking knickers that the women at home were forcing me to wear, however, worked in our favor. Those hideous pants were full and baggy with lots of room in the upper leg area, while the bottom of each leg was gathered and buttoned tightly just below the knee. I would deliberately rip a hole in the lining of my pockets, which would allow me to shove any small piece of merchandise through the pocket flap and let it slip farther down my leg, to a place where the item was practically undetectable. After my pant legs were loaded with loot, I only needed to make a slow inconspicuous walk out of the store and down the street to a safe place where I could unload my loot and cull through it to see if I had picked up anything worth keeping. On the other hand, I also made a few heists that weren't so random. That's when I would zero in on just one particular high-priced toy or novelty that I wanted to swipe for myself. I was finding that the more I stole, the more confident I became, until it reached a point where I thought I couldn't be stopped. I thought no one would ever catch me.

There were times when I gave away what I had stolen just to gain approval and acceptance from the other guys. But to show that my crimes weren't always wanton or senseless, I would brazenly follow the same routine to pick up a gift to give someone on a special occasion. That's how I was able to give Aunt Sophie such a swell autograph album for her birthday. *I am being generous and thoughtful,* I told myself. *I am just doing something nice for someone.* Yet deep inside I wasn't convinced. I knew stealing was wrong.

My family had taught me the difference between right and wrong. But it was a rule I tested. In one instance, when I was able to sneak from under the clerk's watchful eye in the toy section in Woolworth's, I discreetly slid a model airplane kit beneath my bulky winter coat. Clutching the box close against my body, and partially tucking it up under my armpit, I managed to make it out of the store, all the way home and into my bedroom unnoticed. Several days later, assuming the heat was off, I took it from the package and began assembling the tiny pieces of that scale model fighter plane. I was having as much fun as I had ever had, playing alone in my room for hours. It never crossed my mind that I would soon need to explain how I got my hands on such an expensive toy. The unexpected consequences were soon to follow.

Questions ensued for me at home and many of my subsequent answers were lies. Clearly, Uncle Mike had not given me enough money for such a nice gift for Aunt Sophie, and surely I had not earned and saved enough money to buy an expensive model airplane. My mother, Deda and everyone in the family knew the type of fellows I had been hanging around with and what we had been up to. "You're running with the wrong crowd, Eli" I was told. "It's time for us to make some changes. You need more authority and discipline. Time away in a different place with new friends will be good for you." I also heard that I was incorrigible, although I didn't even know what the word meant!

Of course, I was allowed no say in the matter, and it was apparent that the deal was final. The decision had been made for me to go away. But still important points like where and for how long remained undecided. No matter how I measured it, I couldn't see how anything good could come out of it for me.

Am I on my way to a reform school or to some sort of prison for boys? Am I being sent to a camp? What about a military school? Military school wouldn't be such a bad idea. I've seen brochures from a few of them. But, will I ever come back home again? I was frightened and unsure and filled with concerns. I had not even left home before I started to feel the painful sting of loneliness.

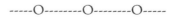

Now, I'll be among the first to tell you that a lot of things have changed over the years, and the world is a lot different from what it was like when I was a youngster. However, there are still many things that have remained constant. Personal values like honesty and integrity will always apply in life, while respect for other people and the property they own will always be required in order for us to live as we were intended. In reflection, I offer no excuses for my shameful behavior as a young boy. But I can now look back over my life with a clear understanding of how difficult and frightening life can be for a child and I can attest to how important it is that children receive proper nurturing, guidance and discipline. Still, I speak from experience when I point out how easy it can be for juvenile peer pressure to ruin the lives of kids today, just as it did when I was young, so many years ago. Growing up was hard. It still is.

CHAPTER 5

SUMMER CAMPS AND BOARDING SCHOOL

No one knew what to do. The entire household was in a state of indecision and I was the cause. I had been caught stealing and trying to lie my way out of it so many times that everyone in the family realized my behavior was spinning out of control. The shameful things I had done were very painful for Mom. She felt responsible for my actions and was at a loss about how to correct them. The pressure on her to do something with me was building. She knew things were changing quickly at home and that time was running out.

Of course, the house where I lived with my aunts belonged to Deda, and at his age, he deserved better. He was close to retirement but was still pulling shift work at the steel mill. Whenever his work schedule allowed, he would get up early to fix our breakfast before I headed for school. Most school mornings, it was a piece of bread in a bowl, covered with sugar and milk; yet it was enough to hold me over until lunch. After working as many years as he had to raise his own family, being responsible for a young male delinquent like me was the last thing Deda needed.

Aunt Mila had married and had already moved out, while Aunt Sophie, who had done so much to care for me, was graduating from high school and was set to start her own life. That left Aunt Mary, who would soon to be the last of the young women left at home. With all of these changes taking place, I knew things would soon be changing for me, too.

Yet as fearful as I was about my future, a voice deep inside kept telling me that I had brought all of this trouble upon myself.

In spite of such dreary circumstances my mother wasn't about to give up easily. She remained persistent, discussing our plight not only within the family but also with people she knew through her work and with some of the folks at church. Mom was open to any ideas she thought could offer even the slightest bit of help. "Growing up as a kid from Slag Valley is one thing, but we can do better than this," I heard her say.

In referring to "Slag Valley," Mom was in no way degrading our neighborhood. The folks there were part of a hard-working, blue-collar culture, which was proud of its ethnic heritage and proud that everyone in the area who was willing to work had a job and paid his own way. The town got its name from the slag and other steel mill waste that was dumped in the area, and yet she was as proud of our community as anyone. But she knew the only way for me to make something of myself was to move me into a totally different social setting. Mom knew I needed to get away from the crowd I was running with and that I needed a source of positive influence. She knew the kind of influence I needed could only come through strong male discipline.

All too often I was overhearing terms like "reform school," "military school," "school for boys" and "boys' summer camp." They were coming up in conversations whenever Mom dropped by the house to visit or after church while I was waiting to go home. The mere thought of any of them sent waves of panic down my spine. From what I was hearing, one thing was perfectly clear, nobody wanted me here and I would be going somewhere else real soon!

Through some means Mom had been given a handful of promotional brochures from a military academy located not far away in Indiana. The glossy papers were quite colorful with striking photographs of boys dressed in sharp-creased uniforms, marching and attending classes. There were also on-the-field photos of their sports teams in action, all of which looked very inviting to me. Yet I was still curious about Mom and how she just happened to drop these pamphlets in places where they couldn't miss catching my attention.

The school was Culver Military Academy, a highly regarded full-military school with a prestigious reputation as one of the finest privately run schools for young men in that part of the country. And needless to say, I was enthralled by the pictures of the huge masonry buildings and boys playing basketball and hockey. My mind wandered as I refolded the brochure and placed it back on the table where I found it. I peered out the kitchen window and for a moment, I imagined how sharp I would look in one of those uniforms. I even had a few quick passing thoughts of how proud my uncles would be, if I could become a cadet. Then suddenly, like a hot poker, the pain of reality seared through my body. *I wouldn't be going there because they want me to. I'd be going because no one wants me here!*

Tears ran down my cheeks as I dashed from the kitchen and headed for my bed. I threw myself down, face-first onto the soft feather-filled pillow, wanting desperately to hide my face. *Maybe if I cry long enough, all of this will go away. Or maybe I will cry myself to sleep, and things will be better tomorrow.* I felt helpless and hopeless and suddenly realized how unprepared I was for life. "What a difference!" I sobbed. "I'm not much of a big-shot after all! This sure wasn't the way I felt when I swiped that model airplane form Woolworth's!"

For the first time, I could remember I was dreading the end of the school year. Normally, I couldn't wait for school to end and summer vacation to start. But from the bits and pieces of conversation I was able to overhear around the house, my summer would be no vacation. From what I heard, it sounded like a sure bet that I would be leaving home as soon as details could be worked out. Nonetheless, the shame and guilt I was carrying made it extremely uncomfortable for me to be around the members of my family, knowing that I had been such a big disappointment to them. Along with my mother, they had all done whatever they could to make life good for me. But even after all of the dishonest things I had done, I still wasn't aware that my life was heading down the wrong path. I had only been doing what every other kid in the neighborhood was doing.

Throughout the spring, my biggest hope was that Mom wouldn't be able to come up with enough money to send me away to any of those dreadful schools or camps. And with the school year drawing to a close, I was clinging desperately to the possibility that if I were given just one more summer at home without causing any more problems, I would be in the clear. Maybe that way, I could buy enough time for the whole troublesome situation to pass. But I found that luck was not on my side when Mom informed me that the local YMCA was offering a summer camp for boys, not far from home for a rate that even she could afford.

I believe it was Mark Twain who said, "Don't go around saying the world owes you a living. The world owes you nothing. It was here first." What a priceless piece of advice! And this quote is just one of the many wonderful gems of wisdom given to us by this great author, known as the "Father of American Literature." Naturally, as a young boy, I would have scoffed at such wise counsel, and because of the ignorance of my youth, I would have also discounted Twain's thoughtful claim that 98 percent of what he worried about never happened. If only I could have known about those odds when Mom told me I was on my way to a summer camp for boys. I fretted and worried until I made myself sick and later discovered it was all for naught.

It was completely different from what I expected. After weeks of allowing my imagination to run wild with horrible images of iron bars on the windows and stern, poker-faced wardens watching our every move, my time at the Lawson Summer Camp for Boys was a great experience. It was two weeks, out in the country, filled with new and exciting activities. We built campfires, pitched tents, played softball and horseshoes and went canoeing on the lake. Each day was filled with fun things to do, from early morning until time for lights out. Unexpectedly, I even learned a few things that weren't on the camp's agenda.

The camp directors and counselors did a good job of organizing and overseeing the daily programs as none of the boys in my barracks were injured, lost or involved in any serious trouble during my stay. However, that's not to say the staff was able to keep an eye on us around the clock. It would have been impossible for the camp personnel to know everything we were up to. Otherwise, there would have been 13 of us in big trouble had they spotted us, sitting in a circle, our shorts pulled down around our ankles as each of us explored himself and frantically experimented with his masculinity. Maybe each of us had something to prove, either to ourselves or to the other campers. And while I was never quite sure about the whole idea behind the incident, it may have had something to do with maturity or manhood or maybe it was just the need to come in first place.

After returning home from Lawson's summer camp and having just a few days to hang around the old neighborhood, I found that Mom had more plans for me. Though they didn't sound as frightening to me as her earlier ideas of sending me away to private schools for boys or military academies, I still had the feeling I wasn't wanted at home and the family was doing everything they could to get rid of me. This time, Mom's plan stirred my interest and had me wanting to hear more about it. It was another trip to another camp out of town, but this time it was all about baseball!

This camp was the Ozark Baseball Camp, located in Ozark, Missouri, just a few miles south of Springfield. It was a three-week camp owned and operated by Carl Bolin, a stern and crusty old baseball vet who, for many years, had worked as a birddog scout for the New York Giants. With the assistance of some of his old buddies who were mostly former major league players, Bolin ran a no-frills camp carved out of the rolling hills of the Ozark Valley. The cabins were topped with corrugated tin roofs and the mess hall was furnished with benches and tables made from wooden planks. Other than the staff office, the open-air showers and a couple of dusty ball fields, there was little else on the property.

The daily competition, along with the in-depth instructional sessions, did a lot to spark my interest in baseball. We were put through drills to learn the finer points of batting, throwing, catching and base running and were expected to apply our newly learned skills each day in a series of controlled games. In the evenings we watched baseball movies and listened as former players who were guests of the camp told us about their experiences in the game. Throughout every waking hour, we were either talking or playing baseball! Unexpectedly, I found myself attentive and receptive to whatever the instructors had to say, and I even surprised myself when I was quick to catch on to some of the pointers they offered. Maybe it was because they were all ex-athletes who had first-hand stories to tell about famous players and important games that caused me to look up to these men and make them my heroes. In particular, it was Jim Bottomley, the former St. Louis Cardinals' first baseman and Most Valuable Player Award recipient, who visited the camp and made a lasting impression on me. It was in his inspirational talk given on his last day at the camp that he told our entire group to "dream big and work hard and you'll get what you want out of life." "Sunny Jim," as he was often called because of his easy-going, sunny personality, left Carl Bolin's Baseball camp that day having a few more fans and admirers than he had when he first arrived. And I was proud to say I was one of them.

After returning home with the experiences from two summer camps, I could tell Mom was pleased with the changes she saw in my behavior and my attitude. She, as well as others in the family, commented on how I was more reserved and more respectful than before. I was "starting to mature," they claimed, and they all agreed it was because of the male authority influence I had received at the camps. With the improvements Mom was seeing in me, she was not about to change course and not follow up with more of the same. While money continued to be the biggest obstacle keeping me from being sent to a private school, Mom remained determined and was not about to take no for an answer. She continued to talk with friends and family, searching for ideas and advice to help keep me moving forward on the path to social conformity.

It was a friend of my mother's, Bob Obradovich, a tall blond handsome fellow she knew from church, who finally came up with a practical solution to Mom's dilemma. We saw Bob from time to time at our local Serbian Orthodox Church, so it wasn't anything unusual to see him chatting with Mom or Deda or others in the family, following morning services. Yet, on this one particularly hot and humid Sunday morning, I developed a sharp sickening pain in the pit of my stomach the very instant I spotted Mom talking with him on the sidewalk near the front of the church. I could sense without doubt that I was the topic of their discussion, and I felt the stabbing pains in my belly intensify as I walked closer to them. I stopped only a few feet away and still couldn't make out what they were saying. I was certain I would throw up right there on the church steps. Their low indiscernible tones and the serious expression on Mom's face told me I wouldn't like the plans they were making. "Come over here, Eli," my mother called out to me. "I have someone I want you to meet." The towering man turned and looked at me. There was no sign of a smile on his face. *Was this a good time to run away?*

As a young boy, Bob Obradovich attended Glenwood School for Boys, a private boarding school located nearby on Chicago's Southside. He was one who proudly looked back at his time at the school as a life-changing opportunity, one that helped him avoid the perils of a misdirected life. Like mine, his boyhood had been a troubled one, lacking the discipline and guidance of a solid father figure. He was grateful, not only for what Glenwood had done to put stability in his own life, but also for what the school was doing for so many other at-risk children in the area. For more than a century, Glenwood has provided a safe structured environment for kids coming from all sorts of troubled circumstances. Bob's recommendations and his offer to help get me enrolled at the school was exactly what Mom had been searching for. It seemed like no time had passed before I was unpacking my suitcase and placing my belongings in a foot-locker at the foot of my bunk in Washington Cottage on the campus of Glenwood School for Boys.

Known for its rigorous academics, Glenwood used a semi-military approach in its educational programs, an atmosphere which set the stage for a harsh and rude awakening for all new arrivals. Naturally, wearing school uniforms, regimental marching and constant strict discipline were all foreign to me. Like any other naive eleven-year-old kid, I wasn't equipped to deal with the differences between the public schools I had attended and a place like Glenwood. I had a lot of adjustments to make and a lot to learn when I first arrived, including how to follow orders and the meaning of the words, "no talking."

Of course, I felt alone. I felt like everyone in the world had abandoned me. I was told that I was at my new home, yet I couldn't find a smiling face or hear a kind word. *What sort of new home had I been sent to?* At first I wanted to cry. But then I noticed how all of the other new boys in my group were just as scared and confused as I was. I felt it would be best if I were to reach out to one of them. "Finding a new friend would help me get off to a good start," I reasoned. "Misery loves company," I've always been told.

It was my very first day at Glenwood. I knew no one's name and couldn't even find my way to the boys' restroom by myself. There must have been at least a dozen of us boys cramped into this small meeting room, each of us nervous as could be, while we silently pondered what would happen to us next. A musty odor filled the place as we sat jammed close together in those old-fashioned wooden school desks.

"You will face the front of the room and there will be no talking!" a petite but hardboiled woman barked from the back of the room. She was a tiny woman with a thin wirey build. Her small frame reminded me a lot of my Aunt Mary. "We will have absolute silence!" she snapped again, in a voice as gruff as a Gestapo officer. The small statue of this woman was misleading and gave us no clue that she was the type of woman who was better suited for wrestling alligators than she was for elementary education.

Without saying a word, this woman paced back and forth behind us as if she were studying the backs of our necks. I suppose the fact that she stayed out of our sight while she rhythmically clacked her heels on the hardwood floor were some of the methods she used to instill fear in our young minds and keep us on edge. I believe she would have loved nothing more than to make all of us cry!

After a short period of silence, I turned my head to take a glance at the boy sitting in the desk beside me. I gave him a quick smile and spoke to him in a voice only slightly above a whisper. "Hi there, where are you from?" I asked innocently. And before I could get an answer...

Wham! Out of nowhere, I was slapped across the back of my head and knocked out of my seat. Onto the floor I crashed! Totally stunned, with my face down and my nose no more than an inch from the floor, I struggled to get up. I tried to push up and raise my upper body, but my arms were trembling from a sudden onset of weakness. I heard what sounded like the garble of someone talking, but the ringing in my ears made it impossible to make sense of it. Off balance, I finally made it to an upright position and with one hand I gripped the corner of my desk to steady myself. I could tell the room was completely quiet as I slowly lowered my butt onto the flat wooden seat. The ringing in my head continued. It sounded like I was listening from the bottom of a deep well when I heard the unmistakable screeching voice of that same five-foot tall sadistic female monster. "Now you know!" she shouted. "When I say 'no talking' there will be no talking!"

I didn't utter a word the rest of the day. There was no one there I could turn to for help, no one I could confide in and no one I could trust. That night, as I pulled my blanket to my chin, my heart ached from loneliness. It was the end of my first day at Glenwood School for Boys and I was dreading the days that would follow. I tried hard to make myself sleep, but my head was spinning with thoughts of the dreadful things that had happened earlier that day and the fear of what might be in store for tomorrow. "Tomorrow will be better," I assured myself. "I just won't speak to anyone!"

CHAPTER 6

GLENWOOD SCHOOL FOR BOYS

The days were long; sometimes the nights were even longer. Washington Cottage, on the campus of Glenwood School for Boys, was a dark and quiet place after bedtime, quiet enough to have your own thoughts. Yet it could be like a prison cell block if your thoughts were filled with sadness and pain. Glenwood was the sort of place I had been dreading. In the past, when I was sent to summer camp or baseball school, I had come away relieved, finding things had not been as bad as I had expected. Those trips away from home had turned out to be fun experiences. Those were the types of things I would have loved to do over and over every summer. But this was no camp, no vacation and no one could say how long I'd be there.

The first few weeks were the worst. Night after night I would lie awake, staring up at the ceiling, afraid to drift off to sleep for fear of what the next day would bring. And with the exception of a few intermittent bursts of noise brought on by the meatloaf from supper and the muffled giggles that followed, the cottage was completely quiet. I would finally be alone with my thoughts, which was the only time I had to myself. But that was when my mind would be bombarded with a whirlwind of thoughts and questions about the circumstances that led up to my incarceration in this place they called a school.

Who was this fellow Bob Obradovich anyway, and how could someone who was no more than a casual aquaintence to my mother, persuade her to put me here? Did he have something against me? I even went as far as to count the years until I would be old enough to track him down and make him pay for this evil injustice. Somewhere between my resentment and fear I would eventually find a place of peace and fall asleep, only to rise too soon and face another day.

"All right, everybody up and moving!" he yelled. The booming voice sounded like that of a military commander. It was our counselor, George Parenti, a tall athletic guy in his teens who bunked in our cottage. He was as regular as the rising sun when it came to getting us out of bed and on our feet. He made that same call every morning, just as the six o'clock whistle sounded. He made sure that within a matter of seconds, every boy in the barracks was up and moving, taking his first steps of the day. George stood about six feet tall and was about six or seven years older than any of the boys in our cottage. He showed a wholesome, yet authoritive demeanor. He observed all the rules and made certain that each of us under his charge did the same. There was no horsing around with this guy. As our counselor, he could be as gruff as any of the other hard-nosed school officials.

George played no favorites and demanded the same from each of us. All the boys saw him as the no-nonsense, in-charge leader of our platoon, especially when he had us in the yard for close-order drills. That's when he would jump down our throats and kick our asses, should any one of us dare to step out of formation or turn the wrong way. He had no problem screaming in our faces or planting his foot squarely in the seat of some kid's pants, whenever his orders were not followed. We all feared him, yet we respected him. If he wasn't busy, he was approachable and was willing to listen. To a few of us, he was like a big brother. Because of his initials, G.P., he was known around the school as "Jeep," a nicknamed that was used a lot more often than his given name. He had been at the school for several years, knew the ropes and worked hard to earn the confidence of the faculty. He could always tell when one of his boys was giving an honest effort and had no problem coming down hard on any who didn't. With Jeep as my counselor, my initial fear of him turned into respect and then into admiration, and I soon found myself watching him as much as he was watching me. He set a positive example, not only through his words, but through his actions. His conduct, his language and his appearance gave us the type of male role model we needed. And with me, it didn't hurt that he was the star player on the school's varsity baseball team.

As much as I resented him, I had to admit that Bob Obradovich had been a straight talker when he told my mother about Glenwood School for Boys, describing it as a semi-military school with an atmosphere of strong discipline. Strict orders and corporal punishment were the constant norm for the school. I quickly learned that an incident like my first-day run-in with the female teacher who swatted me out of my seat was not that uncommon. It was a horrific experience for me, but nothing out of the ordinary for the faculty or administration. At first, I was shocked by the harsh treatment I saw everyday.

It was not unusual for the school's principal to enter our classroom unannounced. Once he walked in and closed the door, we all knew he was there to administer some excruciating form of punishment to any number of us. He was a huge barrel-chested man, who today would put me in mind of actor Ernest Borgnine. Just the sight of him was enough to make the entire class shiver with fear. We knew he had been summoned to our class by the teacher, who obviously didn't want to deny the "big man" the satisfaction of causing young boys to squirm and yelp with pain. The instant he appeared, the teacher would order us to face forward and place our hands flat on our desktops. You could have heard a pin drop as the principal strolled slowly through the aisle between our seats. We couldn't turn our heads, but his heavy footsteps told us when he was getting close behind our chairs. Still, we wouldn't know who among us would be getting a painful "knobby" until it was too late. *Clomp, clomp,* we would hear his footsteps getting closer. Judging by the sound, his shoe size must have been at least seventeen and a half. *Clomp, clomp,* he moved closer to the front of the room. Once the footsteps stopped, it was "Katie bar the door!"

With the knuckle of his middle finger protruding from his fist, he brought his right hand down hard on the top of some poor boy's head, striking that knuckle hard against the top of his skull! Over the years, I'm sure I suffered more than my fair share of lumps and knots on my scalp, caused by those nasty knobbies. Sometimes I never knew why I got them, but that was just part of life at Glenwood.

The school was always billed as a paramilitary school, where boys from ages eight to eighteen are held to the highest academic standards.

And make no mistake about it, academic studies were taken very seriously at Glenwood. Equally as important was the military aspect of our education, which extended far beyond the mess halls, army bunks and uniforms. There were marching and drills and constant checks and inspections, which resulted in severe punishments for even the slightest infractions.

We faced regularly scheduled inspections of our cottage, carried out by a stoic, heavy-set man who never cracked a smile. He was known to us only as "Sarge." He checked our bunk areas for cleanliness, the arrangement of our lockers and saw to it that our beds were properly made. With this fellow, even the tiniest scrap of paper left on the floor or the most unnoticeable wrinkle found in the bed cover was as serious as first-degree murder. Even when on rare occasions our barracks made the grade, the inspection process would continue. The boys would then be ordered to muster for an inspection of hands, necks and elbows, as a way to check for personal cleanliness. Everything, right down to our finger-nails, was examined closely for any signs of dirt and grime. If Sarge found anything to indicate inadequate or infrequent bathing, an old standard military practice known as "G.I. scrubbing" was put into action. Once a boy suffered the agony of receiving a G.I., it was very likely that he would never be a repeat offender. The dreaded process involved having the kid with the questionable hygiene forcibly restrained by other boys who stripped him of his clothes while he was held under a shower or doused with a hose. He would be lathered down, head to toe with strong indus-trial soap. Next, he would be scrubbed by a band of brush-wielding boys who showed no mercy. They used stiff-bristle brushes from the kitchen, along with scouring pads and steel wool to scrub his entire body. It was an extremely painful ordeal for the screaming offender, which resulted in severe skin abrasions and bleeding. Even when the punishment was over, the poor fellow was left cowering on the floor, sopping wet and crying, certainly in no condition to enjoy a hot shower for the next few days.

If there was ever anyone on the staff at Glenwood who seemed to enjoy his job more than Sarge, I don't believe I ever encountered him. This man delighted in doling out doses of violent punishment to young boys as often as possible. He appeared to receive pleasure from hearing us cry and scream with pain. His stone face and his calloused and insensitive deportment made him the perfect character to do his type of work.

At the end of each month, he would saunter into Washington Cottage carrying the hickory shaft from a golf club under his arm as if it were a swagger stick. With his nose cocked into the air, he wandered methodically about the floor, pausing at various spots to take a look around. He looked as if he were expecting to find a bat hanging upside-down from the ceiling or a snake squirming on the floor between the bunks. Eventually, he would make his way back to the front of the building and stop to stare at the platoon roster board that hung on the wall near the door. That was another signal that some of us were about to get a licking.

On the board was an alphabetical list of names of the boys assigned to the cottage. Next to each name were spaces, some open and some filled with checkmarks, which were given whenever a boy neglected his duty or disobeyed an order. Some minor infractions resulted in a black mark being placed in the space, while a more serious offense would merit a red check. Of course, Sarge, in his fiendish mind, had no difficulty in coming up with a conversion system which mathematically determined just how delinquent each boy had been over the past month as well as the severity of his punishment. For every black checkmark next to his name, a boy would be given one lash for each red mark he received seven. Using his golf club shaft as a whipping stick, Sarge methodically administered the beatings, ordering the kid to step to the front of the room, drop his trousers and lean forward over a desk. Next, with only the victim's underwear left to cushion the blows, Sarge reached back as far as he could for leverage before driving his stick forward. He counted aloud after each swat. The sound of that slender hickory rod striking a young boy's fleshy buttocks was enough to make even the most hardened among us cringe. I am happy to say, unlike some other boys in my cottage, I was a quick learner and only faced this treatment on a few occasions. After receiving one of those beatings, I soon concluded I would have been a lot more comfortable in the mess hall if I had been allowed to eat my dinner standing up!

Everything about the school was carried out according to the book. Procedures, rules, drills, schedules and inspections were incorporated into every part of life at Glenwood. Every moment of our lives was overseen by a person of authority that made sure our every move was in accordance with regulations. For a kid like me who had spent a big part of his life alone and free with hardly any discipline, it was a painful transition.

It was a cruel and rude awakening to be uprooted from the unruly streets of Chicago and dumped into a world where I was physically forced to do exactly as I was told. At Glenwood there was no middle ground, and you were given only two options. You could either follow orders or get your ass kicked.

A big part of our military training regimen took place on the parade field, located on campus, not far from Washington Cottage. Like clockwork, our platoon was out there, every Thursday, marching and executing close-order drills. Dressed in our blue uniforms with Fort Knox caps, we moved in unison as Jeep Parenti barked orders. A casual observer would have been hard pressed to tell the difference between our unit and a drill unit from any full military academy. It took time, but once Jeep got us whipped into shape, we performed with precision, yet getting to that point was no easy process. In the early stages of our training, to say our marching drills were poorly executed was a gross understatement. There were times when our ranks were as disorderly as a swarm of roaches scrambling when the light is switched on! It was Jeep who turned us into a platoon that learned to function as a unit, not as individuals. It was through him that we were programmed to think in terms of "we" and not "me."

Even considering the times I absentmindedly stepped out of formation and caused Jeep to put his shoe in the crack of my butt, I saw how he was changing me for the better. I looked up to him, admiring his work ethic, his character and maturity. I began to emulate his mannerisms. I intentionally copied the way he spoke, the way he groomed and dressed. I even began to work harder in the classroom, following his lead and taking my studies more seriously. Jeep Parenti had become my role model.

There was a short time when I started to redirect my thinking and I began to contemplate the future I could have at Glenwood if I followed the example Jeep was setting. Perhaps if I studied more, stayed out of trouble and focused on baseball like Jeep, I could someday be the kind of standout athlete and honor student he was. For a few moments, I even imagined what it would be like to be a counselor for Washington Cottage. But my ambitions would stick around only as long as Jeep was there. The instant I heard he would be leaving, my hopes were dashed and I feared for my future. The positive male influence I had longed for had finally arrived, but it would be leaving much too soon.

With the promise for a bright future ahead of him, I could see that Jeep was eager to get started with his life. Graduation from high school could not come soon enough for him. He was never more proud than when he told some of the guys he was closest to that he would be attending the University of Illinois the very next year and playing baseball on the school's varsity team. It was an exciting time for him. The world was his oyster. Yet, as I shared his joy and was happy for his good fortune, I was crushed by thoughts of losing him and wondering what life would be like at Glenwood without him.

After he left, I kept trying to apply the things he taught me and use the advice he gave me. I even imagined how he would have given me a pat on the back for a high test score or for a good catch on the ballfield. But things were not the same. He had promised to stay in touch and keep us posted on his baseball career. He assured us he would check on us from time to time, to make sure we were all doing our best. But I suppose other things became important, and he became too busy to keep up with us.

Being forced to conform to the authority continued to be one of the most harrowing experiences of my life. On more occasions than I can remember, my emotions would hit their boiling point as I struggled to adapt to this regimented form of existence. I alternated between cursing with anger and resentment to crying from fear and loneliness. I became angry whenever I realized I had so little control over even the simplest things in life, and I was so lonely whenever I thought about Mom and the rest of the family back home.

Sundays, in particular were the days I felt abandoned and alone. It was on Sunday afternoons that the school was opened to guests, as parents, grandparents, brothers and sisters spent time visiting and touring the campus. With no visitors of my own, I kept a constant watch on the entrance, waiting for visitors who hardly ever showed up. Those were some of the loneliest days I can remember. I recall one occasion when my dad came all the way from Texas for a Sunday afternoon visit. After the short time I spent with him, I can't remember when or where I saw him again. Other than that, there were only a few instances when Mom had time away from her job and was able to drive out to the school with one of my aunts for a short unexpected visit. Normally, I was overjoyed to see her and I cherished our times together. However, on one particular Sunday afternoon, she broke the news to me that she had authorized the school to schedule an appointment for me to be circumcised at the local clinic. It was an awful day, one I would just as soon forget.

"I'm twelve years old!" I protested. "What a terrible thing to do to me!" Still, my resistance was futile.

Later that same week, I was driven to the clinic, prepped and left waiting on a hospital gurney just outside the double-door entrance to the O.R. With only a few minutes remaining before I would be put on the chopping block, I lay quietly, thinking only of my impending horrors and fighting to hold back my tears. Nearby, were other young boys, waiting on their gurneys, each scheduled for some sort of surgical procedure for his own illness or ailment.

Suddenly from somewhere down the hall, I heard a boisterous voice, one that was undoubtedly telling others what to do. I lifted my head just enough to recognize it was a nurse, or at least some type of creature in a nurse's uniform. She was pointing her finger and shouting instructions to others on the staff. This woman was gruff, loud and as round as a barrel. She would make Louise Fletcher's character, Nurse Ratched, look like an angel of mercy. As she drew closer to me, she stopped at each gurney, checked the chart attached to the side railing and announced to everyone within shouting distance, the nature of each kid's surgery.

"This one's a tonsillectomy!" she yelled. "This one's a hernia! Oh no, we've got ourselves another tonsillectomy over here!"

Finally, she came to my stretcher, snatched up the clipboard and hastily leafed through the paperwork. For about two seconds, a deviant smile stretched across her face before she resumed her orders.

"Well, whataya know! Today is our lucky day! It looks like this little fellow needs a circumcision!"

Her enthusiasm scared the daylights out of me. I wanted to run, but the anesthesia had taken effect and I was too weak to even move. "How could these people have made the situation more frightening?" I asked myself. "Is this a bad dream? This monster in a white uniform can't wait to get her hands on me!"

Of course, I survived the surgery and thankfully, the gauze bandages were taken off a few days later. As for the results, I can only say the whole operation helped make me a better man!

With another lonely Sunday only a matter of hours away, I reached my emotional limit. My young heart was aching to go home. Not only had I withstood all the orders and punishments I could endure, but I couldn't imagine facing another lonely weekend by myself. I had been hearing stories which were circulating about the school about how one of the kids had pulled off a hastily planned escape. The rumor was he bragged for weeks about how great it was to get a taste of freedom and see the outside world. The story intrigued me and gave me ideas of my own. "If that boy could do it, I can do it too," I assured myself.

The yard adjacent to the school's main building was completely vacant when I ventured out on a chilly afternoon after lunch. What was intended to appear like I was taking a casual walk was nothing of the sort. I felt daring and adventurous. I also felt very desperate. Suddenly, the thought of making a run for it started to feel more and more like a good plan. "Now's the time," I told myself, needing to bolster my courage. I continued my stroll, walking slowly toward the edge of the school property, but I quickened my pace as I got closer to the highway. Suddenly, I was off and running, away from the school, heading for cover in a grove of trees. My heart was pounding as I paused to catch my breath. "I escaped! I finally did it!" I boasted to myself. "Now, I need to be smart and make it work."

Keeping my sense of direction, I emerged from the wooded area and began walking along the road that would lead me back to Southside Chicago. I would have to cover about 30 miles to get back home, but I was confident I could make it. I wanted nothing more than to turn Glenwood into a bad memory. We had all heard about how Glenwood used security officers in black cars to patrol the area and roundup truant boys, so I constantly kept an eye out for any black automobiles in the area. Several times I leaped into the brush or jumped down into a ditch to hide the instant I spotted a black vehicle coming my way. I felt as if I were having another of my crazy dreams. Years later I would often find myself reliving these bizarre childhood experiences whenever I caught an episode of the 1960s drama, *The Fugitive*, on TV.

With each step I looked over my shoulder to see who would be approaching from behind, while I scanned both sides of the highway ahead. Without thinking of the possible consequences, I accepted rides from a few motorists who were going my way and soon I was getting into familiar territory. My instincts told me I was getting close to South

Deering and the Slag Valley neighborhood just as another vehicle slowed down to offer me a lift.

"Climb in son," the driver offered. "I'm heading your way and I'd be happy to help you save some shoe leather." Wearing a white shirt and tie and puffing on a cigar, he appeared to be a businessman, probably a family man with no bad intentions, so I hopped in on the front seat. By this time my legs and feet were aching from the long journey, but I felt safer and more confident as I got closer to my neighborhood. He casually initiated a conversation, asking where I was headed and where I attended school. And while his small talk sounded perfectly normal at first, I grew suspicious as his questions continued. Maybe it was because I was hungry or maybe from a lack of sleep that caused a strange sensation to sweep over me. I knew something wasn't on the level. The smoke from his cigar was burning my eyes and turning my stomach. I wished I hadn't accepted his offer.

"I go to school right here in South Deering," I blurted, trying to keep the conversation going. "I go to Fenger High School!" He took another puff on his stogie and stared directly ahead. I could tell from the eerie silence he wasn't buying my cockamamie story. He knew I was lying and knew I was too young to go to high school. My jaw tightened with frustration; I was sure I had just sealed my own doom. Suddenly my attention was taken by the flash of a shiny silver badge, fixed to a swatch of leather hanging from the knob on his ashtray. After a quick, inconspicuous glance, I was able to make out the engraving on the shield; TRUANT OFFICER - CITY OF CHICAGO.

My entire body went into panic mode. My heart raced and my legs shook with fear. Luckily for me, he needed to tap the brakes and slow down for the red light at the next intersection. With no time to waste, I knew my only hope for freedom was hanging in the balance. I wrapped my hand around the door handle and shouted impulsively as I leaned my shoulder against the door to push it outward.

"I just remembered, this is where I need to get out!" I yelled, my voice quivering. He stomped the brake pedal and reached frantically across the seat to grab the sleeve of my jacket.

"Get back here kid!" he ordered. "Are you crazy? You're gonna get yourself hurt!" Escaping his grasp, I leaped from his automobile and vaulted over a guard railing. For the moment, I held a slight advantage over the officer who was in no position to abandon his car at the busy intersection. I tumbled down a rocky embankment which led to a series of parallel railroad tracks. Running as if my life depended on it, I crossed the tracks and dashed toward an open grassy area which looked vaguely familiar. I stopped only long enough to look behind me and make sure I wasn't being chased. With no one in pursuit, I took a deep breath as I surveyed my surroundings. The place began to look more familiar to me the longer I stood there. Suddenly I realized where I was. I was just a short distance from my old school, Marsh Elementary! I was at the end of "The Swamp," my favorite old play area. At last, I was almost home!

Within minutes, I was dragging my exhausted body up the front steps and onto the porch of the house I had missed for so long. My grandfather must have been taking a nap when he heard me knocking on the front door as it took him a moment answer.

"They sent me home, Deda." I explained to him sheepishly. "They are running out of food at the school and can't keep feeding all of us. I was one of the ones they told to go home."

Even though he had just been roused from a sound sleep, it took Deda only a quick look to see I was muddy and tired. He could tell right away I had been walking through weeds and woods and ditches, and he knew without asking I was scared and on the brink of tears. I'm sure he would have preferred that I not notice the smile that broke across his face as he held the door open for me.

"Come on in here, son, so we can talk this thing over," he suggested.

Of course, Deda never gave that flimsy excuse of mine a second thought, but I believe for the moment, he was proud that his grandson had enough guts to pull off a stunt like this.

I was desperate to break away from Glenwood and it showed. Without having to do a lot of explaining, Mom and Deda saw the need to change things. While I was away, Mom had switched jobs again and had finally worked her way from under some of the financial hardships that had held her down for so many years. With more income and a little more time at home, she was in a better position to have me stay with her. Seeing how her young son was desperate and daring enough to undertake a thirty-mile trek on his own was enough to convince her that Glenwood School for Boys was no longer the place for me. That was the best news I could've ever dreamed of!

Nevertheless, the rigid order and discipline I had been subjected to at Glenwood had forced some positive changes on me which made me a lot more respectful and obedient. Mom and the other family members were surprised by my newly acquired respectfulness and courtesy and by how easily the words like "yes, sir" and "thank you" rolled off my tongue. My time away had changed me into a more manageable child, one who was a lot more pleasant to have around the house.

Operating under a new name, Glenwood School for Boys and Girls is still serving Illinois families today. And while the administration's approach to discipline has softened over the years, the school continues to provide a top-rated academic program which focuses on personal responsibility. Some of the more contemporary programs there include facilities for female students and opportunities for day-students. Glenwood has helped lay the groundwork for many successful businessmen in the Chicago area as well as for individuals who have achieved high-ranking positions in our military. And while I don't want to leave anyone with the impression that my experiences at Glenwood are typical, I must acknowledge that the discipline they instilled in me worked wonders to redirect my life and steer me clear of many social traps that were set and waiting for young boys like me, boys who lacked that ever-important positive male influence.

Like so many others in my life, my mentor at Glenwood, Jeep Parenti, moved on. I'm confident he was successful, and I'm sure he went on to face every challenge that came his way by giving it his best shot and always doing his best. I was happy for the short time I was with him and grateful for the values he instilled in me. I never forgot him and even took time to look for him and contact him later in my adult life. After several attempts I finally found his home and met his mother, a delightful lady who apologized for him not being at home. Yet like any proud mother would have been, she was so pleased to inform me he was away for the season, still pursuing his dream of playing baseball.

However, as amazing as it may be, I still find myself imagining how my life may have been different had I had more time with him. Who knows? It was one of our most controversial and outspoken first-ladies, Eleanor Roosevelt who advised us, "In the long run, we shape our lives and shape ourselves... and the choices we make are ultimately our own responsibility." Maybe I would have handled some things differently. Perhaps I may have done my best in areas where I didn't. Neither George

"Jeep" Parenti, nor anyone else, will ever be made accountable for the paths I chose in my life. I've always done things my way!

BUMPER CROP AT GLENWOOD MANUAL TRAINING SCHOOL
Ell Grba, 12 (left), and Ray Aikens, 12, contemplate a future filled with pumpkin p made from pumpkins they raised themselves on the Glenwood Farms while attend Glenwood Manual Training School at 187th and Halsted sts.

Operating under a new name, Glenwood School for Boys and Girls is still serving Illinois families today.

CHAPTER 7

WE COULD SURE USE A GUY LIKE YOU

———

It would be years before I could appreciate what Glenwood School for Boys had done for me. And while I might have been a little too young to detect all of the improvements in my behavior, the adults who had been around me before I left home and saw me again after my return were impressed by the transformation. The male influence and discipline I received at the school had worked wonders in redirecting my energy and calming the rebellion that had been burning inside of me. Even from my earliest days, I remember being filled with painful anger and frustration, yet I had no clue where it all came from, or who or what I needed to rebel against. But for the time, things were better. I felt at ease and carried myself with a newfound confidence. Simply put, I was more comfortable being me. Rather than make me go back to Glenwood, Deda and my mother decided it was best to have me return to the public school system, so they enrolled me at the local grammar school, Marsh Elementary.

At first, I hooked up with some of the same neighborhood kids I ran with before, the same boys I hung around with when I got into so much trouble. Not a lot had changed for them. They were still up to their old tricks, hanging around town and swiping whatever they could get away with, whether it was something they wanted or not. For a brief time, I rejoined them and took part in the shenanigans. We were back to stealing almost anything, wherever and whenever a store clerk was distracted or wasn't keen enough to keep an eye on us.

Yet for some reason, things were different. The thrills that came from sneaking around, shoplifting and looking to impress my cohorts with my take were gone. There was a subtle voice telling me I could do better and that the time had come to rise above this sort of behavior. I thought about Glenwood and felt an awareness of the values the school had instilled in me over such a short time. It wasn't so much the discipline or the harsh punishments that came to my mind as much as the image of George "Jeep" Parenti and the high standards he lived by. I saw how he demonstrated pride in everything he did and how he shouldered responsibility for his actions without ever looking to lay blame on someone else. I recalled how he seemed to have earned the respect of just about everyone who knew him. Without knowing it, he had become my role model, a position he would hold throughout much of my boyhood. His ethics and integrity made lasting impressions on me, at a time when I was probably too young to know what the words *ethics* and *integrity* meant.

I was about to turn off the table lamp next to my bed when I decided to take one last look at the bracelet I had swiped earlier that day. I had snatched it that afternoon when no one was watching me or any of the other boys as we pervaded the jewelry section at F. W. Woolworth's. I had no good reason for stealing it and even at such a young age I was smart enough to tell it had no real value. I had no plans to give it to anyone in particular and it certainly wasn't something I wanted to keep for myself. Once again I stared at the bracelet as I held it beneath the light. The glass stones sparkled at me, but I couldn't appreciate the beauty of the glimmering colors. I could find no way to justify what I had done. I closed my fingers around the cheap band of metal and cut glass and clinched it tightly in my fist.

"What will happen if get caught again?" I asked myself. "Will I be sent back to Glenwood? And what will happen if Jeep ever finds out about what I did?"

He would be very disappointed in me and I didn't want to think about how much that would hurt.

I switched off the light and crawled into bed. I closed my eyes knowing I had a very important job to do the next day, and that was to get that bracelet back onto the display shelf at Woolworth's. I realized I couldn't undo what was already done, but I was sure going to do whatever it took to make things right. I knew I could do better, and the time had come for me to rise up if I were going to turn out to be like George "Jeep" Parenti.

It was a daring undertaking, but I had no choice. I knew returning the stolen item to Woolworth's would be the only way I could ever hope to erase the senseless misdeed from my consciousness and find peace. So with all the courage I could muster, I went alone behind enemy lines and returned to the scene of the crime, fully aware that if I were found out, no explanation or excuse would suffice. I would be a thief, caught dead to rights. My heart pounded as I walked into the store. Thankfully, the clerks were all busy, working the registers and stocking merchandise in another area of the floor. *If only I knew the on-screen secret of movie star Claude Rains and could suddenly become invisible, then my quest would be an easy job.* I went directly to the spot where I had lifted the object only days earlier. I dropped it into the open display and scurried back toward the front of the store. Realizing I had accomplished my mission undetected, I breathed a huge sigh of relief as I stepped outside onto the sidewalk and turned to head for home. That night, the relief I felt was real. My burden of guilt had been lifted. It was as if a physical weight had been lifted from my shoulders.

I still had another full year to go at Marsh Elementary, but having endured the rigors of Glenwood, I found my final term of grammar school to be more palatable than any I had experienced. No doubt I had received an attitude adjustment while I was away at Glenwood, but I also began to notice how my interests were changing. I wanted to try getting involved in some new activities and I wanted to change from the way I had been doing some of the old things.

While it had been quite a long time since I had seen George Parenti, there was no denying that I continued to emulate him in almost everything I did. I suppose it was my own subconscious way of keeping him alive in my mind and preserving his image as an example for the way I approached things. I recalled what he had said to me about the importance of studying and making good grades and the advice he gave me about how hard work would always be the key to success in athletics. And while the other boys at Marsh Elementary never got to meet Jeep and knew nothing about him, it never kept me from imitating him or wanting to be seen as being just like him.

My dad beamed with pride the day I graduated from
Marsh Elementary School.

The thrills I experienced a few summers earlier at the Ozark Baseball
Camp had not faded. There was still something about the excitement
of meeting Jim Bottomley and the other baseball stars and the fun of
watching old baseball movies each night before bedtime that lingered
with me. The fact that eating, sleeping and talking baseball for three solid
weeks is all we did was a perfect fit for me. I would have been ready for
another few weeks of camp if they would have let me stay. And there was
also Jeep's love for baseball, which he shared with me when we were at
Glenwood. Naturally, I hung onto his every word whenever he discussed
an upcoming game or demonstrated the grip he used for his fastball. But,
my interest wasn't all simply because he was my mentor and I thrived on
his attention. Neither was it because the game was what my father loved

or because it was a topic my uncles talked about whenever one of them walked into the house with a fresh newspaper. I believe I was born with my own fascination for the game of baseball. Surely, there was an assortment of outside influences which pulled me in that direction. But ever since I was a very young boy, baseball has always occupied a big place in my heart.

As I approached the age to enter high school, I began to devote more and more of my time to baseball. In the spring I played pick-up games after school with the boys who lived nearby. But once classes ended for the summer, I played baseball whenever I got the chance. I would have been happy to play everyday, all day long, until it started to get dark and we could no longer see the ball.

Our ragtag teams comprised the same neighborhood boys I went to school with and many of these same fellows had been with me on some of the senseless shoplifting sprees that were staged around town. Yet in spite of the delinquent activities we had taken up at such a young age, I would never say that any of us were the type of boys that should be labeled as hateful or malicious. In fact, everyone in this group with whom I have had contact as an adult has found some degree of success in life. Each has turned out to be hard working and honest, the inherent trademarks of the people from my old neighborhood.

Still, as a bunch of carefree young boys, we played baseball in our overalls, dungarees, T-shirts and sneakers, using slabs of wood, pieces of cardboard or whatever we could find for bases. We played at the school-yard and on sandlots, or in any open area large enough to mark off a diamond. And our equipment, which would be considered antiquated and crude compared to what youngsters use today was also in short supply. However, most of the boys were quick to share and would bring along whatever bats and balls and mitts they could muster. As was often the case, we only had a small group of boys show up to play, so we would find ourselves limited to some of the makeshift games I mentioned earlier, like "strikeout." But still, even those games were lots of fun for me, as I saw them simply as more opportunities for me to imitate my favorite player, the great Ted Williams, whenever it was my turn to bat.

Of course there were times when every boy on the field did not have the luxury of wearing a glove and all the positions on the diamond weren't filled, but those shortages and inconveniences did nothing to dampen our passion for the game or diminish the dreams we all had of one day making it to the big leagues.

He was a little older than I was, but in our early years we were as close as brothers. We first met under some unlikely circumstances; and yet in spite of our age difference, we meshed from the very start. Our friendship is one that has stood the test of time and continues to this day.

He is Ray Aleman, a boy who had already started high school and was recognized by the local kids as one of the best ballplayers around town. Baseball was his lifeblood. For a young boy, he had exceptional determination and a serious approach to the game. He was resourceful enough to have helped organize the Sportsmen, the local team he played on, which was the most formidable sandlot team in the neighborhood.

Some of the Sportsmen players were older than Ray, but almost all of them went to Bowen High School. To the rest of us, the Sportsmen were the elite team, an exclusive club that not only had the most talent, but also the best equipment. And while it was never clear where the resources came from to outfit the team, they somehow managed to come up with an adequate supply of bats and balls for all of their games. To us younger guys who played on ragtag makeup teams, the Sportsmen looked like a troupe of professionals. Not only did every boy on the team have his own glove, but each also had matching T-shirts with the team name emblazoned across the front. To other boys, they presented a classy yet daunting image. But more than anything, it was those sharp-looking shirts that made the Sportsmen the envy of every boy in the neighborhood.

For other teams, getting enough boys together to play a ballgame was a tough job. Once we decided it was time for a game, we had to make phone calls and knock on doors in order to round up boys to play. Even then, we sometimes fell short of having enough to make a full squad. And try as we did, with all positions filled, we managed to play some good ballgames. But we were never much of a legitimate match against the Sportsmen. They were older and had better players than any of the make-up teams I played on, and I'm sure their snazzy uniform tops also went a long way in intimidating us. However, in spite of being overmatched time and time again by the Sportsmen, there was a stroke of good fortune waiting for me. To my surprise there was a lucky break hidden under the discouragement of that dismal losing streak.

We were leaving the field after taking another old-fashioned shellacking from the Sportsmen when I heard a voice calling behind me.

"Hey, Eli, wait up!" It was Ray jogging across the infield, trying to catch up.

I stopping dead in my tracks and turned around, not completely sure that it was me he wanted. Like all the other boys, I knew who Ray Aleman was, but I wasn't so sure he even knew my name.

"You played a good game today," he said in an approving tone. "I noticed how you handled yourself at thirdbase and that you got off some strong throws over to first. It looks like you've got a good arm."

He had caught me off guard. Naturally, I was confused. After all, following such a lopsided defeat, praise from the victors wasn't exactly what I expected to get.

"Thanks, Ray," I finally responded. He placed his hand on my shoulder as if we were longtime friends. I knew he could detect the reluctance on my part.

"You're good at the plate, too," he continued. "You have a nice swing."

Just as sure as summer follows spring, I knew he was up to something. A guy like Ray who plays for the Sportsmen just doesn't stop a younger kid like me and dish out compliments unless something's in the works. *Is he playing some sort of prank on me?*

For the Sportsmen it was business as usual. Ray's teammates were milling around their bench, gathering their equipment and discussing their next game. Not far away, my teammates were huddled together as a group, staring at Ray and me, curiously trying to listen in on our conversation. Sure they were happy for me. There was no doubt they were all pleased by the prospect of one of their own being chosen to move up to the Sportsmen. Yet I knew each of them well enough to recognize their envy. I'm sure any one of them would have traded the world to be in my shoes. It was my lucky day! Ray was on the verge of making his point.

"I'll be honest with you, Eli," he continued. "The guys on our team all agreed when I told them this is no place for you to be playing ball. 'Cause it's plain to see that you're wasting your time messing around with these boys. You can do a lot better. And the Sportsmen are always looking for good players who can hit and throw. We could sure use a guy like you. So whataya' say, Eli? Would you like to play for the Sportsmen?"

Not being prepared for Ray's proposal, I looked toward the boys on my team who were still hanging around. They were whispering among themselves. I turned to Ray and noticed a bit of impatience. He wasn't fooling around. He was waiting for an on-the-spot answer. "Why sure, Ray, of course! I'd love to join the Sportsmen. Who wouldn't?"

Ray had gotten the response he expected and gave me a quick pat on the shoulder. "Okay, Eli that sounds good. We're having a team practice in a few days and you'll need to workout with us before our next game, so I'll be in touch."

Soon, I was wearing one of those great-looking T-shirts and playing third base for the Sportsmen. As the newest and youngest boy on the club, I was nervous at the start. I felt the pressure of needing to prove I was deserving of Ray's offer. But it wasn't long before I discovered I could hit, field and throw just as well as the others, all of whom had advantages over me in both age and experience. Yet, I was able to take my place on the team. I was accepted as a player and became one of the guys. And at such a young age, I was thrilled to find the intense sense of belonging that came to me by joining the team. It was what I needed to help counter the loneliness I carried throughout much of my childhood. Of course there was my family who always loved me through the good times and the bad and accepted me for who I was. Each family member gave me as much of their time and attention as they could. However, my spot on the Sportsmen baseball team was something different and new. For a kid entering his teenage years, it was big and important. It was something I had gained on my own. For once, I stood out from the other boys in the neighborhood. I had been cited for my talents, and finally, I was needed and it was a good feeling to know!

It was the 1940s. The War had finally ended and our country was making giant strides in the areas of electronics, medicine, aeronautics and transportation. America's scientists and engineers had much to be proud of, having made numerous incredible breakthroughs which would enhance the lives of people the world over. Yet, for decades, there has been one proud individual who has laid claim to a discovery of another sort. It was the discovery of a young baseball player who advanced on from the sandlots of Chicago to later apply his skills at the major league level for a number of seasons, as a somewhat successful right-handed pitcher. The pitcher is me, and the person, who claims to have first spotted my abilities on the diamond and caused my professional career to become a reality is my lifelong friend, Ray Aleman.

And you may be right, Ray. Perhaps I owe it all to you. But even away from baseball, you've always been a great friend. And for that, I owe you millions!

CHAPTER 8

THE VOICE OF REASSURRANCE

⸺

In Psalm 91 we read, "For He shall give His angels charge over thee, to keep thee in all thy ways." This is a well known excerpt from the scriptures that some of us may recall reading during our childhood. Yet without carefully contemplating these words, we can easily conjure unintended limitations and restrictions for this passage which were never intended. The verse lists no requirements or conditions and specifies no particular group of people who are entitled to such divine strength and protection. It is God's angels who constantly care for all of us, providing guidance and encouragement to even the most unsuspecting. For some of the more fortunate among us, it can be in our darkest hour, a time when we find ourselves on the edge of despair, that a startling life-changing revelation can occur. And in such a case, an earthly life can be changed forever.

Through her entire adult life, my mother faced a never-ending barrage of hardships. And while she demonstrated strength and courage unlike any other person I have known, it wasn't until I was older that I could appreciate her plight and begin to recognize the hardships that filled her life. There was never a carefree moment, never time to relax and very little time to spend with family and friends. But as a child, I was unaware of her situation. I only knew that I was nurtured and cared for by the most loving mother in the world. I was secure, knowing she would provide everything I would need to go along with a few of the things I wanted. Yet I had no idea of the sacrifices she made to make it all happen.

As it was popular at the time, many of the boys around the neighborhood were sporting dungarees. Made of heavy denim fabric, they were practical for school, the playground or weekend outside activities. They were sewn with heavy stitching and reinforced with rivets and featured extra long legs rolled up into cuffs just above the shoe tops. They were relatively inexpensive and well suited for active boys who loved to run, climb and tumble. There was nothing neat or dressy about them, which may have been the biggest reason my mother didn't care for them and didn't care to have me seen wearing them. Normally, when I left the house, especially for school, I was dressed in some of the finest sweaters, shirts and trousers any boy could have. It was important to Mom that I went well groomed and well dressed to school, to church and almost anyplace. For her, it was a priority. All the while, her own modest wardrobe was seldom updated. Of course, she had nice fashionable clothes for church and family gatherings, but with her hectic work schedule, she had very little time for an active social life. Still, she made sure that my appearance gave no indication of her plight as a hard-working single mother with a low-paying job. There again, she sacrificed so I could have the best.

Her life was always one of fighting to make ends meet. She constantly struggled to keep up with the rent on her apartment, while providing for me and stretching what was left over to cover her own modest needs. Yet despite receiving a regular pittance from my father, there never seemed to be enough money at the end of the month to cover all the bases. As tight as her budget was, those support payments from my dad were probably little more than monthly reminders of the horrible years she had spent with him, suffering cruel abuse at the hands of a violent alcoholic. Those were horrific times that would never leave her memory...or mine.

Her workdays were long and grueling. Whether she was rising early and getting home late from her job as a waitress, or coping with the demands of shift work at the cereal plant, Mom worked very hard, but her wages were low. Still, it was the best she could do. Good paying jobs for women were hard to come by, especially for single ladies with limited education. No doubt, there were times when she received help from the family, maybe a small loan from time to time. But borrowing was never something she preferred to do. It probably caused her to worry even more, until each debt was paid back in full.

It wasn't very often that my mother caught a break with her finances. However, Mr. DeCavitch, her landlord, knew her predicament and often made allowances. He was a serious business man, but was reasonable and understanding when it came to my mother's lease. He knew how hard she worked and trusted her to come through with the rent payment, even if it was a few days late. And like anyone else who knew her, Mr. DeCavitch could tell how things like keeping promises and honoring debts were very important to my mother. She was a lady with strong values and integrity.

Before I went away to Glenwood School for Boys, there were many days I remember Mom coming home completely exhausted after a long tiring day at the restaurant. She would have spent her whole day taking orders, waiting tables and serving meals as quickly as the kitchen could have them ready. She was at the beck and call of all her customers from early morning until the day was done. And by the time she made it home to the old family house on 97th Street and Commercial Avenue, climbed the front steps and grabbed her mail from the box at the front door, her feet were aching as if they were on fire. She would rush directly to her bedroom, loosen the laces of her white service shoes and kick one shoe and then the other under the edge of her dresser. Next, she would empty the money she had collected in tips from her purse and spread it out on the dresser top, counting every bill and coin in the process. I suppose it was her way of determining if her shift had been a lucrative one. As a young kid, going through my stage of rascality and thievery, the exposed cash lying unguarded in the bedroom made an irresistible target for my small, sticky fingers. There had been a few times when I swiped a nickel or a dime, but never any large noticeable amount. I had never been caught, so I got comfortable and started to become complacent with my system.

Once, when Mom was busy at the stove, I snuck into her room and grabbed a half-dollar and quickly stuffed it deep into my pants pocket. I quietly crept past her in the kitchen and without saying a word, bolted out the door. That big silver coin was burning a hole in my pocket. I had no idea how I would spend it, but I knew I wouldn't have it for long. I was neither hungry nor thirsty, but it made no difference. I had money to blow on whatever I wanted.

With no plan in mind, I headed down the sidewalk and ducked into the first corner candy store I came to. It was time for an all-out spending spree. Inside, I handed over all of my loot at once, and managed to come away with a substantial pile of candy and goodies to show for it. I was amazed at how much fifty cents could buy. Back then, a half dollar could buy enough junk food to make a kid sick!

I hurriedly scarfed down a couple of candy bars, followed closely by a bag of chips. I ripped the wrappers from a *Mary Jane* and a *Tootsie Roll* and stuffed them into my cheek. Boy was I in heaven! All of this chewy sweetness was mine! Finally, I washed all of this down with a six-ounce bottle of ice-cold *Coca-Cola*. Out of cash, I had a belly that was full and bloated. I decided it was time to make my way back to the house. With each step, the level of soda seemed to work its way higher into my throat. I began to feel full and queasy in my stomach. I was belching and nearing the point of throwing up. At this point there was no way I could sit at Mom's kitchen table and eat, no matter what she had prepared. *How could I talk my way out of eating dinner?*

Minutes later I walked through the door and discovered my troubles were just beginning. I had a lot of explaining to do. But none of it had anything to do with eating dinner. I quickly found I didn't stand a chance of defending myself against the charges I was about to face. The interrogation began as soon as I closed the door behind me.

"Gerbie, did you take any of the money from the top of my dresser?" Mom demanded. "Did you steal from me?"

I knew from the start there was a chance I could get into big trouble. I knew there was risk involved. But I didn't expect the bottom to fall out of my caper so soon.

"No ma'am!" I answered, completely unprepared. "I don't know what you're talking about."

"Are you sure?" her cross-examination continued. "Did you go behind my back and take money from my bedroom?"

"No ma'am," I repeated. "I wouldn't do anything like that!"

I couldn't tell if she was buying my denials. Then again, she didn't have to. Next, to drive a nail in my own coffin and prove what a lousy thief I was, I played straight into her hand. I made the biggest blunder possible, and offered the most incriminating statement I could have ever made.

"No ma'am, I'm telling you the truth. I didn't take fifty cents from your bedroom!"

"Then how would you know I'm missing fifty cents?" she screamed.

With that, she dealt a sudden open-hand blow to the left side of my head. My ear rang like a fire alarm.

"The last thing I need is a thief for a son!" she shouted.

I was overwhelmed with shame. I had hurt her. I had disappointed my dear mother. Without being told I went straight to my bedroom. I felt about as low as a worm in a wagon rut. I knew it would be a quiet night for the entire household and there would be lots of suspicious looks pointed in my direction. I was so ashamed I made no plans to come out for dinner. But deep inside I knew I would survive. I was still so full of candy and soda. I didn't feel like eating dinner, anyway!

It was instances like this, when I acted like an out-of-control delinquent, that caused me to see how my bad behavior added to my mom's misery. She was an angel of a lady, a description that bears repeating. She loved me with all her heart and proved it over and over, sacrificing what little she had, so I could have a proper upbringing and a fair chance at life. I was just too young to understand and appreciate all she did. I was blessed to have had her in my life for as long as I did. I only wish I could repay her for the needless worry and grief I caused her. It was Ralph Waldo Emerson who said, "The years teach much which the days never know."

My mother was also a woman of great emotional strength. In spite of the hardships and abuse she faced, she persevered. Of course, some of the troubles and complications in her life were the result of her own questionable choices. Yet she kept trying, always searching for a happier life for both of us. Some of the more irrational decisions she made involved the men in her life who, for one reason or another, proved to be misleading or irresponsible and only added to her heartache. Even after surviving the horrific existence of living with my father, other relationships and subsequent marriages which may have appeared promising in the beginning always ended in hurt and disappointment. Still, she was never one to talk about her troubles or show her emotions. However, there were a few occasions, late in the quiet of night, when she buckled under from the burdens of life. As a youngster, I came to see that even my mother had limits and could withstand only so much. It was in those instances that I heard her crying in her room. And as young as I was, I still knew it was the cruel and unrelenting pressures of life that were driving her closer and closer to the brink of despair. But what was I to do, other than listen in silence and hope that she could somehow find the strength to make it through another day?

I was about to graduate from high school when I first noticed an unmistakable change in my mother. And while we each still had our own busy lives, her with her long hours at work and me with school, I couldn't help but notice that Mom had undergone a mysterious transformation that caused me to wonder what sort of experience could have made such a difference in her life. I recall how she enjoyed singing with the church choir and occasionally attended services, but she was never considered to be deeply religious. She was a smoker, but never a drinker of alcohol and never resorted to the use of drugs. However, she had a spiritual faith which served as a source of strength for her life. But suddenly, as if overnight, Mom left the ranks of the downtrodden and abandoned all thoughts of defeat. Her entire being had been renewed. There was a tone of assuredness in her voice and a new air of confidence in her step.

I wasn't the only one who noticed the drastic changes in Mom's personality. Naturally, those of us in the family couldn't help but see the differences as we interacted with her every day around the house. We could only imagine how far-reaching the changes were and how she may have also been like a new person to others like her friends and the people she saw at work. And even though I wish we had been closer, I never got to know much about my mother's thoughts or innermost feelings, so what I eventually learned about her transformation came to me a little later, when I heard about it from my aunts, Sophie and Mary. In their account, the miraculous change we had all seen in Mom was the result of a type of spiritual encounter, an unexplainable phenomenon which occurred at the very moment of her deepest despair. To use my own words, it was an unexpected visit from the spirit world, which was substantial enough to impact her character and demeanor for the remainder of her life.

She had had enough. There was no chance she would fall asleep. Perhaps she had received discouraging news earlier that day or maybe she had heard that another of her payments to a creditor was past due. In any case, her grief seemed insurmountable. It was late and the creaky old Victorian-style house was quiet as she lay in bed, clutching her pillow and sobbing. And for the last time, she was searching for a conclusion, trying to decide if life, as it was for her, was worth the constant struggle. I can only imagine how her shoulders must have quivered as she gasped for each breath. Reaching a point of utter desperation, her weeping turned into loud prayerful sobs and cries for help. With all of her being, she pleaded to a higher power for help. Suddenly, she was quieted by a comforting force that enveloped her. Instantly, the convulsive shaking and sobbing stopped. She raised her head and peered into the darkness of the room, as if she had been ordered to quiet herself and direct her attention into the silence. Out of the stillness a firm yet comforting voice called to her.

"Eva, you will be all right. You will be fine, and so will your son, Eli."

The voice of reassurance had spoken to my mother and her life would be changed forever.

Of course, we could never know what life was like for Mom in the days and weeks that followed. And after such a jolting experience, I am certain she wrestled with the validity of what had happened. Surely she questioned herself, wondering what was real and what may have been a dream. And no doubt, she considered the possible effects exhaustion and fatigue could have played on her mind. Yet, for her, the experience was as real as anything that had ever occurred in her life, and its impact was obvious to everyone close to her.

It wasn't long before we all noticed Mom had much more confidence than before. And unlike her former self, she trusted her decisions and moved forward with life, without seeking the advice and approval of others as she may have done before. She projected a new-found assertiveness which wouldn't allow anyone to belittle or demean her. This new, more aggressive Eva, put her more forceful personality to good use as she began to advance professionally, finding better jobs for herself and earning better pay.

Mom left her stressful and demanding job as a waitress and found greener pastures at the Chicago office of R.R. Donnelley & Sons, a successful printing company which currently holds a Fortune 500 rating as one of the world's foremost producers of paperback books and magazines. She worked there as a proofreader for a few years while I was in high school, and for the first time I could recall, she had a job she truly enjoyed. She no longer came home from work exhausted from being on her feet all day. But instead, she would bring home files of paper in her briefcase, and spend quiet time after dinner with a colored marking pen and a pair of readers on the end of her nose, reading and rereading, wanting to stay caught up with her workload.

Even her interests changed, or perhaps these were interests and ideas she had all along, but never had the time or energy to express. She became an avid reader, particularly on topics such as ladies' fashions, health and nutrition. As I got closer to graduating from high school, she and I talked about the possibility of my getting into professional baseball. With that, Mom had many recommendations to offer relating to my diet, which she felt would send me directly to the big leagues. She cooked steak and explained how it was a good source of protein. She brought home cranberries and told me they were essential in preventing infections and loaded with antioxidants. She also stressed the need to drink lots of water to keep the body purged and hydrated. And keep in mind, she was learning and sharing this information in the early 1950s. The lady was years ahead of her time!

Sometime later, with the help and influence of some of her friends and former customers from a downtown restaurant, she landed an even better job with Poole Brothers, an established printing company, located in the same part of town. The company specialized in the production of maps, schedules and brochures for railroads as well as posters and textbooks. In addition, they published many prominent medical reference books, which were among the work projects my mother was assigned. I never knew her to be more proud than when the directors at Poole Brothers honored her by dedicating one of those medical volumes to my mother, recognizing her for her hard work on the book and her dedication to the company.

After so many years, it remains clear that the message Mom received from her guardian angel provided her with comfort and encouragement. The words of her visiting spirit were true, and for the two remaining decades of her earthly life, she did in fact, make out fine. There is no question, the quality of her later life was far better than the years she struggled through as a younger lady. And I would like to believe the good life she enjoyed was her earthly reward, recompense for the pain and suffering she endured earlier. Now, many years have gone by and she has also received her well-deserved heavenly reward. Surely, there are stars in her crown for the love and concern she had for me throughout her life.

But, what about her son, Eli? Would he be okay? His mother was told he would be and the years would prove it to be true. However, for him there would be many obstacles, hardships, temptations and addictions for him to face before he would ever reach that point in his life

CHAPTER 9
THE NEED TO BELONG

O ver the past several decades so much has been learned about
alcoholism. Findings from recent studies have provided us with a
better understanding about many of the physiological and mental facets
of the disease. Not long ago, researchers scientifically linked the "alcoholic
gene" to beta-endorphin deficiencies, an often hereditary condition, thus
explaining why the dreaded addiction can remain in a family for generations, leaving a trail of broken homes and broken hearts in its wake.
Hopefully, as this information finds its way into the consciousness of our
society, alcoholism will be viewed differently from the way it has been
seen in past generations and will be recognized as the cruel debilitating
disease it really is. As for the disease itself, nothing has changed over
the years. The signs, symptoms and devastating results are still the same.
However, through education, public awareness and open minds, we will
continue to see progress in the ongoing fight to wipe out this deadly
addiction.

I grew up with alcohol all around me. It was part of life at our house.
My grandfather, my aunts and uncles and most of the adults in the family
were known to have a drink from time to time. And it was the males in
particular who drank the most at holiday times and at our family gatherings. Yet, none of them ever seemed to drink so much they lost control
or became loud or violent. Within my mother's family, alcohol was never
the abhorrent problem it had been for my father or for his father before
him. For the grown-ups in our house, drinking, while it wasn't an everyday occurrence, was mostly done at parties and celebrations, and it was

strictly for adults, except for the times my cousin, Marlene, and I would secretly gulp down what liquor or wine was left in glasses, once everyone else had left the room. I was no more than about six or seven years old at the time, but after downing a few of those leftover cocktails, I experienced the effects of alcohol for the first time. The warning signs were there, but no one saw the dangers. Still, it wasn't until years later when I was in my teens that peer pressure became an influencing factor which helped turn my underage drinking into a problem for my mother as well as others in the family.

Since the dawn of civilization, the need for social acceptance has been the most powerful driving force for teenagers the world over. Whether it is music, clothes, hair styles, or even language or behavior, the need to fit in socially with others the same age can be so strong it can drive a young person to the point of helpless despair. During adolescence, the need to belong can be so powerful it can alienate children from their parents and family, and push them to rebel against the established ideals of society. The desire to be accepted can force a teenager to disavow the beliefs and values that are held dear by his parents and teachers and other influential adults in their lives.

I was no exception. Being recognized as "one of the guys" was just as important to me as it was for any other kid. It may be possible to conclude that my upbringing in a household dominated by women may have caused me to push even harder to find my niche with the boys in the neighborhood. That's not to imply my mother, grandfather and aunts didn't provide me with a home environment of warmth and caring, as each of them made a commendable effort to see I felt safe and secure and that I always had a sense of family support. However, I still missed having the positive influence of a father figure in my life, which was the one thing I inadvertently searched for throughout my childhood. Without it, home could sometimes be a lonely place. And loneliness, I would find, would be an agonizing condition I would face all too often in the years to come.

While it wasn't the sort of thing a kid would boast to his buddies about, the whole family was pleased when I started showing interest in music. As far back as I can remember, music played a major role in our family life and traditions. And for our relatives and many of our friends, it was a means for celebrating our ethnic heritage as well as expressing our religious faith, as music was an important part of every service for the

Serbian Orthodox Church. My mother was gifted with a beautiful voice and sang regularly with the church choir. But it was my late uncle Adam Popovich, a natural-born musical genius who, for several years, was the leader of the popular Sloboda Choir of South Chicago. As a professional musician, Uncle Adam, along with his brothers, Teddy and Marco and friend, Pete Mistovich, formed the Popovich Brothers Tamburitza Orchestra, an internationally famous recording ensemble. The group enjoyed remarkable heights of popularity for more than a half-century with notable record sales and live performances all over the country. In recognition for their cultural contributions to the Serbian-American community and for delighting music fans for decades with traditional tambura songs, along with some of their own original tunes, the band was inducted in the Tamburitza Association of America Hall of Fame in 1972. And it's difficult to imagine how Uncle Adam did it all with sheer natural talent. He was self-taught with no formal musical training. He was a man who made the most of the talent God gave him. Incidentally, in 1978, while the group was still actively performing, the life story of my talented uncles was made into a story for a highly rated full-length film documentary, *The Popovich Brothers of South Chicago*, from Facets Videos and director Jill Godmilow.

Since I was a child I have always been drawn to music. As a youngster, hearing a wide variety of songs in church, at school and at home, I learned to enjoy music of all types. There is something unique about music. It has a certain spiritual element, a blending of tones and vibrations that make it a medium of expression, powerful enough to reach across the universe!

While my uncles and some of my aunts and cousins were all blessed with exceptional musical talents, that's not to say the gift was bestowed equally upon everyone in the family. Having a love for music doesn't always translate into having the talent. And while there was never anything notable about my vocal skills, I enjoyed singing. It wasn't a popular activity among all the young people in the neighborhood, but singing was a sure-fire way for me to gain approval from the adults in the family. Mom was thrilled to learn that I was interested in being in the choir, and Uncle Adam, the director, was impressed enough with my wide vocal range that he readily found a spot for me on his row of young male tenors. Thinking I had found my calling, I was delighted to see how pleased everyone seemed to be with my efforts. As the compliments and encouragement came my way, the more excited I became about singing and the more I looked forward to any chance I might get to perform. Then suddenly, with one small flippant remark, my bubble was burst. Just one time being the brunt of Marian Mistovich's teasing and my enthusiasm for singing was gone. It left me behind like a overdue street car!

"What's wrong with your face, Eli?" she jeered.

We had just finished another beautiful hymn and choir practice was about to end. I turned quickly enough to catch Marian looking my way, pointing at me and masking over her laughter with her other hand.

"Why, Eli, you look like you're about to get sick! Why do you have to screw your face up like that?" she taunted. "You're just so funny! Didn't anyone tell you, you don't have to do that when you sing?"

I was crushed. I was completely unaware that my mannerisms had been so amusing. I suppose a few of the higher notes required my best effort and it showed all over my face. I felt my heart sink to my feet. Sometimes it's okay to be told you're funny, but not when you're serious and trying your best!

She continued to mimic me, contorting her face as if she had just drunk a vial of caustic acid. A few other kids joined the frolic, finding her antics to be even funnier than anything I had done. I stepped down from the loft, flipped my hymnal onto a table and left the building.

Sure, I had the approval of every other member of the choir, everyone at home and those who attended the church. These people not only approved, but encouraged me to continue singing. They assured me of my talent as well as my place in the Sloboda Choir for years to come. But to me, none of that mattered. No matter how much I listened to them or how much I believed, as long as it came from grown ups, no amount of positive reinforcement would make a difference. It was acceptance and approval of other young people I was so desperate for. And the hurt that comes from feeling like you don't deserve it can last for a very long time.

There's no rule that says peer pressure has to end when adulthood begins. However, with some measure of hope, we usually expect the compulsive urge to look, act and think like everyone else to diminish somewhat with age and maturity, and perhaps it will for most of us. Or maybe, to justify our actions, we simply refer to it as social pressure, and see it from a different point of view. Regardless, whether it is real or imagined the feeling of being spurned and failing to fit in socially can be as painful as a knife in the back, and it can linger into adulthood. It can bring on dreadful side effects such as loneliness and depression, which can be dangerously debilitating, to the point they lead to alcoholism and even substance abuse. Far too often warning signs are not recognized soon enough. And while assistance and treatment can help so much, it often arrives too late. I know because I've been there. I'm a survivor, and I'm very grateful to say, I am one of the lucky ones!

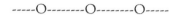

There aren't many things that can help a boy find his way through the awkward years of adolescence like athletics. While wearing the wrong clothes can merit heckles and taunts from an entire classroom and receiving an A+ in mathematics can get a kid labeled the teacher's pet, sinking the winning basket or catching a touchdown pass will go a lot further in helping a young man gain social acceptance from his friends and schoolmates. There's nothing new about it. It's one of the basic laws of growing up that has been around for generations. Thankfully, any athletic skills I had were noticeable at a young age, giving me an advantage over other boys who were not as athletically inclined. I was always an early pick whenever we chose teams on the playground. And in school, I sailed through dodge ball, basketball and all the other games we played in gym class with no problems.

I fell in love with basketball and enjoyed playing every chance I got. I played regularly in league and pick-up games at the local YMCA. The competition was fierce and it taught me a lot about the game. The games at the "Y" could get quite physical at times, yet I learned to hold my own and to be as aggressive as anyone on the court. But oddly enough, when the time came to enter high school, I had no interest or intentions of playing varsity sports. There was something about the daily practices and the rigid game schedule that didn't agree with my free-spirited personality. At that young age, I preferred to play sports on my terms and only when it suited me, which was an immature and a totally irrational concept. As I would learn later, sports would always be about the team, the school, winning and, of course, money.

Coach Harry Pritikin had a knack for spotting a boy whose outlook and attitude were veering off-course, and finding a way to help redirect the young man's energy into a more positive and productive direction. He was a gym teacher, basketball coach and later, baseball coach for the Bowen High Boilermakers for many years. And though his methods may have been questionable at times, his influence impacted the lives of many students and scholastic athletes in the Chicago area for several decades.

He could tell I was athletic and must have been pleased with my height and agility. He liked what he had heard about me playing basketball with the YMCA and wanted me to come out for the school's senior team. If nothing else, his manner of persuasion was annoying enough to keep me away. But he sure was persistent.

"How about it, dummy?" he would tease. "When are you going to come out n' play with the big boys?"

The school had two boys' basketball teams who were separated, not by grade or talent, but according to height. The senior team comprised players 5'- 9" and taller, while the junior squad was made up of shorter players. Yet, it was the juniors who proved to be the real scrappers. The squad included a few Mexican boys who knew the game well, having learned a tough brand of basketball on the courts at the YMCA. The junior team competed in its own division, against teams of comparable height, and each season, they somehow managed to finish with a winning record. On the other hand, things were not so cheery for the taller guys, as the seniors hardly ever won. As I recall, the senior Boilermakers of Bowen High once finished their season schedule with a dismal record of no wins and 17 losses!

With my tall rangy frame, there was little doubt I would be placed with seniors if I gave in to Coach Pritikin's insistence that I play. But believe me, the long losing streak did nothing to make me want to join them. I could see myself enjoying basketball a lot more, playing with the guys at the YMCA, where at least I could be on a winning team.

Now, when it came to playing high school baseball, my feelings were totally different. Even before I finished grade school, I had decided playing baseball for Bowen High was what I wanted to do. No coaxing was needed. There happened to be several older guys who were regulars on the local sandlots with the Sportsmen club that I looked up to. Wanting to be part of their group made me eager join the school team. There was my buddy, Ray Aleman, along with "Gee-Gee" Colella and

Gene Glon, who were among the best high school players in the area. I had closely watched these fellows play many times and checked their every move. I had noticed how, in the field, they could make difficult defensive plays look routine and how each of them could step to the plate, and with some of the most balanced and level swings I had ever seen, effortlessly drive the ball to all parts of the field. These guys even trotted out to their positions with an air of confidence, an unintentional swagger that made them look like winners. I knew early on that I wanted to be part of that.

Of course, it didn't happen overnight. I went out for the team and made the squad my freshman year. But that doesn't mean I got many chances to play. I rode the bench a lot that season and tried to learn as much as I could by listening to any and everything the older players had to tell me. Our coach, Mr. McGinnis was inexperienced and had very little advice to offer his players. So, it was the guys on the team who had a few seasons behind them, the juniors and seniors, who I learned from.

Harry Pritikin coached both baseball and basketball at Bowen High School. For me, he was a difficult person to figure out.

115

After my first year on the team, it was Coach Pritikin who took over as baseball coach at Bowen High. And while he may have been a slight improvement over what we had, he probably did a better job of teaching the basic fundamentals of the game than our previous coach. Pritikin stayed on as basketball coach for the seniors and continued to hassle me about trying out for the team. By that, I figured he must have wanted me to play for his seniors pretty badly, but I just never knew how to take his approach. There were probably other methods he could have used to persuade me to come out for practice, other than harassing me and referring to me as a dummy. And maybe with some other boys his sarcastic style would have been more effective. But for me personally, Coach Pritikin could be a difficult person to figure out.

I was surprised to find how starting high school and trying out for the baseball team were in some ways similar to my experiences at Glenwood School For Boys. There was no question that the structure and discipline I had learned at Glenwood was a big help in preparing me for high school. I had been conditioned to accept the three R's of getting an education; rules, routine and respect. And once again I found myself looking up to some of the older boys who were athletes and good students as well. In much the same way as I had George "Jeep" Parenti as a role model and mentor at Glenwood, I saw fellows such as Gee Gee, Ray and Gene in the same light. To me, they were examples of what I wanted to become. All the kids at school knew them. They studied to keep their grades up, trained to stay sharp on the ballfield and carried themselves with a flair of integrity and confidence. These guys had the admiration of teachers and students alike as they seemed to represent everything that was good about Bowen High. At a time in my life when social acceptance seemed to be as vital to my existence as food and water, I couldn't have chosen a more positive objective than to seek their approval and try to fit in with their exclusive but enviable group. However, it wouldn't be an easy goal to reach. It would take another year or two for me to earn a spot as a regular on the ballclub and by that time those guys would be graduated. Yet in time, I progressed to the point where I worked my way into the starting lineup. And at that time I still tried to be mindful of how Ray, Gee-Gee and Gene would have handled things in my situation.

In the classroom, I tried, but my short attention span presented a big problem. I couldn't seem to help it, as it was just part of my disengaged nature to gaze out the window on a sunny day and daydream about playing baseball or football or anything, rather than concentrate on my studies. Of course, I was never the scholarly type, yet I enjoyed subjects such as Spanish, biology and mechanical drawing. Nevertheless, I simply didn't apply myself as I should have and as a result, my grades were only good enough to get by. And had it not been for sports, I wonder if my marks would have been that good.

Meanwhile, Coach Pritikin continued to badger me, and I finally relented and agreed to give basketball a try. I had stayed out of basketball as far as the school team was concerned, but that's not to say I was away from the game completely. In fact, I not only kept active in basketball at the YMCA as I had before, but I also started playing with our Serbian church team which played at quite a high level of competition. The Eagles, as they were known, featured a roster of older guys with many years of experience, some who had played collegiately and a few who had played at some level in the pros. As the youngest player on the squad, I received what could be termed a baptism by fire as I was given no quarter by anyone in the league. However, it was with the church team that I learned to be more aggressive, to hold my own physically and to push back against my opponent. Just like the other players, I adopted a non-yielding style of play and learned to use my size to gain position and fight hard for every rebound. Fortunately, I was able to take this fierce style of play with me when I played in high school. Beginning with my sophomore year, my first season playing for Coach Harry Pritikin on the Bowen High senior team, I earned the reputation of aggressively driving the boards and clearing a path through the opposition whenever our team needed to grab another rebound.

Following that first season of basketball, I returned for another year of high school baseball. I began to see more action and play a larger role with the team. I was another year older and no longer the bench-riding freshman I had been under Coach McGinnis. As for Coach Pritikin, he liked the fiery competiveness he had seen in me on the basketball court and wanted to see more of it on the baseball diamond. I had what some guys referred to as a natural swing and could hit for power, and though he never told me, Pritikin liked me as a hitter and tried me in different spots in the batting order. On defense, he used me in the outfield and at first base. He also liked my arm strength and had ideas of trying me at third base. But during the entire time I was in high school, we had had a couple of our finest ballplayers at third, and I believed everyone

117

was pleased that the coach chose not to tamper with what worked and left things as they were. Gene Glon, an exceptional athlete, manned the position the first two years I was at Bowen High. Later, Dick Oljenik, a boy in my class from Russell Square Park, a nearby Polish community often called "The Bush," took over at the hot corner and played there with near perfection during our final years in school. I was never more impressed with the ball playing talents of any young boy like I was with Dick. With his exceptional range and agility, he snagged countless line drives and hard-hit grounders which would have eluded any other player. With his abilities, we all felt certain that one day we would be watching Dick Oljenik play third base in the major leagues.

In addition to taking on basketball during my sophomore year, I also went out for football for the first time, which as my third varsity sport, making me a year-round athlete. At first, it was mostly because of to my ability to kick a football that some of my buddies urged me to play football. Our coach, Lou Wasserman, a gruff, coarse Jewish man, had very little to say to any of his players, unless it was to chew out someone who fumbled the ball or missed a tackle, and believe me, I had more than my share of run-ins with the man. Yet, he gave me a lot of playing time, primarily as an end and punter, a couple of positions that kept me close to the action.

Throughout my life I had always done everything right-handed, thrown a ball, signed my name, shook hands, everything. But for some odd reason, I found I did my best punting with my left foot, and punting, along with catching passes became my gridiron specialties. As a receiver, I was pretty reliable, and I could punt the ball a country mile!

In spite of Wasserman, I stuck with football and went on to play three seasons. By the time I entered my junior year I had become somewhat a mainstay on the team and I enjoyed playing football more than ever. We put together two great seasons my junior and senior years. We won a lot of games and I somehow managed to catch a lot of passes. At the same time, all across the country, fans of professional football were buzzing about the amazing heroics of Dante Lavelli, the incomparable pass receiver of the Cleveland Browns. Each week it seemed fans heard how his clutch receptions shaped the outcome of another Browns' victory. "Lavelli has the surest hands in football," sports writers would claim. Cleveland broadcaster, Bob Neal, referred to him as "Gluefingers" for his ability to catch almost any pass thrown in his direction. And like any football thrown within his reach, the nickname stuck with him and followed him into immortality when he was enshrined in the Pro Football Hall of Fame in Canton, Ohio.

Meanwhile, back on the South Side of Chicago at Bowen High School, the football team had a dependable pass receiver of its own. This young fellow made a few good catches and even scored a few touchdowns for the Boilermakers when the game was on the line. However, I'm not so sure that tags such as *star* or even *standout* should be mentioned in describing him. He was definitely no Dante Lavelli. But nonetheless, he liked the new nickname "Gluefingers Grba," which was slapped on him by his teammates as a subtle vote of confidence.

"Throw it to Gluefingers!" barked an anxious player in our huddle.

"We need a quick score, pass it to Gluefingers!" echoed another.

My, but those were some wonderful times! I look back now and see that my years in high school were among the best times of my life. It was special to see how others had so much confidence in me, and it was great to have a place where I belonged.

CHAPTER 10
YOU'RE GOING TO BE A PITCHER!

⟞——⟝

I t was author and humorist Mark Twain who told us "action speaks louder than words but not nearly as often." And it is by this insightful observation that I am reminded of a fellow from South Chicago, who many years ago, gave so much of his time and energy to the well-being and development of others. His name was James P. Fitzgibbons, and from many young boys who grew up in his neighborhood in the late 1940s and on through the 1970s, a great debt of gratitude is owed. Personally, I don't believe I could have ever thanked him enough for the instruction and guidance he gave me or for the number of opportunities that came my way because of him.

All across the country, baseball was never more popular than during the years immediately following World War II as well as the subsequent two decades. It was a time when a majority of American males were baseball fans and a large portion of them who were physically active played the game regularly. With dedication and a willingness to work hard, boys who began playing in Little League Baseball or on the sandlots could move up to high school, American Legion and even to semipro baseball by the time they were young adults. This was the progression so many hopeful young ballplayers in my neighborhood wanted to follow. And because of the efforts of James Fitzgibbons, a few of us got to do it.

My sophomore year was when I first became a year-round high school athlete. After football and basketball were over, I returned for a second season of baseball with Coach Harry Pritikin. Our football team had a successful year, winning a lot more often than we lost, but the same could not be said for basketball. While our team showed signs of improvement and we lost some close games, wins were hard to come by. However, in the spring of 1950, our baseball team was in the early stages of putting Bowen High School on the regional map of scholastic sports. It was a talented bunch of ballplayers that made up that club, and even then the teammates sensed they were on their way to significant accomplishments in local baseball. Bob Jingling, Steve Knezevich, Eddie Liteki and Don Napierkowski were all tremendous athletes with vital roles on that team, not to mention a couple of exceptional right-handed pitchers, Bob Gotovac and Ted Kazek, who signed contracts with the pros and went on to play minor league baseball.

Once the school year ended, I had only a short break from baseball before the start of American Legion Baseball. Being candid, I must admit it was the break from school that appealed to me a lot more than the time away from the game I loved. Having been given a chance to play more during my second season of high school baseball, I somehow caught the attention of James Fitzgibbons, the well-known coach of the local American Legion team, the Sundodgers.

As an amateur baseball team, none was ever more popular or prestigious in South Chicago than the Sundodgers. According to custom, American Legion teams were stocked with players selected from the high schools located within the neighborhood of the sponsoring post. With Bowen High the only high school in the area of Post 11, Coach Fitzgibbons filled the Sundodgers' roster with boys from the Bowen Boilermakers' baseball team. To be chosen as a 15-year-old sophomore was a tremendous thrill for me. And while I knew I would be among the youngest boys to make the club, I was aware that becoming a Sundodger meant I would be part of the finest, most envied baseball team in town. For Fitzgibbons, a strong-willed Irish bachelor raised in the steel mill community of South Chicago, youth baseball was the focus and passion of his life. He worked tirelessly to secure sponsorship money from the membership of Post 11. He prodded officials at the local mills for donations and no doubt, he even chipped in money from his own pocket, just to make sure the Sundodgers had nothing but the best of everything.

With each passing season, I too was becoming more passionate about the game of baseball. I had played with pick-up teams and on the local sandlots. I even had two years of high school ball behind me. Yet, playing for the Sundodgers was more exciting than I could have ever imagined. This team was never lacking for bats, balls, catcher's gear or any other equipment we could have needed. But when Coach Fitzgibbons issued each of us two different uniforms, one for home games and one for the road, I felt as if I had landed in the big leagues!

There was nothing I loved more than being on the ball field, taking my turn at bat or fielding a hard-hit grounder and making a strong accurate throw across the diamond to nab the runner at first. I had found my niche playing shortstop and third base. Except for an occasional game at second base, I was perfectly comfortable playing on the left side of the infield, and wouldn't think of switching to any of the other positions on the field. That's where my heart was, and that's where I thought my future was. However, James Fitzgibbons was my coach, and he had other ideas.

"I don't want to be a pitcher!" I told him, refusing his order again.

"You're going to be a pitcher... and that's the way it's going to be!" the coach demanded. "You've got a great arm, Eli. And if you want to play for the Sundodgers, you'll be a pitcher. Otherwise, you can forget it!"

For the first time in years, I cried. My heart ached at the thought of losing my spot in the infield. With eyes red and swollen with tears, I went home to tell my mother I was finished with baseball, I was quitting.

"I'm not going back, Mom. I'm not going to let him do this to me!"

She had never seen me so upset. Yet, it proved to be just another instance for her to show me what a strong lady she was, offering calmness and reason at a time when I needed it the most. We both paused for a moment of silence and thought before she finally spoke.

"Don't be so quick to react, Eli," Mom suggested. "Why not give it a try? Who knows, you may find you like it. I'm sure you'll make a fine pitcher, and I will be so proud of you!"

I was reluctant, but I went back to the practice field the following day, ready to face Fitzgibbons and eat a sizable serving of crow. To that point in my life, agreeing to give up the part of baseball that I thought was mine and switch to pitching was one of the most harrowing decisions I had ever been forced to make. It took courage, all the courage I could muster, as well as trust and faith. I had finally reached an age where I needed to learn to trust someone with more knowledge and experience than I had, someone like James Fitzgibbons. And I needed to show faith in someone who would always love me and wanted nothing but the best for me, my mother. I had arrived at a turning point in my life where I needed to acknowledge that there were others who may know more about what was best for me.

It would be early August, and just about the time for the dog days of summer to bring on the hottest, most humid weather of the year, that the Sundodgers would switch into another season of baseball and show the entire area of South Chicago that they were more than just another ordinary American Legion team. As our summer vacation sped toward its end, there would be only a few weeks left before the start of football drills. But that's when the Sundodgers transformed from American Legion competition and into one of the most popular sandlot and semipro baseball teams in the area. Using all the connections he had throughout the neighborhood, James Fitzgibbons scheduled games for us against all types of amateur teams, including industrial league teams, semipro clubs, men's church league teams and even other local American Legion teams that continued to play after their regular season was finished. And while we managed to come out winners more often than not, playing with the Sundodgers gave each of us a great opportunity to sharpen our skills against clubs with older players who were more experienced than we were. From a baseball perspective, playing against such tough competition caused every boy on our team to grow up quickly, which only increased our confidence and added to the pride we already had as members of the Sundodgers.

As a pitcher, I was developing rapidly. Unlike many young boys who are learning to pitch, control was not a major concern for me or for Coach Fitzgibbons, who was always supportive and encouraging. I finally proved to myself that my coach had been right all along, and that in fact, I was gifted with a strong throwing arm, so velocity was something I came by naturally.

"You've got all the necessary tools to become a good pitcher, Eli," Fitzgibbons told me. "You just need to keep working."

It was James Fitzgibbons who first spotted my potential as a pitcher and forced me, a hard-headed 15-year-old, to make a difficult change. He was the individual who pushed me into a position, where not long after, a career full of opportunities would come my way. Interestingly enough, it would be only three years later that I would have the stubborn insistence of Coach Fitzgibbons and the reinforcing faith of my mother at the top of my thoughts, as I signed my name on my first contract to play professional baseball. Sometimes, it's others who know what's best.

Other than graduating, which was somewhat of an academic miracle on its own, some of my fondest memories of high school are from the spring of 1951. That was my junior year and my third season of playing baseball for the Boilermakers. It was the year when it all finally came together for us, and at the season's end, we found ourselves in a position to win it all, a chance to become champions. Out of a group of no fewer than 50 member-schools, it boiled down to a single deciding game, a showdown between James H. Bowen High and the powerful Cavaliers of Chicago Vocational High School. It was a game for all the marbles, a one-time opportunity for the winning team to be crowned the 1951 Baseball Champions of the Chicago Public High School League.

For a bunch of energetic young boys still in our teens, our ballclub did a remarkable job of dealing with the fuss and attention that surrounded us as the day of the championship game drew near. We had an outstanding team and a remarkable season record to prove it. But there was no way we would be allowed to approach such an important game being overly confident, as Coach Pritikin would never permit that to happen. Still, it was the pride of our club as well as that of the entire school that was at stake, and the fanfare and build-up by the local press were more than anyone could recall for a scholastic baseball game.

Of course, emotions were running high on the team, as all of us had become year-round teammates, playing together as the Sundodgers American Legion team, and again later in the summer season, as the Sundodgers semipro team. Once spring returned, we were reunited as the Bowen High School team. The familiarity worked in our favor, giving us an advantage over other teams whose players did not play together over the course of the year as we did. We had grown together as a team, and the big game against Chicago Vocational was our chance to prove ourselves. We had won together at each level we played and wanted nothing more than to win the championship together. And just when we thought nothing else could add to the excitement and hoopla surrounding the big game, it was announced that the Chicago Public League Championship would be played on the home field of the Chicago White Sox, Comiskey Park.

Built in 1910, Comiskey Park had been the site of many historical games. By 1951 it had been the host field of three World Series, as well as the site of the first-ever All-Star game in 1933. Since its opening four decades earlier, Comiskey Park had become hallowed ground for baseball fans in South Chicago, and along with the White Sox, had become a vital part of our local culture. Having attended games there with both my mother and my father, I was aware of the stadium's history and had seen in person some of the biggest stars of baseball play there. Knowing I would have a chance to step into the same batter's box where White Sox legend Luke Appling had dug in countless times during his stellar 20-year career was hard for me to believe. And as starting pitcher for the Bowen team, I would stand atop the very mound where the immortal right-hander, Ted Lyons, notched 260 victories over a 21-year span. As the day of the game drew closer, the excitement mounted. At 16 years old, I was facing the biggest and most important baseball game of my life, taking place on the grandest stage I could have ever imagined.

After taking three out of four games from the American League leading White Sox at Comiskey, the New York Yankees left town in second place, but still trailing Chicago by a couple of games. At the same time, the Sox packed up their gear and left the Windy City for an extended road trip, which would keep them away from home for more than two weeks. As soon as the two big league clubs cleared out of Comiskey, the stage was set for Bowen High to face Chicago Vocational in the title game.

Arriving at the stadium a few hours before game time, our team bus rolled into the players' parking area and dropped us off in front of a huge door marked "VISITING PLAYERS' ENTRANCE." Carrying our own bags and equipment, we stepped off the bus and filed through the opening, as an elderly man, perhaps a stadium attendant, held the door and directed us into a dimly lit hallway.

"Welcome to Comiskey Park, gentlemen," he greeted us. "Continue in this direction, fellows, straight down this passage. You will be using our visitors' clubhouse today, and I believe you'll find everything you'll need to get ready for the game and then dress and shower afterwards."

We stepped from the corridor and into a spacious, well-lit open area. The floor was covered with plush carpet and the walls were lined with over-sized, cage-like lockers, which looked to be wide enough and tall enough for me to stand up in. Without dropping our bags, we milled aimlessly about the room, checking out the lockers, each with its own tall swivel chair, and in particular, the names and numbers above each locker, written on tape and left in place from the recent weekend series with the Yankees. There were RASCHI #17, REYNOLDS #22, BERRA #8 and J. DiMAGGIO #5. We wandered about in awe, moving from one locker to the next, reading the names aloud and savoring the way each of them sounded. There were even more for us to discover: MIZE #36 and BAUER #25. The roll call of baseball legends seemed endless. Every player on our team was lost in the moment, deeply immersed in reverence at the very thought of those who had occupied the same room only hours earlier. Suddenly, our enchantment was interrupted. We were snapped back into reality when Coach Pritikin began to clap his hands loudly.

"Come on, guys!" he barked. "Let's get moving! In case you've forgotten, we've got a game today!"

Not ready to let go of the moment so quickly, we gradually broke up our gathering at the lockers and dispersed to go pick out the best spots to suit up for the game. I was about to join the others when I decided to take a final look at the names of some of the greatest players in Yankee lore. Then, out of the corner of my eye, I caught a glimpse of a name and number written on a strip of white athletic tape and applied directly to the wall. It was not placed above a locker like the others, but on the wall, just a few inches above a long nail that was driven in only part of the way, so it could be used as a coat hook. While the name was one we had heard of, it was that of a rookie, a player who at that point of his career was not even deemed worthy of having his own locker. Written on the tape in simple black marker and plastered just above the nail was, MANTLE #6.

I could hardly imagine how, in 1951 Mickey Mantle, the most highly touted prospect in all of baseball, was given nothing more than a nail in the wall. *Was this the major leagues? Was this the mighty New York Yankees?* For years to come and throughout my career in baseball, and even after becoming a teammate of Mickey Mantle's in New York, I often thought of the lesson I learned when I first discovered Mickey's nail in the Comiskey Park clubhouse. For me, that nail was proof that even the most talented players in the game must come up through the ranks, that no one ever starts at the top, not even the hero of an entire generation, not even Mickey Mantle.

"Let's go boys!" Pritikin shouted from the other side of the room. "It's time to get out there! This game's the big one! The starting lineup is on the dugout wall. Now, let's go!"

Baseball is sometimes referred to as a game of inches and often it's the team that gets the breaks that wins. Nonetheless, baseball is never a game of excuses. On that breezy afternoon in May of 1951, Chicago Vocational High had what it took to win a championship game while Bowen did not. From a pitcher's viewpoint, it was not my best game, yet just like all of my teammates, I gave it my best effort. We lost that day by a score of 3 to 1. It had been a great year, but losing that game was a deflating defeat. Finishing out the year just one game short of the championship title was a painful blow to our pride. Realizing that several of our key players were seniors, we had convinced ourselves at the start of the season that 1951 would be our year. For my first three seasons of high school baseball, I had played with basically the same group of boys. During that time, the core of our team had grown and bonded together. And as difficult as it was, after three full seasons together, we had even found ways to cope with Coach Harry Pritikin and some of his questionable tactics.

But that time was over. I would soon be a senior myself. I sure had a lot to think about and some very important decisions to make. I would turn 17 in August and go back to Bowen High for one final year. And then what?

The Bowen Boilermakers of 1951 came to within one game of winning the Chicago Public High School League championship. I'm on the back row, fourth from the left.

CHAPTER 11
I'M HERE TO SEE COACH LINDSTROM

⟡————⟡

I am sure there are very few of us who can say we entered our final year of high school without experiencing some degree of apprehension and uncertainty. The choices we make at such a critical time can impact us for the rest of our lives. And unless our path in life is determined in advance by influencing factors such as our parents, family traditions or industries unique to our hometown, it is up to each of us to lay a solid footing for our future, a truly disconcerting task for anyone so young.

Working in the steel mills of South Chicago was both the life and livelihood for many of the men in my neighborhood. I had grown up around them and knew many of them personally. Some were longtime friends of my family, others attended our church. And while they all had reputations for being honest hard-working men, I admired them for being masculine, able-bodied and mature. Without knowing it, these fellows were role models for me. They set gleaming examples of what adult life could be like for someone like me, growing up in our neighborhood, graduating from high school and staying close to home. To me, it was an enticing lifestyle. I had learned that jobs in the steel industry paid well and came with an attractive package of employee benefits. But I had never experienced the long hours of heat, smoke and noise that came with the job, or thought about the inherent dangers of blast furnaces, liquid molten steel and the heavy machinery involved in the production of shapes and plates. So, like so many of my friends, I was satisfied with the idea that life as a steelworker would be my future. The industry was booming and being part of it was like a rite of passage from schoolboy into manhood. The steel mills had been the work of my father and my grandfather before him.

Hard work was nothing new for anyone in my family. Along with their staunch religious practices, family values and their reputations for honesty and integrity, it helped form the legacy of my Serbian ancestors. And long before any of them left the homeland in the south-central region of Europe, they labored tirelessly and saved their earnings, hoping to one day make the long voyage of almost 5,000 miles to America. It was their desire for jobs and opportunities that lured them to this country, for it was a better life they were in search of, not an easier life.

And if ever there was anyone who exemplified these qualities, it was my mother, an incredibly strong lady who always supported me and loved me unconditionally. Throughout her life, she showed an unwavering willingness to accept responsibility and to work hard, and above all, she always wanted what was best for me. She was a lady of great intellect, someone who found ways to educate herself. Being an ardent reader, she learned a great deal about health and nutrition and became proficient in grammar and writing as well. She refused to settle for physically demanding jobs that kept her on her feet all day as a waitress, or jobs which required rotating shift work, such as tending a conveyor line at the cereal plant. In some ways, Mom was a woman ahead of her time.

She was well aware of the hazards of working in the steel industry. She knew all about the physical demands and the dangerous conditions at the mills and was intent on steering me into a cleaner and safer line of work. In her heart, Mom wanted something different for me, something better.

"Education is the key to success," she insisted. "It opens doors to the best jobs."

There was no doubt that having me go to college was my mother's dream. But while her urging me to study harder and work for higher grades fell on deaf ears, it was a topic she brought up many times during my final years of high school. Still, as I entered my senior year at Bowen, I knew full well I had almost no chance of being accepted by any college unless I was lucky enough to receive an athletic scholarship. There had been several guys in the classes that graduated before me who were outstanding athletes, and a few of them were given the opportunity to take that route. This group was mostly boys I had played baseball with a season or two earlier on the high school team as well as on the Sundodgers. Bob Jingling, Steve Knezevich, Eddie Liteki and Don Napierkowski were all offered baseball scholarships from the University of Wyoming, where Coach Bud Daniel was in the early stages of building one of the finest collegiate baseball programs in the country. But being realistic, I knew my chances of getting an offer like that were slim, which reduced any hopes I had for going to college to nothing more than wishful thinking. And while I would have tried anything to keep from disappointing my mother, I couldn't help but believe I was destined for the steel mills.

For one final time, I returned to Bowen High School in the fall of 1951 to start a school year that began in much the same way as previous sessions. As before, I focused my attention on playing sports. However, while autumn and football season moved by quickly and slipped into the cold months of basketball, I was mindful that each game I played would be among the last for me. The more I tried to savor each game, and even each practice, the faster the time passed.

Over the winter I dedicated a lot of my time to basketball. In a span of just two or three years I had become passionate about the game and was loving it! Not only did I play a full schedule for the school team, but between games and practices, I somehow found time to squeeze in countless pick-up games and league games at the YMCA. Surprisingly, the basketball games at the "Y" were fast and intense, with a higher level of competition than games at the high school level. Many of the players were older and the play was often rough and physical. Yet, I soon learned to hold my own with those guys. It was a good feeling to know I could continue to play at the Y following graduation. And I would, for a few more years to come.

Before I knew it, it was spring and time to start my final season of high school baseball. And while the news headlines were telling everyone how quickly the world was changing, I continued to concentrate on sports. As a high school senior, my priorities were still naive and self-serving. The fact that Prime Minister Winston Churchill announced that Britain had its own atomic bomb, and the notion that President Harry S. Truman's popularity was sinking like a stone because of his handling of the Korean War, were not among my concerns. If there were any items in the news that concerned me, I am sure they could all be found on the pages of the sports section. What grabbed my interest were the reports of how

George Mikan and Vern Mikkelsen led the Minneapolis Lakers to their third NBA Championship in the past four years, and the shocking reality of how, for what would be the first time almost anyone could recall, the New York Yankees would be starting their season without their center-fielder, "The Yankee Clipper," Joe DiMaggio, who was being replaced by a young untested kid from Oklahoma named Mickey Mantle.

Falling just one game short of the championship the year before left the Bowen Boilermakers with a hard act to follow. We anticipated another good season in 1952, but it was difficult to forget how close we had come to winning the title. And having lost several of our best players to graduation, we knew we had missed our big chance. Still, once the season started, we knew we were a team with enough talent to stay in contention and there were others who believed the same, as we couldn't avoid hearing about the number of professional scouts who were showing up at our games. We knew they were there watching us. They were easy to spot as they sat in the stands, chewing on cigars and scribbling in their notebooks. They seemed to favor wide-brimmed straw hats and preferred neckties worn loosely and skewed to the side. Yet, the most telling sign of all was the scout's lack of enthusiasm. His purpose was unlike that of anyone else at the ballpark. The scout never concerned himself with the score, never had a favorite team and never cheered or jeered the outcome of any play on the field. His job was to judge the talent and assess the potential of amateur players, in hope that he would one day discover a diamond in the rough, a boy who possessed the character and talent needed to make it in pro baseball. For a baseball scout, a day at the ballpark was just another day on the job. However, there were a few who were easily recognized and stood no chance of concealing their identity or hiding their business. In some cases, just their mere presence at the ball field was enough to stir the attention of fans and players alike.

By the time I was a senior, almost 20 years had passed since Burleigh Grimes had pitched his final game in the Major Leagues. And after a stellar 18-year career in which he won 270 games, he had established himself as one of the greatest pitchers ever in the game. He would continue to work for many years in baseball as a manager, coach and scout. Finally, in 1964, he would be given his rightful spot in the National Baseball Hall of Fame in Cooperstown, New York.

Even in his late fifties, when Grimes showed up to scout high school baseball in the Chicago area, he was revered by many who spotted him among the spectators. Of course, he did what he could to keep a low profile and avoid fanfare. But he was still well thought of and remembered by baseball fans in the Windy City. After all, he had spent a couple of seasons pitching for the Chicago Cubs near the end of his playing career. And a player like Grimes, known for his competiveness and fiery temperament, could never be forgotten.

I could never say for sure if I was the main reason Mr. Grimes came to Chicago to scout a game I was scheduled to pitch. But, without realizing he or any other scouts would be watching, it was going to be a special game for me, just knowing my mother would be there. At this point in her working life, she had worked her way up to a job with paid leave time, which made it possible for her make it to some of my games. So, having her there supporting me caused me to push even more to do my best. I wanted nothing more than to get her approval and make her proud of me. And now, looking back many years later, I regret that I did not do more to gain her approval in other areas of my life- outside of sports.

In spite of the importance of this particular game against one of our toughest opponents, Hyde Park High School, and the number of scouts expected to be there, I didn't feel pressured or nervous. Actually, when it came to sports, I don't recall ever getting edgy or anxious. I don't remember ever having jitters or butterflies before a big game. Those tendencies were never part of my makeup. For some reason, when it came to athletics I always seemed to have confidence in my ability. Deep within me, I always knew that I could perform as well as any other athletes my age. Perhaps it was my calling and maybe being an athlete was my purpose in life.

As for the scouts, the rules at the time would not permit them to have contact with any high school players until after graduation. We knew they were there, as the topic came up often on the team bus and in the locker room. That's how the players got wind of the rumors about who among us was being watched closely. But I was never distracted by any of that.

With Mom seated in the stands behind home plate that day, I pitched a pretty good game. But, like most of my teammates that day, I couldn't have bought a base hit with a fistful of twenties. In what was a disappointing defeat, we were shut out by Hyde Park 1 to 0 and the loss was especially hard to take after we counted the number of opportunities we had to score runs but failed to cash in. What's more, I felt as if it should be Mom who would be the more disappointed, considering the special effort she made to be there. I wanted to apologize to her the moment I got home. It would be the least I could do for the one person who cared about me the most.

However, when I walked through the front door, I found the situation at home to be quite different from what I expected. Surprisingly, it was my mother who started with an apology. Before I could drop my gym bag on the floor and toss my jacket across the arm of the sofa, she popped out from the kitchen, drying her hands as she walked toward me.

"You pitched a great game today, Son," she said reassuringly. "And I'm very proud of you. I'm just sorry I didn't get to see you win."

With a towel in one hand, she moved closer. She stopped and reached out to me with open arms. Then, using the magical powers that only a loving mother can apply, she gave me one soft gentle hug and that was all that was needed. In a flash, any feelings of failure I may have had were gone. Instantly, my spirits were lifted.

"You sure did a fine job," she continued. "And just so you know, I wasn't the only one who was impressed by your pitching performance today."

After dropping such a subtle comment, Mom stepped back and paused for a moment, waiting for my reaction. It was obvious she had more to say, but I wasn't responding with the curiosity she expected. A few seconds passed before she continued.

"You see, as soon as the game ended, I was approached by a gentleman who introduced himself as a major league scout. He said his name was Burleigh Grimes. Have you heard of him? He's an older gentleman, still fit and trim, and very courteous. He appeared to be in his fifties and claimed to have been a pitcher, himself, years ago. Do you know anything about him?"

At the mention of the man's name, my jaw dropped in disbelief. *Could my mother have really met and talked with the great Burleigh Grimes? And what could he possibly have to discuss with her?*

"Are you kidding? Of course, I know who he is! Why, Burleigh Grimes is one of the greatest pitchers who ever picked up a baseball! What did he say to you, Mom? Did he mention me?"

"I'm not really sure. He may have said something about you," she answered with a tease.

The suspense was overwhelming me. I wanted to hear the whole story right away. Yet, Mom was deliberate, being careful not to give up too much information too quickly. She seemed to be savoring every minute, knowing full well just how eager I was to hear more.

"Yes, Son. As a matter of fact, he did talk about you. He said he watched you throughout the whole game and was impressed with the effort you gave today."

"Today?" I snapped, incensed by the bad timing of Mr. Grimes' visit. "Why today? Of all days? Why did he have to show up for a game I pitched well and still ended up losing?"

"Take it easy, Eli. There's more for me to tell you, and you should stop being so hard on yourself," she cautioned. "First, you should know I mentioned the very same thing to him as we were talking. I told him that you very seldom lose and how unfortunate it is that he came to see you play on such a bad day."

I nodded in agreement. "That's right, Mom. Mr. Grimes could not have picked a day worse than today, if he wanted to see the best I had."

"That's where you're wrong, Eli. As a matter of fact, he explained how he may have seen the best in you today, simply by seeing the way you handled today's loss. He understands you had a tough game today against a tough opponent. But he watched you battle each and every batter. He was impressed by the type of competitor you are. And for him, it is as equally important to see how a young player will continue to fight with every pitch when his team is behind, as it is to see him in a winning situation. As a scout, Mr. Grimes probably knows more about us than either of us realizes. He is aware of your pitching record, from this season, last season and the year before. He knows which pitch is your best. He knows the teams you lost to as well as the ones you beat. And even with the number of people who sat behind home plate at this afternoon's ballgame, he knew which of the ladies was Mrs. Grba!"

As perceptive as she was, my mother gained a great deal of insight into Burleigh Grimes and his work as a baseball scout. As for me, the young, hard-headed, teenage jock, I was totally surprised by what my own mother was able to teach me about baseball, after having just one brief conversation with one of the game's brightest stars.

Since its inception in 1936, the National Baseball Hall of Fame in Cooperstown, New York, has been known for its stringent induction processes which have served to allow only the most worthy and deserving candidates to be enshrined among the immortals of baseball history. Yet, despite the scrutiny given to the records and statistics of so many great ball players, along with the number of explicit requirements each candidate must meet, arguments over who is deserving of induction into The Hall and who is not, is just one of many debatable issues that have helped make baseball the phenomenon it has become. Even today, it is still a game of numbers, long-standing traditions and opposing viewpoints.

Following a 13-year major league career as a star third baseman, Freddie Lindstrom lingered in baseball for many years, long after his playing days were over. He found work as manager for several minor league clubs in the South, but was never successful enough to keep any of those jobs for a significant time. Later, in 1947, he returned to the Chicago area, the place of his birth and became the head baseball coach at nearby Northwestern University. He held that post until the early 1960s, but he produced only three winning teams. Yet, he was able to see several of his standout players sign pro contracts, while a few of them went on to play in the major leagues.

After earning a dramatic victory in the 1949 Rose Bowl Game, Northwestern made a concentrated effort to improve their other sports programs. Not wanting to settle for a reputation as only a football power, the university began working to strengthen their basketball and baseball teams as well. The school dispatched coaches and scouts to check out some of the more promising high school athletes in the Greater Chicago Area, hoping to stock their teams with local talent. At different times, some of us on the Bowen High baseball team heard rumors about scouts from Northwestern, and possibly even Coach Lindstrom himself, being spotted in the stands at some of our games. However, with recruitment rules and restrictions as tight as they were at the time, none of us had personal contact with any of them, so we never found out if any of those rumors were true until about midway through my senior year.

I tend to believe that it was James Fitzgibbons, the longtime coach of the Sundodgers, who put in a good word for me. He had always encouraged and supported me and was known to have many connections with baseball coaches at the collegiate level. Yet, as unexpected as it was, I learned several area colleges had sent athletic ovations and inquiries to review my high school transcripts. Still, I was certain my grades weren't good enough for me to expect any scholarship offers. So you can imagine how surprised Mom and I were when a letter from Freddie Lindstrom arrived at our house just a few days before Thanksgiving.

"On behalf of the Athletic Department here at Northwestern University," the letter read, "I would like to personally invite you to meet with us to discuss our offer of a probationary athletic scholarship,"

A probationary scholarship? Now that was a strange sort of proposal. Neither Mom nor I had ever heard of anything such as that. It seemed that the school was very interested in me despite my less than impressive grades, and was offering to fund a big part of my tuition, as long as I met certain academic standards. We read and reread Lindstrom's letter a number of times, but Mom and I were still unclear on how an agreement like this would work. Yet, we agreed it would be well worth my time to make the trip to Evanston and find out what it was all about. I had grown up on Chicago's Southside and had never before been to Evanston, Illinois, so the idea of making a three-hour journey north to the campus of Northwestern University was, for me, as daunting as if I had been ordered to join the Lewis and Clark Expedition a century and a half earlier.

The start of my trip required I catch a bus and transfer to a second one just minutes later, followed by a short jaunt on the Illinois-Central Railroad. For the last leg of the trek, I boarded the elevated train bound for Evanston. At the rail terminal I asked for directions to the campus and then took off on foot, walking up and down sidewalks for what seemed like miles. At last, I got my first glimpse of Northwestern University, with its delicately manicured gardens, the archways and the magnificent gothic architecture with so many ivy-covered walls. The sight of it all was breathtaking! Suddenly I realized just how unworldly and innocent I really was. As the crow flies, I was hardly more than 30 miles from home. Yet somehow, I had entered what seemed to be a whole new world. The street names, the signs and the building numbers were all new to me, and everyone I spoke with was a complete stranger. Eventually, with the help of some friendly people who knew their way around, I made it to the athletic building and into the office of Freddie Lindstrom.

"We believe you would be a great asset to our sports programs, Eli," Coach Lindstrom suggested at the start of our meeting. "That's why I asked Coach Mike Nixon to join us today. Coach Nixon is working with our football team. We both know that baseball is your primary sport, and I would certainly like to talk with you about playing for me next season. However, Coach Nixon has had an eye on you for our football team. He believes both Illinois and Michigan are going to be tough this year, and if our Wildcats are going to stick with 'em, we're going to have to find a good punter. We feel like you may be able to help both of us if you're willing to play football for Northwestern next fall and baseball the following spring." There was a still silence in the office. To this point, Lindstrom had dominated the meeting. After shaking my hand when he entered the room, Nixon had done nothing more than nod in agreement with everything Coach Lindstrom had said.

The idea of playing two sports was something I had not anticipated. The letter I received was from Lindstrom, the baseball coach, so I had assumed baseball would be the topic of our discussion.

"Of course, we'll be expecting a lot from you, too, Eli," Lindstrom continued. "What we want you to consider is what we refer to as a *probationary athletic scholarship*. It's an arrangement whereby you play football for half of the scholarship and baseball for the other half."

With such an unexpected twist to the offer, I sat quietly, feeling as if I didn't understand the concept well enough to ask intelligent questions. The two men stared at me, studying me as I squirmed in my chair, shifting my weight and crossing and uncrossing my legs. Perhaps this was just part of their normal evaluation process. I felt it was up to me to reignite the conversation.

"Well, what about my grades? I surely didn't think they would be good enough for me to go to a school like Northwestern."

"We've already taken a good look at your grades, Eli, and no doubt, there's quite a bit of room for improvement," Lindstrom confessed. "But we still think you may have a good chance to make it here academically, if you're willing to work hard. That's why this scholarship is offered to you on a probationary basis. As long as you play both football and baseball and maintain good marks in all of your classes, a degree from Northwestern

University can be yours. But should you fail to hold up your end of the agreement, the scholarship will be immediately withdrawn."

In contrast to the warm friendly welcome I received when we first gathered, the atmosphere in the office had changed to a much more serious tone. The faces of both Lindstrom and Nixon had become stern and unforgiving. They had made their point. Both had impressed me as the sort of men you don't screw around with. Growing even more uncomfortable in my seat, I was eager to get back to our discussion.

"This is a big decision for you, Eli," Lindstrom advised. "I hope you will discuss this offer thoroughly with your mother, as your choice could have a big impact on your future. We'll be in touch with you soon to schedule another meeting. Hopefully, by then you will have decided what you would like to do."

I had a lot to think about that afternoon on my trip home from Evanston. For a short time I felt like I had been granted a pardon for not doing as well as I could have in school, for not being attentive in class and for not studying like I should have. *Maybe I was getting a second chance.*

Still, the idea of playing football was troublesome. Sure, they had talked to me about being their punter, but I had been that route before. In high school, I went out for the football team with intentions of limiting my playing to strictly punting. However, after getting caught up in the competition and the excitement of the games, I found myself ready and champing at the bit to get into the action. And with lure and prestige of Big Ten Conference football at Northwestern, I knew it wouldn't take much persuasion to get me back onto the gridiron. *But could I risk the chance of getting hurt?*

All through my seasons of American Legion and semipro, Coach Fitzgibbons had tried to convince me that chances were good that pro baseball could be my future if I kept myself in good physical shape and worked hard. He had always urged me to avoid injuries which could jeopardize my chances in baseball, insisting that I steer clear of any activities as risky as football. He often reminded me I was just one shoulder injury away from pitching my last game. Naturally, my mother was in full agreement with Fitzgibbons's approach to my athletic future, but still she would allow me to choose my own path and leave the final decision up to me. She was strongly opposed to my playing football at any level, even if it kept me from attending a prominent school like Northwestern.

We were only a few days into the new year when, as expected, a second letter from Freddie Lindstrom turned up at our house. Naturally, I was flattered to have another chance to meet with him, as it was not every day that a high school senior received an invitation to talk with one of the most well-known figures in baseball. I was awestruck being in his presence before, and was thrilled to be meeting with him again. But to justify a return trip to Evanston, I explained to my mother how I should at least hear what the university was willing to do, and that I owed it to them to give my answer in person. Nonetheless, against her better judgment, I set out for the campus of Northwestern University on a bright but cold January morning to visit a second time with coaches Lindstrom and Nixon.

Again, I caught the buses and trains to make the tricky trip to Evanston, but this time with a bit more confidence and familiarity than when I made the first journey a month and a half earlier. On this second trip I was a seasoned traveler, with more of a sense of where I was going and where to report. After arriving on campus with a few minutes to spare, I took time to look around at the scenic landscape of the school and checked out some of the markers and monuments spotted along the walkways. For a brief moment I entertained thoughts and visions of what it might be like to live there in one of the men's dormitories and attend classes in the tall majestic buildings. There was just no comparison between Northwestern University and any other college campus I had ever seen.

With my invitation letter in hand, I climbed the steps of the athletic building and walked the hallway that led to the coaches' offices.

"My name is Eli Grba and I'm here to see Coach Lindstrom," I informed the young receptionist.

"I'm sorry but Mr. Lindstrom is not in today," she responded without looking up from her appointment book.

"Well, he asked me to meet with him this morning. And, as a matter of fact, I have this letter from him telling me to be here today to talk with him about a scholarship."

I don't know why I even bothered to pull the envelope from my coat pocket and present it to her as evidence. Obviously annoyed by my mere presence, she flipped through the pages of her calendar and nervously tapped the point of her pencil on the desktop.

"You must be mistaken, young man," she offered bluntly. "I don't see you listed anywhere on Coach Lindstrom's schedule. Besides, he won't be coming in at all today."

I was taken aback not only by Lindstrom's absence, but equally so by the lady's lack of concern for my disappointment and inconvenience. I had traveled all morning to keep my appointment and wasn't about to give up so quickly. I glanced through the open door behind her desk and into the vacant office where I had been interviewed only a few weeks earlier.

"Well, what about Coach Mike Nixon? Could I speak with him this morning?"

"I'm sorry, sir, but he's also out today."

While her artificial apology did nothing to curb my frustration, I noticed how for the first time, she raised her eyes up from her papers and looked at me as she spoke. "I'm afraid you'll have to come back another day. Perhaps you should call and ask for an appointment."

At this point I finally accepted the hopelessness of my situation and uttered a soft, yet insincere "thank you" as I turned to walk toward the door. My mother had taught me to be polite and remember my manners, even when others are impersonal or inconsiderate.

I don't believe I looked out my window even once throughout the entire trip home. The uncomfortable lump in my throat felt like it was as big as my fist. The hopes and dreams I had earlier that same day had been dashed. "It was all just false hopes," I told myself. "How could they do this to me?" I recalled something I had heard many times as a child, something my grandfather said I should always remember.

"A man who keeps his word is a man of integrity," he explained. "And a man is only as good as his word."

But this was baseball, America's favorite pastime, and I had been tossed aside and ignored by one of the best to ever play the game. *Was this only a sampling of what I should expect from baseball? Is this where I want my hopes and dreams to lead me?*

I never again heard from Freddie Lindstrom, the former star third baseman of the New York Giants, who years later, would be enshrined among the other baseball immortals in the National Baseball Hall of Fame. The experience of dealing with him was a bitter pill to swallow, a tough lesson to learn. Yet, in time, I would come to see that someone failing to keep an appointment would be minor and insignificant compared to many of the other setbacks I would experience in my life. I would come to see how a disappointing trip to Evanston, Illinois, would help me be better prepared for some of the other broken promises and bad deals I would encounter later in my playing career and in the years beyond.

I would soon discover that baseball is like any other business. In some instances I found managers, general managers and executives who could be trusted. These were men who kept their promises and demonstrated decency and integrity in their dealings. Unfortunately, I ran into just as many whose words meant nothing. For them, honesty and fairness always seemed to take a backseat to ambition and greed. Today, I extend forgiveness to those individuals, while trying to dismiss what happened and working to move forward.

It has taken many years for me to learn that in order to live free, you must first drop resentment. This is an important rule that unfortunately many of us do not learn until late in life, if ever at all. And even now, it is a principle that I try to remind myself of every day.

CHAPTER 12
"WHERE DO I SIGN?"

E ven the most casual of fans has his favorite baseball story. Each has his own personal recollection a towering homerun, a no-hit game or maybe even an unbelievable play he made himself on a vacant lot that no one else seems to remember quite the way he does. In some cases, baseball stories are handed down through the years, from one generation to another. Often they are passed on by someone who did not witness the feat himself, but heard a first-hand account from another fan, one who claimed to have had a bird's-eye view of the action at the precise moment it occurred. And unlike stories on other topics, baseball stories have a tendency to change with time. Recreational fishermen are probably the only sportsmen known to exaggerate more with their storytelling than baseball fans. And with each passing season, outfield catches always become more spectacular, curveballs tend to bend with greater arcs and homeruns seem to travel higher and farther. It's the stories about the games, the heroes, the goats and the unforgettable characters that have helped weave baseball into our country's fabric for more than a century. And it's these colorful, but sometimes exaggerated stories that will help keep baseball as America's pastime for generations to come.

However, while baseball lore is filled with inspiring tales of record-breaking heroics and glorious days in the sun, there are also stories of heartbreaking mishaps and tragic accidents and illness that leave fans wondering what if? and what could have happened? if a young athlete had not been cut down in the prime of his life, leaving a promising career incomplete and unfulfilled.

Thurman Munson, a perennial all-star catcher with the New York Yankees and the American League's Most Valuable Player in 1976, was only 32 years old when he died in the fiery crash of his privately owned airplane in 1979. The untimely death of this beloved Yankee team captain is often noted as one of baseball's most heartbreaking tragedies.

Still, it's difficult to imagine a sadder time in the game's history than the final weeks of the 1957 baseball season when devoted Dodger fans got their hearts crushed by news of their team's plan to abandon their loyal rooters in Brooklyn and move to Los Angeles. And just when the jilted followers of the "Boys of Summer" were sure things could get no worse, their favorite catcher, all-star Roy Campanella, was left paralyzed following an automobile crash in January of 1958. Campy would spend the rest of his life in a wheelchair.

We have heard how time heals all wounds. Yet for anyone who has seen the 1942 movie classic, *The Pride of the Yankees*, it can be difficult to hold back tears as a ceremony that took place more than 75 years ago is reenacted on the silver screen. Movie fans, even those with no interest in sports, will quickly admit that the scene in which Lou Gehrig, played by Gary Cooper, stood before an overflow crowd at Yankee Stadium and tearfully announced that he considered himself "the luckiest man on the face of the earth," is one of the most emotional scenes ever filmed in cinema history. Ironically, Gehrig, often referred to as baseball's Iron Horse, succumbed to amyotrophic lateral sclerosis (ALS) when he was only 37 years old.

Of course, there are other tragic stories of what if? and what could have been? that surface whenever baseball pundits dig into their files. There is the beaning of Cleveland Indians shortstop, Ray Chapman, in 1920 that is remembered as the only on-field fatality in major league history. And who among us will ever forget the horrible loss of Roberto Clemente, the beloved Pittsburgh Pirate outfielder, whose body was never recovered after the overloaded cargo plane he boarded plunged into high seas on the evening of New Year's Eve 1972, as he and the crew were attempting to transport supplies to earthquake victims in Nicaragua? The pride of his native Puerto Rico, Clemente will always be remembered as a great humanitarian and as one of the best ever to play the game.

Nonetheless, there are many other accounts of tragedy and misfortune in baseball's past that are not so familiar, even to some who are avid students of the sport. Mishaps, accidents and serious illnesses can just as easily occur in the personal lives of lesser-known professional athletes as they can to those who are household names. Yet the pain, sorrow and broken dreams can be just as bitter for the friends, family and fans of a rookie in the minor leagues as they can be for a hall of famer. The terrible misfortune of Chuck Koney is one such example.

He was starting his twelfth season as the second baseman of the Boston Red Sox, but still, Bobby Doerr was showing no signs of slowing down. The only thing working against him was time. Bobby was 31 years old and Red Sox executives could not have been more pleased with his consistent play. However, they were realistic enough to know he still had a few good seasons left, yet they could not expect him to continue to put up all-star numbers forever. It was 1949 and time for the Red Sox to groom a future star to take over Bobby's position.

Chuck Koney had been a Red Sox farmhand since 1943, and had strung together three consecutive stellar seasons for the club's top minor league affiliate, the Louisville Colonels of the American Association, before being slowed by a nagging leg injury in early 1949. From 1946 through 1948 he had proved himself to be one of the top second basemen in the circuit and with Doerr's retirement looming, fans were counting on Koney getting a call to report to Boston once his ailing leg returned to form. Sports writers all over New England were referring to Chuck Koney as the heir apparent of Bobby Doerr. Pitcher, Mickey McDermott, a Louisville teammate, described Chuck as "smart, a sweet hitter and an acrobat at second base." All over professional baseball he was seen as a "can't-miss prospect."

The Colonels were about to visit Milwaukee for a three-game series against the Brewers when Chuck got his team's permission to spend an off-day with his family in Chicago. He had not been home since leaving for spring training almost two months earlier. And while he and his young wife were eagerly awaiting the birth of their second child, Chuck was delighted to get back to his parents' house in his old neighborhood and considered himself lucky to get to return home for even one day during the baseball season. Nevertheless, he had no idea of the danger that waited inside his home. He had no clue that he and his family were being exposed to a deadly volatile atmosphere which was silently accumulating just one level below their living room. To Chuck, everything had seemed to be perfect when his mother, father, wife and two-year-old son greeted him with hugs and kisses at the front door.

Chuck Koney, star second baseman of the Louisville Colonels, was Boston's top prospect and was labeled the heir apparent of Bobby Doerr.

Throughout the evening there had been no hot water in the house, no hot water for showers or bathing and none in the kitchen for washing dishes. His time away from his job was short, but the situation required immediate action. His family was in need. Dutifully, Chuck decided to go downstairs to the basement to check out the situation. He examined the LP gas-powered water heater and found the pilot light was out, a likely cause of the problem. Unmindful of the leaking gas that had gathered near the base of the heater, he struck a match.

The explosion was enough to cause significant structural damage to the house. Chuck's jaw and nose were broken. The blast shot off hot water and shards of torn metal which completely mangled his right leg. His left leg was severely burned and fractured in three places. Following intense treatments, numerous surgeries and extended hospitalization, Chuck agreed to have his right leg amputated.

"Granting permission to have my leg surgically removed when I was only 22 years old was the most difficult decision I would ever make," Koney said years later. "Back then, I would've rather died than lose my leg."

He had his heart set on making it to the Boston Red Sox and the mere thought of living the rest of his life with an artificial limb was a crushing emotional setback for Chuck. However, all was not lost. In an unexpected and indirect way he did make it to the Red Sox.

Boston's general manager, Joe Cronin visited Chuck in the hospital, not only to bring get well wishes from the entire Red Sox organization, but also to deliver a personal offer from the team's owner and president, Tom Yawkey. It was a job offer for Chuck to be a lifetime employee of the Red Sox. Of course it wasn't an opportunity to replace the great Bobby Doerr at second base, as Chuck's hopes of ever playing baseball again were simply out of the question. Yet he would have the chance to remain close to the game he loved, working as scout for Yawkey and the Red Sox for as long as he wanted. Koney accepted Mr. Yawkey's offer and in a few short years became one of the most respected scouts in all of baseball. With an exceptional eye for talent, he helped to coax hall of famer, Carl Yastrzemski and several other star players into the Boston fold. It was a job he would keep until his retirement almost 50 years later. In a 2004 interview with *Chicago Tribune* reporter, Patrick Kampert, Chuck reflected back on his career in professional baseball.

"I was blessed," he told Kampert. "The dear Lord watched over me. The Red Sox have been first class since day one."

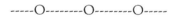

Like every other school year, my senior year of high school was about nine months long, but this final year was unlike any of the others. As I mentioned earlier, it was an unsettling time for me. There was so much doubt about the path of life I should follow and so many crucial decisions to make. It would have been great if I could have slowed down the entire process, and given myself more time to sort through the opportunities, the offers and the advice that bombarded me throughout the year. But at a time when so many people seemed to know exactly what was best for me and what choices I should make, I found myself apprehensive and unsure.

Despite my disappointing experience with Northwestern, I was pleased to learn there were other colleges who were interested in me.

Coach Fitzgibbons, who was among my biggest proponents, was aware of the schools that had scouted me, yet he was candid enough to tell me that their interest was based solely on my athletic abilities and that it was my grades that were my biggest obstacle. I was flattered to learn I was drawing so much attention, but at the same time I was disappointed in myself for not trying harder in school. I had coasted through high school, doing just well enough to pass. Had I studied and applied myself, I could have had my choice from among several good colleges to choose from.

The University of Wyoming could have been one of my possibilities. Several of my former Sundodger teammates were already there, playing on the Cowboys' baseball team. Nevertheless, Laramie, Wyoming, would have been a lot farther from home than I preferred. However, learning that Bradley University, one of the finest colleges in the Midwest, could have been an option, had my transcripts been more impressive, was a sobering disappointment. Located less than 200 miles from home, in Peoria, Bradley would have been ideal. The school was well recognized for its outstanding baseball team, and even more for its men's basketball program. The Bradley Braves had just recently made strong showings in the National Invitational Tournament, finishing fourth in 1949 and second in 1950. With my two favorite sports having such prominence at the school, and the campus only a three-hour bus ride from South Chicago, I felt as if I had missed a golden opportunity and there was no one to blame but myself. If I had only worked a little harder, I could have had so many more opportunities.

Meanwhile, baseball was still in full swing at Bowen High School. We had entered the season with high hopes, but as we moved on into the heart of the schedule, it was obvious we weren't the powerhouse team we had been the year before, but that's not to say we didn't have a winning season. We won our share of games and held our own in the district standings; however, we were never in contention for a return trip to the city championship tournament. Still, more than ever, word was circulating that scouts from big league teams were watching us. And while the rules would not permit any of them to speak to a high school player before graduation, I heard rumors that many of those scouts were there to see me.

I can't remember any of my statistics from my senior year, but I do recall putting up some pretty good numbers. Again, I won almost all of the games I pitched, and saw noticeable improvement with my control. As the season progressed, I was in top form and seemed to be gaining more self-confidence with each game. However, while I was confident and sure on the pitcher's mound, I still wasn't comfortable being myself whenever I was away from the playing field. Like almost all teenagers, I doubted whether or not I was being accepted by my friends and the other kids at school. I was at an age where social status was a major priority and I would have tried almost anything to attain it.

When the season was over, I was delighted to learn I had been invited to play in the Chicago High School Public League All-Star Game. It was an annual event held at Comiskey Park which pitted the best high school players from the Southside of the city against those of the North, and was known to attract scouts from all of the major league clubs. In my mind, this game was going to be the icing on the cake for my career as a high school athlete, and I was still looking forward to another season with the Sundodgers, followed by more basketball at the YMCA. While I wasn't counting on some unexpected lucky break to come my way, I was preparing for a life close to home. I wasn't aware of the number of baseball scouts who had me in their sights.

For me, the day of the game was one unforgettable day! Not only was it my big chance to "show my wares" to the scouts in attendance, but later, I would receive my diploma at the commencement and graduation exercises that same afternoon at the Bowen High School auditorium. *Just how much could I squeeze into one day?*

It was a big crowd for a scholastic baseball game, since much of the lower level of Comiskey Park was occupied. The game had become a Chicago tradition for fans who wanted to see the finest high school players in the area, and the large turnout was proof of the strong local following. There were dozens of area schools represented between the two squads, so just being selected for either of them was an honor. From the moment I received the invitation to play for the Southside All-Stars, I had high hopes of being named the starting pitcher. But as fate would have it, an unavoidable pregame mishap dashed my chances.

In the days leading up to the game, our team was put through a couple of rigorous workouts. On a neutral field not far from Comiskey, we went through the routine drills, including batting practice, infield drills and a periods to run and throw in the outfield, yet with so much at stake, our spirits were high. For such an important game, there were high levels of hustle and enthusiasm. When it was time for batting practice, I took my normal turn in the cage and was getting some good wood on the ball, when suddenly I fouled off a pitch, slicing it down toward the ground. With full force, the baseball made a direct hit on the toes of my back foot. My leather spikes offered almost no protection as the ball struck my big toe, sending shockwaves of pain through my foot and up my right leg. It was as if my toes had been smashed by a blacksmith's hammer! I shrieked in pain and leaped from the batter's box. I began hopping on one foot, keeping my throbbing right foot off the ground. My first thoughts were to stifle my reaction, to do nothing to draw attention to my injury. The last thing I wanted to do was give the coaches a reason to suspect I was hurt and unable to play. I had to be ready to pitch my best and I didn't want to miss my chance. But it was too late. Several teammates who had been hanging around the batting cage waiting to take their cuts came running to offer help. The coach sauntered over to check on me, while a trainer bolted from the bench and made a dash for me. In no time, I was on my butt, sitting in the red clay at home plate, watching as he removed my shoe.

"I'm okay! I'm fine! Just let me get up and walk it off," I fussed. Perhaps, I was doing a poor job of hiding my pain. The trainer and none of the coaches were buying my act. They helped me to my feet and watched intently as I tried to put weight on that aching right foot.

"Just give me my shoe," I ordered the trainer. "Let me get back in the box and finish my swings."

My foot felt like it was about to explode, yet I somehow managed to slip it back into my shoe. Using my bat like a cane, I took a few short steps, gingerly making my way back to the cage. I wanted to finish batting practice.

"Don't worry about hitting," the coach ordered. "Grab your glove and shag a few balls in the outfield. That right foot is your push foot, and you'll need to have it in top shape if you're going to pitch effectively."

By the time I tied the laces on my shoe and picked up my glove, the throbbing was beginning to subside. My big toe was badly bruised and the soreness lingered, but I found I was able to throw with only minimal pain.

"No, I'm fine," I repeated. "I'm here to pitch, so let me get on the mound and throw batting practice."

Several anxious onlookers stood by as I lobbed a few pitches to a teammate. There was no denying the pain, but I made a deliberate effort not to show it. I began adding a little more velocity with each toss. I was determined to pitch that day and willing to take the mound even if it killed me!

"I'm fine, Coach," I announced, using all the optimism I could muster. "I'll loosen up a little more and I'll be ready to go."

Warding off the pain, I went on to pitch BP for the rest of the session, which took about a half hour. Near the end of the drill, I began to notice a twinge of soreness in my right shoulder. For the first time I could recall, I was experiencing pain in my pitching arm, an on-and-off condition I would become a lot more familiar with over the course of my career. Without saying a word to anyone about my injuries, I was sure the tenderness in both my foot and shoulder would soon go away if I were to take it easy for a day or so and rest my arm until game time.

Sure enough, I was feeling much better, when just moments before we took the field at Comiskey, I stretched my arms and shoulders as I suited up in the clubhouse. The rules for the all-star game called for each boy to play only three innings, which would give every boy an opportunity to play. "Surely, I can pitch three innings," I assured myself. "That will be just long enough for me to show the scouts what I can do." It wasn't until the coach called for everyone's attention and announced the starting lineup that I got blindsided by a surprise I will never forget.

"Batting fourth and playing right field, Eli Grba," he read aloud from his card without looking up. His eyes never left the clipboard as he continued to call the names and positions of the other starting players. Still, it wasn't until he got near the bottom of the batting order that the true purpose behind the lineup change became evident, and the coach sheepishly announced his own son as the starting pitcher!

I was floored by his decision. To make sure I heard correctly, I even checked the lineup card for myself after he taped it on the dugout wall. "Of all the nerve!" I whispered. "This guy saw the break he needed when I fouled that ball off my foot in practice, and now he is taking full advantage of it." Shocked to learn I would be playing in the outfield, I started up the dugout steps to begin warm-ups when he gave me an unexpected pat on the back.

"We gotta take care of that foot, Eli," he reminded me, with all the sincerity of a desperate politician. "We need to play it safe."

Without turning to acknowledge him, I headed for my position. I pounded my fist into my glove and sprinted across the grass. "You're right, Coach. Play it safe, my ass!" I mumbled under my breath. I didn't want to believe the worst, but I had no choice. His backup plan seemed to be in place well in advance. I recognized his ploy for what it really was: a chance to push his own kid into the spotlight.

Throughout the game, I tried hard to keep my thoughts away from the missed opportunity and the fact that I was relegated to outfield without getting a chance to pitch. I could have pitched that day; I know I could have, at least for a few innings.

I can't recall many of the details from that game, as I suppose the combination of my frustration at the time and the passing of so many years have worked together to cloud my memory. However, I do remember how much I wanted to give that coach a piece of my mind when I was taken out of the game after three innings. I passed the dugout of the opposing Northsiders who were equally surprised that I was finished for the day without taking the mound.

"Where are you going, Eli?" they questioned me. "Why aren't you pitching today? Are you hurt?" They seemed to be as taken back as I was. Yet, as I left the field, I found I wouldn't need to confront the coach myself since I had a family member there who was more than ready to speak up on my behalf.

It was my mom's brother, Uncle Mike, who had come to see me play, who was no doubt infuriated well past the point of my own disgust. He held nothing back and showed no restraint when it came to letting the coach know exactly what he thought. I was about to head down the steps of our dugout when I spotted Uncle Mike leaning over the box seat railing and screaming his head off. Or perhaps I should say I heard him long before I spotted him!

The coach could not duck back into the dugout quickly enough to escape the wrath and anger of my Uncle Mike. He called that man everything in the book and then some! He even went on to drag practically everyone in that poor coach's family tree into his tirade of ugly names. The tongue-lashing was rough enough to make a sailor blush. Why, I recall a trio of young ladies who were seated behind the dugout, who covered their ears with their hands, just as Uncle Mike was about to shift his language into high gear!

Had it not been for my own ill feelings toward the coach and the obvious pleasure he took in moving me to the back burner, I may have been embarrassed, but I wasn't. While the actions of my uncle were crude and repulsive, it was good to see how he had no reservations about supporting me. While his violent rage was uncharacteristic of him, it was the first and only outburst of that type I ever saw from anyone in my family. It went against the principles that were taught and upheld in our family. On the other hand, I was reassured to know there was someone in my corner. Uncle Mike saw how the circumstances had been manipulated against me and was ready to fight to expose it. And as a 17-year-old with no clear direction in life, I could have used all of the support I could get.

Even at the end of such an unforgettable experience at Comiskey Park, there was still a lot of drama left to go on that day in June of 1952. After leaving the game, I didn't have a minute to waste in stopping at the house to change clothes and make my way to the school auditorium for my long-awaited graduation.

The exercises were already underway when I hopped out of the car in front of the school. A round of applause erupted as I pushed through the double doors and strutted up the aisle, sore foot and all. I slowed my pace as I neared the front of the room, searching for the "G" section of the several hundred excited seniors who were seated alphabetically.

"Nice of you to join us!" one classmate jeered.

"Grab yourself a seat, Grba!" yelled another.

The speaker was forced to pause until I found my place and got seated. In spite of my late entry, it was still a long ceremony and a long time to be cramped elbow to elbow in a stuffy auditorium. We could hardly wait until the final address was done and we could finally sling our caps and tassels to the ceiling!

At last, we had broken free from the chains of education and it was time to celebrate. And like any other graduating class on our final night, we split into separate groups of our closest friends for one last evening of rip-roaring partying. Of course, some of the celebrations may have been a little more subdued than others, but for me and my cronies, it was a night of all-out hard drinking and carousing. It would mark the last time many of us would see each other or even get together as longtime buddies, teammates and classmates. It was our intention to make it a time we would always remember. I saw it as a final shot to find my place socially, to fit in and be accepted as one of the gang. I gave it my best try by foolishly drinking myself into a drunken stupor.

I can only guess how I made it home safely, but it was the wee hours of the morning when I staggered up the steps and into the house. The windows had been open, but the weather had been unusually hot with very little breeze, which caused the upper floor to feel as sultry as a Turkish bath. To escape the heat, my mother appeared to be asleep on a pallet in the hall just outside of her bedroom, yet with so little light, it was hard to say for sure. I would like to think I made it past her without her knowing. But it's a lot more likely that she knew what was going on, and was all too familiar with the routine. After all, she had put up with a drunk in her home for too many years and had been hurt too many times not to recognize the sound of a drunken man's footsteps.

My head was spinning like a whirlwind and I was nauseated. I closed the door to my room and by the street light beaming through the window, I stumbled to the dresser and gripped the corner with one hand to steady myself. In the darkness, I felt for the handle on the top drawer. Just in time, I slid it open as far as I could and vomited onto the freshly laundered socks and underwear my mother had lovingly folded and placed there. I somehow made it across the floor to the bed and collapsed. The room was rolling like a ship in an angry storm. I had seen this happen many times before, but not to me, I had sworn I wouldn't allow it. I was young, but I had already been a witness to the ugly side of alcohol.

"I'll never go down that road!" I promised myself.

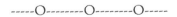

It was soon clear that the North-South All Star Game and all the chaos that came with it would have no bearing on my prospective future in baseball. I don't recall ever crossing paths with that coach again, and by the grace of God and Uncle Mike, I assume he lived to coach a few more seasons of high school baseball. I suppose many of the professional scouts in the area had already checked on me prior to that game, and saw enough of what they wanted, as they sure seemed to have no trouble finding our house, once graduation was over.

It was the Yankees who came calling first, or maybe it was the Cubs. Nevertheless, they were among the first of the major league clubs who had scouts pay me a visit. At first it was surprising to find out how much they knew about me. It was obvious each of them had watched me play on numerous occasions and had done their homework. As I pointed out before, there were rumors of scouts attending many of our games, but I never realized I was being scrutinized so closely. According to the rules of professional baseball, with graduation behind me, I was finally eligible to be contacted by scouts and free to negotiate and entertain all offers.

For several weeks, scouts visited me at home, each having basically the same encouraging compliments along with a long string of reasons why their particular club had the most to offer and would be the perfect fit for me. Naturally, I would have liked to have teamed up with one of the local clubs, the White Sox or Cubs, but their offers were not much different from any of the others. All of the contracts called for something in the range of $2,600 to $2,800, with the New York Yankees leading the pack with an offer of $3,000. It was all very confusing for me. There was so much talk of bonuses and salaries and club options that I wasn't sure who to trust or whose advice I should take. That's when I got a call from my trusted friend, Coach James Fitzgibbons.

"You'll be hearing from the Red Sox soon, Eli. And it would be good if you don't sign anything until you talk with them," he advised. "You remember Chuck Koney, don't you? He's from right here in town and since that terrible accident a couple of years ago, he's been working as a scout for the Boston club. He will visit you soon to offer you a contract. And you have my word, he's a fellow you can trust!"

It was only days later, as Coach Fitzgibbons predicted, that Chuck Koney came to our house with an offer from the Red Sox that was, by far, the most generous offer I would receive.

In keeping with the strict guidelines that Major League Baseball implemented at the time to restrict signing bonuses for young players, a limit of $6,000 was ruled to be the maximum amount that could be offered as a bonus/salary package without classifying the new player as a "bonus baby." Should the contract exceed $6,000, the club would be required to place the bonus baby on their major league roster before the end of the season, or give the player free-agent status, whereby he could be claimed by other teams. The process was often very unsettling to veteran players at the major league level who resented losing their spots on the roster to unproven first-year players.

"This is as high as we're willing to go," Koney assured me. "Making you a bonus baby wouldn't be fair to you or to the team, yet we will be giving you the maximum we can offer and still stay within the guidelines. And believe me, Eli, as I speak from experience when I tell you there is no finer organization in all of baseball. There is no ball club that cares more for their people than Mr. Tom Yawkey and the Boston Red Sox... and I'm living proof!"

There was a silent pause as I pondered what felt like a once-in-a-lifetime opportunity. "This is as good as it gets!" I told myself.

"Okay, that's proof enough for me, Mr. Koney," I conceded. "Where do I sign?"

Chuck Koney assured me that the Boston Red Sox
were the finest organization in all of baseball.

CHAPTER 13

OH, TO BE YOUNG AND FULL OF HOPE!

———

The word spread like wildfire and folks from all around the neighborhood were happy to hear the news. The prominent local newspaper of South Chicago, The Daily Calumet, even found enough space on the front of their sports section to run a photo of me in my Sundodgers uniform along with a headline banner across the top of the page declaring, "GRBA SIGNS WITH RED SOX." The article went on to say how unique it was for me, a hopeful young prospect from the local area, to be signed by a Chuck Koney, a professional scout from the same hometown. Even before his untimely accident, Chuck had been revered as somewhat of a local hero, not only for his once promising career as a ballplayer, but also for the way he worked his way through his life-altering injuries, his attitude throughout his therapy, and the way he continued to move forward with his life.

"It's my job to find the best players for the Red Sox," he told a reporter. "And I sure hope I can do it. I owe it to Mr. Yawkey and the ball club for all they've done for me."

For the brief time it lasted, it was great to be the "talk of the town." The attention, the good wishes and encouragement had me flying high with emotion. And it all came at a good time, following a not-so-flattering quip in the Chicago Tribune which ran a week or two earlier. It was written by a Tribune sportswriter who blasted Major League Baseball for stealing the most talented players from under the nose of area colleges and universities by offering incredibly high salaries and signing bonuses to unproven young prospects. To make his point, the writer cited the University of Illinois, who had had their sights on local standout, "George" Grba until they learned of the lucrative offers he received to turn pro. Of course, the fact they couldn't even get my name right was a blow to my pride, not to mention I was never aware the school was interested in me. Still, I would soon recognize this as my first chance to see how the press could be both a friend and a foe to a ballplayer. A writer's praise can be inspiring, while his criticism and misquotes can be damaging and hurtful. Experience taught me it was usually best to ignore what the media had to say and allow public opinion to fall where it may. It was no easy lesson to learn, but it was an important one.

I suppose it was only natural for friends to question me about why I didn't sign with either of the hometown teams, the Cubs or White Sox. And while I had numerous visits from Vedie Himsl, a fine gentleman who scouted for the Cubs, the Chicago White Sox, for some reason, never contacted me. Still the Cubs, like all the others, did not come close to Boston's proposal. "Their terms just didn't compare to what the Red Sox offered me," I would explain. And once I mentioned how I was signed by local favorite, Chuck Koney, there were very few doubts about my hometown loyalty.

Through the rest of the summer and the months that followed, my most important job was to stay healthy and avoid injuries. At the time of my signing, it was made clear that I was property of the Boston Red Sox and it was my responsibility to have myself in top physical condition when I reported to training camp. But perhaps I didn't follow their orders as closely as I should have. I stayed on with the Sundodgers for their entire semipro season, but played only as an outfielder. Coach Fitzgibbons, who had been supportive and had advised me through the uncertainty and confusion that came with all the scouts and their offers, was not about to let me risk injuring my pitching arm, just as I was about to start my professional career. Still, the season turned out to be lots of fun and one of the most exciting I can recall.

For me, the most memorable game of the summer was a road game we played against an all-inmate team at the Joliet State Prison. Located about 30 miles from my South Chicago neighborhood, the infamous facility built before the Civil War was home to some of the most hardened criminals in that area of the country until it was finally shut down in

2002. The prison, which was always filled to capacity, had no room to spare. The huge limestone buildings situated on less than a dozen acres of state-owned land left very little open space on the grounds. However, a sizable area was designated for a clean, well-maintained baseball field. The prison team, which was stocked with some very talented athletes, played all its games at home and often hosted exhibition games against minor league clubs and semipro teams like ours. The inmates took pride in keeping the field in good shape and ready for play, and on game day, the area behind the backstop and in foul territory along the baselines would be jam-packed with hundreds of boisterous prisoners who loved baseball and were happy for a chance to let off a little bit of steam.

The news about me signing with the Red Sox had already reached Joliet long before the Sundodgers arrived for the game. And no doubt, many of the guys imprisoned there were sports fans just like anyone else. But like everyone else, they often had more appreciation for the truth after it has been stretched. And so it was with the details of my contract, as some of the more vocal but uninformed spectators positioned along the right field line had it in their heads that my agreement was worth as much as ten times its actual value.

"Hey, Grba!" one yelled. "How about loanin' me a piece of that sixty-grand you signed for?" There was hardly time for the frolicking and laughter to subside before another heckling inmate chimed in.

"Hey, kid! Don't go spending all that big league dough in one place!"

I was surprised to find out those fellows at Joliet knew about me and the news about my contract, even if they were a little mixed up on some of the facts.

It was the summer of 1952, my last carefree summer. My time was my own and I had no responsibilities. America was beginning its love affair with television, as almost half of the households in the country owned a set. However, while many families were sitting in front of their bulky cabinet models, tuned in to programs such as "Dragnet" and "I Love Lucy," American moviegoers were flocking to theaters to catch "High Noon" and "Singin' in the Rain," and other great Hollywood classics. But as a 17-year-old who stayed on the go, I didn't stay still long enough to watch TV or go to movies. Baseball and the Sundodgers took up all of my time and energy that summer. The following season I would turn pro, and I was determined to make the most of what would be my final summer at home with my boyhood buddies.

The Sundodgers had another successful season, good enough, in fact, to receive an invitation to play in a tournament with other semipro teams in Cleveland, Ohio. As a team we played a fine tournament. And personally, I felt as if I was playing at the top of my game. I was pleased with my all-around performance in the tourney, both at the plate and with my defensive play in the outfield. But without knowing it, I had played well enough to catch the attention of a scout from the Cleveland Indians, who caught up with me after the final out of our final game. With a hearty handshake, this middle-aged gentleman introduced himself and told me how much he had been impressed by my play on the field.

"Well, young man, I'm here to talk with you about playing for the Indians," he offered. "We could sure use a young outfielder with your talent and we're ready to do whatever it takes to sign you."

"I've already been signed," I confessed sheepishly. "I'm under contract with the Red Sox." Thinking I was finished having to deal with scouts and their confusing proposals, I was caught by surprise.

Suddenly, there was quiet pause. Like an unexpected splash of ice water, my response brought an abrupt end to our conversation. His efforts foiled, the scout pulled a crumpled handkerchief from his back pocket and dabbed his forehead.

"Well, that's too bad," he finally spoke up. "Our club was prepared to top all other offers you may have received," he concluded. "But I guess none of that matters at this point."

He was right. At that point, none of that mattered. There was nothing left to discuss. Yet, he walked away leaving me to wonder, with doubts and questions that would never be answered. *Was he truthful when told me the Indians would have topped all other offers? Would I have been better off as an every-day player, playing in the outfield? Should I have waited a while longer before I signed?*

"This is not the time to look behind," I told myself, working to keep a positive outlook. "I'll be reporting to my first spring training in a few months and I have my entire career in professional baseball in front of me. And regardless of what this fellows says, I'm still going to make more money than I ever dreamed possible, and I'm going to do it playing for the Boston Red Sox." *Oh, to be young and full of hope!*

It was basketball at the YMCA that kept me in shape over the winter months. It was a great way to keep physically fit and prepare for spring training. However, considering the fierce competition in these games, I was undoubtedly taking a chance with my health. The Red Sox had urged me to stay in shape and be ready for training camp, but insisted that I choose my physical activities carefully and avoid any needless injuries. And while basketball at this level was probably not the wisest means of off-season conditioning, I was lucky. Still, after our team made it to tournament play for our area's District AAU title, I ran into more good luck. As I ran onto the court for the start of the opening game of the tournament, I suddenly recognized one of the referees as a scout for the Philadelphia Athletics, the same scout who had offered me a contract to play for the A's just a few weeks earlier. Of course he was aware I had signed with Boston and I was considered a professional, making me ineligible for the tournament. He gave me a wink and a quick smile, as if to say "It's okay, Eli. Your secret is safe with me." It sure was great that he allowed me to slip by, or I could have been in big trouble. Otherwise, except for the usual number of bumps and bruises, I played out the league schedule unscathed. Still, I couldn't wait for spring and the arrival of warmer weather.

But like any other winter season in Chicago, we had more than our share of bitterly cold temperatures and sharp gusty winds during the winter of '52 and '53. The fact that this particular winter was one of the few Chicago winters on record that did not bring subzero temperatures to the area, did little to warm my spirits. However, on one of the coldest snow-blown days of the season, a check from the Boston Red Sox was delivered to our house by registered mail. It arrived just in time for the holidays and nothing could have done more to get my mind off of the icy Illinois weather. It was in the amount of three thousand dollars, half of my bonus package, and it was more money than I had ever seen in my life. I had money to burn! In the privacy of my room I held the check in the light of my bed lamp, examining it and contemplating it as my first paycheck as a professional and as tangible evidence that I had been accepted into the life I had always dreamed of. *Would there be other checks? Could I make the grade? How many seasons would they want me?* These were all questions I was asking myself. Yet I would soon learn they were some of the same questions I would ponder again and again over the years as I would deal with the highs and lows of my career in baseball. It was Hall of Fame pitcher, Stan Coveleski who summed it all up so perfectly when he told a writer: "The pressure never lets up... So, you worry all the time. It never ends. Lord, baseball is a worrying thing."

I owed her more than I could ever repay. She had stood by me through both the good and bad, proving that her love for me was unconditional. I could not have had a mother who would care for me or love me more. So, when I received that first check from the Red Sox, I had no hesitations or second thoughts about sharing it evenly with her. After all, without her, many of the opportunities I was offered as a youngster would not have been possible. Still, my remaining share of $1,500 was more than I could comprehend and more than I could manage on my own. "What to do with such a windfall?" was a question I rolled over and over in my mind. U.S. Savings Bonds or a savings account at the local bank were among the wise suggestions I heard from Mom and family members. But my thinking was not nearly as mature or conservative. Some may refer to my approach as "instant gratification" or "living for now, not tomorrow," but I see it as the typical mindset for a boy who just turned eighteen.

"A new car!" I told my mom. "That's what I'd like to buy with my money. I'd want my own new car!"

Taken by surprise, Mom was not prepared for my idea or for the enthusiastic way I presented it. But she could see how intent I was, and that there was no chance of reaching a compromise. Buying a first automobile is a "guy thing," a rite of passage for all American males. And this was a time when I could have benefited by having a strong male influence in my life. But like in every other important event of my youth, Mom was there, guiding and supporting me, working hard to fill the roles of both my mother and father. And she did a remarkable job. And when the subject of buying an automobile came up, she knew the ideal person to call on.

His real name was Steven G. Lalich. He was a former boxer and a long-time friend of our family. Around the neighborhood he was called Tom-Tom, because of the rapid-fire jabs he often landed on his opponent, but to boxing fans, he was better known as Denny O'Keefe, a popular ring name he used throughout his career. He continued to go by Tom-Tom, even after he started his second career as a car salesman at Yates Ford, one of the largest and most popular auto dealerships in South Chicago. He was a friend to everyone in the Serbian community and was well known for the generous deals he tendered, even if it meant he made very little for himself. Mom was willing to take a few hours off from work to go with me across town, to meet Tom-Tom at the dealership. She was confident we would be treated fairly and get sound advice. So it was no surprise when he popped out of his office and greeted us like long lost family members. He was a real go-getter and a fast talker, who jumped quickly into his sales pitch before we could grab a seat.

"Man, have I got the perfect car for you!" he began. "The fellow who owned it took real good care of it, it runs great and it has low mileage."

"Wait a minute," I interrupted. "It was well cared for and has low mileage? Is this a used car?"

"Sure it is, but it's like new. The tires are good and the body is in perfect condition, and I'm sure I can give you folks the best deal you'll find anywhere!"

Even after he ran down the list of selling points, I remained silent, squirming in my chair, studying the color posters of the new model Fords on the wall behind his desk. I guess I wasn't as excited as either he or my mother had wanted. Still, I couldn't keep my eyes off those posters. *The new Crestline Victoria is sharp looking. And the Sunliner is so cool with the convertible top and the V-8 engine!* Suddenly, my wishful daydream was interrupted by Mom's rationality.

"Come on now, Gerbie. Buying a used automobile is a good idea," she proposed. "Buying a new car would take all of your money, besides; you don't even know how to drive!"

Of course she was right. I had never driven a car in my life. But the remark was a stinging one. It was a blow to my immature male ego. No guy would ever want the word to get out that he couldn't drive a car. There was no call for her to say that or bring up something that had nothing to do with our conversation. Or, at least that was my reasoning.

Then Tom-Tom noticed I was uneasy and came to my rescue. "Oh that's no problem, Eli," he assured me. "You'll be getting your license and driving all around town before you know it. Now, let's go outside and take a look at the car I have in mind. I think you'll be quite pleased."

It certainly wasn't the prettiest car I'd ever seen and not very sporty but it wasn't bad. It was a 1949 Dodge Wayfarer sedan. The paint was a dull dark gray, but the tires looked new. He was right, it looked like it was in great shape, no significant dents or dings anywhere. The car was beginning to grow on me, but Mom was still reserved and had a few more questions. "If you don't mind me asking, how much does this one cost and how could we get it from here to our house?" Sidestepping her questions, Tom-Tom pretended not to hear and went on with his delivery. He knew his biggest hurdle was to win me over. He knew if he could sell me on the deal, the rest would come easily.

"It has a radio, Eli. Come check it out. It also has the new Gyro-Matic transmission. You're going to really like that!"

The more he talked, the more interested I became. I began to imagine what the boys would say once they saw this machine parked in front of our house. Even if it wasn't a hot rod, I would still be the only guy in the neighborhood with his own set of wheels. Mom could sense that I was getting excited and figured it was time to get some answers.

"And what will this cost?" she pushed. "You know, we have insurance and taxes to think about too. And how will we get it home?" The smile left his face. He was trying his best to appear earnest and forthcoming in giving us the bottom-line figure.

"Look, I'll be honest with you and tell you exactly what my boss said. He doesn't want to let this automobile go for a penny under $700. But we've been friends for a long time, and I want to help Eli all I can, so I'll go out on a limb and let you folks have it for $680. Now, how does that sound? I wish I could do more, but I have to answer to my boss."

"But what about getting it back to our house?" Mom pried again. "You still haven't told me."

"Getting it over to your place is no problem, Eva," he assured her. "I'll drive it myself, or better still, Eli can drive and I'll ride with you and I'll have someone drive over to pick me up. I'm sure Eli will do just fine." His vote of confidence did nothing to change Mom's feelings, but it made me eager to hop in and hit the road.

"That's right, Mom," I finally spoke up. "I'll have to learn sometime soon. I'll be leaving for spring training in a few weeks, so I just as well start now." After another round of shaking hands the deal was final.

I filled in my personal check to Yates Motor Co. for "Six Hundred Eighty and 00/100 dollars." It was the first big check I would ever write. And with the stroke of a pen, that four year-old car was mine, bought and paid for. And while I had seen Mom happier on many occasions, she reluctantly climbed into the back seat of that Dodge as I got behind the wheel, preparing for a ride neither of us would ever forget. It was with God's protection and the daring patience of Tom-Tom Lalich that we safely made the five-mile trip home. It wasn't exactly legal, but we made it.

Over the weeks that followed, I cranked up the motor from time to time and kept the body waxed and polished. And though it never left our driveway, I was proud to show off the car to friends whenever they would drop by. However, it wasn't until the following fall, when I returned home from my first season of pro baseball that I got my operator's license and started driving. The car was fun, inexpensive and my buddies loved it and over the next few years it sure served its purpose. At that point of my life a car was something that I had to have, a true necessity. After all, who ever heard of a professional ball player who didn't have his own automobile?

CHAPTER 14

THERE'S ANOTHER WHOLE WORLD OUTSIDE OF ILLINOIS

———

I had never been more excited. I would be going farther away from home than I had ever been in my life to do what I loved more than anything, and that was to play baseball! The contract the Red Sox sent had been signed and mailed back, and the day I was scheduled to report to spring training could not come quickly enough. And while those days were filled with excitement and anticipation, I was also dealing quietly with more than my share of apprehension and doubt. Each night I went to bed realizing I was another day closer to leaving home, and falling asleep was no easy job with so many questions running through my head. *Will I run out of money? What should I pack? Will I make new friends? Will I be on time to catch my flight?* Why, just the thought of boarding an airplane for the first time and flying from Chicago to Tampa, Florida, was enough to keep me tossing and turning.

According to Will Rogers, "Worrying is like paying on a debt that may never come due." And so it was with my situation in the spring of 1953. I was probably as anxious as any young man in my shoes would have been. But just the same, it was all wasted energy. The arrangements for my trip were well planned and for whatever details the Red Sox did not cover, my family stepped in and took care of them. Mom made sure I packed everything I would need. Aunt Sophie's husband, Uncle Ostoich, promised to take good care of my car and keep it safe, while Uncle Mike assured me he would drive me to Midway Airport in plenty of time to catch my flight. I really didn't have as many concerns as I thought.

On the final evening before I left home, my aunts and uncles and other family members gathered at the house for my grand send-off. They were all proud of me and wished me well. I can't recall another occasion when I received so many good wishes and so many hugs and kisses and pats on the back. But just as the celebration was winding down, my grandfather, Deda, got up from his easy chair and pulled me aside. In a discreet whisper, he suggested that we step outside for a moment. "Let's take a little walk," he urged me. "It won't take long." As a man who had always placed high values on the virtues of integrity and hard work, he wanted a chance to further influence my future. He wanted time alone with me to pass on some of the wisdom of his advanced years and to warn me of the evils of the world.

"Come with me, Sonny," he coaxed, in his strong Serbian accent, the dialect he brought with him from the old country many years before. "I have a few things to tell you."

Side by side, we strolled along the sidewalk. I turned up the collar of my jacket and pushed my hands deep into the pockets. Like always, Deda was serious and direct. I gazed down at the cracks in the damp mossy concrete and waited for him to start our conversation.

"Your mother has worked very hard for you," he began. "She is very proud of you, so you need to be a good boy. Watch your money," he cautioned. "And send some of it home when you can. Watch your drinking and watch your women. Just be a good boy."

His advice was simple and straightforward, and it could have been among the most precious things I would take with me, had I only been smart enough to heed it. A wise man once said, "Advice can be given, but not the sense to use it."

There's no way we can fairly compare air travel of 1953 to that of the present day. The speed and luxury enjoyed by passengers on today's jetliners were still decades away when I took my first flight at 18 years old. Perhaps there are positive things to be said for the old days of commercial flying, when it came to efficiency, service, leg room and yes, even food. While traveling on today's modern airlines on a flight delayed at least an hour, I can sit jammed into a tiny seat and wonder if my luggage was even loaded onto the same airplane. Later, at the midpoint of my trip, I will expect rations of salted mystery nuts and canned soda poured into a disposable cup. Whenever I experience these typical conditions of present-day travel, I am forced to recall my first flight ever, Chicago to Florida, when precisely at mealtime, a tall beautiful stewardess passed down the center aisle, pushing a food cart loaded with the biggest, leanest roast of beef I had ever seen. The very sight of it made my mouth water. However, my inexperience as a traveler became evident to everyone around me when she asked, "How would you like your cut?" Confused and completely out of my element, I was unable to speak. I looked up at this gorgeous specimen of a lady and made some weird indiscernible sound.

She recognized the predicament I was in and immediately covered for me in my embarrassment. "Okay, sir," she offered with smile. "I'm sure I can cut yours just the way you like it." It was the thickest, juiciest cut of meat I had ever eaten, and the beautiful lady who served it to me was even more memorable. *If this is what it's like in the life of a pro ballplayer,* I reasoned, *I can get used to this real fast!*

There were several of us rookie farmhands who arrived at Tampa International Airport later that same afternoon. To a man, we each had the same clueless look of confusion on our faces as we wandered nervously about the terminal. Yet it was easy to tell we were all ballplayers, many away from home for the first time. We hardly spoke to each other, but were afraid to stray away from the herd, for fear we may miss our contact from the ballclub. At last, in a loud gruff voice that would have rivaled the orders of a drill sergeant, an overweight, middle-aged guy with a clipboard called for our attention.

"Okay fellows, heads up!" he barked. "You boys with the Red Sox, gather over here with me and answer up when I call your name." It was all routine for this fellow. No doubt, he had been through this same procedure many times before. But for us, a bunch of green rookies, barely old enough to shave, it was a new adventure. "You boys may want to hit the can before we leave," he added as a last-minute suggestion. "We got every bit of a 100-mile ride ahead of us, and unless we break down or get another flat tire, we won't be stopping." Outside, the bus was warmed up and waiting to transport us north on Route 301 to the quiet picturesque town of Ocala.

As we quietly lined up like baby ducklings and stepped aboard the bus, none of us could help but notice a fit, well-groomed man who appeared to be no more than 40 years old, standing near the door of the vehicle. He seemed to be no stranger to airports or to traveling, as he rambled on to the driver about his late flight into Tampa and how he had rushed to meet us with his suitcases and oversized trunk, which by this time, were stacked nearby on the pavement. He was dressed to the nines, decked out in a colorful shirt and sport coat, a wide-brimmed hat, white cuffed trousers and white buck shoes. And just by overhearing bits and pieces of his conversation, we knew he was an ex-player and someone of importance within the Red Sox organization.

To the south, along Florida's west coast, the Red Sox established their spring training headquarters in Sarasota. It had been the base camp for their big leaguers and upper level minor league clubs for several seasons. However, for those of us starting in the lower classifications, there could not have been a more ideal setting than Ocala. It was the model small city, but growing quickly, much in part because of the thoroughbred racehorse industry, which had gotten a foothold in the area a few years earlier. Along with a number of lovely artesian springs near the Silver River in the Silver Springs community, and the incredibly curious reptile farms spotted just outside the city limits, it was unlike any place I had ever visited. There were lots of fun things to see and enjoy. For many of the locals, it was as much a vacation spot as it was a place to live and work. The townspeople were warm and patient. They spoke in a much slower and softer tone than what I knew back home. Things seemed more relaxed and low-keyed. And from the very moment I stepped off the bus and got my first whiff of the sweet fragrance of orange blossoms, I realized there's another whole world outside of Illinois, one I had never experienced, but one I could easily fall in love with.

Once we arrived in camp, there was never a wasted minute. We had a team meeting, learned the names of our coaches and were given a few basic do's and don'ts about the operation of the camp. We soon learned that the well-dressed fellow who rode on the bus with us from the Tampa airport was none other than Charlie Wagner, a former Red Sox pitcher, who had been a fixture on the team for about 10 years, from the late 1930s until the late 40s. Charlie, we learned, was the club's assistant farm director, and he would be staying with us for a couple of weeks overseeing our training. Still, our curiosity was high. None of us rookies could start to guess why one man would need so many suitcases and a huge trunk for just a few weeks of spring training. Finally, some of the guys got a chance to see Charlie as he opened his luggage and began to unpack. The big trunk, as well as all of his travel bags, were stuffed with expensive shirts, jackets and trousers, not to mention the stylish hats and ties, which went along with the alligator shoes and belts. He had brought with him the biggest, most elaborate wardrobe any of us had ever seen. Charlie was a one-man fashion show! For those of us who were new to the Red Sox, the pieces began to fit together, and it all started to make sense once we learned that Charlie's nickname was "Broadway." No one in all of baseball ever looked sharper or dressed finer than our friend, "Broadway Charlie Wagner!"

However, there was no room for doubt concerning the schedule and daily routine at our camp; our manager, Warren G. "Sheriff" Robinson, was the man in charge. A hardened military veteran of World War II as well as professional baseball, he had paid his dues as a minor league catcher. Although he never made it to the major leagues as a player, he came close on a number of occasions and eventually was promoted to a coaching position with the New York Mets, where he served under managers, Casey Stengel, Yogi Berra and Wes Westrum. Nevertheless, while working in the low minors for the Red Sox in the early 1950s, he wore a lot of different hats, filling various roles for the team. His official job title may have been minor league manager, but he was a coach, an instructor, a trainer and even a part-time bus driver. For some guys who had difficulties being away from home, he was a father, advisor and counselor, not to mention a disciplinarian and babysitter. The Red Sox sure got their money's worth when they hired Sheriff; he was a hard worker. Strangely, his nickname had nothing to do with him ever being an officer of the law. Ironically, he was given the moniker as a young boy, after his father failed twice to get elected sheriff of his hometown in Maryland.

There were also several former major league stars in camp who worked as instructors. For us rookies, just meeting them and getting advice from them was a thrill. Mace Brown, who spent much of his big league career pitching for the Pittsburgh Pirates, but finished up with the Red Sox, was well known among fans who kept up with baseball during the 1930s and 40s. Even more popular as a pitcher from that same period was ex-Yankee, Johnny Murphy. A three-time American League all-star, he was actually the director of minor league operations for the Red Sox, but he never seemed to mind working hands-on with rookie pitchers. Johnny was one of the first pitchers in the majors to find success as a relief specialist. He carried the nicknamed "Fireman," because of his uncanny knack to stamp out enemy uprisings whenever he was called on to bail the Yankees out of threatening situations. Combining to pitch in more than 800 games at the major league level, these two men had much to offer young boys who were about to pitch their first games in Class-D baseball. Myself included, the young pitchers in our camp were in awe from just having an opportunity to work out with these guys. These men possessed the knowledge and experience it took to make it to the top of their game. And best of all, they were patient and willing to share that knowledge with young players who stood to gain so much from it.

After just a few days in camp, things began to lighten up. Our activities and drills became routine. The guys learned each other's names, began to interact more freely and make friends. While there were some boys who were private and reserved, there were some who talked openly about most anything. Some boasted about how much money they were getting and openly discussed their contracts and bonuses. There were a nosy few who went to great lengths to know other people's business and scrutinize the operations of the organization. For such personal matters, it was surprising to see how some players were as interested in the salaries of others as they were their own. On the other hand, while I preferred to stay out of the affairs of others, I was lured into such a discussion when I carelessly responded to some probing questions as part of a roundhouse discussion of "who's making what" took place on the practice field. It was the sort of conversation I should have avoided, knowing nothing good would come of it. Contrary to my better judgment, I hung around, and the more I heard, the more anxious I became.

"Yeah, they just made some changes at the winter meetings," one guy explained. "That's why those fellows are getting such big money without becoming bonus babies."

"That's what I heard, too," a second fellow added. "That's how guys like Jerry Zimmerman, Don Buddin and Jerry Casale got the big cash. Maybe the scouts told them what was going to happen," he speculated further. "And the rest of us didn't find out until it was too late. Those fellows didn't sign their contracts until after the bonus restriction rule was changed!"

"There's no doubt about it!" another chimed in. "It's the West Coast boys, the guys from California who are the fat cats!"

I listened a while longer to the discouraging grumbling. The very idea that some of those fellows received five-figure offers was enough to make me curse under my breath. My heart sank. Sure, the Red Sox were one of the top-paying clubs in all of baseball, but personally, I could have done much better if I had waited just a few weeks more before I signed. I had no way of knowing.

"What's done is done," I told myself. I left the group and walked across the grass of the infield to begin my workout. It was time for me to get my mind on other things. I gazed upward and squinted at the bright Florida sun. I drew in a deep breath of the warm spring air and again, I noticed the sweet aroma of flowering orange trees. I had work to do. It was time to concentrate on baseball.

I needed to be reminded that the work I contracted to do was on the field. It was my job to listen to my manager and coaches and apply their teachings to my own game. I was in camp to learn the fundamentals of baseball and to learn how to play the game "the Red Sox way." In those times, it was best for a young ballplayer to learn to focus only on execution, the part of the game that takes place on the field, and leave the business of money and managing the club to those who are in charge. Back then, players had no voice and were nothing more than pieces of property, which the team could sell, trade or release as they saw fit. There was no strong union or bargaining power for players like there is today. We were simply bound to play under the terms offered by the ballclub or quit and go home. The days of free agency were still many years away.

Red Sox management had many of us first-year players confused and concerned as soon as we arrived in camp. Like me, many other rookies had mailed in their contracts just prior to leaving home, contracts which specified an assignment to play Class-D baseball for the Hi-Toms of the North Carolina State League, a Red Sox farm team located in the adjoining cities of High Point and Thomasville, North Carolina. However, once in camp, we soon learned that the Red Sox had terminated their working agreement with the North Carolina State League and relocated their team about 30 miles west, to Salisbury, a small town nestled in the middle of Rowan County, North Carolina. Again, it was the business side of baseball, a matter of no concern for players. It's a standing rule that ballplayers will stay totally confused if they try to rationalize and make sense of the business of baseball.

Weeks later, we broke camp and headed north to start the season. We had to pack up our personal gear as well as the team's equipment and cram it all into a tiny bus that looked as if it had missed its chance for the junkyard many years before. I squeezed myself and my suitcase onto that worn-out rumble-heap and tried to get comfortable for an all-day trip from Ocala, Florida, to Salisbury, North Carolina. With 24 other nervous rookies onboard, the ride was loud and noisy, much like a rowdy high school field trip. For more than 500 miles, we kidded each other, exchanged magazines, counted telephone poles and held in-depth discussions on every subject from hot rods to fishing to girls.

Whenever I hear someone use the expression, "one half of the world doesn't know how the other half lives," I am reminded of some of the eye-opening sights I encountered during the first few hours of this long journey. It was along the winding country roads of northern Florida which reach up into Georgia that I saw for the first time a cultural side of America I never knew existed. There, in the open fields and swamps, were hundreds of small, crudely built shacks lining the highways which, as difficult as it was for me to imagine, were homes for the countless poor black families in that region of the deep South. Young and old alike, men, women and children, barefooted and dressed in tattered remnants of cloth, could be spotted walking along the roadside, or milling about outside of their makeshift houses made of unpainted boards and scraps of tar paper with dilapidated roofs of corrugated sheet metal. The sight of them was like nothing I had ever witnessed. Of course I had seen for myself the ghettos and the government funded housing projects of the southwest districts of Chicago. I would pass through some of these neighborhoods on my way to Comiskey Park. Nevertheless, the culture shock I received that day as we made our way northward along the East Coast was unforgettable. It was a sobering experience to realize the landscape I was seeing through an open bus window was part of our United States, and the people who occupied that land were Americans! It was a striking lesson in sociology that I wasn't expecting. It was cause for a period of quiet personal reflection in the midst of a long bumpy bus ride.

Onboard, we had at least one experienced authority on every topic that came up, or at least a persuasive liar who would make us think so.

We were the Salisbury Rocots, the newest entry in the Tar Heel League. "And what's a Rocot?" you may ask. Oddly enough, no one among our busload of young experts could come up with an answer for that one. And it wasn't until some 60 years later after I received a credible explanation from Mike London, a prominent sportswriter in the Salisbury area, that the mystery behind the name was finally made clear.

"It was an odd acronym that made up the team name," London explained. "The RO and CO are short abbreviations for Rowan County, the sprawling rural area enveloping the city of Salisbury. The T simply stands for team. The words Rowan County Team were inadvertently shortened to ROCOT, thus, the team name Rocots. It's just another little-known fact, misfiled and almost lost from the ancient records of small-town baseball trivia."

Even though we went into the schedule with enthusiasm and confidence, it didn't take long to see we weren't the world-beaters we may have thought ourselves to be. It was Sheriff Robinson's first season as a manager, and perhaps the Red Sox didn't stock his roster with sufficient talent to be competitive in a league that was new for Boston's farm system. At a few of the lower points of the year, the team went so far as to activate the 31-year-old Robinson, who sometimes inserted himself into the lineup or put himself in games as a late-inning pinch hitter. Still, none of these moves helped. We struggled from opening day until Labor Day.

At the very onset of the season, I was tossed into the fray, as Robinson put me in his four-man rotation of starting pitchers. Over the course of the summer, I became the workhorse of the pitching staff, starting more games and logging more innings than anyone on the club. I also made a handful of relief appearances and chipped in with a batting average well over .300, which was impressive considering the limited number of times I came to the plate. At year's end my pitching record stood at seven wins and eleven loses, which was indicative of the type of season we had. We finished dead last in the ten-team league. When the curtain came down on what was my first year in professional baseball, the Rocots had won only 44 of 111 games. Our dismal performance was enough to land us 31 games out of first place! We had given the faithful fans of Salisbury, North Carolina, nothing to cheer about. However, the Red Sox organization had a few positive points to offer.

"We saw a lot of potential on this club," Robinson told us after our final game. That means most of you boys will be back with us next spring. And while we want to win as many games as we possibly can, the Red Sox won't judge the future success of the organization on the number of games won in a Class-D league. At this level, it's about more than just winning. It's about individual development and progress," he stressed. "We're looking for development."

Robinson's season-ending pep talk was good for building my confidence and encouraging me for the following year. So were some of the things he had to say during the year. "Stay in shape and keep working hard, Eli," he advised in a one-on-one conversation. "You've got a great arm and all the other necessary tools you'll need to be a big league pitcher." These were words I was sure to take with me as I headed home for the winter.

I couldn't wait to get home. I had friends and family and a '49 Dodge waiting for me. But I also had lots of experiences to share and stories to tell. I had tales about riding on long, hot bus trips, meeting Johnny Murphy, flying on airplanes and visiting reptile farms in Florida, all great experiences I would have never known had I stayed home in Chicago. For a guy who had just turned nineteen, my life was exciting. In professional baseball, I was still wet behind the ears with a lot to learn and a long way to go, but over a period of seven months I had grown and matured. I wasn't the same naive teenager who had left home that spring. I had seen a lot and learned even more, and I could hardly wait to do it all again. In the meantime, I was eager to tell my buddies that I had discovered another whole world outside of Illinois.

CHAPTER 15

NEXT TIME YOU MAY NOT BE SO LUCKY

⟋⟍

S o much seemed the same. In the words of Yogi Berra, "It was déjà vu all over again." I spent another winter playing basketball at the YMCA and hanging out with my buddies in my old South Chicago neighborhood. And just as the holiday season rolled around, I signed another class-D contract with the Red Sox, this one calling for a monthly salary of $225. It still wasn't a lot, but was a nice increase over the money I received in 1953. I even saw a slight bump in my meal money for road trips, which raised my allowance to a whopping $2 per day. For me, the extra food money meant I could start looking forward to more variety in my diet whenever we traveled, and not having to relegate myself to so many bacon, lettuce and tomato sandwiches. However, the only unexpected provision in this contract was a significant one. It was my assignment to play in a small town in south-central New York for a team I had never heard of, the Corning Red Sox of the class-D P.O.N.Y. League. The Pennsylvania - Ontario - New York League had been around for years, but the team, the Corning Red Sox, was a new one on me.

Even before the 1953 season ended, there were rumors afloat, suggesting that the Salisbury ballclub was on shaky financial ground. And though it wasn't common knowledge, the situation was much the same throughout the entire Tar Heel League. With money hard to come by, the Red Sox chose not to renew their working agreement with Salisbury and withdrew from the league, leaving only four teams in what had been a ten-team circuit the year before. The ill-fated Tar Heel League made a desperate attempt to stay afloat for another year but was forced to shut down less than two months into the '54 season, when creditors became too many and paying customers were too few.

However, on the heels of terminating their affiliation with Salisbury, the Boston Red Sox, under the guidance of their farm director, Johnny Murphy, elected to increase their minor league operations and go with two class-D teams in lieu of just one. It was Murphy's plan to expand the lowest level of the organization in order to accommodate a larger number of young prospects. In addition to Corning, New York, another team was placed in Bluefield, West Virginia, as an entry in the financially solid and well-established Appalachian League.

In many ways it seemed like the Salisbury club of the previous year was being kept intact and being relocated to Corning. Again, in the spring of 1954, I reported to Boston's minor league training camp in Florida, only to find myself among many players who had been my teammates the season before. Both Mace Brown and Johnny Murphy were back in camp working with us, along with Sheriff Robinson, whose role with the organization was not clear until just days before we broke camp and final assignments were given. It wasn't until then that we learned Len Okrie, a veteran catcher who had a brief career with the Washington Senators, would manage the Bluefield club, while Robinson would be our skipper at Corning, which was a bit of news I was pleased to hear. Of the Boston farmhands I had played with in Salisbury in '53, most were back for another year of basic conditioning at the class-D level. But for the '54 season we were separated, with about a dozen of us getting orders to head north with Robinson to Corning, while only about half that many were assigned to Bluefield.

Each year, at a time near Memorial Day, it was customary for many big league organizations to undergo a "cutdown," a point in the season when clubs were known to make an increasing number of player transactions in order to set their rosters for the stretch run of the schedule. It was a time when players were traded, sold, reclassified to lower levels, or in some cases, released outright. For many ballplayers it was a milepost of the season which was nervously awaited. Yet, depending on the outcome, a young man's future in baseball could be made secure for a while longer or he could be cut and sent home on the spot. And for each personnel move made by the front office, a ripple effect would be felt throughout the system, as for each player demoted, roster spots had to be cleared at the lower level, until some unfortunate youngster at the end of the chain lost his job. This whole process is just another of the cold realities players face in the harsh world of professional baseball.

I had been riding high during the first few weeks of the '53 season until the May cutdown occurred, which gave me a totally unexpected reality check. I was coasting along after winning my first three decisions, when suddenly my confidence was rocked after several veteran players with experience in some of the most advanced leagues in the country, landed in the Tar Heel League. These were older guys, a few who had been in the professional ranks since before World War II. And had their careers not been put on hold because of the war, some would have likely made it to the majors. Most of these guys realized that 1953 would be the final year, and by willingly accepting a demotion to the Tar Heel League, some were returning to their hometowns, playing before their friends and families and helping their club increase home game gate receipts. At that time, each team was permitted to carry as many as six veteran players on their rosters, which could substantially improve the overall talent level of the league. With the addition of these older, well-seasoned players, the THL was no longer simply a league for brand-new baseball recruits, but a stage for final curtain calls for some very talented but aging minor league stars.

At that early point of my career, my arsenal of pitches was adequate for competing against first-year boys in a class-D league. However, I soon found out it would take more than a straight fastball and a bush-league wrinkle of a curveball like mine to get these veteran players out. Suddenly I found myself overmatched as my win-loss record dropped like a rock, from three wins and no losses to a record well below.500. I was in a tight pinch and I would have to come up with a different approach to pitching if I wanted to keep my job.

Norm Small was a 39-year-old veteran who had played as high as class-AA in the New York Giants organization, when he signed on with the 1953 Mooresville Moors of the Tar Heel League. In a game against the Moors, I tried my darnedest, time and again, to throw my best fastball past him, just as I had done many times to young rookie batters over the previous few weeks. My strategy didn't work with an experienced batter like Norm. At the very moment I served up my fastest pitch to him, a straight ball over the heart of the plate, about belt-high, he unleashed his powerful bat, making solid contact with the defenseless baseball in a manner, which was no less impressive than the notorious swing of the greatest of all batters, the Splendid Splinter, Ted Williams. In comparison, Small's astonishing blow took off as if it had been shot out of a cannon! It cut through the humid North Carolina night air like a rocket heading for the stars. It continued in its upward path, gaining altitude until it reached the height of the stadium light tower located just beyond the centerfield wall. The incredible flight and distance of that drive combined to make Small's homerun as impressive as any batted ball I had ever witnessed. I will never forget the Baptism by fire I unwillingly received that night at the hands of a veteran slugger twice my age. In that season, his last in professional baseball, Norman Small would go on to finish the year with an incredible .340 batting average to go along with a tobacco wagon full of homeruns. Surely, his batting accomplishments from that one particular season were enough to keep baseball fans in that tiny town in Central North Carolina buzzing for years to come.

At six feet, seven inches tall and weighing well over 200 pounds, James Balentine was another of the experienced players in his 30s, who came into the Tar Heel League after the cutdown. With his powerful bat he quickly made lasting impressions on me and a few other young, wide-eyed rookie pitchers. He signed up with the Marion Marauders for what would also be his final campaign in the pros. Years earlier, Balentine had played as high as class-B baseball in both the Yankees' and Indians' farm systems. Nevertheless, after seeing what he could do with his bat, I couldn't understand why he never went higher. To many of us rookies, he had all the makings to become another legendary slugger, one on the order of hall of famers Jimmie Foxx and Babe Ruth. In one memorable game, soon after his arrival in the league, James blasted a towering homerun off one of my Rocot teammates, another defenseless first-year pitcher who was left quaking in his shoes by the time the ball returned to earth far beyond the centerfield fence, some 505 feet away! The very sight of Balentine's monstrous clout sent a shiver down my spine and reminded me of the tremendous wallop Norm Small had hit off me just a few days earlier. There were several other older fellows in the league who devoured inexperienced pitchers like me. We stood no chance whenever they came to bat. There was also outfielder Red Mincy, who at 37 years old could hit the ball a country mile. Red, a veteran of the higher leagues, signed up with the Shelby club for '53. What's more, we faced the Tar Heel League's 1952 Most Valuable Player, Don Stafford, a tall first baseman who had batted above .400 with Salisbury to win the award. Don remained in the league for one last year with the '53 Lexington Indians and contributed a lot to my miseries. "I had no business playing in the same league with these guys!" I told myself. My confidence was shaken, and for the first time in my life, I was doubting my ability to pitch.

"If old guys like Balentine and Small, in the twilight of their careers can feast on pitchers like me," I reasoned, "then how will I ever make it to the big leagues?" To use a term originally coined to describe battle-weary combat vets, I was "shell-shocked." I was dreading taking my next turn in the pitching rotation. I was desperate and needed to get help fast, but wasn't sure where to turn to get it.

Even a year later, when I was starting my second season in pro baseball, I had no good reasons to believe my situation would improve. I was returning for another year at the class-D level with the same organization, the same coaches and many of the same teammates. "With so many things remaining the same," I asked myself, "What did I have to be optimistic about?"

Fortunately, with Sheriff Robinson, I had a manager who was caring and perceptive. He wanted each of his players to benefit from his years in the game and wanted each of us to learn and progress. He knew how I struggled through the second half of my first year, yet he never seemed to be alarmed or never lost his patience. He never lost his confidence in me and continued to give me more innings of work than any other pitcher on his staff.

"You just need a little extra work," he hinted when he saw that my frustration was mounting. "We'll get you some help with your curveball and you'll be fine."

Right away I began getting personal help from our pitching instructors, Johnny Murphy and Mace Brown, along with Charlie Wagner, a roving instructor in our farm system, all former pitching stars who attributed much of their success to mixing an effective curveball with a well-located fastball to keep opposing batters off-stride. The time and attention I received from these fellows did a lot to assure me that I was on the right track.

After being shown the "tricks of the trade," I spent a big portion of my time in the 1954 training camp working to perfect the new techniques I had been shown. I was constantly working on the grip, the wrist action and the arm motion, all the ingredients needed to produce a major league curveball. Obsessed with my newly discovered pitch, I worked to improve it at every opportunity that came along, which was whenever I could find someone willing to catch me. I tried it out with teammates as we limbered up during pregame warm-ups. I worked on it in the bullpen, during team workouts and even after practices, if I could persuade another player to stick around a few extra minutes. I was encouraged by how quickly I developed the spin and rotation necessary to make a baseball drop and curve. Through experimenting, I found I could vary the movement of the ball by applying more pressure with my middle finger and by altering the snap of my wrist as I released it. Control was soon to follow, as I reached a point where I could use it in games with relative confidence and found I could throw my curveball for strikes. Instead of relying solely on my ability to overpower batters, I suddenly had the added advantage of forcing them to consider the possibility of seeing a breaking pitch and being ready for it at any time. Possessing a good curveball, I found, will give any pitcher the upper hand mentally, even if he uses it sparingly.

On an individual level, my new-found success bolstered my confidence and renewed my hope for a future in baseball. My numbers for my sophomore season reflected significant improvement over those of 1953, as I placed among the league's pitching leaders in several categories. In July, I was selected to the all-star team and by the year's end, I had one of the circuit's best records at 14 wins and 10 losses, to go with a sharp earned-run average of 3.36. Sheriff Robinson continued to make me the workhorse of his staff, using me almost exclusively as a starter and calling on me so often that I led the entire league in innings pitched, not to mention, how at the plate, I helped my own cause by batting a lofty .379 and socking a couple of home runs to boot!

Instead of trudging through a disappointing repeat of the previous season, 1954 was the year my baseball career turned the corner. Entering training camp with the same manager, instructors and many of the same players who finished dead last the year before, I had anticipated similar results. However, I found I was in for a huge surprise. For me personally, it was incredible to discover what a difference a new pitch can make. As a team, we edged out the Jamestown Falcons, a squad of Detroit Tiger farmhands, for the 1954 P.O.N.Y. league championship.

Up in Boston, our parent club ended the season with a disappointing fourth-place finish, but managed to produce a few bright spots along the way, as Frank Sullivan, a tall right-handed rookie pitcher, chipped in 15 victories and first-year first baseman, Harry Agganis, "The Golden Greek," captured the hearts of Red Sox fans with his impressive offensive stats and his near-flawless glove work. At 35 years old, Ted Williams turned in another great performance as he continued to roam the outfield, shun the press, banter with fans, fight off injuries and hit at an astounding .345 clip. It was still a great time to be part of the Red Sox organization. I was more hopeful and encouraged than ever, after having had a productive season and feeling as if I had contributed to the overall success of the club. As a group, we had gone from worst to first, which was enough to cause all of us go home for the off-season with our chests out and heads held high. Meanwhile, considering the progress I had made and how I had matured as a pitcher, I had to consciously remind myself throughout the winter not to be over confident concerning a promotion to a higher level. Shortly before the season ended, Sheriff Robinson hinted that my chances were good, but I wanted to be cautious and not count my chickens too soon. Nonetheless, I could not have helped but be disappointed if I didn't get bumped up to a higher classification to start the '55 season. After all, I definitely felt like I had earned it.

As much as it was the responsibility of each player to keep himself in good physical shape during the off-season, he was directed to do so in a safe and reasonable way. "It was part of our job," we were told, "to stay fit during the winter and report to spring training in good shape and at a suitable weight." It was the ballclub's way of reminding us to stay active, avoid overeating and not get hurt. Personally, I had no problem following those rules, except for the rough-and-tumble style of basketball I played each winter at the YMCA. The brand of basketball played in those adult league games surely put me at risk of being injured, but thankfully, except for a few strains and sprains here and there, I made out fine. Between the basketball league and the winter jobs I worked with Wisconsin Steel during my first off-season and Ironworkers Local #395 the next, I found baseball season to be safer and a lot less physically demanding.

Since its inception in the mid-19th century, the steel industry has been among the most hazardous jobs in our country. Injuries from heavy materials and equipment, burns from molten metal and serious respiratory diseases caused by the inherent smoke and dust within the mills are only some of the dangers steelworkers face each day. Having grown up with many of her friends and family members working in the industry, there weren't many ladies who were more familiar with those hazards and safety risks than my mother. We knew folks around town who had been injured or made ill as a result of working in the steel mills. Yet, in spite of the attractive wages and generous benefits the industry was known for, the mere thought of her son having a career in the mills or as an ironworker made Mom uneasy. I tried to reason with her and persuade her to see my side of the argument, but I was fighting a losing battle. There was no question that life as a "punk" with the ironworkers was hard. It was my job to run materials for the mechanics and specialists working up top, and answer to their every beck and call. I was in the best physical shape of my life. My body grew lean and muscular. Yet, night after night, my back and shoulders ached after climbing stairs and ladders all day, carrying buckets of rivets to workers on the higher levels. Nonetheless, clearing $90 each week on my paycheck was enough to keep me on the job. "What's four times $90?" I questioned Mom, trying to make my point. "It's a lot more than I make each month playing baseball!" Still, she would have none of that. She wanted something better, something safer for me. And as the outlook of my finding a career in professional baseball became a bit more hopeful after two seasons in the minor leagues, her less than favorable opinion of me having even a seasonal job in the mills or with the ironworkers grew even more impassioned.

Once, while working at the mill, stacking an order of heavy steel angle bars onto a loading platform, my coworker, another young laborer, was fascinated by my having completed my first season in pros. He had a constant stream of baseball-related questions for me. And the more lengths of steel we stacked, the more engrossed the two of us became in our baseball conversation. Finally, he was distracted to the point where he lost his grip on his end of one of the bars. Unable to steady the weight of the entire piece by myself, the heavy steel came crashing down onto the stack, squashing one of my fingers in between. Thankfully, I suffered no broken bones, only minor swelling and discoloration. However, when I got home from work that evening with my finger wrapped in a protective splint, my mother saw my mishap as no minor incident. To her, it was an omen, a clear warning sign for me to quit my job immediately. "Next time you may not be so lucky," she warned. "A more serious accident could have cost you a career in baseball!"

At Mom's insistence, the day of my injury was my last day working at the steel mill. And in the weeks that followed, I suppose I missed the Wisconsin Steel Company a lot more than they missed me. But more importantly, I missed the chance to clear 90 bucks a week. However, in timely fashion another Red Sox contract arrived at the house as expected, just before the holiday season. This time, the promotion I hoped for had come through. I had been assigned to the class-A Montgomery club of the South Atlantic League!

The advancement to class-A along with some of the other provisions in the agreement were a lot more than I had expected. In addition to having me skip over both the C and B levels and raising my salary to $325 per month, the correspondence which accompanied the contract also commended me for the good job I had done during my first two years as a Red Sox and mentioned how, as one of the club's "prospects," they were looking forward to continued progress from me. Furthermore, I was to report to a special training camp which the organization was conducting in Sarasota, Florida, in February. The camp, reserved for only selected players, would start a month prior to the beginning of spring training and would provide each of us additional opportunities for instruction and evaluation.

Was this real, or was it all too good to be true? Was I ready to move up to the "Sally League," and pitch in one of the fastest minor leagues in the country?

Sure, I had my confidence back and I was ready to go. Apparently, the Red Sox thought the same. But need I remind you, in baseball, nothing is for certain and again, only time would tell.

CHAPTER 16
WHAT DO YOU MEAN YOU'RE SENDING ME TO SAN JOSE?

In the 1950s it was a place many folks referred to as a "boomtown." While luxury resorts were being built and opening for business at an alarming pace, land values in the area were skyrocketing. Beachfront acreage was being gobbled up by speculative investors and opportunistic businessmen who were keen enough to cash in on the bonanza. It was among the fastest selling resort property Americans had seen since World War II.

It was all happening in Sarasota, a small beach city situated on the southwestern coast of Florida, and by February, 1955, the building boom was well underway. There were still long stretches of open shoreline which had yet to be developed and most of the hotels, restaurants and seasonal homes were either under construction or only in the planning stages. Much of the town was developed by a couple of famous brothers, John and Charles Ringling, who had earned their fortunes in the circus business and chose Sarasota as the company headquarters and winter home for "the greatest show on Earth," the Ringling Brothers Barnum & Bailey Circus. It was the younger brother, Charles, who created his own bank and granted affordable loans to help establish new businesses in Sarasota, a city which saw its population almost triple during the 1950s.

Charles Ringling's own hotel, the Sarasota Terrace, a stately downtown landmark built in the 1920s, was the team hotel of the

Boston Red Sox each spring for more than 20 years, until the Dodgers came to town for spring training in 1959, followed by the White Sox in 1960. No question, Sarasota has long been a baseball town, but it has also been a wonderland for boaters, beachgoers, sports fishermen and golfers, not to mention carefree 20-year-old baseball players looking for a good time.

I was overjoyed with the contract offer I received over the winter. The salary increase was really nice, but equally as pleasing was my assignment to class-A Montgomery. The sizeable raise, along with the promotion, were very inspiring, leading me to feel that my progress had been noticed and was being acknowledged by the ballclub. Plus, I was excited to be invited to the pre-spring training camp in Sarasota, which was open only to the top prospects in the Red Sox organization. The fact that I was leaving home a month earlier than usual was no problem, not for me; I was honored just to be on the list of invitees.

It was Mike "Pinky" Higgins who was heading up the special camp, a former star third baseman for the Athletics, Tigers and Red Sox, who had become a close friend of team owner, Tom Yawkey, during his stay in Boston. Higgins had found his professional niche with the Red Sox, managing and coaching at varying minor league levels and ultimately being picked to be the manager of the major league club just days before the start of the prospects' camp in Sarasota. After holding the helm of the Red Sox for several more seasons, the easy-going Texan would continue to work in the team's front office until the mid 60s. He was a good fit for Mr. Yawkey and the Boston Red Sox as well as for all of us young players reporting to Sarasota.

"We've got work to do, fellows," Higgins told us when we arrived in camp. "But you ain't going to the big leagues yet, so you might as well have some fun while you're here. So enjoy yourselves, get out and see the area and take advantage of all there is to do. Make the most of it, because we have another long season ahead of us."

Not that we needed any extra encouragement, but that was exactly what we wanted to hear. We could go out on the town, to the beaches, the bars, meet girls, whatever we wanted to do and we had the manager's blessings! "Just don't get yourselves into trouble and don't embarrass the organization," he cautioned us.

There was so much for us to do and see in Sarasota, we didn't know where to start. The city was home to the greatest of all Red Sox stars, Ted Williams, who dropped into camp from time to time. He was often spotted around town, shopping and trying out the latest in fishing gear at local sports shops. And thanks to the Ringling family, there was always a circus in town. But among the most exciting features of the town was the breathtaking Lido Beach, with its sparkling blue waters, fine white sand and all the young good looking girls!

Still, at almost 20 years old, I was not as worldly or experienced as many of the other guys on the ballclub, so I used a lot of my free time in Sarasota to satisfy my curiosity and further my exploration by getting to know some of the local young ladies. Please keep in mind that there are very few creatures on earth that are more sexually obsessed than a human male in his teens, and I was certainly no exception. I was on the prowl, always keeping an eye on the girls, and there was certainly no shortage of them on the beaches along the west coast of Florida.

It was teammate Don Buddin, a handsome South Carolinian, who seemed to be at ease and handy with the ladies. And not only did he brim with confidence when it came to dating, he had unlimited use of a mini-limousine, which belonged to a doctor who worked in the team hierarchy. With Don behind the wheel and a few girls who were willing to come along, we often drove to the water's edge to go parking. And more than one occasion, while we were busy making out, the gulf tide rolled in unexpectedly, leaving us with an expensive luxury automobile stuck axle-deep in the wet sand and no way to get back to our hotel! But we didn't care and neither did the doctor who owned the vehicle. It was just part of the fun of growing up and being irresponsible.

On the other hand, young baseball players were often targets for the girls living in the area. Many of us were naive, didn't know our way around town, had no transportation and very little money. Yet any of us would be happy to have a girlfriend for the season, especially one who was a little older and had her own car. Knowing we would only be around during the season made dating ballplayers more enticing for some girls, while simply dating a professional ballplayer was trophy enough for others. Still, the most dangerous trap any young player could fall into was getting involved with a married woman. And, as one of my teammates found out the hard way, no one could cause more trouble for a player or his ballclub than an angry husband!

Nonetheless, it wasn't until I left home and was in my first few years of pro baseball that I took the giant step of having intimate relations with a girl. Simply explained, the strong sexual urges of my adolescence were more than I could manage, and the words of wisdom, given to me each spring by my grandfather were subsequently ignored and fell by the wayside. But I was young, it was springtime and love was in the air. Alas, as I look back on the excitement of my early romantic encounters, I can also recall moments of frustration and embarrassment that I would just as soon forget.

It was a thrill just getting invited to the Red Sox pre-spring training camp. The roster of players was like a list of the top-rated prospects in the organization, the guys who got the biggest salaries and the most bonus money to sign. And while my contract didn't compare with the others, it was still a special feeling to be included in the group. Considering the reputation the Red Sox had for paying well, I knew I was in the company of some of the highest paid minor league players in all of baseball. There was big Bruce Weaver, a long ball hitter from Reading, Pennsylvania; Jerry Zimmerman, a standout catcher from Oregon; infielder Don Buddin; and right handed pitcher, Bob Adubato from New Jersey, who posted a 16 and four record the previous year at Corning. These were the caliber of young players sportswriters flocked to, hoping to create a good working rapport before any of them reached stardom. But, because of injuries, attitudes, personalities and other uncalculated factors, it is nearly impossible for anyone to predict which minor leaguers have a shot at the majors, much less who the star players of the future will be.

The one-month prospect camp was fun. We worked hard, yet it was all done in a laid-back atmosphere, but on a well-planned schedule. It gave us all a jump on the upcoming spring training, as well as a head start on our suntans. And just as Pinky Higgins suggested on the first day we reported, we went out and enjoyed ourselves. But as far as I know, none of us got into any serious trouble. We had a great camp and everyone gave it his best. Things seemed to run smoothly throughout the spring, even after we joined the other minor leaguers for regular spring training in Ocala. However, none of us had any idea of what was about to erupt during the final days in Ocala, just as we were about to break camp and start the regular season.

"What do you mean you're sending me to San Jose?" I screamed, not giving Johnny Murphy enough time to close the door to his office. "Is that what you called me in here to tell me? I signed a contract to go to Montgomery, and now you guys aren't going to keep your word! Is that right?" My heart was racing as I felt the veins in my neck bulge with anger."No, Johnny, I won't try to calm down. And I don't care that you need to stock the San Jose club with top-level players, and I don't care how many of the others will be going out there with me. You told me I was going to class-A Montgomery and now I find out it's all a big lie!"

I stormed out of Murphy's office, slamming the door hard enough to generate a seismic reading on the local Richter scale. Mad enough to eat nails, I made my way down the dimly lit hallway and stomped into the locker room under the stands of our spring training home, old Gerig Field. There I found a gathering of indignant players, ranting and cursing. These guys had already received the same ugly news.

"I'll quit and go to hell home!" one shouted, as he punched the door of his locker. Yeah, same goes for me!" echoed another. "We can't let them get away with this!" a third chimed in.

The outrage spread through the team like wildfire, until every man on the squad got word of the club's double-cross. While the underhanded reassignment orders actually affected only a handful of the players in camp, the entire clubhouse was ready for an uprising and I quickly became one of the hottest firebrands of the group. Not a single one of us immature hotheads stopped to consider the fact that we didn't have a leg to stand on and had no say about where the club assigned us. Any action we took would surely have come back to bite us and would have likely have ruined our careers.

Nevertheless, we continued to talk it up and fan the flames until we took our discontentment with us when we left the clubhouse. In my own way of handling my disappointment, I simply clammed up and refused to speak to any of my coaches or instructors. Two or three days went by when I wouldn't even talk to Johnny Murphy. I would rudely walk away whenever he tried to start a conversation. But it was pitcher, Bobby Adubato, who had also signed a class-A contract, but was reassigned to class-B Greensboro of the Carolina League, who held nothing back and proved to be the most vocal of us all. It was Bobby who came back to our hotel late in the night after soaking up a few beers and began storming up and down the hallway, yelling, cursing and pounding on the door of Murphy's room. "Wake up, Murphy, you lying SOB!" he shouted. "How can you sleep after screwing every player on your club?" No doubt, Bobby's rant was loud enough to wake up every guest in the building, but Johnny Murphy never once stuck his head outside the door. It was early the next morning that Murphy sent word for me to meet with him "just to talk."

"I don't even know why I'm here, Johnny," were my first words as I walked into his office. "We have absolutely nothing to discuss," I pushed, not giving him a chance to speak.

"Hold on a minute, Eli," he offered. "I understand. I only want to ask you a question."

I took a deep breath. The room suddenly became quiet as I paused to consider my options. "Okay, Johnny," I relented. "What is it?"

"I just want to know how much money you're making," he asked sheepishly.

"Why is that important?" I shot back. "Besides, you know what I make. You have a copy of my contract!"

"You're right, I could check that for myself. But you're very upset and I want to do whatever it takes to make things right. So tell me, Eli, how much are you making?"

"Three hundred and twenty-five a month," I confessed.

"Well, that's not too bad. But, what if... what if, we increase that amount by a hundred bucks and raise you to four hundred and twenty-five a month?" he offered. "Would you be okay going to San Jose at that salary? I want to be fair, Eli, and I want an honest answer."

Murphy's willingness to treat me fairly and increase my salary was a much bigger concession than I anticipated. Moving up to class-C ball was still a nice jump and there were lots of things I could do with an extra hundred bucks a month. But I didn't want to let Johnny think I could be easily swayed. I didn't want to appear overly excited or accept his proposal too quickly.

"I guess that will be okay, Johnny," I said. "Send me to San Jose and at $450 a month I'll give it my best effort."

"Okay, Eli, class-C San Jose it is. We're going to stock that club with some of the best talent in our organization, so it should be a lot of fun and you guys should win a lot of games out there in the California League."

The more I listened, the more I liked Murphy's proposal. He caused me to feel as if the Red Sox cared about me and were including me in their plans for the future. But it wasn't until I walked out of his office and closed the door behind me that I pumped my fist into the air and privately celebrated my good fortune. "So what if I wasn't going to Montgomery?" I asked myself. This isn't a bad deal. I'm heading for the sunny West Coast and getting a lot more money, to boot!

Those last few days in spring training camp were a breeze. But in keeping with the deal I made with Johnny, I kept the terms of our agreement under my hat. I had a new attitude and a more positive outlook on my future. I was surprised by how much of a difference my talk with him had made. As much as anyone in camp, I was optimistic and ready to start the season. Once again, I felt lucky to be a Red Sox.

My season at San Jose turned out to be my finest year in professional baseball. I found the California League to be very fast and loaded with talent. Getting back together with old teammates Marlan Coughtry, Jim Mahoney and a few of the others helped create a familiar clubhouse atmosphere. But more than anything, having Sheriff Robinson as my manager for the third consecutive season really put me at ease. He was calm and even-tempered and I always took him at his word. Yet, that's not to say that Robinson couldn't be tough at times, especially when the behavior of his players warranted strict discipline. On one occasion, it was me and my partner in crime, Jim Mahoney, who tested the limits of our manager when our team was on the road, staying in a hotel in Bakersfield. We discovered "the sheriff" to be a lot slicker than we thought.

Jim and I were returning to our rooms just minutes ahead of curfew when we passed by the open entrance to the hotel bar. There inside, we spotted a couple of attractive young ladies seated at the bar, chatting away, giggling and enjoying drinks. Obviously, they were on the lookout for some male companionship.

"We have a few minutes left, let's go in and see what they're up to," Jim suggested. "It might be worth the time. You never know what might happen."

Before I knew it, we were parked on a couple of barstools on either side of these two ladies, introducing ourselves, serving up some big talk and otherwise, doing our best to impress them. Suddenly, Jim checked his wristwatch and realized we were almost out of time.

"Hey, I've got an idea," he announced. "We've got adjoining rooms upstairs. Why don't we all make our way up there and have our own little private party?"

For the moment, Jim's idea seemed to be a good one. Our little party was in high gear. We were having a lot more fun than the rules allowed. We were both getting exactly what we were looking for, as these gals turned out to be as hot as the desert winds of California. I still recall the astounding sight of seeing just how versatile Jim's new girlfriend was. She was like no girl I had ever seen before. I will never forget seeing her nonchalantly chomping on an apple while in the act of making love with my indifferent and still energetic teammate!

To liven up our frolic, we decided to call downstairs to have the bar deliver a bottle of Scotch and a bucket of ice to our room. Never did we stop to consider that Sheriff Robinson was a shrewd baseball man and knew what to expect from young players. He had ways we never imagined to find out what his boys were up to. Later we would find out we were in trouble with him long before we knew it.

With only night games scheduled for our stay in Bakersfield, it was our plan to sleep late and recuperate from our late-night shenanigans before preparing to go to the stadium. But we were never given the chance. A ringing phone woke us early the next morning. It was a fuming Robinson on the other end.

"You two guys are to be at the ballpark extra early tonight," he ordered. "I want you and Mahoney on the field, suited up and ready to go at 6 p.m. sharp! "Is that understood?"

There was no doubt that our normally affable manager was displeased with us about something. His voice was stern and unyielding.

"But, Skip," I pleaded. "It's going to be really hot again today. That's why they don't start the games here in Bakersfield until after eight o'clock. What's this all about?"

"You fellows don't need to worry about any of that. You just need to be on the field at six, if you know what's good for you!"

At precisely six o'clock Mahoney and I left the clubhouse and stepped onto the sun-scorched field at Sam Lynn Park. This old stadium, which was known as the hottest, stickiest and most uncomfortable stop in the California League was in traditional August form. The sun was still high and the temperature was pushing the century mark.

"Okay, boys!" Robinson barked. "We're out here to get in some much needed work on running down fungos. So, hustle out there on the field and let's get started!"

Without a word, Sheriff hit one fly ball after another to us, forcing us to run in all directions, all over the outfield, chasing down the ball and being forced to make running catches.

"For any you drop, we'll add on five more!" he shouted.

With my temper as hot as the late-day temperature, I threw the ball back at him as hard as I could. Jim and I were tiring fast in the extreme heat. Our uniforms were heavy and soaked with sweat. I was so angry, I wanted to remove Robinson's head from his shoulders with my return throws.

"For every throw like that, Grba, I'll add on five more!" he warned. "I can do this a lot longer than you guys can."

Finally, after almost an hour of grueling exercise and the two of us nearing heat exhaustion, the manager relented.

"Okay, that's enough, boys! That will do it until the next time you decide to throw a party and have booze and ice brought up to your rooms at one o'clock in the morning! Now, Mahoney, go get ready for the game, you'll be starting at shortstop again tonight. And Eli, you go to the bullpen. You'll be the first one I call for tonight, when we get in a jam. And by the way, fellows, in case you were wondering, I was at the bar when the bartender took your call. He gave me the number of the room that placed the call. I knew it was you guys. And I wanted to make the delivery myself, but liquor laws and hotel rules wouldn't allow it. But if anything like this happens again, you'll be lucky if you get off with a fine. I'll put you both off the ballclub!"

Sure enough, I was called in from the bullpen in the middle innings and had my worst outing of the year. In relief, I was the losing pitcher, while Jim Mahoney went hitless that night at the plate. We had learned our lesson well and it was the last time either of us underestimated Sherriff Robinson or his managerial skills. It was the last time either of us would try to pull a fast one over on him.

Following that incident, it became clear to both of us that we could have his respect, but only after we gave him ours. Sherriff Robinson was a no-nonsense guy who took his job seriously. He was a terrific manager and coach and was as fair as any man I would ever know.

In the minor leagues, Warren G. "Sheriff" Robinson was my manager for three consecutive seasons.

With those things aside, we still had a fine club at San Jose. Among our strengths, our team included some of the best pitchers in the league.

Jack "Ozzie" Osborn, a right-hand pitcher from San Diego, won 21 games for us in '55, while another righty, Stan Willis won 19. Ted Wills and Ted Bowsfield, who were both future major league pitchers, enjoyed productive years, while I had my most successful season as a pro, contributing 17 wins and finishing with one of the lowest earned run averages in the CL, at 2.67.

Once again, we played hard for Sheriff Robinson, but found it impossible to keep pace with the Fresno Cardinals, who won an incredible 104 games during the season compared to our 98. The St. Louis farmhands played consistent winning baseball for the entire year, largely in part because of their strong starting rotation, which featured two 20-game winners, Tom Hughes and Glen Stabelfeld. We gave the Fresno club a run for their money, but finished in second place, 5-1/2 games behind them.

Oddly, it was the Stockton Ports, a club that worked with no major league affiliation, which came in third in the 8-team circuit. The Ports boasted a couple of right-handed pitchers, both bound for the big leagues, who had career-years in 1955. Nineteen-year-old, Ernie Broglio logged 20 victories for his manager, Roy Partee, a former Red Sox catcher. Ernie would later spend eight years in the National League with the St. Louis Cardinals and Chicago Cubs. However, it was his teammate, Charlie Beamon, a future hurler for the Baltimore Orioles, who turned in one of the most sensational seasons any professional pitcher would ever record. Beamon appeared in 16 games for Stockton that year and finished with a perfect record of 16 wins and no losses! Fittingly so, his amazing E.R.A. of 1.36 was, by far, the best in the California League.

Near the end of the 1955 season, manager Sheriff Robinson alluded to the idea that we would likely cross paths again in the spring. But considering the impressive year I had at San Jose, he felt I would likely see another promotion once I received my next contact. "You're on your way, Eli," he assured me. "The Red Sox have plans for you. Just keep working hard."

I trusted him and believed whatever he told me. His words were encouraging. I went into the off-season excited, waiting for my contract to arrive and eager to find out where my next stop in the Red Sox organization would be. Yet at the same time, I had the feeling that Robbie and I might not be together when the '56 season started. He had not only been my skipper the first three seasons of my career, but he had also been a father figure to me, someone I admired and a good friend as well.

Soon after the season ended, I was back home in South Chicago, getting ready for another long brutal Illinois winter. And just like other recent winters, it always seemed that it was on the coldest and snowiest days that I found my mind wandered the most, drifting to thoughts of spring training, warm temperatures and baseball. But this particular year, as I anticipated what the next season might bring, I wondered what changes lay ahead and just how far I could go in this game I loved. I had lots of questions running through my mind: *Where would I be assigned to play? How much money would I make? And what would my life in baseball be like, if my manager is someone other than Sheriff Robinson?*

CHAPTER 17

THE ODD MAN OUT

I was entering my fourth season of professional baseball, and I couldn't have been more pleased. I was satisfied with the progress I had made, and every indication I received from the Red Sox led me to believe they were pleased with me as well. At this point of my career, I had no reason to suspect that the relationship I had forged with the Boston club was not a permanent bond, an everlasting match made in heaven. But even at 21 years old, I was probably a little more naive than I should have been.

For me, the lower levels of minor league baseball were a part of my life that was fun and I was socially comfortable. Most of the players were still teenagers, with only a small number of us at or nearing the age to legally purchase alcohol. In many ways, my first three seasons in baseball had been a lot like hanging out with the guys back home. We hooked up after games and workouts, just to mess around and do a lot of the same crazy things kids all across the country were doing after school or work. We gave very little thought to the changes that waited for us right around the corner. As much as anyone, I made the most of those fun times and enjoyed each day as if they would last forever. Yet, as we grew up together as ballplayers, we matured socially as well. And surprisingly, I would find it to be social factors, such as living arrangements, marriage, children and of course, money that would categorize us off the field and distance me from many of my teammates.

From Babe Ruth to Jimmie Foxx, from Lefty Grove to Ted Williams, the Boston Red Sox was an organization rich in history and built on tradition, and in the spring of 1956, I had dreams of one day becoming part of that tradition. "Keep working hard," I was told. "You have all the tools needed to be an outstanding pitcher." I was receiving encouragement from everyone involved with the ballclub. I was viewed by many in the media as one of the top pitching prospects in the Boston system. And following the great season I had at San Jose, I started to believe the things I was hearing and started to believe in myself more than ever. My hopes of becoming a star pitcher in the big leagues were soaring. However, as I moved closer to realizing my dreams, I was blindsided by an unexpected enemy, a foe that would, over time, grow to be more powerful and destructive than anything I would ever face. I never imagined that simply being alone, day after day, in a strange place could have such a damaging effect on someone's life.

Today, doctors at the Betty Ford Center in Rancho Mirage, California, conclude that while loneliness may not be a direct cause for addiction to alcohol, it can definitely be a contributing factor. It is their finding that if a person who suffers from loneliness develops alcoholism, it usually means that the person has a genetic predisposition to the disease. I was coming off another all-star season in which I won 17 games and posted an earned run average of barely two and a half. So, my memories of the horrific, self-destructive life of my father were not what was on my mind. Moreover, it was those very recollections and images that I would spend a lifetime trying to forget and erase from my thoughts. And today, without placing blame, I live on to cope with those memories as well as memories of other painful and regretful experiences, brought about with my own doing. Still, it's an ongoing condition which never really goes away. It's the reason I ask God for strength every day as I continue to wage my own personal battle against a very powerful addiction.

By the winter of 1955-56, rumors had spread throughout the world of baseball that the major leagues would soon be expanding to the West Coast. While there were several established franchises which were considered to be possible candidates for relocation, there were no real favorites. But Los Angeles and San Francisco were prime targets, as both cities had reputable histories in minor league baseball, each having operated in the Pacific Coast League since 1903.

Of course, there were big league clubs which openly expressed their plans to move to the greener pastures in California. However, much of that commotion was seen as merely empty threats, used as promotional ploys to ignite local fan bases. The struggling Washington Senators, as well as the Athletics, who had just moved from Philadelphia to Kansas City a year earlier, were among those accused of resorting to such tactics. But when the Brooklyn Dodgers and New York Giants dropped hints about their plans to move west, the sports world paid attention, and for good reason. But the majority of sports reporters and baseball insiders remained hesitant and treated the rumblings as nothing more than speculation.

On the other hand, it was the Boston Red Sox who had no intentions of moving, who created a wave of suspicion when general manager, Joe Cronin traveled to his hometown, San Francisco to, as he put it, "See the old neighborhood and visit with old friends." Still, some reporters would have no part of Cronin's claim and conjured up their own reasons for his trip.

"He's going out there to do the spade work for his boss, Tom Yawkey, to clear the way for the Red Sox move," one Boston beat writer submitted. "This is only their first step toward the west."

But as time would prove, there was no basis for the suspicion. The Boston club would stay put and it was soon revealed that Cronin was actually on assignment during his West Coast visit. He had been dispatched by owner Tom Yawkey to finalize the Red Sox's purchase of the San Francisco Seals and turn the previously unaffiliated team into the top minor league club in their farm system.

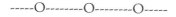

With the frigid temperatures and blustery winds of Chicago notwithstanding, it had been a pretty good winter. I went back to my usual off-season job "punking" with Ironworkers' Local 395 out of Hammond, Indiana, where this time my work was a breeze. Along with a few other seasonal employees who played local sports, I was kept away from the more strenuous and hazardous jobs. The company knew our backgrounds and was aware of our potential as future athletes. They accommodated us and were willing to help safeguard our futures. We just weren't smart enough to take advantage of a good thing.

The preferential treatment lasted only until a bunch of us were caught horsing around on the job. The work manager, big Pete Parker, showed up unexpectedly during one of our impromptu weightlifting contests, just as we were lifting bars of steel over our heads, using the style of a basic military press. The light-hearted competition was our way of showing off and impressing each other with our manly physical feats. However, our boss was not so impressed when he caught us pumping iron. And in no uncertain terms, his displeasure came through loud and clear in his angry, facetious tone.

"You boys need exercise to keep warm?" he asked, tongue in cheek. "Great! I'll see if I can find you a job that will keep you warm and keep you moving!"

Later that same day, we were working our butts off! We were back to our old jobs, lugging buckets of bolts up and down ladders, carrying materials to the worksites and stacking pallets with angle bars and plates of steel. Again, it was hard work, but nothing any of us couldn't handle.

We were a fit and able bunch of young men. Our group included boys who would soon prove themselves to be outstanding athletes in the years that followed. In particularly, there were two who were offered scholarships to play high-level college basketball: Don Laketa, who starred at both Kansas State and Wichita State, and George Stepanovich, who signed with North Carolina State. Following college, Laketa moved on to a successful career coaching basketball in the scholastic ranks, while Stepanovich, who pitched briefly in minor leagues for the Baltimore Orioles, will always be remembered as one of the great rebounders in NSU Wolfpack basketball history.

Meanwhile, on another winter day, complete with the normal gray cloudy skies, sub-freezing temperatures with mounds of snow piled along the streets of South Chicago, my much anticipated piece of mail, bearing a postmark of Boston, Mass., finally arrived. It was a relief to know that the answers to so many doubts and questions I had worried myself with since the last day of the season would finally be put to rest by the contract inside. For me, waiting to receive my contract offer each winter was always the most worrisome, nerve-racking time of the year.

Naturally, I was looking to get a raise in salary, as well as a promotion to a higher classification. But surprisingly, the terms of my 1956 contract exceeded my expectations. I still remembered the cross-up that occurred the year before when my offer called for me to go to class-A. But things were different and I was confident that there would be no more last minute assignment changes like the type that disrupted an entire squad of young players the season before. This new contract placed me with the Red Sox top farm club, the recently acquired San Francisco Seals and increased my monthly salary up to a whopping $650 per month! I could not have been more delighted unless the Red Sox had added me to their big league roster and that was the goal I was ultimately striving for. But I was ready to cope with the idea that reaching the majors might still be a year or two away.

The "Coast League," as it was commonly known, was often thought of as a league on parallel with the major leagues. Certainly the level of talent was there. Every club was stocked with veteran players who had paid their dues in pro baseball, many having years of big league experience to list on their resumes. As odd as it may seem, the Coast League had an abundance of players who were offered contracts to play Major League Baseball, but opted to stay where they were to avoid taking a pay cut. Many star players chose to spend their entire careers playing in the P.C.L., which had more to offer in terms of level of play, salaries and popularity than some of the long-established big league clubs. For decades, the Pacific Coast League provided our country with the finest baseball west of the Mississippi River and I often thought it curious why it was never recognized as a third major league.

Unlike my teammates at the class-D or C levels, the fellows in this league were an older, more mature breed. They were men who were seasoned in the ways of pro baseball and knew the ropes. Of course, there was the much younger group, consisting of Ted Bowsfield, Jim Mahoney, Stan Willis and Jack Osborn who had been with me at San Jose, but most of the Seals were in their 30s, married and had families. They knew each other well and had their own circles of friends. They were familiar with the cities in the league and the hotels, restaurants and night spots in each of them. Not to mention, they had been in the game long enough to earn big salaries, so they could easily afford to enjoy the best of all of these things. I was surprised to discover the wide divisions that existed among players in the upper levels of professional baseball and that the separation between the old and younger ballplayers was so evident, not only on the playing field but to a greater extent in our social lives. When I arrived in San Francisco I soon found that baseball had its own social levels and its own unique off-the-field pecking order. As unsuspecting as I was, I failed to realize how difficult it would be to find my place among my own teammates and how hard it would be to deal with this new lifestyle on my own.

It was a good thing I didn't take time to examine too closely the team rosters of the P.C.L. or I would have been frightened out of my jock. On every club there were players who most baseball fans would have easily recognized. And equally as intimidating was the number of ex-big leaguers who, after games, were showering and getting dressed only a few feet away from me in the Seals' clubhouse. Former White Sox players, Max Surkont and Don Lenhardt, were now my teammates, while longtime American League infielder, Jerry Priddy was on the club as a part-time second baseman.

Also, joining the Seals of '56 was the Red Sox's much heralded third baseman, Frank Malzone, who had played part of the previous season on the big team in Boston. But sadly, after he and his wife lost their infant daughter, Suzanne, to a persistent illness over the winter, he was sent to the minors, where, as a valued prospect, he could continue to play every day without having to face the day-to-day pressure of trying to establish himself in the Boston lineup. Personally, I viewed this whole arrangement as a compassionate gesture on the part of our organization, and another example of how caring and considerate our boss, Mr. Yawkey, could be to his employees during the most difficult of times.

All around the circuit, I found the level of play to be incredibly fast. But it was the Los Angeles Angels who outclassed all other clubs and sewed up the league championship by mid-August. They won an unbelievable 107 games and outdistanced the second-place Seattle Rainiers, the top Cincinnati Reds' farm club, by a whopping 16 games. The Angels' lineup was powered by first baseman, Steve Bilko, who batted at a .360 clip and belted 55 homeruns with 164 RBI, certainly a performance of historical proportions. But Big Steve was not the only Angel to put up heavenly numbers in '56. Outfielder, Jim Bolger smashed 28 homers and batted .326, while second sacker and future major league manager, Gene Mauch, had the finest offensive year of his career, contributing a .348 average along with 20 homeruns. Under the direction of manager, Bob

Scheffing, the Halos batted .297 as a team and featured six batters who turned in 20 or more homeruns for the year. With such a potent arsenal, the mere idea of having to face the Angels was nerve-racking and scary enough to give a young pitcher like me a severe case of jitters. Yet, the more I think about it, I'm sure it had to be that way for every other pitcher in the league.

As another part of the Red Sox-San Francisco connection, Eddie Joost was handed the job of managing the Seals for the 1956 season. He had just retired from a long and successful career as a major league shortstop, which over the span of 17 seasons as an active player, included notable stints with the Cincinnati Reds and Philadelphia Athletics and one final year with the Red Sox in 1955. As soon as the news became official that the Seals would become the top farm team for the Red Sox, general manager Joe Cronin wasted no time in naming his good friend and fellow native San Franciscan, Joost to the position. Baseball fans in the Bay Area were delighted to hear that one of their own would be taking the helm of the hometown team, especially after the Seals, who had played no better than even baseball over the past few seasons, had dropped to below .500 in 1955. With Joost and the Red Sox having taken over the club, the future looked bright for baseball fans in San Francisco.

Eddie was a pioneer of sorts by being among the first big leaguers to break a longstanding baseball taboo which prohibited players from wearing eyeglasses while on the field. Yet he was always quick to point out the dramatic rise in his batting average, once he agreed to wear his glasses during games. However, following his playing days and during his time as manager, his vision may have become too sharp for his own good.

But after a less than impressive start of the season under Joost's guidance, the Seals sunk even further in the standings by losing 9 games in a row in late June. Eddie blamed his team's streak on an array of what he termed "sloppy calls" by umpires. Showing no restraint and making little effort to curtail his thoughts or emotions, he was ejected numerous times for his sometimes violent protests. "I'm the guy wearing glasses," he told reporters, "but they're the ones who really need 'em!"

In the following weeks, in what must have been a difficult and awkward situation for the general manager, Cronin was forced to fire his good friend and select a new skipper to replace Joost for the remainder of the season. His choice to fill the opening was one of the all-time great second basemen ever in the game, former all-star with the New York Yankees and Cleveland Indians, Joe "Flash" Gordon.

With a more settled demeanor and his own personalized approach toward our remaining games, Gordon's hiring gave the Seals a short-lived boost which lifted our record to within a game or two of the break-even mark in early August. But just as it was earlier with Joost as manager, my role on Gordon's pitching staff remained basically the same. Joe used me often, yet my work was almost exclusively out of the bullpen. I got into 45 games over the course of the season, but logged less than 100 innings. Getting only an occasional spot-start, my role had obviously changed to that of relief pitcher, which was a big change in plans from what the Red Sox had laid out for me earlier.

Still, in spite of the initial optimism, the mid-season change in managers and a few brief winning streaks in the second half of the schedule, the Seals could only pull off 77 wins and limped across the finish line in sixth place, not so impressive in the eight-team league. Yet, it was reported that the Red Sox were very pleased with the development of many of their young prospects in San Francisco and dropped hints that some possible big league call ups were being discussed for the upcoming year.

Even so, I was pleased to have made more appearances than any other pitcher on the club and to have finished the 1956 season with a record of seven wins and four losses. Taking into account the high level of play of the P.C.L. and the relatively short time I had been in professional baseball, I felt as if I had had another successful year.

Over the season, I learned a lot about the game and the art of pitching. I also learned what life could be like in a strange city, if you're always by yourself. I experienced loneliness like I never knew before and took off on my own to find answers. I only wish that taking control of my lonely life away from the ballpark had been as simple as controlling one of my fastballs.

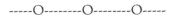

It was nothing lavish or extravagant but it was a nice apartment, and with four of us splitting the expenses it was affordable. As roommates, we agreed to contribute equally toward the rent and food, take care of our own laundry and each do our share of the housework. The apartment was situated in one of the oldest sections of the city, the Mission District, not far from Seals' Stadium. It was a great arrangement for the four of us, with fair and equal terms.

The oldest and most experienced among us was second baseman, Ken Aspromonte, an Italian, who at 24 years old, had already traveled around the world. "Chip," as he was known, had served 22 months with the U.S. Army in France during the Korean War, which was long enough to cause him to take the methods of the military with him into his civilian life. It was evident in his dress, the way he made his bed, polished his shoes and the way he kept his room in perfect order.

"Don't worry, fellows," he would warn us. "Each of you will be drafted soon and Uncle Sam will whip you guys into shape in no time, just like he did me!"

This native of Brooklyn, New York, was tidy and meticulous and always jumping on the rest of us whenever he noticed a dirty dish or spotted a piece of trash on the floor. After finishing the year with the Seals, Ken would move on to play 7 seasons in the major leagues, followed by a couple of years in Japan. He topped off a lengthy career in baseball by serving as manager of the Cleveland Indians from 1972 to 1974.

Also Italian and also from Brooklyn was pitcher, Jerry Casale. About two years younger, but having grown up in the same neighborhood as Ken, the two of them had lots to talk about and quickly became good friends. Jerry had a great year in '56, picking up 19 wins for the Seals, including 16 complete games. However, his hopes were put on hold, when just as Aspromonte predicted, Jerry was drafted into the army and would spend most of the next two years in Europe. Upon his return in September 1958, he would earn a promotion to Boston for what would be the start of his five-year big league career. Oddly enough, Jerry and I would be reunited as teammates on one of the American League's new expansion teams in 1961, the Los Angeles Angels, for a season neither of us will ever forget.

And I could never leave out our remaining roommate, Jim Mahoney. The handsome, slender-built shortstop from New Jersey was the one guy who had been with me nearly every step of the way through the Red Sox farm system. "Moe" and I had quite a history, starting when we were first together in class-D Salisbury and then for part of a season in Corning. We partied and played together when we were with San Jose in the California

League and all through the spring trainings in between. He was always one of the team's fair haired boys and was always a lot of fun.

In Jim's favor, barring injuries or other setbacks, he was pretty much assured of making it to the majors, as Boston had placed a sizable investment by giving him a hefty bonus at signing. We knew he had a place in the organization and was considered to be part of the Red Sox plans for the future. He would finally get his call to report to Boston in the middle of the '59 season and from there, go on to play for several other major league clubs before calling it a career.

But in 1956 things were different. I suddenly found that being roommates no longer meant what it did when we were in the lower classifications of baseball. Of course, the four of us were still friends, but we were all maturing and our interests and priorities were changing. We were seldom ever together at the house or out on the town. I sometimes saw more of my roommates at the ballpark than I did at our apartment. And while I often envied these guys, I never once begrudged any of them because their social calendars were always full or because they were always on the go.

Mahoney had his own car and so did Jerry and Ken. They had all driven to San Francisco in the spring and had their automobiles with them for the season. Their cars provided them with the luxury and freedom to go and come as they pleased, whenever the team was at home. Besides, they each had their girlfriends in town, which was all the more reason for me to see so little of them. In the apartment, I quickly discovered that a person can watch only so much TV and eat only so many meals by himself, and as the odd man out, I would need to come up with other ways to occupy myself.

One thing that a professional baseball player can sometimes have too much of is time. While players may be required to report to the ballpark several hours before game time, once the game is over and he has showered and dressed, the rest of the night and most of the next day are all his. This can be an over abundance of time for a lonely young man in a big city.

I began to check out the nearby restaurants, bars, novelty shops and galleries. The Mission District was full of such places, along with many antique stores and exhibit halls filled with sculptures and paintings. This particular section of town was known as the art district of the city. But as much as I enjoyed them all, I could only visit so many shops, galleries and restaurants before I was forced to change my routine. I had to find something more. That's when I made the costly mistake of visiting too many bars too often and without noticing the pattern, I began to drink more frequently. At first, I resorted to alcohol to soften the pain and ease the burden of being alone. I would downplay my drinking as nothing more than a temporary solution to help get me through a difficult time. *It was nothing I couldn't handle.*

"This is no serious problem," I tried to convince myself. "A few drinks here and there will help me get through this. I'll be going home in a few more weeks and my life will get back to normal."

In the beginning it worked. For a brief time, following a game or on an off-day, I would find myself feeling more comfortable with my situation and more accepting of myself with the help of a few beers or a couple of drinks. However, at the stadium with a crowd of noisy fans, I had no problem. The ballpark was where I belonged and baseball was still my comfort zone. But it was my time away from the game that I dreaded. That was when I felt lost and lonely in a city full of strangers. Those times were my weakest moments. Nevertheless, whenever I entered a bar, I would think about my father and recall the pain his drinking had caused. I would remember the horrible violence that wrecked our family and remind myself that it all stemmed from alcohol abuse. But those memories, as painful as they were, were still not enough to change my course. Without realizing it, I was developing a dependency.

With nothing better to do before heading to the ballpark, I would often stop by a small ice cream parlor just down the street located not far from where we lived. That particular shop had some of the best sundaes and ice cream sodas I had ever tasted. Blum's it was, a quiet, friendly place to relax and pass the time of the day, but for me, perhaps a little bit too friendly. I was caught off guard each time I walked in and couldn't help but notice the glances and stares I got from some of the other customers who were all males.

On what would be my final visit to Blum's, I finished my soda, left the table and strolled toward the cash register to pay my bill. As I reached for my wallet I was suddenly questioned by a cute young cashier stand-ing behind the counter, who was likely no older than her early twenties.

"You're not one of them, are you?" she blurted.

"Excuse me," I answered. "I don't understand what you mean."

"I mean you're different from the other fellows who come in here. The other guys who come in here are all queers, and you're not like them!"

"No, I don't suppose I am," I responded in a low whisper. "But I must thank you. You just answered all my questions and told me all I need to know."

This is just another example which illustrates how lost and naive I was at 21 years old and just how misplaced I was in the big city so far from home. Needless to say, after that little incident, I began checking out the ice cream at some of the other soda shops around town.

CHAPTER 18

"MONKEYS AND SNAKES AND IGUANAS? NO, THANK YOU!"

I wouldn't want to imply that my time in San Francisco was completely filled with unhappiness and despair. And it would be misleading if I did not mention a few of the more positive things that happened to me during the 1956 season. San Francisco is a great city, rich in culture and history, and I wish I had taken more time to visit the nearby sights and attractions when I had the chance. Maybe I would have ventured further and seen more, but this huge "City by the Bay" was all new to me and I wasn't so eager to go touring by myself.

As a ballplayer, I was comfortable, even if not fully satisfied with my performance for the year, and from all indications, it seemed that the Red Sox were pleased with my development as a pitcher. I felt good having finished with a winning record and I saw significant improvement with my control. I also used a wider variety of pitches which helped raise my confidence. But surprisingly, it was when I was away from the game that I made some of my most treasured memories of the summer.

As alone as I was, I suppose it was only natural that I missed my friends and the neighborhood back home. I missed my family even more. And with each passing season, it became more special whenever someone from home showed up at one of my games, but those instances were all too few.

For many years, my Uncle Eli was employed by the U.S. Government, working for the O.S.S., the Office of Strategic Services and even later when the agency evolved into the C.I.A. He was a world traveler. He was seldom home and because of the nature of his work, none of us ever knew where he was or when we would get to see him next. He was always one of my biggest supporters. Whenever we had a chance to get together, he would ask about my career and was quick to offer encouragement. When I was playing for San Jose in the summer of '55, Uncle Eli took a vacation trip out west to visit a friend he worked with at his home in San Mateo, California. On four consecutive evenings, he and his friend made the one- hour trip south to the ballpark in San Jose to see me play. I was delighted to see him and proud to have him there. Knowing he cared and supported me made his visit a special occasion for me. However, it was the following summer, when my mom came to visit me in San Francisco that will always be one of my fondest memories.

Mom flew from Chicago to San Francisco and stayed in town for about four days. Her visit not only gave us time to tour and see some of the sights of the city, but to enjoy each other's company. Some of our time was spent talking over coffee or simply strolling through the park. By this time I had matured to the point where we could relate to each other like never before.

She brought me up to date on what was happening with the family back home and told me about her latest job. As proof of just how much our relationship had evolved, I even worked up enough courage to share with her the thoughts and feelings I had for a special girl I had been dating.

The girl, Dottie Dayton, was an airline stewardess living in El Segundo, who I had met through Ken Aspromonte. Ken had been dating Dottie's roommate, also a stewardess, and was quick to suggest that we be introduced and the four of us go out together. Working around the erratic schedules of a baseball player and a flight attendant wasn't easy, but Dottie and I still managed to see each other. After just a few dates I was smitten by love. In no time I found myself under her spell, falling fast and hard for this beautiful young lady. I was eager to tell Mom about her and share my hopes for our relationship. Mom and I were together, yet alone in an unfamiliar city. We experienced a new type of closeness while seeing each other from totally new perspectives.

However, my most treasured memory of that special time with Mom is of an afternoon visit to one of the movie theaters in the Mission District. On a whim, we decided to catch a matinee showing of Walt Disney's *Fantasia*. Originally released prior to World War II, it reached a new wave of popularity in the 1950s. It was a film Mom and I had seen together back home years earlier when I was a child, and by seeing it again, we were both looking forward to a short trip down memory lane. It was our attempt at revisiting a special and happy time in our past. But for me, I had no idea just how magical the experience would be.

Perhaps it was the vibrant colors, the artful animation or the powerfully charged symphonic music, enhanced by Disney's own innovative new sound system, *Phantasound,* which captured me during the opening scene. Or maybe it was the combination of all of those things, along with the sentiment of having my mother sitting beside me as I revisited my past. The movie enveloped me and took me on a two-hour emotional journey filled with sound, color and feelings of nostalgia. *Fantasia* is truly one of the most wonderful films ever made, a full-length cartoon intended for young audiences. But as unusual as it may seem, I was not merely entertained for an afternoon, but swept into an awareness of making special memories with my mother. As we sat in the theater, I began to sense that Mom and I might not have many more opportunities to experience things like this together and that this special day was one to be cherished. Even now, I can relive that afternoon over and over in my mind as often as I like, and through my thoughts I can transport myself back to that unforgettable day.

After all of these years, it is a comfort to know that some things have not changed with time. I suppose it's part of my personality or in some way an extension of my soft sentimental side, but I still carry a strong appreciation for classical music and the power it has to evoke memories. I consider it a blessing to be able to enjoy the qualities of symphonic music and how it can touch me and impact me like nothing else can.

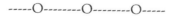

When the 1956 season ended, everyone on the club had had enough baseball and was ready for the off-season. With the L.A. Angels finishing so far ahead of the rest of the pack in the P.C.L., there was no need for us to stick around for any sort of post-season play. Instead of flying or taking a train home, I took Ken Aspromonte up on his offer to ride along as he drove east to go back to his home to Brooklyn. Ken had sunk a big chunk of his bonus money into the purchase of a brand new green Oldsmobile convertible, so the idea of traveling with him as far as Chicago sounded exciting. By striking a deal with Ken to go fifty-fifty on the gasoline, I was not only saving a few bucks on travel costs, but with more than 2000 miles of open highway between San Francisco and my home in South Chicago, I figured the possibilities were limitless and we would be in for all sorts of adventures. But the three-day trip turned out to be relatively uneventful. The scenery along the route was incredibly beautiful, but we didn't experience as much as a flat tire or a speeding ticket. The highlight of the whole drive, if you could call it that, occurred when the pair of us drove up in front of Mom's house and honked the horn before Ken shut off the engine. Friends and neighbors came rushing from all directions to see who could be motoring through our quiet little, no-frills section of town in a fancy new convertible. It was fun to be at the center of so much attention.

I was pleased that Ken got a chance to see where I lived and that he got to meet so many of my friends and family. We were all happy to have him visit for a short while before taking off for his home for what would be the final leg of his journey. Unknowingly, it would be the last I would see of him for quite some time; yet for Ken, there were some very exciting events about to take place in his life.

During the final weeks of his second season with the Seals, where he led the team in batting and helped carry them to the 1957 P.C.L. pennant, he married his stewardess sweetheart and in the days that followed, he finally received a long-awaited promotion to the Boston Red Sox. Ken's career had turned the corner. After getting that late-season call-up in September 1957, Ken would remain in the big leagues for many years to come. He would go on to enjoy a relatively long and rewarding career as both a player and manager, with stops in both the American and National Leagues as well as Japan. All things considered, Ken did very well for himself in baseball, leaving his own personal mark on the game and finding success which could not have come to anyone more deserving.

I brought home a lot of things to think about over the off-season. My mind was jumbled with questions and uncertainty. First and foremost,

I missed Dottie and wanted to see her. I couldn't imagine being without her for very long. The Red Sox also wanted me to play winter ball.

During my first few days at home I spent hours stewing about what to do. *Turning down such an offer will surely jeopardize my good standing with the Red Sox.* Yet I felt like I was nearing the end of my emotional rope. And as if I didn't already have enough issues complicating my life, a letter from the United States Selective Services System showed up at the house, notifying me that I was draft eligible.

Before I settled in at home with a winter job or went away to play winter ball, or God forbid, got drafted into military service, I wanted to see Dottie. She would be exactly what I needed. She would have some good sound advice and I could trust her as much as anyone. Surely she would be the one who could calm the storm of uncertainty which had quickly moved into my life. Making a return trip across the country to be with her didn't seem unreasonable, and it wouldn't have been, had she felt the same way I did.

A few of my old buddies from the neighborhood were happy to have me back in town for the winter. After being away since spring, I enjoyed hanging around with them, especially after a long season of spending so much time alone in San Francisco. But through it all, some of them could tell I wasn't my old self. They could tell something was weighing on me and they persuaded me to open up and talk about what was on my mind. That's when I discovered what a great bunch of friends I had.

Johnny Kapovich had been a close pal since high school. He was an easy-going sort of guy who did just enough to get by in school while spending most of his time tinkering under the hood of his souped-up hot rod. By this time, he had become one of the better known race car drivers on the local circuit and had also earned the reputation of being a pretty fair mechanic. Over the years he had spent hanging around the speedways and working at repair garages, Johnny had picked up a tough, hard-ass demeanor. Yet under his grimy coveralls and the grease beneath his nails was a good friend with a kind heart. And it was at his urging that I packed my bags and joined him on a hastily planned trip to the West Coast.

I had another old friend from the East Side neighborhood, Bob Gotovac, who had moved out to California a few years earlier. A former local baseball standout, Bob had signed with the Washington Senators, hoping for a shot at a the pro career. But by 1956, he had put those dreams to rest and was attending Santa Monica Junior College when he caught up with me at a Seals' game in San Francisco.

"If you ever decide to move out here to be near your girlfriend, just give me a call," he insisted. "You can stay with me until you find a job and get settled."

With Johnny's offer to drive and Bob's invitation to stay at his place, everything was in place for me to go. I said good-bye to Mom and phoned Dottie one final time. And just before we hit the road, a couple of my good friends, Roger Kristovich and "Beer-Beer," showed up at the house and decided at the last minute to go along just for the fun of the ride. With tires squealing and rubber burning, we sped out of the driveway, the four of us, on our way west to the Golden State. Johnny drove like crazy, stopping only for a quick burger and gasoline and then it was back on the highway. In his barely-legal, fuel-guzzling street rod, Johnny established what was likely a new land speed record on that trip, rumbling into Santa Monica less than 24 hours later.

At first, it looked like the ideal arrangement. California was beautiful year round with warm sunny weather, which provided a welcome contrast to the harsh winters of Chicago. Rooming with Bob turned out to be sweet deal. Yet within a few days, I had found myself a place to stay, a small dumpy place, but it served its purpose. I landed a temporary job as a mail carrier, working the nearby Lomita neighborhood. The hours weren't bad and the pay was okay. And while Dottie still kept a busy work schedule, we were able to find time to be together whenever she was home between flights. Even while she was away, she let me drive her car to go wherever I wanted to go. Normally, I used it every Sunday to drive to services at a local Serbian church.

Living on the West Coast was a great change of pace for me. I didn't give a thought to winter baseball or military duty. I just wanted to take it easy and clear my mind. For a short time, I was beginning to think that my life was finally coming together. But it wasn't long before changes occurred and things started to unravel. Out of nowhere, it suddenly became obvious that Dottie and I had different expectations. It was apparent that I was a lot more serious about our relationship than she was. Things reached a point where she needed to be honest and say exactly how she felt. It was difficult for her to tell me, but even harder for me to hear.

"I have to do what I think is best," she explained deliberately, "not just for me, but for both of us."

As painful as it was to accept, no one could have ended a relationship more delicately than Dottie. She seemed to do everything with dignity, which was one of her qualities that attracted me to her in the beginning. She would never be one to purposely mislead me. But the message was clear. She was breaking up with me and I would have to deal with my personal predicament on my own.

My spirit was broken. The hurt and disappointment were excruciating. Things had not gone the way I had anticipated, and I had no idea how to handle such an emotional dilemma. I had no alternative plan and had never once stopped to think I would ever need one. As naive as I was, I had assumed that Dottie would be my future and be the one special person who would add purpose and direction to my life. But now my heart and my hopes were crushed. I felt like a cork bobbing on an open sea, not knowing which way to turn and longing for someone to point me in the right direction. After only a few weeks in California, I was ready to head back home. The time had come for me to face reality. I returned home with a heavy heart. I felt rejected and dispirited and wasn't in the mood to do much of anything.

At a time when I needed nothing else to further complicate my life, I had been back home only a day or two, when I got an unexpected phone call from, of all people, the New York Yankees! It was Billy Shantz, the coach and coordinator of the Yankees' winter league team calling, asking about my interest and availability. Billy, a former big league catcher with the Athletics, was the younger brother of Bobby Shantz, the outstanding pitcher with the same club, who had received the American League's Most Valuable Player Award in 1952. A native of Pottstown, Pennsylvania, Billy was on the downside of his career as an active player and had been hired by the Yankees to organize a squad to play in an instructional winter league. Billy sounded enthusiastic on the telephone.

"Some of our scouts have had an eye on you for the past couple of years, Eli," he confessed. "And they have been impressed by the progress you have made as a pro."

Normally, Billy's compliments would have been uplifting and inspiring, like music to my ears. But at this particular time, in my depressed state of mind, there was probably very little anyone could have said that would have lifted my spirits. There was a noticeable lull in our conversation as Billy allowed time for me to respond. He knew he had put me in a jam.

"Now, the Red Sox have recommended you," he resumed. "They have given us the green light to invite you. But, it's all up to you, Eli. The decision is yours to make. You will be getting a salary of about $700 per month plus daily meal money, and we'll take care of all of your airline tickets and living accommodations, free of charge."

I had been blindsided by Billy's proposal. I felt like a dummy, unable and unprepared to give him any answers. I wasn't sure if he knew how totally confused I was, or if he thought he may have called some nitwit who didn't know how to use a telephone. Regardless, he didn't give up. He continued to provide more details.

"We'll be holding a short, one-week training camp in Miami, Florida, and once that's over, we'll fly down to Panama to start the winter season."

I couldn't believe what I was hearing. I was flattered to receive such an offer, yet the whole deal was daunting and made me nervous. The idea of traveling abroad made me wary, and I wasn't ready emotionally to spend more time away from home, alone. I wouldn't have been more startled if he had suggested that I go to Moscow! Billy was good at his job. He had dealt with many young ballplayers before me and knew when to back off. He knew I would need more time. But he still threw in a few final words to help support his case.

"Talk it over with your mom and call me back. It's instructional baseball," he reminded me. "We'll have a great time down there, and it will be a great way to gain experience and sharpen your skills."

Several days passed. I had started back to work at my old winter job with the ironworkers and was playing basketball again at the Y as often as I could. My spirit was dragging bottom, and I needed to make a change. It took all the resolve I could muster, but I pushed myself to phone Billy Shantz. I told him I would accept his offer, meet him and his team in Miami for a short training camp and then spend the next two months playing ball in Panama. I believe had I been in a better frame of mind, I would have appreciated the invitation to play winter ball a lot more, but at the time I was in no mood to appreciate anything. Little did I realize that I was about to embark on what would be a wonderful paid vacation.

I caught my flight and arrived in Miami on time for training camp. Physically, I was in great shape and ready to play ball. But mentally and emotionally I was very much out of sorts. Not knowing anyone on the club seemed to push me back into a familiar but difficult social situation: that of being alone. I reverted to my old habit of going out on the town alone and spending my evenings at the local bars and pubs. I drank heavily, and at times literally cried in my beer. For me, Miami was just another lonely city. My depression soon led to bitterness and anger, to the extent that if someone in the bar spotted me in such a despondent condition and asked innocently "Are you okay, Mister?" or "What's the problem, buddy?" they would either be cursed or challenged to a fist fight.

From Miami, we flew to Panama, a small Spanish-speaking country at the southern tip of Central America, which at the time had a population of only about one million. Nevertheless, since I chose to doze off or stare out the classroom window during much of my time back at Bowen High School, these basic geographical facts were all new to me. Yet like everyone, I had heard about how ships passed through the U.S. controlled Panama Canal, but that was about the extent of what I knew about the country. I had no idea what a beautiful place it was, especially the constant blue skies and balmy temperatures. I was also surprised to find so many Americans there, many in the military, stationed at the larger U.S. Army installations, such as Fort Clayton and Fort Amador.

It took a few days to get into the routine, but once I paused long enough to assess my situation, I decided to give Panama an honest chance. I consciously paused to notice the beautiful white sandy beaches that stretched endlessly along the shoreline. I filled my lungs with the salty air and took a closer look at the tall palms bending in the tropical breeze. It was then that I decided to appreciate where I was and the reason I was there. It was as close to paradise as any place I had ever seen. My thoughts drifted to my buddies back home, and I quickly realized that any of them, if given a choice, would jump at an opportunity to trade places with me. Sure, I thought about Dottie, and quite often, but I decided to concentrate on other things. I was forcing myself to move on.

I met one fun-loving gal who was more than happy to show me a good time, taking me to some the more remote parts on the beach. She was very attractive, a little older than I was and obviously a lot more experienced. She seemed to know the shoreline like the back of her hand. She knew about the most secluded spots on the beach, places where there were no other people, which caused me to suspect that she had been doing this sort of thing long before she met me.

I frequented a nearby night spot, the Balboa Club, and learned a few Latin dances. I was getting my tan, playing baseball two or three times a week and enjoying what for me, was a long fabulous vacation. But suddenly, at a time when I had little more than sun and fun on my mind, a most disturbing piece of mail arrived, a letter from the only relative I would have preferred not hear from: Uncle Sam!

"Greeting:" it read. "You are hereby ordered for induction into the armed forces of the United States." The notice included further orders, directing me to report to my local induction station for my physical examination. *What lousy timing! I should have known my life of leisure in the tropics was too good to last!* Although this piece of registered mail had been originally received at my home address in Chicago, by the time my mother forwarded it to me in Panama, the deadline for reporting had passed. I was already in hot water with the government without knowing it. With the letter clinched in my fist, I rushed to the closest army post. The sooner I pleaded my case the better off I would be.

The army doctors deemed me fit for military service and classified me 1-A. Before I could get back into my civilian clothes, I was told to expect orders to report for active duty at any time. "What should I do in the meantime?" I asked. With that, no one seemed to hear my question, or maybe no one cared to answer. "I guess I'll just have to put my entire life on hold," I told myself. "I'll just lay low and wait to hear from them."

A colonel from Fort Clayton, polished and buffed, with a column of hash marks on his coat sleeve and huge serving of fruit salad on his chest, was standing nearby. He had been in the examination area for several minutes, quietly observing my examination. While everyone seemed to be aware of his presence, he kept his distance and did not interfere. As I finished getting dressed, I happened to look up and noticed him walking toward me. I quickly buttoned the top button on my sport shirt and rose to attention just before he had a chance to speak.

"Well, Grba," he snapped, "I understand you're a baseball player. You're with the Red Sox and you're here in Panama to play winter ball, is that correct?"

"That is correct, Sir!" I admitted respectfully, my voice cracking. "I've been in the Red Sox chain for four years."

"Yes, I know all about that. You're a right-handed pitcher and you were in the Coast league last year, if I remember correctly."

"Yes Sir! That is all true, Sir!" I could sense that every eye in the room was on the two of us. I had no idea why he was questioning me or where this inquiry was heading.

"I've been a baseball fan for long time," he continued. His eyes began to soften. His thoughts seemed to drift away from the present, which indicated to me that he had other passions in his life beside the United States Army. He took a quick look around the room. It appeared he had more he wanted to say, but his superior rank was putting a damper on our conversation.

"Come with me, soldier," he ordered. "I need to have a word with you."

I followed the colonel through the door of the medical building and outside onto the sidewalk. Once out of the range of curious ears, he appeared to be a bit more relaxed. He pushed his hand beneath the lapel of his coat, searching for a cigarette.

"So tell me Grba, would like to stay here in Panama?" he asked in a friendly tone. "Would you like to continue playing baseball here?"

"Yes, Sir! I sure would!" I blurted, being caught totally by surprise. "I'm in love with this place. The beaches, the weather, the people... it's terrific here, Sir!"

"Well, I'd like to have you stationed here, so you can play on our post team. I'm sure you would be a great addition to our ballclub, and we'd be happy to have you. But you know, to do that, I would have to arrange for you to take your basic training here. Of course, you'll need to complete your first eight weeks of basic boot camp and then move on to another eight-week period of AIT, your Advanced

Individual Training. Once you're in AIT, you'll be trained in the most up-to-date techniques of jungle warfare, by some of the world's best combat instructors. It will all be conducted right here in Panama. Now, how does that sound?"

"It all sounds good to me, Colonel," I responded, not knowing the full details. "I have a strong connection to the army because of my Uncle Eli. He enlisted in the army many years ago and did very well for himself," I boasted. "If I am not mistaken, he is currently working for the CIA."

"Well, Grba, as you may have heard, this Jungle Warfare Training Program is a tough one. It's certainly no picnic. During the last few days of that training, you'll get a chance to apply all the survival skills you've been taught. You and a partner will be dropped in the jungle for a one week test. You'll live off the land, using what you were taught along with your own wit, to show us that you can survive on your own out there. It's a tough challenge, no doubt, but you'll be a real soldier when you're done."

"A whole week in the wild, living off the land?" I asked naively. "Where do you sleep and what do you do for food?" With those questions, the colonel took another puff from his cigarette and his face broke into a smile.

"Oh, you'll do okay," he assured. "You'll be taught how to find water and you'll learn the various leaves and berries that are edible. You'll be taught to trap and kill birds, iguanas, snakes, monkeys and other wildlife. And you'll probably lose a few pounds over the duration of the test. But you'll be fine."

"Monkeys? I'll have to eat monkeys and snakes and iguanas?" I asked in astonishment. "I can't imagine anything like that!"

"That's right, Grba. But it's not all that bad. You'll discover that you're a lot tougher than you thought and you'll find you're more of a soldier than you ever thought you could be."

He stared at me in silence, waiting for a response. I found myself awkwardly short of words, searching for something to say. The colonel sensed my predicament and came to the rescue.

"If you think you can handle it, drop by my office and let me know. I'll arrange to have you on our baseball team when the season starts. Remember, Grba... just let me know."

Suddenly, the colonel's proposition wasn't quite as appealing to me as it had been a few moments earlier. *A week in the jungle? Having to find my own water and trap my own food? Eating monkeys and snakes and iguanas? No, thank you!*

The whole idea, which at first sounded like a great way for me to follow in my Uncle Eli's footsteps had suddenly struck me as being a bit too much for a city boy like me to handle. From the time I was a small child, I had always looked up to Uncle Eli and admired him. For as long as I could remember, he had been my role model. But after what the colonel described to me, I decided it might be best that I seek other ways to gain his approval and make him proud of me.

Once the winter baseball season was over, I returned home, tanned, with my hair still bleached from the sun. Once my flight landed in the States, I found everyone bundled up in heavy winter coats and mittens. The difference in climates was staggering. But I also brought along an unwanted souvenir from my tropical stay, a very painful one.

On what was our final day in Panama, teammate, Dave Jacobs, an infielder in the Pirates' system, joined me on a fishing excursion, which had been offered to the two of us at no charge. A friendly charter boat captain, Captain Terry, a big baseball fan, took us out to sea to one of his prime spots, urging us to try our luck at hooking some of the incredible fish found in that part of the world. Dave and I had a blast that entire afternoon, soaking up the sun and bending our rods on some of the biggest fish either of us had ever seen. We were both lucky enough to have reeled in our fair share of red snapper, along with an assortment of other fish, mostly grouper and tuna. After his final catch of the day, Dave pulled a small-size snapper from his hook and underhandedly tossed the fish in my direction, wanting me to place it the cooler with the rest of our haul. As I made a half-assed attempt to catch the fish before it fell to the deck, a needle-like spine from the snapper's dorsal fin stabbed into the middle finger of my left hand. In an instant, I felt the excruciating pain of the spike entering my flesh, driving itself inward, almost to the bone. Captain Terry ran to my aid, rinsed my hand with solution of bleach and water and applied a bandage of gauze and adhesive tape. "You'll be okay in a day or two, Eli," he assured me. "A stick like that should heal up soon, if you keep it clean."

Even after several days at home, I continued to struggle with the pain. At times my entire left hand throbbed, keeping rhythmic time with my heartbeat. I was unable to curl my fingers or make a fist. And like any other mother, Mom was worried silly and wouldn't rest until I took a trip to the local doctor's office to have it treated. A doctor examined me, probing the wound and flexing the painful joint. Finally, with the help of fluoroscopy imagery, he determined that a piece of the spine was still imbedded in the tissue near the knuckle. Yet it was his opinion, that as long as there was no infection, he should leave the spine in its place and allow time for the irritating fragment to work its way out of the wound. In the weeks and months that followed, the pain finally began to subside. Yet I continued to pick at the injured joint, hoping to work the spine to the skin's surface and restore some degree of flexibility to the finger.

Weeks later, in the dead of winter, another contract from the Red Sox arrived at the house. This agreement, for the 1957 baseball season, would be my fifth such contract offer from the same club. "I must be doing something right," I told myself, tooting my own horn. "And this registered letter from Boston is written proof." However, just as I had anticipated, there were no surprises in the terms, no big promotion and no big raise in salary. I was being reassigned to the Pacific Coast League for another season with the San Francisco Seals. The modest boost in salary would lift me to more than $700 per month, which wasn't bad, and I was comfortable knowing I would start the year with basically the same bunch of guys I had been with the previous season. By far, the majority of players on the San Francisco club were good guys, personable and easy to get along with, and the coaching staff had been helpful without being overbearing. In my mind there was no doubt that the Red Sox had plans for me. But I couldn't forget the number of veteran players who, over the years, pulled me aside and warned me, "Never get too cozy with any one club," they would advise. "There's no security in professional baseball. Just when you think you've found your spot, that's when they ship you out!"

With a move that pleased everyone on the ballclub, the Seals relocated their spring training camp to Anaheim for the 1957 season. It was a great change of scenery for the players and much closer to the team's home city than our old training site in Florida. Disneyland, which had opened only a year earlier, was operating at full speed, which was great for the players who had their families join them for the spring. And personally, I couldn't wait to get out there and become friends with Mickey, Donald and Goofy.

I was in great shape, my pitching arm felt great and my tender finger was slowly improving. Naturally, I still thought of Dottie from time to time, but emotionally, I was getting stronger and my hopes were high for another good season. But still, I was puzzled. I had heard nothing more from the draft board. *Had Uncle Sam forgotten about me, or was my luck about to run out?* A tiny voice inside my head told me I would be hearing from him soon. I began to recall how, about a year earlier, my roommate, Ken Aspromonte, shared with me the benefit of his military experience by giving this warning:

"Make no mistake about it, Eli," he cautioned me. "The army will know where to find you... and sooner or later your ass will belong to Uncle Sam!"

CHAPTER 19
"SEE YA' LATER, YANKEE!"

Most baseball historians agree that Hall of Fame pitcher, Leroy "Satchel" Paige, was 59 years old when he pitched his final game in the major leagues in the mid-1960s. But oddly, "The Ageless Wonder," as he was often referred to, could not provide with certainty, the true date of his birth when he joined the Cleveland Indians in 1948. Being pressed over and over by sports reporters who wanted to resolve the issue of his age, Satchel finally relented and responded with an insightful, rhetorical question of his own, one which wasn't intended only for those who were there with him, but a question meant for all of us to consider. "How old would you be," he asked them, "if you didn't know how old you are?" His crafty, but provocative reply caused each of them to start scribbling frantically in their notebooks. For once, roles had been reversed, and the writers had been charged to answer. The question "Ol' Satch" proposed to them quieted much of the concern they had about his age and prompted them to redirect their inquiries into the more customary aspects of his game.

The grand old game of baseball itself is seen as timeless. Unlike other sports, there is no clock, so time never runs out. The final outcome is never decided until all opportunities are exhausted and the final out is made. Baseball is also timeless in its history, traditions and rules. And while records may be broken, new names are introduced in the lineups, and even though uniform styles and colors continue to evolve, the game remains much the same. Yet, how ironic it is that on Opening Day each year, the players on the field are always another year older, but the fans in the stands are all still the same age as before.

I believe ice cream, fishing and Disneyland are among them, but there are very few things in life which can help us maintain the exuberance of our youth the way baseball can. Any combination of items from that short list could, no doubt cause any of us to feel as young as we could ever imagine, short of resorting to time travel. So in 1957, when I reported to the San Francisco Seals' training camp in Anaheim, located not much farther than a long flyball from the entrance gate of Disneyland, I felt like a kid again-- strong and healthy, optimistic and ready for another productive year with the Red Sox.

It was great to see a bunch of familiar faces when I walked into camp. Several guys who had been my teammates the year before were among the first to greet me: catcher, Eddie Sadowski; first baseman, Bob DiPietro; and outfielder, Gordy Windhorn were among the first. Manager, Joe Gordon, the former Yankee great, was back for another year, having done a commendable job of turning the club around in mid-season1956 after replacing Eddie Joost. Among the new fellows in the camp was 35-year-old Harry Dorish, a right handed pitcher who, after ten seasons in the major leagues had been given his release by the Red Sox over the winter. However, rather than let Harry return to his home in Pennsylvania to look for another line of work, Boston signed him to a minor league contract, with the understanding that he would be activated to pitch from time to time, but that he would also work as a pitching coach for the Seals, imparting his wisdom and experience to the younger hurlers. Reporting to minor league training camp may have seemed awkward for an experienced veteran like Harry, but I was happy to see him there and considered it an honor.

I had long been a fan and admirer of Harry's, dating back to the times I had seen him pitch for my hometown White Sox, back in the early 50s. Recalling how he reached success in the big leagues as one of the finest fielding pitchers in the game, who could attack batters with a vicious assortment of breaking pitches, I was excited to find out that we would be on the same team, and I was eager to see what I could learn from him.

I had been throwing for several minutes from the bullpen mound, but in the warm, dry air of Southern California, I had yet to break a sweat. It was during the first few days of camp, so I was trying out both my fastball and my curve, being careful not to overthrow or overwork myself. Harry had been standing by, quietly watching my every pitch. I was delighted to find that he knew who I was and called me by name when he stepped closer.

"That's a pretty good curveball you have there, Eli," he said approvingly. "It's one of the better ones I've seen lately." His tone was positive and complimentary, just what I was hoping to hear from a guy who had been one of my boyhood heroes. "But your fastball is as straight as a string." It was a candid comment coming from Harry, but he was being tactful by emphasizing the positive before addressing the negative, an effective training method too often ignored by coaches and managers. "Let me see how you're gripping your fastball," he coaxed. I held the ball up, turning my wrist, permitting him to view it from every angle. "Hold it across two seams, like this," he explained. "Leave your index finger where it is, to stabilize and guide the ball, but add a little more pressure with your middle finger to make it break." I watched and listened intently while he continued with his instructions. "That looks good," he said encouragingly, as he examined the position of each of my fingers. "Now, throw it using the same delivery you use with your fastball, and let's see what happens. With that particular grip, the ball should sink like crazy!"

Harry stepped behind me to get a good look at my first attempt. I toed the rubber with my right foot and stared in at the catcher's mitt, focusing on the target he provided. Stepping back, I shifted my weight to my left foot. Hands joined over my head, I rocked forward and pushed off hard with my right leg, driving my entire body in the direction of the plate. Not sure of what to expect, I released the baseball just as I had a million times before. Whoosh! It left my hand like a missile, maintaining both its velocity and altitude until it reached a point just a few feet short of the catcher. Suddenly it sank as if it had been rolled off a table! I was astonished! The abrupt downward movement of that pitch was so much sharper than I expected. "That's it, Eli!" Harry exclaimed. "That was a good one; now let's see you try it again."

Harry stood by watching as I continued to throw one sinker after another. "You've got the hang of it!" he assured me. "Now, keep playing around with it and experiment a little. Once you learn to control it, the hitters in this league won't know what to do. They'll be reaching for that ball and swinging like they're wearing shackles!"

Like anything else I was ever introduced to, I set out to perfect the sinkerball with a passion. I threw it incessantly, pitching batting practice, throwing in the bullpen, and playing catch in the outfield. Even in the dugout and in the clubhouse, I kept a baseball in my hands and practiced my grip, noting the placement of my fingers and the pressure I was applying. It wasn't long before I had developed enough confidence that I decided to try my newfound pitch in some of the first few exhibition games of the spring. I was amazed at the results, as the sudden drop of my ball caused unsuspecting batters to lunge forward, hoping to make contact with a letter-high pitch, which quickly and unexpectedly sank to a level below their knees. "That sinker is exactly what you needed," Harry confided. "That one new pitch makes all the difference in how these other clubs will approach you from now on. You're giving them something new to think about."

"But you're the one who deserves the credit," I commended him, feeling like I owed him a debt of gratitude. "You're the one who taught me."

"I think Gordon has plans for you," he mentioned subtly, wanting to change the subject. "Joe feels that you have the bulldog attitude that's needed to be a good relief pitcher. He feels that with your tough, aggressive mindset and your great sinkerball, you'd be great coming in from the pen. And I'll have to admit, Eli, I agree with him. I think that would be a great role for you."

Learning that I was being considered for a specific spot on the pitching staff boosted my confidence and gave me a new optimism for the upcoming season. *Working strictly as a reliever could become my specialty and perhaps be my ticket to the big leagues.* I couldn't wait for the regular season to begin.

The light breezes and the warmth of the early afternoon California sun were enough to make for a beautiful day, the sort of day that made me thankful that I played baseball for a living. I was tossing batting practice to a few of the guys, working off the mound, pitching from behind a portable protective screen. It was my idea of a perfect day. But looking back, I recognize my mistake. I was caught up in the moment and had thoughtlessly allowed myself to get a little too comfortable with where I was and the people I worked for. For a brief time I let my guard down. I wasn't mindful of the advice I had heard numerous times from some of the veteran players I had met along the way. "Don't allow yourself to feel too secure with the team that signed you," they warned me. "Once you get cozy with your ballclub, that's when they ship you out!"

"Hey, Grubsy! Take a break, I need to see you." It was Joe Gordon, yelling to me from the dugout. There was no apparent urgency in his voice, so I lobbed one last pitch to the batter and dropped the other balls I had in my hands, one by one, back into the ball basket. I grabbed a small towel draped over the edge of the screen and headed for the bench. "What's up, Skip?" I asked, as I stepped across the baseline. "What's on your mind?"

Joe trudged up the steps of the dugout and out onto the grass to meet me. "See ya' later, Yankee!" he greeted me, extending his hand.

"What's going on?" I wondered. "He's gotta be kidding me about something."

He grabbed my hand and gave it a hearty shake. "See, ya' later, Yankee!" he repeated.

Now, starting with his arrival on the Seals, Joe razzed us over and over about the superiority of his former team, the Yankees, and their dominance over Boston. Naturally, I assumed this was just more of his needling. "Yankee, my ass!" I snapped back. "I'm no Yankee! You know I hate those SOBs!"

"Well, you better get used to the sound of being called a Yankee because you've just been traded!" I looked directly into his face and saw that he was serious.

"You're not kidding are you, Skip?" I asked in disbelief.

"No way, pal! You're part of a two for one swap," he continued. A friendly smile broke across his face. "I suggest you start packing right away!"

It was no joke. Everything Joe told me was true. When I got out of bed that morning, the thought of being traded to another team was the furthest thing from my mind. But the unexpected had occurred. I was on my way to the Yankees, along with Gordy Windhorn, in exchange for Bill Renna, a big right-handed-hitting outfielder. Gordy and I were told to report to the Yankee training camp right away.

Just months earlier, the Yankees had won the World Series, taking the Brooklyn Dodgers in a seven-game series, which included a perfect game tossed by their own unlikely hero, Don Larsen. They won the 1956 A. L. pennant by a margin of nine games, due in part to their 24-year-old center fielder, Mickey Mantle, who captured the Triple Crown Award and was voted the American League's MVP. Their everyday lineup featured other heavy hitters who were rated among the best in the game, including Yogi Berra, Bill Skowron and Hank Bauer. So, by taking into consideration such a list of credentials, being traded to the Yankee organization was definitely not the worst hand a young player could be dealt. It was the emotional jolt of being uprooted, sent across the country and having no say whatsoever in the matter, which was upsetting. Yet, it was the usual sort of player transaction which occurs every day in baseball. But still, it was the first one that involved me.

Leaving behind the great weather and attractions of Anaheim and landing in DeLand, Florida, was a culture shock, to say the least. Located between Daytona Beach and Orlando, DeLand was never a bustling metropolis by anyone's standards, especially when I arrived there in the spring of 1957. The town's biggest attribute was that it provided the Yankees with a training location close to other clubs training there in Florida. Nevertheless, for years it was home to their minor league spring training facility.

As soon as we reported, Gordy and I learned that, even though we were both there to play at the Triple-A level for the Yankees, we were going to be separated when camp ended, playing for different ballclubs. He was placed with the Richmond Virginians of the International League, and I was assigned to their other top farm team, the Denver Bears of the American Association. It was uncommon for a baseball organization to have the financial means to operate a farm system with two AAA teams. However, much like today, there weren't many organizations that could compare with the New York Yankees.

My manager was ex-Yankee catcher, Ralph Houk, a highly decorated combat veteran of World War II, who had risen to the rank of major. He was a quiet, no-nonsense gentleman who, after coping with the horrors of war, was very rarely upset or excited in civilian life, unless there was a situation which involved a visually impaired umpire. He was a well-read man who appreciated well-tailored suits and fine cigars. From the first time I was in his company, he had my respect. I sensed an air of dignity and refinement about him. Perhaps, even then, at 22 years-old, I was still inadvertently searching for the father figure missing in my life.

The players on the Denver club were a great bunch of guys, but they were all new faces to me. Their roster was loaded with sluggers, such as Norm Siebern, Johnny Blanchard, Marv Throneberry and Jim Pisoni, who could all hit the ball a country mile. The Bears were also well stocked with pitchers. Zach Monroe, Ryne Duren, Mark Freeman and John Gabler were the likely favorites to fill the spots in the starting rotation, while Jack McMahan and Ben Flowers were also expected to see a lot of action. Despite the backlog of good pitching, Houk confirmed that I would be given every opportunity to prove myself. "Believe me, Eli," he assured me. "The Yankees would not have traded for you, if they didn't have a need for you."

Ralph Houk was a highly decorated combat veteran. From the first time I was in his company, he had my respect.

Of course, every club in baseball has its own preferred ways of working its players into shape, conducting drills and operating a training camp. But for the most part, the basic elements are always the same, making the transition from one team to another nothing more than an unavoidable inconvenience. It is a lesson every player usually learns for himself, after just a few seasons in professional baseball. However, this being the first big move of my career, I was surprised how quickly things began to fall into place. After just a couple of days of adjusting to my new environment, getting familiar with my new coaches and adapting to a new set of training drills, I was beginning to understand that there are many things that could happen to a ballplayer which are a lot worse than getting traded to the Yankees. But still, this time was no time for me to be comfortable or satisfied. As an amusing old saying goes: "Life is full of surprises, but never when you need one." I was about to get a big surprise, one that I could have very well lived without. It was another letter from the U.S. Army. Uncle Sam wanted me to report for active duty right away!

Once again, my mail was slow getting to me. By the time this letter reached our home address in Chicago and Mom had forwarded it to me in Florida, the date I was scheduled to report had already passed. *What was I to do?* I had yet to put on an army uniform and I was already in deep trouble. I nervously read and reread my orders. Each time, the sick, gnawing feeling in my belly only got worse. My best bet was to talk it over with Houk, I concluded. Who would know more about dealing with the army than "The Major" himself?

I sat quietly at his desk as he carefully studied my letter. With his reading specs perched on the end of his nose, he squinted at the calendar hanging on the wall. "You're late, Eli, that's for sure. But I still think we might be able to get this whole deal straightened out. We'll need to talk to someone at the local draft board office and see if we can get you an *active duty forbearance* or what you may call a *deferment*. There's no guarantee, mind you, but I think it'll be worth a try." Based on what Ralph told me, I was unable to draw any conclusions about our chances of meeting with success. But having someone go with me, someone who used words like "forbearance" and "deferment," had to give me an added advantage.

"We'll head out first thing in the morning," he suggested. "And we'll take my car. The closest draft board is in Bartow, so we're looking at a two- or three-hour drive. Be sure to wear a sport coat and tie because no matter where you go, it never hurts to dress like a Yankee." Ralph was brimming with confidence and had a detailed approach all planned. Perhaps he had helped other young players with this sort of thing before.

The sleeves of my sport coat seemed a little short. But my black loafers were polished and shined and my borrowed necktie, tied in a perfect Windsor, looked pretty snazzy. I don't think I had looked so sharp since our senior class photo day back at Bowen High. We parked on the street in front of the office. As I stepped out of Houk's automobile and onto the sidewalk, the colorful image of Uncle Sam taped on the inside of the plate-glass window snagged my attention. "I WANT YOU!" it read across the top of the broadside. The wiry old fellow sporting stringy white hair and a tri-colored top hat seemed to be pointing his finger directly at me.

As planned, Ralph did all the talking. He introduced himself and explained the purpose of our visit to the uniformed corporal seated at the front desk. We were led down a short hall to the rear of the building and to an office at the very end. A homely old lady in a floral print dress was seated behind a desk just inside the door. With a manner and air, which would have made Ma Kettle seem like a beauty queen, she ordered us to be seated. "I'll be with y'all in just a moment," she drawled. Ralph and I cautiously lowered ourselves onto a couple of rickety folding chairs and waited for her attention. "What are y'all looking to do today?" she finally demanded.

Ralph began presenting our case by bringing up his prior service, being in the 9th Armored Division, serving as an Army Ranger and retiring from the army at the rank of major. He went on to outline how we were with the New York Yankees and how baseball was my primary means of earning a living. "It's his livelihood," he offered. "And our season is about to start. Missing a whole year could jeopardize this man's career, maybe his entire future." He paused long enough to check her reaction. Seeing no signs of making progress, he continued. "Now, if you were to grant a deferment, he could report for active duty in the fall. What difference will a few months make, anyway?" he proposed. Unmoved by Ralph's presentation, she continued to glare at us from across the desk. He offered her my letter. The two of us sat quietly, occasionally looking at each other, as she lip-read her way all the way to the bottom of the page. Ralph tried to offer another solution, but she cut him off in mid-sentence. "Well, suppose he were to..."

"Well, Mr. Grabber," she interrupted, "is that how you say your name? Grabber?" She didn't pause long enough to give me a chance to correct her. "It looks to me like the Yankees will have to get along without you for the rest of this year," she said matter-of-factly, "and probably next season, too. But I'm gonna do you a favor and make it easy for you. I'm giving you 72 hours to report to Fort Jackson, South Carolina. But this time, you had best show up on time. Do you understand me, Mr. Grabber?"

I could sense the pleasure she derived from giving orders and controlling the fate of others. Perhaps she thrived on authority, or maybe the power of her position was stoking her ego. Nevertheless, Ralph and I both knew when we were beaten. We realized it was a hopeless cause. We got up from our seats and headed for the hallway, only to find that this woman had not finished belaboring her point. "You may think playing baseball is an important job," she went on, "but it's not as important as defending our country."

As we turned to leave, she got up from her desk. She pointed her boney finger at me, wanting us to remain long enough for her to make one final remark, one which revealed to us why our efforts to present a reasonable, legitimate case were doomed from the start. Her face grew even harder. "You know, Son, we've had a lot of our Rebel boys from here in the South who got drafted and they all had to go into the army. And there ain't no good reasons why you Yankee boys from up North shouldn't have to do the same!"

We couldn't get out of that place quickly enough! Without speaking, we hurried to the car. Ralph's cheeks glowed bright red from frustration and disgust. He slammed the driver's door. His hands trembled as he missed his mark again and again, trying to insert his key into the ignition switch. Driving away, Ralph stared straight ahead at the street and oncoming vehicles. He gripped the steering wheel as tightly as he would squeeze the handle of his bat on a three-two pitch. Emotional pressure was building inside him. It was only a matter of time until he would erupt. "Damn it, Eli! We didn't stand a chance with that ol' bitty! Someone needs to let her know that the Civil War ended a century ago!"

"You're right about that, Skip," I agreed. "How could she not know about that? I'm sure it was in all the papers!"

Ralph didn't react. He was in another world. I gazed out the window at the Florida countryside. We had a long drive ahead of us. My body was numb with shock and disbelief. *How did it all happen? How could I go from Disneyland to the U.S. Army so fast?*

"Fort Jackson, South Carolina," I whispered sarcastically, "that sounds like a fun place to go."

CHAPTER 20

THE ARMY IS FULL
OF SUPRISES

◦────◦

I t was a journey that covered nearly 500 miles. For seven hours on a north-bound train, I listened to the chatter of a bunch of nervous recruits, all of us on our way to Fort Jackson. The stiff, high-back seat and the half-cooked boxed meal made the trip seem even longer than it actually was, yet none of us were in a hurry to get off. One kid looked like he was about to burst into tears. Another sat quietly, stone-faced, as if it were all a bad dream. Some of the others told horror stories they had heard about life in the army. However, if truth were known, none of us had the slightest idea of what was waiting for us at our destination. It had been a long tiring ride, but try as I may, napping was out of the question. With the constant rocking and swaying of the train and the apprehension and uncertainty of what lay ahead, sleep was impossible. We finally rolled to a stop sometime after midnight. I was sleepy, dead-tired and feeling like I was going to throw up. But I was about to get my first taste of life in the United States Army.

We were led into a building where a huge first-floor area was filled with rows of folding cots. "These are temporary quarters," a sergeant barked as we were lined up for orders. "Your barracks are being overhauled and refurbished." He was very animated and gruff. His voice sounded like he had eaten gravel for dinner. Nearing the brink of exhaustion, I clenched my teeth to keep from yawning. I felt my knees begin to quiver. He handed each of us a scratchy wool blanket and a pillow case, and ordered us to grab the first rack we came to. "Listen up, men!" he shouted. "You best get all the sleep you can, 'cause you're gonna need it! We're gonna get an early start tomorrow, and tomorrow will be your first day as a soldier in the U.S. Army!"

I had hardly closed my eyes before the quietness of our makeshift bunkroom was shattered by loud voices and heavy footsteps, as a line of soldiers scurried past our cots and up the stairs to the second floor. A ceiling light above the stairwell had been turned on, allowing me to see that these responders were medical personnel and military police. "Remain in your racks!" someone yelled, as more men rushed in, "there's nothing to see here!"

In minutes, a young fellow, strapped to a gurney, was brought down the stairs and wheeled out the door to a waiting ambulance. I heard the words "attempted suicide" mumbled softly by one of the attendants. "Why would he do such a thing?" asked another. "He was only in for six months." I laid motionless on my cot, staring up at the ceiling, my thin, scratchy blanket pulled to my chin. *What had I gotten myself into? Is this life in the army?*

The next morning they had us up at the crack of dawn. After early chow, our heads were buzzed to the scalp and we were issued boots and fatigues. For the next few days, running and calisthenics took up a lot of our time, but since I was already in pretty good shape, I didn't have the problems that some others had. Yet, the routine was physically grueling, while mentally, we had our personal identities taken away. Our hair was cut off, we dressed the same, and we moved from place to place as a unit. We were permitted to have only certain items in our footlockers and we were constantly berated and shouted at for falling short in just about everything we did. And to add to our humiliation, our barracks were nothing more than six-man tents, set up to be used as our temporary quarters. I bunked there not only with five other recruits, but with every type of flying and crawling insect known to man. With all the bugs and the damp night air, sleep was hard to come by.

Early in camp, we were each issued a standard M1 rifle, our personal weapon which we were responsible for until the end of basic training. From that point on, our rifles were with us at all times. For weeks without firing a round, we worked at becoming familiar with our gun. We broke it down, cleaned it and reassembled it repeatedly, until we could quickly perform the whole process blindfolded. It wasn't until the second half of training that we finally got to fire our first live rounds at the qualifying range and it was then that I encountered my first real problems with my first-sergeant, Sergeant Watts.

Watts was among the officers who enjoyed riding and harassing athletes under their charge. These guys saw to it that athletes were assigned the dirtiest, most demeaning jobs and spent more than their share of time on KP, working the mess halls and kitchens. It was the officers' way of letting us know they weren't impressed with anything we might have done prior to being drafted, and reminding us that ballplayers were nothing special.

"You're no ballplayer, you're just a marble player!" Watts would taunt me.

Still, I was able to hold my own and keep up with the rest of the pack, until we began our target training exercises on the firing range. That's when Watts really got on my case. Making no bones about it, he let me know right away that I was the worst marksman he had ever seen.

"I don't believe this, Marble Player!" he screamed. "You couldn't hit a bull in the ass with a spade!" And whether or not he spoke the truth didn't matter. In reality I was terrible, and I didn't need anyone to tell me.

A hardened career-soldier, Sergeant Watts was a lifer who had seen more than his share of combat in Korea. He had been captured, abused and tortured by the enemy in unthinkable ways. At this point, nearing his retirement, he was still tough and wiry, short on patience and would never hesitate to make a spectacle of a recruit who failed to perform up to his standards. Each day, no matter the drill or exercise, there was always someone in our platoon who got his butt chewed.

On the firing range, it was me who didn't measure up to his expectations and he wasted no time in making an example of me. He watched as I missed the mark time and again. His face began to turn a shade of fiery red and it wasn't long before he erupted, yelling and cursing. He was all over me like a cheap suit. Calming down only long enough to make his case, he proposed a wager, betting me that I couldn't hit my target seven consecutive times."I'll tell you what, Marble Player, I'll bet you seven dollars, you can't do it!" he challenged.

The entire platoon gathered around, eager for the contest to begin. "You can do it!" they chanted, egging me on. From behind his dark glasses, Watts gave me a devilish grin, waiting for me to respond. "No bull's-eyes, no dead-ons," he reminded me. "Just hit the target with seven rounds in a row. Any knucklehead can do that!"

All firing had stopped. An unusual silence had come to the firing range. I gazed around to see that all eyes were on me. I squinted across the range at my target. At 100 yards away, the bright cardboard rectangle, or what little of it I could see, appeared blurry and out of focus. "Maybe there's a problem with your rifle," the sergeant sneered. He grabbed my weapon from my hands and began to examine it closely. "Why, it looks like the sight is out of alignment," he remarked with a gibe. "That could be the reason you're having trouble. I'll just make a few minor adjustments and you should be okay." Turning his back, I could tell he was fidgeting with my rifle in some way, but no one could clearly see what he was doing. "There you are!" he told me, handing it back to me. "That should fix your problem."

I raised my rifle and placed the butt squarely against my right shoulder. I squinted at the target, and seeing only a fuzzy image at best, I squeezed off the first two or three rounds and hit nothing, except the earthen bank behind the row of targets. After each shot, "Maggie's drawers," a red signal flag, was waved to indicate that I missed the entire target. A chorus of chuckles came from the onlookers. With arms folded, Sergeant Watts, watched contemptuously, shifting his weight, rocking from heels to toes. "You still have a few rounds to go, Marble Player," he announced for everyone to hear."Let's see what you can do with what's left in that clip."

Humiliated and embarrassed, I rapidly fired the remaining rounds, not even taking time to see if I came close to the target. "Okay, Sarge," I admitted with disgust, "you've made your point. I owe you seven bucks."

"You got that right!" he shot back. "I even adjusted your rifle and you still can't hit shit! You do pretty good when it comes to doing anything with a ball. You can kick a football and throw a baseball. Why, hell, you're probably even good at playing marbles! But when I go to war, I don't need a marble player, I need a soldier!" He paused and looked upward at the sky, as if he was looking for more degrading things to say to me. "I can't believe it," he finally continued, "you gotta be blind to be that bad!"

As dispirited as I was, I began to count the days until boot camp would end. I didn't know what to expect or what to hope for, but I was confident that whatever followed basic training would have to be better. But for the time being, I would have to make the best of it. No doubt, Sergeant Watts would be with me every step of the way, always making my life a little more miserable than it needed to be. Some guys said he was just doing his job, while others felt he enjoyed that part of his work a bit too much. He was a coarse and crusty individual who knew no life other than the army, the sort of individual who would tamper with the sight on another man's rifle, just to win a bet. And while he may have been seven bucks heavier in the pocket for a short time, it was a sure bet that the money I lost to him went to replenish the private stash of liquor he kept hidden in his locker. Nonetheless, to his credit, Watts had made a valid assessment when he attributed my deplorable marksmanship to poor eyesight. In the training room, I couldn't make out diagrams and charts at the front of the class. In the field, I had trouble seeing signs, signals, targets, anything at a distance. Finally, reaching his limit, Watts arranged to have me visit Lieutenant Fox, the optometrist at the base infirmary.

Using beams of light, liquid drops, charts and an assortment of lenses, my eyes were tested and retested. I was issued a pair of prescription eyeglasses which were to be the end-all solution to my vision problems. But as I would soon learn, the army, through a combination of red tape, bureaucracy and paperwork, could always find ways to make things more confusing than they needed to be. Or perhaps, the work required to maintain accurate patient records is a lot more complicated that I ever imagined. Regardless, with my new spectacles, my vision was worse than ever. Somehow, the Coke bottle-thick lenses they prescribed were incorrect, and I was given the wrong glasses. I slipped them on and right away I knew something was terribly wrong. I could hardly see my hand in front of my face! "It may take time," I was told, "but you'll get used to them." What nonsense! After a couple of days of stumbling and bumbling, I was back for another examination and another pair of glasses. This time, with the new ones, I immediately noticed a big improvement. This time, when the fitting was done and it was time to leave, I was able to find the door by myself.

As the weeks dragged by, I continued to mark the time, anticipating our graduation from basic training. In the final weeks, I started my

MOS (Military Occupational Specialty) training to become, of all things, a clerk-typist. Something I could never understand was the reasoning behind my getting that particular assignment. But like so many other things that happened while I was in the army, it was just another surprise. After enduring the rigors and physical conditioning of boot camp, I often wondered why they placed me in an office, training for such a cushy desk job, knowing I could only type 19 words per minute!

Meanwhile, I began to hear stories about other athletes who, after completing their basic training, moved to other bases where sports were a priority. Fort Gordon, near Augusta, Georgia, was a hotbed for basketball and had a room full of championship trophies to prove it. Fort McPherson, just outside of Atlanta, was known far and wide for its formidable baseball team, with many of its core players having arrived there after completing basic training at Fort Jackson. While Fort Jackson on its own was considered a powerhouse among army football teams, I was amazed to learn about the importance that some base commanders placed on sports and the extent to which some were willing to go to secure the best athletes. They were like baseball scouts in search of the best players. They were proud and very competitive, and for these people, winning was a high objective.

With a few weeks still to go in basic training, our unit was involved in grenade combat exercises on the base training field. The guys were lined up, each of us waiting to make our first try at lobbing a live fragmentation grenade. Watts had gone over all the basics of gripping the grenade in the throwing hand and inserting the index finger of the other hand through the pull-ring to remove the pin. "You should be good at this, Marble Player!" he interjected, just to hound me. "You have no problems throwing a baseball or passing a football, so you should have no trouble with this."

I was at the front of the line, about to take my turn, when we were all distracted by a jeep bouncing across the field and speeding directly toward us. In a cloud of dust, the driver brought the vehicle to a skidding stop just a few feet away from where we stood. It was no ordinary motor pool jeep. As we could see from the white star and other markings, this jeep was from the base commander's office. As the dust cleared, the driver hopped out and charged straight for Watts. "Sergeant, I'm here for Private Grba. He's to report to headquarters immediately!" Watts snapped to attention. "Yes sir, right away!" he complied.

With no clue of what was going on, my first thoughts were of my family back home in Chicago. I jumped into the jeep, next to the driver. He jammed the shifter into first gear and popped the clutch, leaving the platoon in another plume of dust and sand. If I were in trouble, I would have been picked up by the MPs, I surmised, so something must have happened to my mother or maybe Deda. The driver looked straight ahead as we sped across the open field.

"Do you mind telling me what this is all about?" I finally asked. "Is there something wrong?"

"Oh, you have nothing to worry about," he assured me. "Aren't you the guy who plays baseball for the Yankees?"

"Well, yes I am," I replied. "But I still don't understand why you're taking me to headquarters. Am I in some sort of trouble? Are you sure there's nothing wrong with my family?"

"Just take it easy, pal. There's nothing for you to worry about. The general just doesn't want you to get hurt. They couldn't risk you ruining your arm messing with those grenades.

"Hurt my arm?" I shrieked. "This is crazy! What does my arm have to do with anything?"

He adjusted his rear-view mirror and peered into it long enough to admire his stylish aviator sunglasses. Pleased with his reflection, he smiled with a hint of conceit before he answered.

"In case you forgot, our baseball team has a big game tomorrow and you're the starting pitcher!"

"Starting pitcher!" I exclaimed. "Are you sure? I didn't realize we had a game tomorrow."

"Well, you know now, and you'd better be ready. We're still in the running for the base championship, so you need to be at your best."

We coasted into a reserved parking space just outside the base command office and headed for the entrance. My driver took one last admiring glance into the mirror.

"You'll get used to it, buddy," he remarked as we walked through the door. "It may take a while, but you'll learn for yourself. You'll soon find out that the army is full of surprises."

-----O--------O--------O-----

Other than a handful of spring training games, we were never teammates, but like me, Don Buddin, an infielder from South Carolina, had spent several seasons in the Red Sox farm system before being called to report for active duty in the military. He had been in the army almost a year when he phoned me from Fort McPherson, where he had been stationed since completing boot camp at Fort Jackson. "It's not too bad down here," he advised me. "We're only a few miles outside of Atlanta, so there's always lots to do. Plus, we've got ourselves a pretty good baseball team here on the base. This year we have another full schedule of more than 100 games, and we sure could use another good pitcher. So, think it over, Eli," he proposed. "I think you'll like it here."

"What's there to think about?" I replied. "I'll be ready to go as soon as basic training is over. Just tell me what I need to do."

"Just keep it under your hat for now," he suggested, "and let me see what I can do. Steve Korcheck, the big catcher from the Senators, is our manager and I'm sure he knows all about you. I'll let him know that you're interested and maybe he can pull some strings. For now, let's just wait and see what happens."

Sticking to our plan, I followed Don's advice and kept the whole idea to myself. Somehow, I managed to survive Sergeant Watts and the final weeks of basic training, and just prior to graduation, I was delighted to receive orders which sent me to Fort McPherson. I was relieved to have the toughest, most difficult part of my hitch behind me, and happy to be moving on to what Don had described to me as "a totally different world."

While the distance between Fort Jackson and Fort McPherson is hardly more than a couple hundred miles on the map, the differences between the two army bases were like night and day. I arrived at Fort McPherson feeling like I had entered the Garden of Eden. The Fort McPherson Colonels, the post's baseball team, had yet to finish their 1957 schedule, so I was immediately added to the roster and got to pitch in a few games soon after I arrived. The Colonels were an incredible ballclub, which featured players with professional experience at almost every spot on the field. Our player-manager, Steve Korcheck, a big leaguer with the Senators, was our starting catcher. Right-handed, Jim Owens, who had been in the Phillies' farm system for several seasons and pitched for them in the majors in both 1955 and 1956, was the workhorse among the pitchers. He had been at Fort McPherson since the start of the season and had the highest totals in wins and innings pitched on the staff.

The list of other pros on the club included Gordy Coleman, a big first baseman from Duke University and the Cleveland Indians system, who could hit the ball a country mile! After getting out of the army, Gordy's name would appear regularly in big league box scores for nine seasons, mostly with the Cincinnati Reds. Marv Breeding was a flashy defensive second-sacker from Alabama, who had played minor league ball for the Orioles and was listed among their prized prospects. Marv, a future major leaguer, was another player who finished basic training at Fort Jackson before getting orders to come to Fort McPherson. However, the speedster of the club was outfielder, Al Spangler, a farmhand for the Milwaukee Braves who, like Coleman, attended Duke University before being drafted into the army. In his early 20s, Al could run the bases and chase down fly balls as well as anyone in the game. And he would continue to do so until the early 1970s, when his 13-year career in the major leagues would come to a close.

With such a talent-laden club, the Colonels seemed to have all the right ingredients to take the All-Army Baseball Championship for the second consecutive season in 1957. Pitching, speed, defense, slugging and hitting for average were all in place as we traveled to all parts of the country, defeating the teams of every army base in our path. Unfortunately, our Waterloo was waiting for us in the form of a power-hitting team from Fort Carson, Colorado, a team stocked with future major league players, who were still relatively unknown at the time.

Future sluggers, Willie Kirkland, Leon Wagner, J.C. Hartman and George Altman were all in the batting order of Fort Carson, while their pitching corps included Bob Bruce, a minor league right-hander from the Detroit Tigers and a singing knuckleballer named Charley Pride, who was about to become one of country music's brightest recording stars. But it was Bruce, who would go on to play nine years in the big leagues, who shut the Colonels down by pitching a three-hitter against us, relegating Fort McPherson to runner-up status for the '57 season.

The U.S. Army provided me with what turned out to be the wackiest two years of my life. I met men who were characters, revolting and unsavory. I also met men of character, men who exhibited honesty and integrity, men who garnered my respect. I played another season of baseball at Fort McPherson with many of the same guys from the previous year. And sure, it wasn't the pros, but at least it was baseball.

However, the time each of us lost from our individual baseball careers to fulfill our military obligations is time we could never recover. And military service, while it is both a necessary and noble duty, will always be a primary reason why there are so many "what ifs" that can be justly inserted into discussions about baseball records and history. Nevertheless, in my case, it was a matter of only two years spent in the army. But for other, more notable players who had a significant impact on the game, record-setting careers were often selflessly sacrificed during times of war. These men left the game of baseball to protect and defend our country, risking their lives as they served willingly, claiming it was their patriotic duty. It is these individuals who served in all branches of our military, who will always have my utmost admiration and respect.

The Ft. McPherson baseball team of 1957 was loaded with talent. Several players on the club would be signing major league contracts soon after completing their military obligations, including: back row (left to right) Jim Owens, Phillies; Gordy Coleman, Reds; me, Yankees, Marv Breeding, Orioles and Tom Cheney, Cardinals (top right).

CHAPTER 21

"I BELIEVE YOU'RE READY FOR THE BIG LEAGUES!"

———

I t is impossible to fathom the powerful influence a father can have on his growing son. Even when he is least aware, a father is continuously fostering and teaching his son by the example he sets. There is no way for a father to escape the eyes and ears of his young son, which are always open and ready to receive and process everything his father says and does. It's been said, "Every father should remember that one day his son will follow his example instead of his advice." Yet it is important to note that this should not be perceived as a broad-brush justification for anyone's attitudes or behaviors. Nor should it be used as an excuse by any man who refuses to be accountable or responsible for his plight in life. God has given each of us a free will to choose between right and wrong. Moreover as individuals, we each make choices which will ultimately shape our destiny and determine our life's path.

A father should be close by to provide instruction and guidance throughout his son's formative years. He should be involved in everything, from kicking a football to fixing a flat tire. A boy should also have the benefit of observing his father's temperament and language when reacting to things such as burnt pancakes or misplaced car keys. In my particular situation, I had uncles and a grandfather who did a wonderful job of recognizing the voids in my upbringing and took their time to do what they could to fill them. However, there is no viable substitution for a true father.

Because of Dad's absence for much of my life, I missed out on a lot of father and son experiences, which may have better prepared me for both the working and social worlds I was about to enter. As a teenager and even in my 20s, I was clueless when it came to things such as girls and dating, using basic hand tools, building a fire or even tying my own necktie, basic things that every boy should know. Not knowing about many of these things clearly put me at an early disadvantage, but with determination, maturity and the help of others, I was able to find my way through many of life's social obstacles. But the more painful and deep-rooted emotional impact which I have lived with for so long stems from the vicious physical attacks my dad perpetrated on my mother, along with all the other life-ruining effects brought about by his abuse of alcohol. Yet, this man was my father, and because of that and what I have learned and lived through myself, I continue to blame the alcohol, not the alcoholic.

With all of his weaknesses and his inability to ward off such a devastating disease, my father was a good man. He was a hard worker, a gifted athlete and honest in his dealings. He had many friends, good intent and a kind heart. And knowing him as I did, I am certain that in times of sobriety, his heart ached when he acknowledged the hurt he imposed on those who loved him. Surely, he felt the pain and regret whenever he reflected on the chance he once had to be a husband and father, and whenever he looked back at the life that could have been.

Nevertheless, a father's example will often do more to set a pattern for his son than serve as a warning. Australian novelist, David Gregory Roberts, wrote, "Fate's way of beating us in a fair fight is to give us warnings that we have, but never heed."

I am sure my dad felt pain and regret whenever he reflected on the chance he once had to be a husband and a father, and whenever he looked back at the life that could have been.

Once I left home to play baseball, I began to drink more frequently. During my time in the army my drinking increased. With alcohol available almost everywhere, it was pleasantly alluring, and it appeared harmless. Moreover, I was never pressured or coerced by anyone to drink; not by friends, family, teammates or anyone. It was a path on which I started willingly.

Looking for fun along with some of my baseball buddies at Fort McPherson, I played beer-gulping games, placing bets to see who among us could slug down the most beer before having to make a desperate dash for the men's room. We even went as far as to donate our blood just to pick up a few extra bucks for beer! Suddenly without realizing it, the fun and games of drinking had become a lifelong addiction.

So what were the warning signs that I missed, and which ones did I ignore? Were they the same ones that were overlooked by my father and his father before him? I was vulnerable, naive and in denial. And sadly, there are even greater dangers and temptations out there in today's world waiting to claim another victim. Still the search for answers goes on and researchers continue to work to zero in on causes and solutions for this dreaded addiction.

Denial is one of the first warning signs of any addiction. It is a transparent way for an addict to lie to himself and justify to others. And during the time I spent conjuring explanations for my drinking, I was denying myself a chance to a look at the real root of the problem. "This is just a temporary phase," I told myself. "I don't have a problem, and even if I did, I'd be the first to know."

In a 42-year-career, which began with enlistment in 1916, General Thomas F. Hickey experienced just about everything the U.S. Army had to offer. He fought in both World Wars and Korea. He was wounded in combat and was highly decorated, receiving an assortment of prestigious medals and awards. And prior to his retirement in 1958, he enjoyed the last years of his career in peacetime status as commander of the Third Army, headquarterd at Fort McPherson. A lifelong baseball fan from Boston, General Hickey devoted a great deal of his time and attention to the game at McPherson and worked hard to put together some of the finest teams ever to compete in army baseball. Moreover, it was his love of the game that made life good for the ballplayers stationed there. Other than keeping our barracks clean and in order and an occasional close-order drill, our work centered around baseball, traveling to road games and keeping the Fort McPherson home field ready for play. Of course General Hickey attended our games and was known to drop by the ball field while we were caring for the grounds and during workouts. He knew all the players by name and would often start friendly conversations with us, which as a rule infuriated our direct officers. But what could they say? We were just living the coveted and privileged life of a baseball player at Fort McPherson, Georgia.

I got out of the army in March, 1959, and immediately headed to DeLand, Florida, to join the Yankees in spring training. By this time, the Yankees had dropped their minor league affiliate in Denver and were back to operating only one AAA club, that being the Richmond Virginians of the International League. My contract assigned me to the Richmond club, a team which was a sure-fire winner on paper, but would go on to finish the season in fourth place in an eight-team league.

The 1959 Virginians were managed by Steve Souchock, a former first baseman and outfielder who had played eight seasons in the American

League, mostly with the Yankees and Tigers. But, of course, it was the one season he spent in a White Sox uniform that I remember most. I always seem to recall the guys who played in Chicago more readily than the others, even if their stay in the Windy City was a brief one. Even before his playing career had ended, Steve had set his sights on becoming a manager, and the Yankees sure gave him a legitimate shot. With many of his clubs finishing in the second division, he managed at just about every level in the Yank's farm system, but AAA Richmond would be as high as he would ever go.

Overall, the Virginians were well stocked when it came to offensive firepower. Outfielders, Deron Johnson, Jim Pisoni and Jack Reed were all capable of hitting the long ball. And first baseman, Frank Leja, a tall lefthanded-hitting slugger from Massachusetts, was getting as much attention as any prospect who had come through the Yankee chain in years. Frank hit for both power and average in the minor leagues, but because of injuries and other problems, he was never able get on track as a big leaguer. Nonetheless, during his time with Richmond, he was one of the most feared batters in the IL. The Virginians could also count on steady hitting from infielders, Fritz Brickell, Clete Boyer and Curt Roberts. All three had previous major league experience and were top-notch defensive players.

The pitching corps was anchored by starters, Zach Monroe, Jim Bronstad and Bill Short, who all had outstanding seasons in '59. But it was right-handed reliever, Johnny James, who proved to be a model of consistency. Souchock called on him more than anyone else in his bullpen and Johnny responded brilliantly, leading the International League in appearances and finishing the year with the circuit's second best earned run average.

Working primarily in a relief role, I was given a lot of chances to pitch during the first half of the season. I was happy to find that my sinker still had that sudden downward break, which helped me pick up more strikeouts and ground ball outs. When I first arrived at spring training, I had been concerned that I might have lost some of my sharpness while serving in the army. However, I was pleased to find that I had good command of all of my pitches, and my control was as sharp as ever. By mid-season I had won five games and lost only one, and the speculative rumors about who among us should expect a call to join the big club were starting to circulate around the Richmond clubhouse.

As a club, the Virginians of 1959 never lived up to their full potential, but it was still a great time to be part of the International League. The league was very competitive with each team carrying a combination of experienced veterans and promising young prospects. However, one of the most engaging features of the league, and one that made it truly international, was the geographical locations of the eight clubs. With our home ballpark, Parker Field in Richmond, being somewhat a central point, the other cities represented in the league extended as far southward as Havana, Cuba, and as far to the north as Montreal. Southern road trips also took us to Miami for games against the Marlins, the Orioles' top farm team, while northern swings included stops in Buffalo to play the Bisons as well as the Maple Leafs in Toronto.

Even though Fidel Castro had come to power in Cuba just a few months earlier, the Havana Sugar Kings, the AAA affiliate of the Cincinnati Reds, stayed on as an entry in the International League and it was our visits to Havana that I recall for having as much fun as any place my travels in baseball ever took me.

In the spring of '59 downtown Havana was still a bustling resort city, a trendy hot spot for vacationers, gamblers and tourists. On practically every street corner, there was a nightclub, restaurant or casino. But it was the Capri Hotel and Casino which was the most popular of all the nightspots in the city, even if it was the most difficult for gaining admittance. Hollywood actor, George Raft, who was known to have connections with the criminal underworld, worked as the front man for their club and casino operations, and he was usually there mingling with patrons and gamblers each evening until the wee hours of morning. At the same time as our stop in Havana, the cast and production crew of the box office hit, *Our Man in Havana*, were in town for the filming of the movie, of which several scenes were actually filmed on location at the Capri. Maureen O'Hara, Alec Guinness, Ernie Kovacs, Burl Ives and other cast members were regularly spotted in the club after-hours, generating a lot of attention from the public. Still, the hotel security staff saw to it that these celebrities were well guarded from all their fans and nosey admirers. Yet I found it amusing how once local reporters learned that a New York Yankee farm team was also staying in town, some of us players suddenly achieved popularity and were invited to meet a few of the stars. How ironic it was, when the following edition of the morning newspaper ran a large photo of me, teammate Johnny James and the lovely Ms. Maureen

O'Hara, posing together on the rooftop gardens of the Capri Hotel. For that brief moment, I was keeping grand company!

A few weeks later I had another unforgettable on-the-road experience when we visited Montreal to play the Royals, the Dodgers' top minor league team in a weekend series at their stylish old ballpark, Delorimier Stadium. While this situation was just as memorable as having my picture taken with Maureen O'Hara, thankfully, it was never publicized, nor was it nearly as dignified.

Our team was staying downtown at the Mount Royal Hotel, one of the oldest and most elegant hotels in the entire city of Montreal. Over the years, the guestbook at the Mount Royal had included as guests famous luminaries, ranking heads of state and even royalty from other nations. Naturally, the accommodations there were well above the standards of anyone playing minor league baseball. Everyone on the ballclub was grateful that the Yankees chose such a ritzy place to put us up, especially since they were covering the tab.

My roommate was veteran backstop, Billy Shantz, the same guy, who years earlier was coordinator for the Yankees' winter league team in Panama. But by this time, he was in the part-time role of backup catcher for the Virginians. Billy had reached his early thirties and was playing out the string on what had been a relatively lengthy career in professional baseball. He was happy to still be playing ball and enjoying the good life and all the benefits that were part of his chosen profession. Billy loved the travel, dining in the best restaurants and staying in the finest hotels. He knew that for him, it wasn't going to last much longer.

It was midmorning when Billy and I finally left our room and headed out for breakfast in the hotel dining room. Perhaps we weren't fully awake when we sauntered out into the hallway, as it took a few moments of pressing the same button over and over for us to realize that the elevator we were hoping to ride had been shut down and taken out of service. Not to be denied, we stepped to the side and began pressing the button for the adjacent elevator. It was a long way to the ground floor, we figured, and still too early in the day for a couple of able-bodied athletes to have to tromp down the stairwell. With no other passengers onboard, the second elevator soon arrived at our floor, the doors slid open and we stepped in, giving no thoughts to why the power had been shut off to the other car. Billy and I had no clue that minutes earlier, the hotel had been put in security mode. With no one to warn us, we had just wandered into a restricted off-limits area.

Without stopping at any other floor, our car descended. With no idea that Queen Elizabeth II, the Queen of England herself, was visiting the Mount Royal Hotel, Billy and I were silently whetting our appetites for the hot coffee and omelets we were about to enjoy when we came to a stop and the doors slowly opened. At first I noticed the trail of bright red carpet on the floor, running from the elevator door and extending far into the lobby. It seemed to go on forever. There was a crowd of onlookers standing there facing the elevator door, watching and waiting for something special and exciting to happen. The red carpet immediately put me in mind of the top rated TV program, *This Is Your Life!* which was peaking in popularity at the time. The live, real-time show was known for treating their guests like royalty, giving each one the red carpet treatment as they were brought onto the set. Stepping out of the elevator and onto the red carpet, I quickly spotted the faces of a few of my teammates among the gathering, Johnny James and Billy Short among them. The group was obviously anticipating the arrival of someone a lot more important than the two of us, but that wasn't enough to stop me from missing a chance to ham it up and try to get a laugh from the folks looking on. I walked boldly down the red carpet, one step after another. With my head held high and my arms stretched forward, I announced to everyone within earshot: "Eli Grba... THIS IS YOUR LIFE!"

Before I could take another step, members of the Queen's armed Royal Guards lunged at me from out of nowhere and in an instant, they were all over me like spots on a firehouse dog! Guards grabbed me by each of my shoulders. They each took one of my wrists and quickly snapped my arms upward behind my back. An uneasy stillness fell across the astonished bystanders as I was manhandled and hustled away to another part of the room. Yet, I couldn't help but pick out my good buddy, Johnny James, at the front of the crowd, pointing at me and laughing his butt off.

It took a few minutes, but I finally satisfied the guardsmen with answers which convinced them that I was, in fact, nothing more than a clueless baseball player who didn't know when to quit horsing around. Billy was also detained, but was never questioned to the extent I was. Perhaps the bodyguards considered his mature demeanor to be less threatening to the Queen's well-being than my attention-grabbing antics. Once they were satisfied with our innocence and accepted our story of how we had simply been in the wrong place at the wrong time, we were allowed to continue on our way to the dining room. I could feel the blood rush to my face as I followed Billy to our table. I surveyed the room just long enough to see that every eye in the place was on us as we were being seated. I took a sip from my water glass and peered over my menu only to see Johnny James approaching our table, flaunting a grin that extended from one of his ears to the other.

"Good mornin', boys," he greeted us, bobbing his head flippantly. "I see you guys have already made your presence known this morning. And it's too bad, Eli, that you've already stolen the show. Queen Elizabeth is about to step off the elevator at any moment, but there's no way she can make a grand entrance that will compare to the one I just saw!"

"Don't be so annoying, Johnny," I told him. "Go sit down and enjoy your breakfast!"

"Sure thing, Eli," he agreed unconvincingly. "But first, I just want to say that as I was watching your live version of *This Is Your Life,* I couldn't help but notice how nicely your red face matched the Queen's red carpet!"

My bottom jaw tightened. Trying to ignore him, I stared down at my menu, pretending to read each item until he finally walked away.

All these many years later I look back on my career and somehow I don't think I would have ever made it in baseball had it not been for great teammates like Johnny James. He was the sort of guy who was always there when I needed him. Best of all, he's still a great friend today.

That same season of 1959, we made another northern road trip, which took us back to Canada, and as usual, we made back-to-back stops in the cities of Montreal and Toronto. Under the management of ex-Brooklyn Dodger star, Dixie Walker, the Toronto Maple Leafs were beginning to slip in the IL standings after having been one of the showcase clubs of the league in recent seasons. Still, Toronto was a great baseball city with a friendly, old-styled ballpark and a solid following of devoted fans.

With a couple of hours to relax before I needed to be at the ballpark for a night game against the Maple Leafs, I returned to our hotel after a late lunch. Stopping in the lobby to pick up my room key, I soon found myself engrossed in small talk with a lovely young Canadian girl working the front desk. And while she was probably about the age of twenty or so, she had an adorable gleaming smile, which radiated the charm and innocence of a young schoolgirl.

"Are you one of the baseball players?" she asked, passing me the key.

"It all depends," I answered playfully. "It all depends on whether being a baseball player is a good thing or a bad thing."

"Well, I guess you are," she admitted shyly. "You just didn't seem to be like the others. The other ballplayers who stay here at this hotel aren't nearly as courteous and friendly as you."

Enjoying the playful chitchat as well as the flattering compliments, I didn't want the conversation to end. Like me, she seemed to be in no hurry to go anywhere, so I decided to ask the only obvious question I could think of.

"Well, tell me, are you a baseball fan? Do you go to many games?"

"I'm not sure," she answered, stringing me along. "I've never been to a real game."

"Well, we can change that very easily," I offered. "If you're free tonight, I can leave a ticket for you for tonight's game at the gate of Maple Leaf Stadium. You can come as my guest. All I will need is your name."

I'll never know for sure if it was really her first game, but she did show up at the ballpark that evening. The next day, we had another friendly conversation at the hotel, where she invited me to drop by her place for a visit. Things were progressing very quickly. We had met only two days earlier and I already had her phone number and the address of the house which she shared with her mother. This relationship was about to shift into high gear and move into the fast lane.

Wearing my best sport shirt and a splash of Ice Blue Aqua Velva, I stepped out the taxi, handed the driver a couple of bucks, which included a generous tip, and headed up the sidewalk to her front door. I felt a swagger of confidence in my walk. I was excited by the possibilities that lay ahead.

With that same wholesome yet inviting smile, she welcomed me inside and led me from the small foyer into the living room. There her mother was sitting in a large fanback chair, quietly reading a magazine. A very attractive and well dressed lady in her forties, she was friendly and pleasant as well. In spite of her age, this middle-aged mom still had everything necessary to turn a man's head. It was easy for me to see how alluring beauty ran in their family. After a quick introduction, I was taken by the hand and whisked out of the room.

"We're going to my room for a while, Mother" she advised. "We won't be going out anywhere."

"That's fine, dear," the mother replied without concern. "I think I'll be staying in tonight, too. And by the way, it was nice meeting you, Eli," she added.

I was led down a short hallway to her bedroom. She closed the door behind us and pulled down the shade of the only window in the room. Soon the fires of physical passion were flaming high. At first, we only sat on the edge of her bed. But in no time, we were squirming and writhing from one side of the four-poster to the other. Using just one hand, she began to systematically unfasten the buttons on my new sport shirt and with the other, she removed my glasses. This little innocent white lily was proving to be a lot more aggressive than I had ever anticipated. With each of her advances, I became more aroused. My heart was pounding like a bass drum. Suddenly, she hopped up from the bed, startling me. She stood facing me and with her blouse completely unbuttoned, she started to douse the flames of passion. She wanted to stop.

"We can't, Eli, we have to stop!" she exclaimed. "We can't do this!"

"What do you mean? What's the problem?" I asked, baffled and confused. "Is it your mother? Is it me? What's going on?"

"It's very difficult for me to talk about," she explained. "It has nothing to do with you and it's not about my mom. But I..."

Before she could continue I reached out, took her hand and pulled her closer. I gently brushed a tear from her cheek, trying my best to console her. Naturally, as a 24 year-old male, I also had my own interests in mind, and I wasn't about to let the curtain come down on this romantic escapade so soon, not if I could help it.

"There now, it's gonna be all right," I assured her. "Let's just take it easy and let nature take its course," I urged. "There's no cause to be upset."

In no time we were both back on the bed, passionately kissing, caressing and rolling about, well on our way to a session of steamy, vibrant lovemaking. All the while, her mother remained just down the hall, making for an eerie situation for me but one of little concern to my lover. "Oh, well," I thought, "Different people have different ways of doing things." It was one of the most bizarre evenings I can ever remember. I only wish I had been smarter and a lot more careful.

The next day, following our final game with the Maple Leafs, we flew back home to Richmond. Our road trips to the north usually had us playing games in four different International League cities before returning home. Sometimes these trips would often take as long as two weeks and by the time we returned home, everyone on the club had had his fill of traveling. By then everyone was looking forward to sleeping in his own bed. Regardless of the number of games won or lost on the road, it always felt good to get back home.

After getting a day off for travel, we resumed our schedule with the start of a homestand at Parker Field, the home ballpark of the Virginians. A quaint little two-level stadium built during the Great Depression, Parker Field was situated in the central portion of Richmond, just north of the James River. In the clubhouse, prior to the first game of the series, I was at my locker, suiting up when our skipper, Steve Souchock, came scurrying past. "Hey, Grubsy!" he called as he hurried by, "Get ready, big guy!" Before I could slow him down and find out what he was up to, he was gone and out the door. *That sure was strange. When did anyone ever have to remind me to get ready for anything?*

We were outside on the field going through our usual pregame drills. I did my normal amount of running in the outfield with the other pitchers and followed that up with a few minutes stretching. I spent a short time throwing from the mound in the bullpen, just enough to loosen up my arm, but I could tell something wasn't right. I didn't feel well, and I knew it was more than just the long tiring trip back from Toronto that had me feeling weak and exhausted. Sure, it was early July and the East Coast heat and humidity were beginning to settle in for the summer. But after such a light, easy workout, my energy level was surprisingly low. I went back to my locker to put on my game top. I paused to take a few gulps from the drinking fountain and stepped into the men's room to take one last leak before the start of the game. That's when I knew something was dreadfully wrong.

The painful burning was excruciating! I stopped for a moment, took a deep breath and tried to go again, but the sting was too much. I couldn't bear to finish. I was sweating profusely and my knees felt like rubber. I zipped up my fly, picked up my glove and started outside. I wanted to grab a seat in the bullpen, get off my feet and take it easy as soon as I could. Just as I walked past the dugout and onto the field, Souchock yelled to me again. "Hey, Grubsy, get ready!" By this time I wasn't feeling well enough to even bother myself with what he was saying. Perhaps it was just more of his annoying pep talk. Besides, I was preoccupied by a much more serious matter. I was becoming more anxious by the minute. I was certainly no doctor and had no medical training. But I knew enough to suspect that I was in big trouble. There was no doubt, I had contracted a sexually transmitted disease, the one souvenir I wish I hadn't brought back from Toronto. "How dumb could you be!" I scolded myself. "How could you be so careless?"

It was a long night in the bullpen, but somehow I survived and made it through the game. As uncomfortable as I was, I considered myself lucky that Souchock didn't even call on me to warm up, or much worse, bring me in to pitch. Once the final out was made, I headed straight for the clubhouse. I didn't wait for any of the other guys in the pen or stop to speak to anyone along the way. I had one thing on my mind and that was making my way to the men's room. I needed to go badly, and I was determined to go, even if it killed me!

After finishing that very painful task at the urinal, I trudged slowly over to my locker. I was intentionally ignoring the buzzing activity going on around me. I just wanted to get dressed, get back to my apartment and crawl into bed. *Maybe it will all be better in the morning.*

"Hey, Grba!" Someone yelled from across the room. "The skipper's been looking for you. He wants to see you in his office right away."

"Oh, boy!" I mumbled. "That is just what I need, a meeting with the manager." I slammed the door on my locker, slung a clean towel over my shoulder and started for the office. I wondered what sort of trouble I was in this time. I found the door open, so I walked right in without saying a word. Souchock was seated behind his desk.

"Come on in, Grubsy," he offered. "And close the door behind you."

"What's up, Skip?" I asked. "You wanted to see me?"

"Why sure, Grubsy. I got a little bit of good news for you, but you don't seem to be feeling well. Is everything okay?"

"Sure it is," I answered, trying to use a more convincing tone. "I guess I must still be a little tired after the long road trip."

"Well, that's to be expected, Grubsy," he said, getting up from his seat. "That's fine. Just turn in early tonight and I'm sure you'll feel a lot better after a good night's sleep."

I didn't know when I had ever seen Souchock so upbeat and chummy. Normally Steve didn't speak to me unless he was being a wise ass. At least it was good to learn that I hadn't been called in there to be chewed out.

"Well you know, I've been telling you to get ready," he reminded me. "And I hope you are, because you going to the big leagues tomorrow!"

My jaw dropped in disbelief. I couldn't believe what I just heard. The mere thought of going to New York to join the Yankees made me lightheaded. It was what I had worked for all my life, and suddenly it was like a dream come true. And that's exactly how I felt, dizzy, as if I were in a dream. "Are you sure?" I asked, needing assurance.

"Sure I am," he answered forcefully. "The big club has been wanting to call you up there for quite some time, and now they have an open spot. Now you'll need to come back here tomorrow and clear your locker," he continued, reaching to shake my hand. "Your airline tickets will be waiting for you. You are to fly into LaGuardia Airport tomorrow afternoon. They are expecting you at Yankee Stadium in time for tomorrow night's game." He paused, waiting to get a reaction, but I just sat there speechless. Well, what do you think about that, Grubsy?" he prodded. "Are you ready for this?" My head was swirling. I had so many thoughts rushing through my mind, I couldn't muster an answer. "Well, I think you are," he affirmed, giving me a hearty pat on the back. "You sure deserve it, Grubsy, you really do. I believe you're ready for the big leagues!"

CHAPTER 22
THE PITCHER WITH THE FUNNY NAME

It was supposed to have been my time to shine, my moment in the sun. Making it to the major leagues was the one goal I had strived for since Chuck Koney signed me to my first pro contract with the Boston Red Sox six years earlier. I was on my way to New York to join the Yankees at their home, the place known as *The House That Ruth Built*, Yankee Stadium. It was a spectacular day, the kind that schoolboys dream of, but very few ever get a chance to experience. It was to be my golden moment, but things weren't going quite the way I had envisioned. I had always anticipated that my arrival in the big leagues would be a happy event, a day that I would cherish and remember the rest of my life. And it could have been a wonderful day, had it not been for the misery I had brought upon myself for being so dumb and careless.

During the flight from Richmond to New York, I was still feeling slow and listless and the dreadful pain I experienced every time I went to the bathroom was almost unbearable. Unsure about what I was dealing with and what to do about it, I was growing increasingly concerned and apprehensive. "I'm about to miss out on the opportunity of a lifetime," I told myself. "There's no way I can pitch in this condition."

Our descent pattern was well underway, and we were only minutes away from landing at LaGuardia. I watched nervously out of my window as the glittering lights of New York City grew closer. It had been a relatively quiet late-day flight, but as the landing drew near, the cabin came alive with activity and conversation. Trays were being secured in the upright position while some folks fidgeted with the reading lamps above their seats. Other passengers who had been asleep since we boarded the airplane in Richmond were roused from their naps by the snapping and clacking of overhead compartment doors.

"This is not the way we normally approach LaGuardia," I overheard a remark. "I'm on this flight every week and this is the first time we've flown directly over The Bronx. The observant passenger took another look through his window across the aisle. "Yeah, usually these pilots will veer away from the most heavily populated areas," he continued. "It's all about safety, you know, and I used to fly planes years ago," he boasted. "But we could never get away with anything like this."

While most people sitting nearby ignored this talkative old guy, some seemed to be miffed by getting an unsolicited lesson on aviation. I wasn't sure if he knew what he was talking about, but to me, he sounded reasonable. Unexpectedly, the plane, flying at an even slower speed, banked to its starboard side, dipping its right wing. The captain turned on the plane's speaker system and asked for everyone's attention.

"Ladies and gentlemen, we'll be landing in just a moment, but as we make a southerly approach from The Bronx into LaGuardia, look to your right and you'll see Yankee Stadium. It's one of the great landmarks of the city and the home of the World Champion, New York Yankees. Also, on behalf of the entire crew, I want to say thank you for choosing to fly with us."

As if to take a bow and pay tribute to a sacred shrine, the pilot again lowered the starboard wing, pointing the green navigation light on the wingtip directly at the stadium. The view was breathtaking! The stately old ballpark, fully illuminated and rising high above her surroundings, seemed quiet and still, but ready to receive the tens of thousands of Yankee fans who would soon be passing through her turnstiles. It was a Wednesday night, and the visiting opponents for that game were, of all teams, the Boston Red Sox. Suddenly the question occurred to me. *Why was this alternative approach route being taken into LaGuardia? And could it be possible this pilot knew that one of his passengers was the newest Yankee? Could he have gone out of his way to give me a special unique look at my new place of employment?*

Suddenly my mind was filled with thoughts of some of the great Yankees of the past who had played in that historic park. I recalled the things I had heard about the rich history and longstanding traditions associated with the Yankees. The names Ruth, Gehrig and DiMaggio popped into my mind. Those names are at the top of the list of baseball's all-time greats. Yet at the same time, I began to question my own worthiness. *Is this where I belong? Do I deserve to put on the pinstriped uniform like these immortals wore? Should I even be on the same field with Mickey Mantle, Yogi Berra and Whitey Ford?*

I had been in New York for only a short time when I realized I had landed in a different world. The icy indifference and the impersonal hustle n' bustle, which are just as much part of life in the Big Apple as Broadway shows and the Statue of Liberty, were the sort of things I had prepared myself to expect. However, I wasn't prepared to be cast into the public spotlight quite so soon. I quickly saw for myself just how seriously fans in New York took their baseball. Of course, the wounds caused by the Dodgers and Giants leaving town were still fresh, and the arrival of the expansion Mets was still a few years away. So New York baseball fans were thrust into the unfamiliar and precarious position of having only one big league team: the Yankees. And for four years, 1958 through 1961, the Bronx Bombers were subjected not only to the praise, but also to all the wrath and ire that the press and fans of New York could produce. For Yankee players, it was life in a fishbowl!

After retrieving my luggage from the airport carousel, I caught a taxi for the eight-mile-trip from LaGuardia to the ballpark. With my one suitcase, I climbed into the back seat and reached for the handle to close the door behind me. The door was no sooner shut than the driver grabbed the lever on the dash, resetting his meter. "Where to, Mac?" he asked impatiently.

"Yankee Stadium," I replied impassively, hoping to sound as detached as he did. However, my answer perked his attention. This time, he looked at me in his rearview mirror as he spoke to me.

"Well, tell me deh, buddy, are you with da' Yanks? I mean, do you play for 'em?" Now this guy's big city accent was as heavy as they come, but his tone toward me was becoming a lot more personable.

"Yes, I do," I responded proudly. "And I don't have a lot of time. We've got a night game with Boston."

The young cabbie was quiet as we made our way to the airport's exit ramp. I could sense he was putting the pieces of the puzzle together in his head. He took another quick glance at me in the mirror, struggling to put a name with my face.

"You must be Goi-bah, da new pitcher they just called up. Aw you him?"

"Yeah, buddy, that's me," I conceded, trying to hide my surprise.

"Well, it's in all da papers," he continued. "And papers all say they can sure use some help outta' da bullpen."

It was tricky, but I managed to sit quietly for the rest of the drive, acting as if being recognized was nothing new, just another everyday occurrence. In about 20 minutes we rolled to a stop at the players' entrance at the stadium. Like a flash, the driver hopped out of the cab, grabbed my bag and brought it around the car to the sidewalk. "Good luck to ya', Goi-bah," he said, shaking my hand like I was his best friend. "I'll be pullin' for ya'."

I took a few steps toward the door, mindful of the significance of the moment. "This is it," I whispered to myself. "This is what you've dreamed about since grade school and now, I've finally made it to the majors."

Who knows what's waiting inside that door? Will anyone be expecting me? Do these guys talk to rookies? Will they have a locker ready for me? I hope arrangements are all set and they're waiting for my arrival. Wouldn't it be great if these guys read the newspapers as thoroughly as a New York City cab driver?

I suppose it was because of TV or newspapers that a few of the guys in the clubhouse looked familiar. But with everything I was dealing with, I was in no frame of mind to start trying to put names with the faces. Pitcher, Jim Bronstad, a long, tall Texan who had been called up to the Yankees a couple of weeks earlier, must have seen me when I walked in, noticed how lost and uncertain I was and came to my aid. We had become good friends at Richmond, so he was quick to give me a hearty welcome. We had both been pitching pretty well before getting promoted to the big club, but he was obviously disappointed with the way things had gone for him so far with the Yankees.

"I hope you're bringing me good luck," he said half kiddingly. "So far I've had a rough time of it. They've given me a couple of starts and

I've pitched my ass off, but somehow, I dropped both of them. So, who knows how much longer I'll be up here?"

"You'll be okay, Jim," I assured him. "You'll turn it around. But tell me, who do I need to talk to? "

Without getting as much as a curious nod or a scrutinizing stare from anyone, I followed Jim across the room to a short corridor. "Right in here, Grubsy," he pointed. "The first door is Casey's office. Just go in and let him know you're here and he'll get you fixed up."

Bronstad walked away, leaving me to fend for myself. The partially opened door was only a few feet away. I stepped closer and tentatively rapped on the door. Inside that office was Casey Stengel, one of the most famous managers in baseball history. That's when the significance of the moment struck me. My throat became dry, making it difficult to swallow. I was about to meet the man who had led the Yankees to seven World Series Championships and two American League pennants in the past ten years. With no concern about who was knocking on his door, he invited me in. "Just come on in," he offered. "The door's open."

There, behind the desk sat the one and only, Casey Stengel, the "Old Professor," a fellow almost 70 years-old, who had played his first game in the major leagues in 1912. With a pencil in one hand and another resting behind his ear, he sat mumbling to himself, seemingly frustrated with his paperwork. He slowly looked up and quickly realized he had permitted a stranger to enter his office. He began giving me the once-over, staring at me, scanning me from head to toe. I suppose my suitcase gave it away, but he finally concluded who I was.

"How do you do, young man?" he asked with a slightly Midwestern accent. "You must be the new fellow up from Richmond, the pitcher with the funny name."

"Yes sir, that's me," I replied. "I'm Eli Grba... pronounced Ger-bah."

"Sure, I've got it," he assured me. "Ger-bah ...Ger-bah," he repeated, filing it away in his memory. "That name's a little different, but it shouldn't be too difficult to remember."

From the very moment I walked into his office, Casey seemed distracted. No doubt, he was dealing with other, more pressing issues than meeting a new rookie pitcher whose name he would never remember. The first time I met him would be the only time he would call me by my name as from then on I was simply, "the pitcher the funny name." But I would soon find that anytime I spoke to him, or he with me, he would always appear to be uninterested and preoccupied by something more important. Fortunately, it only took a few minutes for Casey to tell me everything he had to say. I was still dealing with a pressing issue of my own. I was feeling terrible and in desperate need of medical help for a condition which was only getting worse.

Yankee manager, Casey Stengel, played his first major league game in 1912. The first time I met him would be the only time he would call me by my name as from then on I was simply, "the pitcher with the funny name."

With the help of "Big Pete" Sheehy, the Yankees' longtime clubhouse manager, I found my locker, but spent only enough time there to drop off my suitcase and see that he had provided me with everything I needed to suit up. An engraved name tag with GRBA had been mounted above the locker. Placed inside was a cap, stirrups and belt and a complete home uniform: white with navy blue pinstripes and the number 47 sewn on the back of the wool flannel jersey. For decades, the Yankee uniform had remained unchanged, featuring its trademark logo, the interlocking N and Y, symbolic of the most revered uniform in all of professional sports. Suddenly, my thoughts became reflective. It was difficult to imagine how far I had come to reach this point. It had been a winding, treacherous path, but somehow I had made it all the way to the New York Yankees. "Now is the time to do your best," I reminded myself. "But first I need to get help."

Across the room I spotted a partially opened door with an attached sign reading "GUS MAUCH -- TEAM TRAINER." I walked closer and got a whiff of liniment and rubbing alcohol. Inside I could see shelves stocked with jars and bottles. There were stacks of clean white linens and towels. Without giving it a lot of thought, it seemed like a good place to start. I stuck my head inside and tapped on the door. "Are you in here, Gus?" I asked politely. "Are you open for business?"

From behind the door, Gus stepped into view, drying his hands with one towel, while a second one draped across his shoulder. "Yes sir, I'm always open for business," he answered in a pleasant voice. "And what can I do for you?" Before I could reply, he took a quick look at me and knew immediately who I was. "Oh, you must be Eli, the new pitcher from Richmond," he concluded. "Welcome to the Yankees."

I sheepishly explained my predicament to Gus, and to my relief, he passed no judgment, reassuring me I wasn't the first to ever come to him with such a problem and I surely wouldn't be the last. "It's going to take a week or more for us to clear this up," he predicted. "But, I have a plan and we will need to get started soon. After tonight's game we'll be heading to Boston for a five game set. So, while we are there, you come to my hotel room each night for a penicillin injection. It won't be fun, but after a few shots, you should be feeling a lot better."

For my first game as a big leaguer, I was nothing more than a spectator with a free seat. However, I was provided with one of the best spots in all of Yankee Stadium from which to watch the game. Pitching coach, Jim Turner, had me spend the evening sitting in the Yankee dugout, observing the Boston hitters. It was an assignment that kept me busy from the start, as the visiting Red Sox sent a dozen batters to the plate in just the first two innings. Yankee starter, Don Larsen, was unable to survive the top of the second, being promptly replaced by left-hander, Bobby Shantz.

In contrast, while Larsen showed no likeness to the pitcher he had been three seasons earlier, when he tossed a perfect game in the '56 World Series, Bobby was in top form. With masterful control of a variety of pitches, he went on to finish the game for an 11 to 5 Yankee win. At first, I wanted to believe that my mere presence on the ballclub brought good luck to the Yankees, who had come from behind to win that Wednesday night game. But it would be nearly a week later before we would pick up another victory.

The following afternoon we arrived at Fenway Park in Boston to resume a string of six consecutive games with the Red Sox. And much like Larsen the night before, our starter, Bob Turley was hit hard in the early going. Again, Stengel was forced to go to his bullpen much sooner than he would have preferred, causing me to think I may get my first call to work in relief, but I would have to wait until the following night to see my first action. This time, due in part to a barrage of Boston homeruns, the Yanks were dealt a stinging defeat, losing 14-3!

As planned, I kept my appointment with Gus and stopped by his room for the first of my injections. I trusted Gus and felt safe in taking his treatments. Simply knowing that this was the same trainer who, in years past, treated the injuries and ailments of Yankee greats such as Babe Ruth and Joe DiMaggio helped cause me to feel that I was in good hands. Still, there was nothing pleasant about getting a needle in the buttocks every 24 hours, but thankfully I began to feel better after just a few doses. It took several days before the pain and infection began to go away; however, by that time, I had already come to realize that I was getting off easy, considering how serious the disease could have become. I had no one to blame but myself. I had taken a senseless risk and made a dumb mistake, one I would ever make again. In my case, it was the words of Academy Award-winning actor, John Wayne, which rang so true: "Life's hard. It's even harder if you're stupid."

It was our third game in a row with the Red Sox and the second of our five-game visit in Boston. For a Friday night game, the crowd was a good one, filling Fenway to about three quarters of capacity. After starting the season in sluggish form, the Yanks had put together a successful streak in late May and early June, winning 11 of 13 games, improving their slate to as many as four games above the .500 mark. But the recent slump, which began prior to my arrival, had put the club in danger of falling back to an even record, but our hopes of reversing the trend were high. Whitey Ford, who had been one of the more dependable starters of late, was taking the mound for the Yankees and was a solid bet to cool off the red-hot Red Sox hitters. All the while, a formidable batting order, which included such capable hitters as Ted Williams, Pete Runnels, Frank Malzone and Jackie Jensen would be no easy lineup for any pitcher to solve.

Staked to an early 1 to 0 lead, Whitey breezed through the first three innings, making easy work of the Boston batters. Then, as if he were the victim of a mysterious spell, he surrendered a string of base hits, including a two-RBI single by the opposing pitcher, plus a rare throwing error of his own which quickly gave the home team a 4 to 1 advantage. The pendulum of momentum had suddenly swung to favor the Red Sox, who had the flustered Whitey Ford on the ropes. With only one out in the inning, Coach Jim Turner stepped slowly out of the dugout and asked for time. He made his way to the mound just as the phone rang in the Yankee bullpen. Within seconds, someone yelled in my direction, "Let's go, Eli, you're up!"

The call for me to warm up came as no surprise. After being passed over during the lopsided route the night before, I had anticipated that Stengel would have to use me sooner or later, even if he couldn't pronounce my name. Besides, the next several Red Sox batters would all be hitting from the right side, which would make for a sticky situation for a left-handed pitcher like Whitey. Still, my heart began to pound as I reached under my chair to grab my glove. "This is it!" I mumbled to myself. "It's the moment I've been waiting for!"

I stepped up onto the bullpen mound and made a couple of light tosses to the catcher. To help loosen the muscles in my shoulder, I lifted my pitching arm, extending it high above my head. Then swinging the arm faster and faster, I began to rotate it in a circular, windmill-like motion. From the corner of my eye I noticed Turner had finished his conversation with Whitey and was trudging slowly back to the dugout. When play resumed, my old army buddy, Don Buddin, the Boston shortstop, was next to step up to the plate. Sensing the urgency of the situation, I began to increase the velocity with each pitch, when suddenly my concentration was interrupted by the roar of the Fenway crowd. Buddin had lined a sharp grounder off the glove of second baseman, Bobby Richardson, for the third New York error of the inning. Before Bobby could retrieve the baseball from shallow right field, another Red Sox runner had crossed the plate. Their lead had been increased to 5 to 1.

With another right-handed batter due up, I expected Stengel to pop out of the dugout and make a pitching change, but that was because I had yet to learn to expect the unexpected, when it came to Casey and his managerial moves. With no further instructions, I continued to warm up. Meanwhile, out on the field, Whitey, being the savvy pitcher he was, somehow managed to pull a rabbit out of his hat and fan the next two batters. These two outs finally brought an end to Boston's fourth inning, five-run eruption.

To get back one of our runs, right-fielder, Hank Bauer led off the Yankees' half of the fifth with a homer. As Hank rounded the bases, word reached our bullpen that Ford was finished for the night. "Okay, Eli!" called an unidentified voice behind me. "You may want to shut down. Whitey's finished, and you're going in to mop up." I threw one final off-speed pitch and turned to walk over to the drinking fountain. I grabbed a paper cup and partially filled it with cold water. I sloshed the water around in my mouth for a few seconds and dramatically spit it on the ground. "This is it!" I mumbled to myself, as I crumpled the cup in my fist and dropped it on the wet grass at my feet. "This is what I've been dreaming of!" My career as a major league pitcher was officially underway!

After Bauer's homerun, our next three hitters were retired in order, leaving me with no time to waste in getting to the mound to take my allotted eight warm-up pitches. While the distance from the pen to the mound was only a couple hundred feet, it seemed to take forever to get there. We were down by three runs, and it was my job to keep us close. I only hoped I had not left my best pitches in the bullpen. It was the fifth inning, but there was still a lot of baseball yet to be played. I toed the rubber and took my warm-ups from the mound, relieved to see that my control was sharp, and my hard sinker was dropping like a rock. "You only get one chance to have your first game," I told myself. "You need to make the most of it!"

Dick Gernert, Boston's big first baseman, stepped into the box as home-plate umpire, Nestor Chylak pulled his mask over his face and crouched forward, hovering just above the shoulder of catcher, Yogi Berra. Gernert was a right-handed pull-hitter, so I wasn't about to give him anything hittable over the plate. He laid off a couple of fastballs, which were outside; however, he couldn't resist my tempting sinkerball. The next pitch, a sinker, came at him fast, about belt-high on the outside part of the plate. Suddenly, at the last split second, the ball dropped and broke even farther to the outside. Surprised that he had managed to make contact, an addled Dick Gernert drove the ball downward into the dirt in front of home plate, sending a slow bounder to third baseman, Hector Lopez, who easily threw out the slow running first baseman.

The result was much the same for the next batter, the American League's reigning MVP, Jackie Jensen. Jackie was also incapable of making solid contact with a sinker. He produced nothing more than a couple of foul balls and a weak grounder to shortstop, Gil McDougald, who made another easy putout.

From my earliest recollections of baseball, I had always idolized the Red Sox's legendary right fielder, Ted Williams. I had followed his career closely, memorized his stats and emulated his batting stance countless times on the playground. It had been in New York just a few days earlier that I saw him in person for the first time. And here he was, in the flesh, about to become the third batter to hit against me in my first big league game. His posture, his grip on the bat handle, his swing, and how his bat seemed to coil about his body in his follow-through, even the number nine on his back were all familiar to me. It was as if pictures and news reels of "the Splendid Splinter" had instantly come to life before my eyes! A surreal, almost eerie feeling enveloped me as he took a couple of practice swings glared out at me. Even as he stood 60 and one half feet away from me, the very sight of him was more intimidating than I could have imagined. Hero or not, he would see the best I had. I would throw him nothing but sinkers, if that was what was needed. But he would have hit my best pitch, if he were to beat me.

With a mixture of fastballs and hard breaking balls, I went for the outside edge of the plate, hoping to tempt Ted to go for one. And even then, he impressed me with his uncanny knack to make good contact with a ball well away from him. Always one to take his cuts and never to settle for a base on balls, Ted claimed "a walk is nothing more than charity on the pitcher's part." So he strived to earn his way on base the honest way. Thankfully, each time he connected with any of my offerings, he sliced the ball hard, just outside the foul line for a loud, but harmless strike.

The count had run full on Williams at three balls and two strikes. I nodded in agreement when Yogi put down the sign for a slider and set his target low and away. Perhaps Ted didn't count on a rookie, pitching his first game, being brazen enough to use breaking stuff in a full count, or maybe it was a change in fortune and lady luck was with me. My 3-2 slider cut the heart of the plate and tailed away ever so slightly to the outside corner. It was a called strike three!

In disgust, Ted flipped his bat to the ground. He subtly mouthed his disagreement to Chylak. But the veteran ump responded with nothing more than a nod, as if to reaffirm that he had made the correct call. I left the mound with my head down, pleased and proud, but careful not to show it. I walked down the steps into the dugout to a round of congratulatory handshakes and slaps on the back. "Of course, it was a strike!" I assured my new teammates. "Chylak called it a strike, didn't he?"

The early deficit proved to be too much to overcome and the Yankees lost the game 8 to 5. Yet from a personal standpoint my major league debut had been a successful one. I had shown composure under fire, setting down three of the AL's best batsmen in order, including the league's current MVP and a future first-ballot Hall of Famer. I was overjoyed to get off to such a great start, but I had pitched only one inning. It would take a lot more than one good outing to become an accepted member of the close-knit Yankee fraternity. I was happy to have gotten that first game behind me, but I would still have to prove myself worthy if I were to keep wearing a Yankee uniform.

The following day, in a Saturday matinee, the offensive firepower for which the New York lineup was so well known, was apparently AWOL once again. We scratched out three runs in the top of the first frame, but would not score again until the ninth. The Yanks were clinging to a shaky 3 to 1 lead, but our starting pitcher, Duke Maas, who had struggled with his control was pulled after five innings, and that's when I got my second call to action. I viewed this assignment as a slight vote of confidence, whereas unlike the night before, I was charged with protecting a precarious lead against the heart of the Boston batting order.

In spite of yielding a hit and a baseball on balls, I escaped my first inning of work without giving up a run. Jensen and Malzone both drove hard line drives to straight-away centerfield. But after recording the third out, I walked off the field with illusions of grandeur, holding my chin up, having coaxed Ted Williams into a harmless ground ball out. *I am off to a good start, but how much longer will my luck hold out?*

I was sent back to the mound to pitch the seventh, this time to face the lower third of the Boston order. I gave up another needless walk, but our two-run lead was still intact. "We're looking to get at least one more inning from you," Jim Turner mentioned in the dugout between innings, "And you'll be up against the big boys again, so work 'em carefully." But as I had come to learn over the years, a coach's advice can only go so far. It remains up to the pitcher to deliver the right pitch, in the right location, in the right situation. Failing to do this can cause a quick shift in the course of a game. Then suddenly, without warning, a dumbfounded pitcher can find himself out of the game and back on the bench, with no idea of what went wrong.

After striking out the first hitter in the bottom of the eighth, Vic Wertz, a veteran left-handed power hitter, slashed a single up the middle for a base hit. He promptly moved up to second base on a an infield groundout, which placed a runner in scoring position with Ted Williams about to come to bat. To this point, I considered myself fortunate to have retired my boyhood idol in the two plate appearances he had against me, so I had no reason to suspect that my allotment of rookie luck was about to run dry.

Without delay, the left-handed-hitting Williams brought the Fenway faithful to its feet, with a line drive single to right field, which sent Wertz sprinting home from second base. Ted's running-scoring hit could have easily been stretched into a two-bagger, had it not been for the fine defensive effort of a well-positioned Hank Bauer in right field. Trailing now by just one run, the Red Sox fans had been awakened and were becoming increasingly louder by the minute. Yogi slid his mask to the top of his head, asked for time and strolled slowly out to the mound for a quick conference. It was all part of an obvious stall tactic, a deliberate move on his part to allow a relief pitcher time for a few more warm-up pitches in the pen.

With the noise in the stadium approaching a near deafening level, Berra returned to his spot behind the plate. Working from a stretch position, I took a quick glance over my shoulder at the pinch runner sneaking away from first. Before each delivery, Yogi positioned his target low and away from the righty-hitting Frank Malzone. Still, I missed the mitt and proceeded to walk Frank on four consecutive pitches. The crowd roared again. This time it was because Casey was on his way from the bench to give me the hook!

Before reliever Ryne Duren could restore order and secure the final out of the inning, Boston scored twice more to take a 4 to 3 edge, a margin which held until one of the Yankees' brightest young stars of the time, Tony Kubek, homered in the ninth to send the game into extra innings. However, hope was short-lived for the Yankees that afternoon, as my former army teammate from Fort McPherson, Don Buddin came up big for Boston in the bottom of the tenth inning, smashing a walk-off grand slam home run, making the final score 8 to 4. Buddin's blast sent New York to a third straight defeat and lowered our season record to .500, an unbecoming mark for any Yankee team.

With a couple more games left to play in Boston, the Yankees' woes continued. The losing streak reached five games before returning home for a home stand with Cleveland and Chicago scheduled to visit. Other than a few warm-ups, I wasn't called on to pitch in any games for almost a week. Jim Coates, Ryne Duren and Duke Maas were Stengel's first choices from the bullpen and got the bulk of relief work during that stretch. This unexpected layoff may have been what I needed and worked out in my best interest.

By the last day of the homestand, when I was given a starting assignment for game two of a Sunday doubleheader, I was feeling well physically for the first time in weeks. Thanks to Gus Mauch, I was healthy again. The sky was clear and the warm conditions were just right for me to pitch my best and make my mark in the major leagues. The stadium was packed to the rafters for the Sunday twin-bill. The front-running Chicago White Sox were in town and 53,000 Yankee fans were eager to see the home team pull two full games closer to the top spot in the AL standings.

In top form, Whitey Ford pitched brilliantly to win the first game, narrowing the gap by one game. In the nightcap, I faced off against Billy Pierce, a seasoned left-hander who already had a considerable amount of big league experience to his credit. The pitching match-up would feature the crafty veteran versus the rookie in his first starting role.

By the middle innings, with the Yanks up 5 to 0, Pierce was out of the game. Yet, with a balanced combination of fast balls and curves, I was able to keep the Chicago batters off-stride most of the game. I was also the beneficiary of offensive support from Mickey Mantle and Bauer, who chipped in with home runs along with three base hits from Bobby Richardson, which helped provide me with a comfortable lead to work with. Nevertheless, had it not been for three untimely errors which led to four unearned runs, the White Sox would not have scored. I made it into the seventh inning, where I gave up back-to-back hits, followed by a rare fielding miscue by Mickey Mantle. The Yankees held a 6 to 4 lead when Casey came to get me.

Art Ditmar and Duren took over the pitching duties and preserved the two-run lead. As a ballclub, we had taken a giant stride toward catching the White Sox and Indians who were trying to run away with the league lead. The doubleheader sweep put us back to one game above .500 and in good shape to leave on our long upcoming road trip, which included Cleveland, Detroit and Chicago. After limiting Chicago to just three base hits over 6-2/3 innings, I anticipated getting another starting assignment soon. But with Casey, who could say for sure?

Four days after my first big league win, I was called upon to relieve Ralph Terry in our third and final game in Cleveland. Ralph had been staked to a 4-0 lead, but was flirting with disaster. With two out in the sixth and a runner on first, I entered the game needing to get just one out to calm the Indian uprising. Perhaps I left my best pitches in the bullpen or maybe I should have simply just stayed in the hotel and stayed in bed. For me, it was nothing short of a nightmare.

For starters, I gave up a sharply hit single to center field to Tribe catcher, Russ Nixon. I walked the next hitter to load the bases and followed up with another base on balls to force in a run. After a short visit to the mound from Jim Turner, I faced one of the most dangerous hitters in the American League, Minnie Minoso. Minnie, "the Cuban Comet," was a strong, high-average hitter and a perennial all-star, who batted from the right side. Making solid contact with a sloppy hanging curveball, he sent the baseball flying over the left field wall like a meteor for a grand slam homerun! I surrendered two more consecutive hits before Casey mercifully came out to retrieve me from this Indian massacre. I faced six hitters without recording an out. After this embarrassing appearance my E.R.A. ballooned from less than 1.00 to 4.50! My confidence was dealt a serious hit. Could I really blame Casey if he never called on me again? Now he had no good reason to learn to pronounce my name.

I suppose it's always the first few big league games of any player's career that are always the most memorable. It is from those games that even the smallest details can be recalled in surprising detail and the events of each contest can be accurately replayed over and over in the player's mind. Even decades later, when the scores are nothing more than trivial numbers in a record book, the memories can remain alive, accurate and indelibly etched in a man's mind. It is the thrill and excitement of making it to the major leagues that helps keep the memories of those first days in the big leagues vivid and true. After years of struggling in the minors and finally reaching the summit of baseball, every interaction with managers, coaches and teammates, along with every play of every big league game, can be remembered and cherished as part of having personally experienced the thrill of having a lifelong dream that finally came true.

CHAPTER 23
PITCHING AND ACTING LIKE A YANKEE

According to Transcend Recovery Community, a well known addiction recovery organization headquartered in Beverley Hills, California, addictions start out slowly and innocently. No one sets out to have an addiction. Yet, if the right things are in place, an addiction can grow, especially if one is genetically prone. Transcend also points out that their list of contributing conditions includes the following four primary psychological factors which are evident in almost every case: how you deal with stress; who you allow in your life; what you do in your spare time; and how you think about yourself. And after carefully considering each of these points and recalling the type of person I was, I see how of each of them helped place me on the downward spiraling path to alcohol abuse.

In recent years, great strides have been made in the war against drug and alcohol addiction. However, most of this progress has been made in the areas of recovery and treatment programs. Because of recent breakthroughs in medical research and clinical studies, alcoholics and drug addicts are being rescued and redirected to a life of sobriety at a rate never seen before. But there is still more work to be done to discourage this abuse from ever occurring in the first place. This can be done only through increasing public awareness and education, a cause I intend to advocate and promote as long as I possibly can.

Being genetically prone, there is no doubt I was at a disadvantage from the moment I was born. Yet, at the time I first entered professional baseball in the 1950s, little was being done to prevent alcoholism. There were no public service announcements on TV and no recovering alcoholics speaking openly about their experiences. There was no one to warn young people of the pitfalls that were waiting to lure them into a life of addiction. Today, Major League Baseball has programs in place which include counseling for players and testing for substance abuse. And while I'm not about to blame anyone but myself for my own personal misery, who's to say that programs like these could have made a difference in my life as well as that of many others from my era?

Still, I can see how by the time I entered professional baseball, I dealt with stress carelessly and irresponsibly. To reward myself for pitching a good game, I drank. To cope with the disappointment of a bad game, I drank. The friends and girlfriends I allowed into my life, usually brought me trouble and heartache. To alleviate the pain and drown my sorrows, I drank.

After finally making it to the Yankees, I found myself on a ballclub with mostly older guys. Many of these fellows were married and had their own seasonal apartments in New York or just across the Hudson River in New Jersey. Following the end of the school year, many of them had their wives and children living with them until the end of the summer. These guys were busy with their families and I often ended up alone, looking for somewhere to go and someone to hang out with in my spare time. I soon found out for myself just how lonely a big city like New York can be. And as a means to cope with the loneliness, I drank.

As professional athletes, we are taught to ignore both the cheers and jeers of the crowd, disregard what we read or hear in the news and to go about our business, playing baseball with no thought of who may be watching or who may be reporting. Still, it takes a thick skin to ward off the effects of unkind remarks made by sports writers, which in turn, can help perpetuate disparaging comments from spectators. Nevertheless, I sometimes allowed criticism from both the press or public to get to me and took it personally. Thoughts of self doubt would flood my mind. I felt bad about myself and I drank to restore my confidence.

In retrospect, I can see how I unsuspectingly met all four of the primary factors mentioned above. I was unaware of what stress was doing to me or that my remedy for it was equally as damaging. I didn't realize how certain people I allowed to get close to me only added to my stress level. There were many times I was by myself with too much spare time on my hands. That's when I made the costly mistake of allowing a bottle of liquor to become my only friend. And without considering how fortunate I was to be in the big leagues, living the life that every other young man in America could only dream of, I felt bad about myself. I wanted more for myself and I turned to alcohol to find it. Without realizing it, I had become an alcoholic.

Of course, anyone can have a bad day, but after my disastrous showing against the Indians, I wasn't sure if Stengel would ever let me pitch again. The Yankees' losing ways continued as the long road trip dragged on, taking us out of Cleveland, to Detroit and on to Chicago. All the while, the White Sox and Indians were winning, staking their claims on the two top spots in the American League standings. Inconsistent pitching by the Yankees was the cause cited by most sports reporters as New York sank into a fifth place tie with Detroit. With two months left in the season, the press was predicting the end of Yankee dominance. "Casey's too old for the job!" they claimed. "And the Yankees need new blood!"

I spent a week in Casey's doghouse, without getting as much as a call to warm-up during any of the games. But surprisingly, I got another start, this time in Chicago against the first-place White Sox and their 39-year-old all-star pitcher, Early Wynn. A no-nonsense veteran who already had more than 200 career wins to his credit, Wynn would go on to win 22 games that year as well as the 1959 Cy Young Award.

Lucky for me, I held my own that Thursday night, pitching in my hometown, with a large turnout of friends from the old neighborhood looking on. Trailing 2 to 1 and the Yankee hitters handcuffed by Wynn throughout the game, I was lifted for a pinch hitter in the top of the eighth inning. In my seven innings of work I limited the White Sox to five hits, but still I was the losing pitcher. The loss dropped my personal record to one win and two losses. But more importantly, it put the Yankees in the unfamiliar position of being three games below .500, an uncomfortable spot for the team which had dominated baseball for much of the decade.

Back home, several days later in New York, I was given another start against Detroit. For that evening, our opposing pitcher was Frank Lary, "The Yankee Killer." And like Early Wynn, Frank was also a right-hander from Alabama, who garnered his nickname by consistently beating the Yankees. Regardless of where the game was played, and no matter where the two clubs placed in the standings, Lary always got the upper hand and found a way to win. During the late fifties and early sixties, no pitcher in the AL was credited with disappointing more Yankee fans than the Tigers' ace, Frank Lary.

There is an old adage that says, "Inconsistency is the only thing in which men are consistent." And being entrusted to get our week-long homestand started on a positive note, I realized the truth of those words the moment I threw my first pitch. From that point, things never improved. I struggled with wildness through the first two innings and was pulled from the game in the third, trailing by a 4 to 1. Reaching a final score of 4 to 3, Frank Lary continued his mastery of the Yankees while I picked up my third defeat of the season. Frustrated by my up and down performances, I knew I would have to prove myself to be more dependable if I wanted to keep my spot on the big league club.

Later in August, when Casey found himself in a jam, I filled in a couple of times as a spot starter and both of these opportunities turned into nightmares, games I wish I could forget. In a home game against Boston, I was plagued with wildness and taken out in the third inning. This lopsided win for the Red Sox lowered my record to 1-4. A few days later in Detroit my control problems continued and I lasted only one third of an inning. Thanks in part to outstanding relief work by Whitey Ford, the Yankees came from behind to win, but this game would mark the last starting job I would see for a long time.

For the remainder of the 1959 season, I was relegated to the bullpen and cast into the dubious role of mop-up pitcher, entering games after the outcome was pretty well decided. And even in situations when I was given a chance to make a difference, I could never find the command and effectiveness of the pitches which had helped me earn a promotion to the big leagues in the first place.

Thanks to an eleventh inning home run by Mickey Mantle against the Indians, I got my second win on a cool Sunday afternoon in New York. However, about ten days later, in the next to last game of the year

I failed miserably, getting shelled by Baltimore in another extra-inning game. The Orioles scored runs off me in the eleventh, tagging me with my fifth loss and bringing down the curtain on a disappointing rookie season in the major leagues. By this point, the Yankees had been eliminated from the pennant race, mired in third place, 15 games out of first. With the benefit of an effective pitching staff, led by Early Wynn and Bob Shaw, the Chicago White Sox took the American League crown, outpacing the second place Cleveland Indians during the final week of the schedule. The 1959 season had been a frustrating one for the Yankees, an uncharacteristic campaign for the club that had won the AL title the past four years in a row. It was also a stinging disappointment for me personally, knowing I had done so little to make it better. Finishing with a 2 and 5 mark and earned run average above 6.00 didn't make me feel good about my chances of returning to the Yankees in 1960. But only time would tell.

It was the dawning of a new decade, the 1960s, and the lives of Americans were changing like never before. A young senator from Massachusetts named John F. Kennedy was dropping hints that he may be interested in making a run for the White House, while Prime Minister Fidel Castro was settling into power in Cuba. With full support of the Soviet Union, Castro's Communist regime wasted no time in erecting an arsenal of nuclear missiles, aiming them directly at the U.S. mainland. For me personally, it was the off-season and a time of reflection. It was time for me to look back at my disappointing season as a first-year Yankee and on my own determine what had happened and what went wrong. My confidence in my ability to pitch had been destroyed and I needed to find out why. It was a strange predicament, one I had never been in before.

However, for some guys, 1959 had been a fantastic year. In music, Bobby Darin held the top spot on the pop charts with his trademark hit, "Mack the Knife." In sports, Wilt Chamberlain of the Philadelphia Warriors, set a basketball scoring record for rookies, averaging almost 38 points per game. And in professional football, the high-scoring Baltimore Colts, led by quarterback, Johnny Unitas, defeated the New York Giants in the NFL Championship game. But still, the baseball world was unsettled, and so was I. The Yankees were not on top. The normal flow had been disrupted and I wasn't sure what needed to be done, from a team standpoint or from a personal level.

But personally, what puzzled me more than anything was how my best pitches, even when I spotted them in the best locations, were still getting swatted all over the ballpark. In too many instances, it seemed as if batters knew what pitch was coming. But was someone picking up my pitches? Was someone stealing my signs? And after recalling how ineffectively I had pitched, especially against the Red Sox in Fenway Park, I believe I had good reason for my suspicions.

On the mound in Boston, there were times I turned my back to the plate, and while rubbing up a new baseball and gazing toward left-field, I spotted one of the attendants in the old manually operated scoreboard, glaring intently through an opening. With his eyes fixed on me, he studied me like a hawk watching his prey. And perhaps, with the help of a spyglass, he could have been picking up the catcher's signals. Or maybe it was my imagination, and maybe I was overly paranoid. In any case, those Red Sox hitters sure had my number.

To prevent the opposing club from decoding a catcher's signs, it has been a longstanding practice for catchers to use a different set of signs, whenever a runner reaches second base. While a base runner on second has an easy look at the signals, it's a simple way to keep him from stealing signs and letting the hitter know what pitch to expect. Yet, whenever Yogi Berra was catching, I never had that advantage. Yogi would never agree to use an alternate sequence or a different set of signs, even when a base runner had a clear view of every signal he gave. "Ahh, it won't make no difference!" he would argue. "It'll just makes things complicated."

Perhaps he was accustomed to working with a staff of experienced pitchers, veterans such as Whitey Ford, Vic Raschi and Ed Lopat, and he wasn't about to take suggestions from a rookie pitcher who was fighting to keep his spot on the team. But while I was still learning to adapt to baseball in the majors, I expected to use the fundamentals I had been taught in the minors, the basic principles of baseball which could be beneficial at any classification. However, Yogi refused to budge. On the other hand, if Johnny Blanchard or Ellie Howard were working behind the plate, they would insist on changing the signs. These guys wanted to use every advantage available. And to this point, while Berra may have had more than a dozen years with the Yankees and was a three-time MVP, some claimed he had earned the right to be stubborn. However, in this situation, a little cooperation may have gone a long way to help bolster my confidence.

We were on the road in Chicago, with a few weeks remaining in the season, when the star shortstop of White Sox, Luis Aparicio, spoke with me briefly about my interest in playing winter baseball in his native Venezuela. As an organizer for this off-season league, Louie was working to get as many big league players as possible to fill the rosters for each team. He explained that the league would be staffed with credible coaches and the experience of playing there would be beneficial to my career. It all sounded like a good deal to me, but it was the $1500 per month salary he spoke of that sealed the deal for me.

I came to love Venezuela. The countryside was beautiful and the people there were warm and friendly. However, in the fall of 1959, the country was in a state of political turmoil. It was an election year, and there were as many as a dozen political factions vying for power, each of them campaigning with a win-at-all-costs approach. A Democratic government had recently taken control, but resentful Communist Party supporters were still making their presence known with gunfire in the streets of the capital city, Caracas. Their ill feelings toward Americans were no secret, and a good reason for any of us there to be nervous and edgy.

I played for Licoreros de Pampero, a team sponsored by the Pampero Rum Company, one of the world's leading producers of fine rum. We were one of four teams in what was a very fast, competitive, short-schedule league. Sluggers, Johnny Callison and Norm Cash, who were teammates of Aparicio on the Chicago White Sox, were in the league along with other big leaguers from the U.S.

In spite of pitching fairly well, I lost my first game. I felt like Lady Luck was still avoiding me and my pitching struggles would continue. After that game, I showered, got dressed and left the beautiful stadium on the campus of Caracas University, where we played our home games, and decided that before turning in, I would drown my sorrows by having a few late-night drinks. I checked out a downtown bar, where I chugged down some good Venezuelan rum and contemplated the pitches I wished I could take back and the other miscues that had led to my loss. The joint was full of beautiful working girls who served drinks and accommodated male customers with just about everything else they wanted. This one girl was exceptionally attractive; a sexy, well-built Eurasian with high cheek bones and a flawless complexion. She knew I was a ballplayer, and we became quite friendly before I had finished my first drink. We ended up spending the night together. And in the early morning hours, when I left her to return to my hotel, she assured me that my luck was about to change. "You will ween next time, Elly!" she promised in broken English. "You come back here to tell me."

Just as she predicted, I did well enough to win my next game, and for the first time in a long time, I had cause to celebrate. To share the good news and celebrate with more of those great rum-based drinks, I went back to the bar the following evening. The news was already out and this girl was set to celebrate with me. She had listened to the game on the radio and knew about my win. The moment I walked through the door, she ran across the room to greet me and began hugging and kissing me. "You deed it, Elly, you ween!" she cried. "I knew you would ween!"

Like so many other ballplayers, once I discovered a routine that worked I stuck to it. It was nothing more than crazy superstition, but as long as I was winning, I would do things the same way until my luck changed. For good luck, some guys would avoid stepping on the base lines at the ballpark, while others would eat the same foods before each game or wear the same undershirt, game after game without washing it. The strange ritual would continue until their luck ran out; at which point, some other peculiar practice would begin. If I thought anything would improve my chances of winning, I was willing to give it a try. So after earning my first win of the winter season, I went back to see this same girl at the rum house and won a second game my next time out. Before each game I pitched, I spent the night with her, and before I knew it, I had a six-game winning streak, a winning record and a successful season of winter baseball to my credit.

By the time I was done with winter ball and got back home to Chicago, there were only a few weeks remaining before the start of spring training. Waiting for me, along with all the other mail Mom had saved for me while I was in Venezuela, was an envelope from the Yankees. It was my contract offer for the 1960 season.

Inside the envelope was an cordial letter from the Yanks' Assistant General Manager, Roy Hamey, inviting me to report to spring camp with the major league club. In itself, that was a relief, considering my less-than-impressive showing at the end of the '59 season. Over the winter I was very uncertain about what the organization might do with me. From my standpoint, getting sent back to Richmond was a strong possibility. However, the paltry, rock-bottom salary of $7000 Hamey offered was unchanged from what I had received the year before. Instead of being rational and fair-minded about the deal, and thankful that I was still on the major league roster, I was incensed.

"Why, this contract is nothing but an insult!" I roared, tossing the papers into the air, scattering them about the living room floor. Startled by my outburst, Mom dashed in from the kitchen. She dried her hands on her apron, slowly raised her finger and stuck it in my face, only inches from my nose. She then proceeded to scold me in a way that no one else would have ever been allowed to do. I was 25 years old and stood six feet-two inches tall, but she was still my mother.

"You need to stop and think, young man! Do you realize how lucky you are to have the job you have? Who do you think you are!" Her voice was stern and forceful. I had not been dressed down like this since I was in grade school, when she found out I was a shoplifter.

Mom was right. I needed to be put in my place. But still, I wasn't about to drop my pride. I wanted to prove myself. I wanted to show her I was my own man, a mature man who could handle his business dealings without advice.

"I'm going to mail this contract back to the Yankees, unsigned!" I ranted. "I can't let them get away with this. I was paid more money than this to play winter ball!" Mom stood silently and glared at me before turning to go back to the kitchen. She knew as well as anyone how mulish and unbending I could be, but she also knew when to give up.

"Well, do whatever you want," she conceded as she walked away. "I only want what's best for you and I only hope you don't make things worse."

"This is what all the guys do, Mom," I offered, trying to lose my angry tone. "Nobody accepts the first contract offer. It's how you negotiate."

I got only a flippant shrug as she left me. Her silence told me she was disappointed and that she wanted no cross words with me. *How could I be so unreceptive and bullheaded with the person who loved and cared for me more than anyone?* I wanted to kick myself.

Nonetheless, I needed to make my point. Without signing it, I mailed the contract back to the Yankees and attached a short note to Mr. Hamey, pointing out how, after having spent more than half of a season with the big league club, I felt I was entitled to more than the minimum salary. I went on to explain that this upcoming season would be my second as a Yankee, and I thought I deserved to be paid like a Yankee.

It only took a few days for me to receive a reply from the Yankees' front office. The original contract was returned, unchanged. With it was a brief, straight-to-the-point letter from Hamey, worded very much like the following:

> Mr. Grba:
>
> Our original contract offer for the 1960 season is herein returned for your review and approval.
> Regarding your request to be considered for a salary increase, I personally assure you that once you start pitching like a Yankee and acting like one, you will be compensated like a Yankee.
>
> Sincerely yours,
> H. Roy Hamey
> Asst. General Mgr.

Needless to say, I was cornered into giving my mother some red-faced answers, but I scribbled my name at the bottom of the contract and dropped it in the next day's mail. The execution of this agreement was typical of the take-it-or-leave-it approach of baseball management in that era. Baseball's longstanding reserve clause was still in effect and free agency was still years away. Players who had an exceptional season were sometimes successful in their negotiations, but those were rare cases. Player agents were unheard of and bargaining with team officials as an individual was a daunting proposition. The major league players of today have no idea of the price paid by their predecessors in the game to establish the players' union, the pension plan, free agency and so many other benefits and privileges they now enjoy. The sacrifices made back in the 1950s and 1960s, by courageous baseball players who were willing to put their careers on the line, are what made it possible for major leaguers to earn astronomical salaries today. On the other hand, it is sad to see how the efforts of those who stood up and fought for players' rights so many years ago are all but forgotten.

Spring training in 1960 exceeded all my expectations. My arm was in great shape and I was throwing the ball harder than ever. Our new pitching coach, Eddie Lopat, who had just been brought up from the Richmond club, was very pleased with my performance and even Casey seemed to be impressed judging by some of the positive comments he made about me to the press. So, it came as a huge surprise when Stengel called me aside to tell me I was being optioned to the Richmond club for the start of the season.

Training camp was over and we boarded a northbound train to start the season. We had brief stops scheduled in Richmond for an exhibition game with our AAA minor league team, and another against the United States Military Academy in West Point, New York. We had no sooner pulled away from the station in St. Petersburg when I spotted an old girlfriend on the train, a great-looking Southern girl, who was once queen of the Cherry Blossom Festival in Washington, D.C. She was happy to see me and invited me to have a seat beside her. We had a few drinks, sparked a few memories, and before our train rolled into Jacksonville, we were together in her sleeper compartment, just the two of us, along with a very expensive bottle of wine. Around four o'clock in the morning I finally emerged from her room and with the help of a friendly porter, found my way back to the Yankees' team car and climbed into my berth undetected, or so I thought. In just a matter of hours, I went from being on top of the world to the depths of disappointment. It was the following afternoon when we reached Richmond and Stengel gave me the bad news.

"I know you had a great spring and everything, but we need to take a look at this kid, Gabler," he explained, getting straight to the point. "We only got to see him in a couple of games late in the season and we need to take another look at him and see what he's got."

"What he's got?" I shot back angrily. "Johnny Gabler hasn't got anything close to what I showed you this spring! This is wrong, Casey, and you know it!" This sort of conversation was nothing new for Stengel. Over the years, he had sent lots of confident young ball players back to the minors. So delivering bad news and following it up with a few words of hope and encouragement were routine for him, just another part of his job.

"It's just going to be for three or four weeks," he assured me. "Then, we'll call for you to come back to New York."

"Are you on the level with me, Casey? Because if you're not, I want you to give me the truth right now!" I demanded boldly. "The least you can do is give me the truth."

Of course, I had no bad feelings toward Johnny Gabler. He had been pitching well, was a fine teammate and he deserved a fair chance. Besides, he had a name Casey could pronounce and remember. But I had just come off my best spring training ever, and had been rewarded with a trip back to the farm. Still, the whole deal seemed fishy to me and left me with a lot of unanswered questions.

I never had the nerve to ask if anyone knew about my little rendez-vous on the train. I knew how harsh Stengel could be dealing with players who violated curfew rules, but I thought I was in the clear and had gotten away scot-free. Yet I never found out for sure if Casey or any of his informants saw me when I snuck back to the team car. It all seemed very suspicious that having pitched as well as I had all spring, I was demoted to the minor leagues just as the season was about to start.

With the Richmond Virginians, I was resolved to vindicate myself. To me, the assignment was insulting and I set out determined to make the Yankees regret their decision. But I would have to do it on my own. The Yankees got off to a great start, winning five of their first six games, including a start by Gabler who pitched a masterpiece in Boston. I wanted them to need me. I wanted to be their solution, their deliverance. However, after the first couple of weeks of the season, the Yankees were sitting on top of the American League, thanks in part to good pitching from Jim Coates and Bill Short. This scenario placed destiny in my own hands. I would need to pitch well enough that I couldn't be overlooked. It would be up to me to force their hand and take away any excuses they may use for leaving me behind.

As I suspected, my sentence, which Stengel assured me would not exceed three to four weeks, had long passed. And by mid-June, the Yankees, in spite of winning nine games over a span of ten, were clinging to third place, fighting tooth and nail to keep stride with Cleveland and

Baltimore. It was clear they would need to make changes soon if they were to avoid embarrassing themselves like they did a year earlier. Meanwhile, I was posting numbers which placed me among the pitching leaders of the International League. In the roles of both starter and reliever, I had won seven of eight decisions and paced the IL in earned run average at 1.80. The big club could no longer overlook my performance at the AAA level. I was recalled to the major leagues on June 18th and joined the Yankees on the road in Chicago. I thought it unusual that my call-up included a pay raise, a jump of $500, which increased my annual salary to a whopping $7500. "Why now?" I asked myself. "Perhaps they expect me to start acting like a Yankee. And in case no one noticed, I had been pitching like a Yankee ever since the start of spring training!"

"Put him to the test!" was Casey's response, whenever asked about how to use a newly acquired pitcher. "He's up here to do a job," he would quip. "Let's throw him out there and see what he's got."

In keeping with his usual practice, Stengel called on me right away, bringing me in from the bullpen to relieve Bob Turley and to protect a 4 to 3 lead over the White Sox. In what I recall as one of the most gratifying games of my career, I surrendered only two runs over six innings of work to pick up a 12 to 5 win. Although the Sox's first sacker, Roy Sievers, tagged me with a two-run homer in the eighth, it was my old nemesis, Early Wynn, who took the loss for Chicago, lifting the Yankees into first place, even if only by percentage points over the Orioles.

Making only a couple of short relief appearances over the following three weeks or so, I was given a starting assignment for game two of a Sunday doubleheader at home. Some 60,000 fans squeezed into Yankee Stadium to see us battle the White Sox, who had just reclaimed the league lead, knocking us out of the AL's top spot earlier in the week. To the delight of the full house, I pitched all nine innings for a complete-game win, defeating left-hander Herb Score 8 to 2.

On what was a day I should have stayed in bed, I dropped my next start at home against the Kansas City Athletics, giving up a three-run dinger to KC's catcher Danny Kravitz, a long fly which barely cleared the right-field wall. In spite of the loss, we were left in a virtual tie for first with Chicago, as the once-hopeful Baltimore Orioles slipped further in the standings. In the time that followed, I was back in the bullpen, keeping loose and staying ready to answer the bell. And I was fine with that job. At the start of the season, I had mentioned to Casey that my preference was to be used as a spot starter whenever needed, but to work as often as possible out of the pen. He agreed that pitching in relief was my stock in trade.

I got myself back on track, working in relief on a hot, sticky Saturday afternoon in old Griffith Stadium in Washington. As the beneficiary of a Moose Skowron two-run homer in the top of the 11th inning, I improved my personal record to three wins and one loss. My confidence was back and the Yankees were back in first with a game and a half lead over Chicago. After winning a few games in the big leagues, it was good to see how many reporters and fans had learned to both spell and pronounce my name, even if my manager still couldn't do either one.

CHAPTER 24

BASEBALL IS A WORRYING THING!

———

I t's a popular phrase these days: "My job is secure, nobody wants it!" You see it on T- shirts, coffee mugs and bumper stickers. In professional baseball, it's quite the opposite. Of course, there are some players today who have the luxury of working under a multi-year contract, but in baseball there is fierce competition for every position on every club. It makes no difference how many years a player may have in the game, every spring there is a rookie ready to step up and take a veteran's place. And management is always ready to give the young guy a shot if he shows any signs of potential.

Hall of famer, Stanley Coveleski, who won more than 200 games in his brilliant career, summed up the situation very well, "The pressure never lets up. It don't matter what you did yesterday, that's history. It's tomorrow that counts. So you worry all the time. It never ends. Lord, baseball is a worrying thing."

Even in his heyday in the 1920s, Stan found out that management would never acknowledge his accomplishments, that his heroics on the field would never be enough to assure him of a place on next year's team and that even pitching and winning three complete, nine-inning games in the 1920 World Series earned him little more than a standard raise at contract time. Too often, owners, general managers, managers and even coaches will avoid saying anything positive to one of their players, as if paying a compliment or giving a pat on the back will be too costly. It took me a while, but I learned that people like that will dish out nothing but criticism even after an outstanding performance.

In the midst of all my troubles in 1959, I started the second game of a Sunday doubleheader in Yankee Stadium against the Athletics. I had pitched a whale of a ballgame, taking a 1 to 0 lead into the top of the eighth inning. After retiring the first two hitters in the eighth, I gave up a bloop-single to KC's centerfielder, Bill Tuttle. The next hitter, Russ Snyder, a rookie outfielder not known as a power hitter, stepped into the batter's box as I went to the stretch position, eyeing the base runner, Tuttle, over my left shoulder. Suddenly, as I peered in at my catcher, Ellie Howard, to get my signs, negative thoughts began to flood my mind. *Is this the end of the line for me? Am I running out of gas?* The confidence that had taken me through 8-2/3 innings was gone and had been replaced with doubt. Having lost my concentration, I floated my next pitch down the heart of the plate and Snyder promptly belted it over the wall for a two-run homer! The baseball had hardly had time enough to come down in the left-field seats before Casey was on his way to give me the hook. While Bobby Shantz was being summoned from the bullpen and was making his way to the mound, I stormed off the field and down the dugout steps. I began looking for an out-of-the-way place to sit alone and brood. The idea of having pitched my best game since coming to the Yankees and seeing it end in disaster was a bitter pill to swallow.

With just a couple of pitches, Shantz got the elusive third out which put the brakes on the Kansas City rally. With the Yankees now trailing 2 to 1 in the home half of the ninth, Yogi Berra came to the rescue and pulled the game out of the fire. Down to our last out, Yogi entered the game as a pinch hitter and slammed a dramatic, game-tying homer, knotting the score at 2 to 2 and sending the game into extra innings.

Using no more than six or seven pitches, Bobby put down the A's in order in the top of the tenth, giving the Yanks a golden opportunity. And as if he were following the script of a down-to-the-wire drama, Elston Howard led off bottom of the frame for New York with a climactic line drive homer, down the left-field line, giving the Yanks a come-from-behind 3 to 2 win! As Ellie went into his home-run trot, I jumped up and hurried toward the clubhouse. I didn't want to speak to anyone. I was in no mood to celebrate.

I sat dejectedly in front of my locker, my head in my hands. My heart was as heavy as lead. *How could this happen?* I had been in the zone, almost unhittable, pitching to a perfect rhythm for almost the entire game, only to get knocked out of the box with one out left to go. Coming from the dugout tunnel, my teammates began to file into the room. Yet I continued to stare at the floor. I just wanted to shower and go somewhere for a few drinks. Out of nowhere, I felt a pat on my shoulder, followed by unexpected words of praise from some of the guys passing by.

"Good job, Eli!" I heard from one. "'Way to go! You kept us in the game and gave us a chance to win!" said another. The overall consensus was one of appreciation and approval. Soon there was a gathering of players around my locker, all of them happy for me and pleased with my day's work. Even pitcher, Bobby Shantz, who had just picked up a win the easy way, came over to express himself. "You did all the hard work, Eli," he admitted. "You did a great job and you deserve this win a lot more than I do." He reached out and shook my hand and sheepishly looked away. "I'm sorry, Eli. I wish there was something I could do."

Coming from a well-respected, veteran pitcher, Bobby's thoughtfulness and his taking time to talk with me meant more to me than he realized. Our little talk and the happy mood of my teammates lifted my spirits. A few of the guys continued to hang around my locker, talking and rehashing the game, and I was enjoying every minute. The more we talked, the more I started to see how hard I was being on myself, that I was the only one disappointed in my performance until Jim Turner, our pitching coach just happened to pass by. He stopped in his tracks, paused directly in front of me and placed his hands on his hips. He must have heard the commotion and noticed the attention I was receiving and was obviously annoyed. "Well, Grba, I see you can't handle pressure," he blurted indignantly. "A good pitcher would have won that game one to nothing!"

A hush fell over the room as he turned and left the area. Stunned by the disparaging comments, the gathering dispersed, no one saying a word. It was like someone had popped open a jar of ants at a family picnic. "That sure was inspiring," one of the players mumbled sarcastically. "That shows how much management appreciates what we do!"

Turner's remarks infuriated me. My blood was boiling. My first impulse was to fight. I wanted to punch his face in. I sprang from my chair, my fists were clenched. It took all the self-restraint I could muster to keep from going after him. "Take it easy, Eli, it's not worth it," one concerned teammate urged. "Don't get yourself in trouble."

"What's wrong with these people?" I snapped. "Why are they so negative? Why is nothing ever good enough?"

I realized then that life in baseball would be tough, that keeping a job in the major leagues would be no easy task, and that malicious criticism and backbiting would be such a part of it. Often, it was difficult to tell who wanted to see me succeed and who was set to see me fail. It was hard to tell friend from foe. And while newspaper and magazine articles and TV and radio broadcasts can do a great job promoting the positive image of baseball, the typical fan has no idea of the impersonal, hard-nosed business that underlies our national pastime.

Today, baseball is more lucrative than ever for both players and club owners. Salaries and profits have escalated to levels that would have been considered unimaginable just a few decades ago. And while so much about the game has changed over time, some things have remained constant. Even now, as games are won and lost every day, so are starting positions and spots on team rosters. Whenever one player is promoted to a higher level, another is released. And in spite of the many changes made over the years, the modern player will surely agree that the words of Stan Coveleski still ring true: "Baseball is a worrying thing!"

The Yankees would go on to finish the 1960 regular season as champions of the American League. In what would be the final pre-expansion season, wherein each team played a schedule of 154 games, the Yankees finished 40 games above .500, crossing the finish line eight games ahead of the second-place Baltimore Orioles. In contrast to the season before, the Yankees were like a new team. Team morale was higher; we won more games and our winning steaks were longer. In particular, it was the club's offense that made the biggest difference. Led by Mickey Mantle with 40 and newly acquired Roger Maris with 39, the team's home run count improved by more than 40 over the 1959 total. The Yankee swagger was back in 1960, and while the entire club played more aggressively and with more confidence, I too approached the season with determination and a new attitude.

I was a different pitcher. Even after having to start the year at Richmond, I went about my work knowing I had what it took to get back to the major leagues and stay there. I was throwing harder than ever before. My pitching had advanced to a point where there was little difference in the velocity of my breaking pitches and my fastball. My control was sharper, and I had worked to get rid of any quirky habits which may have been revealing my pitches. I was ready to take my place in the big leagues.

After my mid-June call-up, I returned to the Yankees with a vengeance. With a mixture of both starting and relief work, I ran my record to 3-1. However, in late August with the Yankees in first but Chicago close behind, I started a crucial night game against the White Sox in New York and again, my opponent was Early Wynn. At forty years old, "Gus" was as sly and cunning as ever. He pitched a complete game, limiting us to just one run, a home run I hit off him in my second at bat. Had it not been for several errors committed by the Yankee infield, the game may have developed into a low-scoring pitchers' duel, but the 5 to 1 win for Chicago brought them one game closer to us in the race and gave me my second loss of the season.

Following my satisfactory showing against the White Sox, Casey kept me in the starting rotation for a while longer; however, the result was not nearly so positive. When Detroit came to visit Yankee Stadium, I was unable to survive the second inning of what turned into a rout by the Tigers. And while I fared a little better when Boston came to town, going five shaky innings in a win for the Red Sox, my once impressive record had quickly dipped to three wins and four losses.

It was a time when the Yankees needed every win they could get. The American League race was neck-and-neck, and with the White Sox still within striking distance, we couldn't afford to let up. But after suffering a three-game sweep in Baltimore, in which the Yankees scored a total of two runs against the Orioles, Chicago grabbed first place. My personal slump had come with bad timing, if I were to contribute to the Yankees winning the 1960 pennant.

Fortunately, the Yankees got back on track and so did I. The club's offense suddenly caught fire and overall, our pitching was sharper and more consistent than it had been all year. In relief, I picked up a win in Cleveland, thanks to a Mickey Mantle homer in the 11th inning. And in another 11-inning affair, I won a 2 to 1 game at home over the Senators. The Yankees were playing like the Yankees of old. We went on to pad our lead over second-place Chicago by as many as eight full games, winning 19 of our final 21 games, including the last 15 in a row! With more than a week to go in the season we had won the AL crown, yet we continued on our winning path, soundly thrashing Washington on the road, where I gained my final win of the year, and Boston at home, where we ended the season on a high note.

All the while, over in the National League, the Pittsburgh Pirates were in the driver's seat, but were still having to wait for two stubborn teams, the Braves and the Cardinals, who dropped out of the picture in the final games. When the dust finally cleared, the stage was set for the Yankees to meet the Pirates three days later, in game one of the World Series in Forbes Field, Pittsburgh. The odds makers had us as heavy favorites. And with the brash self-confidence which resulted from the long, season-ending winning streak, we had no idea that we were about to experience what is remembered as the most bitter defeat ever recorded in New York Yankee history.

"The past should be left in the past, otherwise it can destroy your future." These are wonderful words which we should all strive to live by. But letting go of a regrettable past is difficult for even the strongest among us. For members of the 1960 New York Yankees, the World Series of that year is still the most disappointing memory any of them can recall. And while vivid mental pictures of a bad-hop grounder hitting shortstop Tony Kubek in the throat, the Clemente chop, which landed between two undecided fielders and the unforgettable sight of Yogi, his back to the camera, watching helplessly as Bill Mazeroski's home run sails over the left-field wall, are all etched in the mind of everyone who witnessed these mind-boggling occurrences; no one was more stunned than the Yankee players themselves. Yet from my perspective, the most astonishing indication that things were about to come unglued occurred when Stengel called both me and Duke Maas into his office for a little pre-series meeting.

"You guys are done pitching for the year," he informed us. "But I want the two of you to throw batting practice throughout the series, and to help get our boys ready, Duke, I want you to throw as much like that pitcher, Bob Friend, as you can. And Grba, I want to you to pitch like their other big guy, Vern Law."

Duke and I were dumbfounded. We couldn't believe what we heard. *What sort of warped reasoning was this?* For the season, the two of us had combined for about 60 games and 150 innings of work and we were being instructed to throw BP during the World Series! "We need to save your arms to pitch winter ball," he told us. As disheartened as we were, Duke and I followed our orders. We went about our jobs prior to each game, throwing from behind the protective screen with all the meanness of a couple of angry vipers. Needless to say, our teammates were given nothing easy to hit, seeing nothing but a steady stream of blazing fastballs and hard sliders.

Now more than a half-century has passed, yet the heartache lingers for those of us left from the 1960 Yankees and our fans. Many choices that were made have never been justified, leading to questions that have never been answered. Nevertheless, much of what went wrong in that seven-game series for the New Yorkers can be chalked up to chance. However, in retrospect, it is quite evident that with sound decision-making and fundamental baseball strategy, many of the unfortunate things that took place could have been avoided. The Yankees should have never been put in such a position, their backs to the wall in a seventh game. The team was far too talented for that to have happened. And it is with the same staunch belief that I place much of the blame at the feet of manager Casey Stengel, not in a way to attack his character, but to question his astuteness as a team leader at that point in his career.

Of all of the questionable choices he made in the 1960 Fall Classic, it was the use of his pitching staff for which Stengel is still most heavily criticized. His most questionable moves relate to the pitchers he selected as well as the timing and sequence in which he used them, the most glaring being his choice of starting pitcher for game one.

Picking the game one starter is one of the most crucial decisions a World Series manager will make. The first game pitcher will not only set the tone the remainder of the series, but should the series reach a seventh game, the number one starter in the rotation will be available to work games four and seven as well. And while Art Ditmar had turned in a great season for the Yankees, winning 15 games and losing nine, it was Whitey Ford, a veteran of five previous World Series who was the obvious choice. Ford, a perennial all-star, who had won three games over the final two weeks of the season, all in convincing fashion, was passed over. Instead, Ditmar was called on to start games one and five and failed to pitch beyond the second inning in either of them. On the other hand, Whitey was named the starter for games three and six. In each case he was outstanding, throwing two complete-game shutouts, winning 10 to 0 and 12 to 0. With such commanding leads in both of those game, it is curious why Casey never went to his bullpen, as there was a full complement of relievers, both righties and lefties, available and ready to work. Nonetheless, after pitching 18 innings in those two games, Whitey was done for the series, which further limited Casey's options for the rest of the series.

With Ditmar being as ineffective as he had been all year, we fell behind early in game one. Trailing 3 to 1, another right-hander, Jim Coates, had to be brought in to relieve Art and get us out of the first inning. At this point, as if he hadn't raised enough suspicion, Casey then made the unheard of decision of calling for a pinch hitter, with no one out in the top of the second inning.

Following consecutive base hits to open our half of the second, Yankee runners were aboard at first and second when third baseman, Clete Boyer was unexpectedly called back from the on-deck circle. Clete had started the game, played one inning defensively and was listed in the seventh spot of Stengel's lineup. But before getting his first chance at bat, he was taken out of the game and replaced by Dale Long, a left-handed hitting reserve who had seen limited action during the regular season. Facing the ace of the Pirates' staff, Vernon Law, Long promptly lifted a lazy fly ball to right field which was caught easily by Roberto Clemente for the first out of the inning. The next two outs came quickly as New York failed to score. But to complete this awkward piece of strategy, Casey was then forced to bench Long for the rest of the game and insert Gil McDougald into the lineup to replace Boyer at third. It was a bumbling move to make at the instance of an ideal scoring opportunity. Our manager's unorthodox call accomplished nothing other than totally humiliate Clete Boyer. The Yankees dropped the opening game 6 to 4.

The following day the bats of the Bronx Bombers exploded in game two, hammering Pittsburgh pitchers for 19 hits for resounding 16 to 3 win. Mickey slammed two home runs as the Yanks scored seven runs in one inning to embarrass the host team. But here again, just as Ford would be kept on the mound to go the distance in lopsided games three and six, starter Bob Turley was staked to a 16 to 1 advantage when he left the dugout to begin the ninth inning. Unable to complete the final frame, Turley would need help from Bobby Shantz who got the final two outs of the game in the 16 to 3 New York victory. Yet to this day, I am completely baffled by how a big league manager would push his best starting pitchers to pitch nine full innings when he has a commanding lead of 10 or more runs!

The Pirates took a three games to two advantage, winning game five 5 to 2 in front of a stunned Yankee Stadium crowd of over 62,000. Ditmar was given another chance to start, but again he gave Pittsburgh an early lead. In this situation Stengel called to the bullpen for 21-year-old rookie Bill Stafford, who had less than a dozen big league games to his credit since getting a late-August call-up from the minors. Stafford did a great job of keeping us close, pitching five scoreless innings. However, it remained evident that for reasons unexplained, Casey was ignoring some the relief pitchers who had been his go-to guys during the season. Ryne Duren, who had arguably been the most reliable fireman all year, would be used twice, and only then when the Yankees were trailing, to mop up the final innings. The same applied to regular relievers, Duke Maas and Luis Arroyo, who throughout the year had been a couple of Casey's workhorses. Each of these guys would get to make only one brief appearance in the post-season. However, in my case, I suppose I was the biggest hound in Casey's doghouse.

In game six, I was sent into the game in the second inning, as a pinch runner to replace Elston Howard, who had been struck on the fist by a Bob Friend fastball. As exciting as it should have been to be playing in the World Series, it was equally as insulting to me to be used as nothing more than a replacement base runner. To this point, I had been ordered to warm up twice in the bullpen, but never called into a game. So with hardly any enthusiasm, I took my sweet time getting out to first base. There was a pause on the field while trainer Gus Mauch took a long look at Ellie's busted fingers. Just as play was about to resume, I recall hearing my name on the PA system at old Forbes Field, being introduced as a pinch runner and how embarrassing it was that the announcer informed the crowd that I was the final player on the

Yankees' roster to get into the 1960 World Series. However, Whitey Ford was masterful that day, pitching a seven-hit shutout and evening the series at three games each.

Some baseball historians have referred to the final game of the 1960 World Series as "the greatest game ever played." And depending on perspective, it can be described as the crowning jewel of Pittsburgh Pirate lore or the darkest day in Yankee history. Of course, the story has been told thousands of times, the story of how, with Bobby Shantz pitching in relief, the Yankees came from behind to take a 7 to 4 lead in the top of the eighth, only to give back five runs in the home half of the same inning. Suddenly, Shantz, one of the greatest defensive pitchers in baseball history, surrendered three runs and was given the hook and replaced by right-hander, Jim Coates; a surprising switch which raised a lot of eyebrows. As a manager well known for platooning his players to gain an advantage in pitcher-hitter match ups, why would Casey bring in Coates, knowing the next two hitters would both bat from the left side?

Nevertheless, working carefully, Coates got two quick outs and the Pittsburgh rally seemed to be quenched. But a leak in the Yankee defense would allow it to continue. The next Pirate hitter, Roberto Clemente, a young, 25-year-old outfielder from Puerto Rico, made an awkward, chopping half-swing that softly dropped the baseball on the infield grass, spacing it equally between Coates and first baseman, Bill Skowron. Both Yankees went to recover the ball, with neither of them going to cover the bag. Clemente was safe without a play at the base. With Pirate runners now on the corners, catcher Hal Smith stepped up to the plate to face the crafty Coates. Smith, a right-handed hitter with good power, worked the count to two balls and two strikes before undoubtedly swinging through a high fastball which National League umpire, Bill Jackowski, called ball three. Confident that he had Smith struck out, Coates started off the mound, only to be sent back on the hill to make a three and two pitch to Smith. With a mighty cut, Smith redirected Coates's next delivery skyward and deep toward left field. The baseball sailed into the trees beyond the outfield wall, giving Pittsburgh fans a 9 to 7 lead and a thrill they would never forget.

The seventh and final game, played in Pittsburgh on October 13, 1960, has been written about, read about and discussed as much as any other game in baseball history. For the New York Yankees, the bitter 10 to

9 loss was a string of miscues, indecisive plays, a freak injury and a poor call by the home plate ump mixed in for good measure. Could Bobby Shantz, a Gold Glove Award winning pitcher have made a difference had he been left on the mound to field Clemente's chopper? Why was one of our best relief pitchers, Ryne Duren, left sitting on the bench the entire afternoon? What if Whitey Ford had been allowed to start three games instead of two? And how could Bill Mazeroski, a career .260 hitter, win it all with a homer in the bottom of the ninth? These questions have fueled hot-stove arguments for a long time and likely will continue to be hashed over by serious baseball fans for years to come. It was during a friendly visit not long ago that my old buddy, Jim Coates, summed up our rueful recollections. "It just wasn't meant to be, Eli," he confided. "For us Yankees, it just wasn't in the cards."

Baseball stories are often exaggerated and sensationalized, and with team loyalty they can be told from a biased point of view. Yet, the memorable 1960 World Series, with its abundance of bizarre circumstances and unflattering miscues, combined with an assortment of inexplicable managerial decisions, is a story I would never intentionally alter. And because I was able to watch all except two-thirds of an inning from the Yankee bullpen and witness the unfolding of this crazy, but incredible nine-day drama, I hope to share some of my own insight and personal thoughts about this disappointing period in my life, before any more time slips away.

Following the World Series, it took the Yankees less than a week to get rid of Casey. His age was the reason they gave for his firing. Yet as their manager, he had won ten American League pennants and seven World Series titles. "They fired me for turning 70," he told the press. "I'll never make that mistake again!"

His dismissal would mark the end of a long successful relationship between Stengel and the Yankees. However, within a couple of years, he would resurface again in the same town, this time, across the Harlem River from Yankee Stadium at the Polo grounds, as the skipper of the newly formed New York Mets.

Unknowingly, 1960 would also be my final season in a Yankee uniform. And fortunately, I too would resurface in baseball with another team. But unlike Casey, who would be packing up and moving just a few blocks across town, my journey would take me all the way across the country, to a brand-spanking new ball club located some 3,000 miles away, a new team with old players, a famous cowboy for an owner and odd-looking halos encircling their caps!

Unknowingly, 1960 would also be my final season in a Yankee uniform.

CHAPTER 25

EXPANSION OF THE AMERICAN LEAGUE

I remember well how we clinched the league title one late September Sunday afternoon in front of a capacity crowd at Fenway Park. Ralph Terry had pitched a brilliant game to beat the Red Sox, and the win put us out of reach of both the Orioles and White Sox, with only a half dozen games left to play. After the final Boston hitter was retired, several of us who were relatively new Yankees rushed from the bullpen, across the field and into the clubhouse. And although the group of us had never experienced anything such as this before, we had all heard tales about rowdy locker room celebrations with the popping of corks, flowing beer and champagne, and teammates dousing one another with foam and spray. It had been a tradition in club houses of championship teams since the early days of the game. So it was only fitting that we expected a time of joyous celebration following our pivotal win over the Red Sox. We had just become the 1960 American League champions!

Beside me were Johnny Blanchard, Jim Coates, Dale Long, and a few others who, until this point, had never been on a major league pennant-winning club. We couldn't wait to burst through the clubhouse door and get the party started. But we had no idea of the letdown we were in for. Just inside, we quickly discovered that for the older guys, it was business as usual.

For many of the Yankee veterans, winning the flag was simply the job they set out to do. Winning another league championship is what they had confidently put their sights on as far back as the start of spring training. It was what was expected of them, as well as what they expected of themselves. And perhaps, for players, such as Yogi, Mickey, Whitey, Gil McDougald, Bob Turley and Bill Skowron, winning five pennants over a span of six seasons may have taken some of the luster away from what was an incredible string of accomplishments.

Yet, for us first-time champions, the clubhouse was surprisingly subdued. There may have been a few more handshakes and pats on the back than usual, and maybe some guys who normally rushed to the showers paused long enough to pop open a can of beer, but it was disappointing to find hardly anyone who was in a mood to celebrate. No one seemed ready to share our excitement.

Finally, it was Gil McDougald who noticed the bemused look on our faces and tried to do what he could to enliven an awkward atmosphere. Stripped to his undershirt and with a towel draped over his shoulder, he came to us with a cold can of beer raised high above his head.

"We need to salute you boys," he announced. "All you young fellows who played a part in helping us win the pennant!" Taking the hint, some guys, already wrapped in towels and heading for the showers, turned around and walked back to join us. Others, still at their lockers, rose from their stools and sauntered across the room. With drinks in hand and what may have been perceived as a slight tone of indifference, the small group gathered around just long enough for McDougald to give an impromptu toast and for everyone to take another gulp of beer. Had it not been for Gil's efforts to mark the occasion, capturing the A.L. title would have been like another day at the office for most of the Yankees, while not being able to celebrate the moment as the highlight of the season to that point, was quite disappointing for the rest of us.

Since the days of Gehrig and DiMaggio, Yankee tradition demanded dignity and professionalism from every player. Historically, the organization would settle for nothing less than being crowned World Champions. Nevertheless, in 1960, there were eight clubs which competed for the American League title, and the Yankees managed to finish at the top of the A.L. standings for the 25th time in 40 years. The World Series was still a few days away, but so what. I believe winning the league championship the way we did, on the road and in the middle of a red-hot winning streak, was reason enough to celebrate. I think it would have been great to get doused with champagne just once.

I returned home for the off-season, despondent and disappointed. I had discovered that being a New York Yankee wasn't exactly all of what I had expected. Dropping the World Series to Pittsburgh was a very painful experience, and even winning the American League pennant, I found, was no big deal for most of the ballclub. Still, I went home to Chicago as the local hero. I lived it up big, having extra money to burn from my World Series bonus. For those few short weeks, I was playing the part of the big man in town, yet I never took the time to notice the warning signs that were popping up all around me. Signals, which I believe, were sent to me to warn me that my life was heading in the wrong direction.

I had planned to spend a big part of my bonus on a new automobile, and there wasn't a dealership in the entire Chicago area who wasn't willing to take my money. But I went back to the same dealer, Yates Ford on South Chicago Avenue, and talked with the same salesman who had sold me my first car, the '49 Dodge Wayfarer, a few years earlier. It was former boxer, Steven G. Lalich, "Tom-Tom," an old friend of the family, who I trusted to give me the best deal possible. Tom-Tom assured me he would do whatever was necessary to put me in the car of my dreams.

I had my heart set on a new '61 Thunderbird, but Yates Ford had none on their lot or in the showroom that matched up to my expectations. However, with Tom-Tom's assurance that he could order exactly what I wanted and have it delivered to his dealership within three weeks, we made a deal. The total cost of my dream car would run just a little over $3,000!

In the meantime, Tom-Tom furnished me with a loaner car, a sporty late-model to drive around town until my car was delivered. It would be mine to use as I pleased, but he firmly insisted that I get myself a short-term auto insurance policy, just in case something unexpected happened while the car was in my care. Unfortunately, I wouldn't realize the value of his advice until it was too late.

After an evening that started innocently with a couple of games of handball at the Y, I went out with the boys to have a beer, and before I knew it, the night turned into one of heavy drinking and chasing girls.

By the dawn's early light, I tried to drive home. I was fighting to stay awake and keep the new automobile on the highway. But, the combination of handball, alcohol and staying out too late with the ladies proved to be more than I could handle. I approached an intersection, stopped at the stop sign, and for what seemed like only a split second, I nodded off behind the wheel. Suddenly, I was startled by the impact of a violent crash. I was jolted back into reality when my head was forced forward into the steering wheel, cutting my mouth and breaking off several of my front teeth. At considerable speed, another vehicle had rammed the front end of my car. My vision cleared just in time to see the other driver speed away from the scene. My car was heavily damaged and stranded in the middle of the intersection. The weather was bitterly cold, but I set out on foot, wanting to make it back home before daylight. After a five-mile walk in the frigid temperatures, I reached the house, where Aunt Sophie opened the door and gasped in horror at the sight of my bloody mouth and chin.

"Please don't tell Deda," I begged her. "It's nothing serious. Besides it's time for our Orthodox Serbian Christmas. There's no need to upset my grandfather on such a special holiday."

In the peace and quiet of that Sunday morning, Sophie somehow found a way to sneak a phone call to our local dentist. And after explaining the situation, he agreed to see me later that same day in his office. He had me in his chair for what seemed like hours. He straightened and realigned a couple of my teeth which had been knocked out of place, ground and filed the rough edges of a few that were broken and extracted the ones he could not salvage. The work he did was both extensive and expensive. I left the dentist's office that afternoon in pain, my mouth packed with gauze and my wallet empty. I realized right away that keeping my condition a secret from Deda would not be easy.

Later in the evening, I emerged from my room. Aunt Sophie was working in the kitchen, preparing food for our Christmas celebration. As usual, Deda was seated quietly at the table, spreading out his playing cards to start another game of solitaire. To make things appear normal, I walked into the kitchen and made conversation with both of them, carefully covering my mouth and lips with my hand to hide my injuries when I faced Deda to speak to him directly. I should have known that such a ridiculous scheme as mine would not fool someone as intelligent as Deda. He was a very perceptive man and would see right through it.

In keeping with our Christmas mealtime traditions, Sophie placed the entire head of a cooked pig on a large platter and carefully arranged colorful garnishes around it. The dish and the arrangement, which were for decoration only and not to be eaten, had been part of the holidays at our house for as long as I could remember. It was just one of the many Serbian family traditions we enjoyed each year at Christmas. To keep things lighthearted and festive, I began to joke with Aunt Sophie about the pig's head.

"Nobody ever eats the head," I laughed, poking at it with my finger. "Maybe this year, we should give it a try." Aunt Sophie rolled her eyes and patronized me with a girlish giggle. Still, Deda was quiet and never looked up from his card game. I could sense that he wasn't in a pleasant mood. "Maybe we could start with the eyes," I continued. "If I ate the eyes, they might improve my vision and I would never have to wear eyeglasses again!"

And just as if he had drawn a losing hand in a high stakes poker game, Deda slammed the cards down on the table. He was disgusted and the tone of his voice was proof.

"Well, why a' don't you eat a' his brains?" he fumed in his broken English. "Then a' maybe you will be smarter than you were last night when you knock a' your teeth out!"

My grandfather knew what had happened! It was useless to try to hide anything from him. He was a very wise man who had tried hard to give me direction and guidance, and it was painfully disappointing for him whenever I failed to heed his advice. He wanted what was best for me, even when I didn't. More than ever, I appreciate my grandfather's insightful wisdom and everything he tried to do for me. He had so much to offer and I should have been paying attention.

Nevertheless, I was lucky to have survived that accident. I could have been critically injured, crippled for life or even worse. I have no doubt that I was spiritually protected when I fell asleep at that stop sign. Yet, like so many other times in my life, I was unable to accept the indisputable warnings I was offered. I failed to see how I was being told again and again to change the direction of my life. But by this point, my addiction to alcohol had tightened its grip and I was making little effort to fight back. It is with such regret that I failed to heed these warnings and see them for what they were.

-----O--------O--------O-----

It was the fall of 1960 and the National League had already made it official. They had announced plans for expansion, awarding new franchises to the cities of New York and Houston, which would increase the number of teams in the league to ten. With the two additional clubs which would begin play in the 1962, the NL also announced it would be switching to a new, extended schedule for that season, one that would require teams to play 162 games instead of 154.

Not to be outdone, the American League jumped headfirst into the expansion business. They had stood by and watched as the NL took control of the West Coast baseball market by moving the Dodgers and Giants to California in 1958 and they weren't about to allow themselves to fall even further behind, monetarily or geographically. No sooner had the National League's expansion plans been made public, than the AL hastily announced that they would also be adding two new franchises. One of them would be a replacement team in Washington D.C. and the other in California, and both new clubs would be up and running in time to start the 1961 season. Considering the short span of time the America League imposed on itself to put it all together, the results were quite impressive.

The Washington Senators had been operating in the red for years. They had last appeared in the World Series in 1933 and with the exception of a couple of seasons during World War II, the club had not enjoyed a winning year. To go along with the dismal play, poor attendance made it practically impossible for the club to stay afloat financially. The AL granted Washington's tight-fisted owner, Calvin Griffith, permission to relocate his team to the Minneapolis-Saint Paul area, where they were renamed the Minnesota Twins. However, the move left a gaping vacancy in the Nation's Capital.

After hearing from a new D.C. based ownership group which had the financial means to back such a deal, American League President, Joe Cronin, acted quickly. He scrambled to establish a new replacement team of Senators in Washington, while simultaneously working to secure authorization from Major League Baseball's Expansion Committee to set up another new franchise in Los Angeles. With only four months to go before the start of the 1961 baseball season, Cronin had a lot to do with no time to waste.

Following the Thanksgiving weekend, the "New" Senators were getting their ducks in a row. They announced that Edward Doherty would be the club's general manager and ex-American League batting champ and all-star first baseman, Mickey Vernon, would serve as field manager. Meanwhile the Los Angeles club still had no committed ownership and were a couple of weeks away from taking their first steps as an organization. However, in early December, a chain of events occurred which were almost too good to be true.

Throughout the decade of the 1950s, cowboy film star, Gene Autry, had expanded his own business empire by purchasing numerous radio stations in Southern California. Several of his stations had been parts of the Los Angeles Dodgers' Baseball Network, broadcasting Dodger games each year, all season long. But after the 1960 season, the Dodgers cut back on the number stations that would be allowed to carry their games and several of Autry's stations were among those dropped.

Not to be denied, Autry attended the baseball winter meetings. It was his intention to rub elbows with club owners and executives, as well as any representatives of the new L.A. team of the American League who may be there. He was looking to negotiate a deal which would permit him to carry games of the new team on his network of stations. Decked out in his unmistakable white Stetson and his custom-made Western boots, the affable "Singing Cowboy" strolled into the winter meetings with the idea of signing a broadcasting contract and walked out as the principal owner of the new Los Angeles Angels!

Gene Autry knew that the key to running a successful team was to surround himself with knowledgeable people to handle operations both on and off the field, people competent in all areas of the business. The first person Autry coaxed into the Angels' fold was his good friend, Fred Haney, a crafty third baseman in the 1920s who had since picked up ten years of experience as a big league manager. Under Haney's direction, the Milwaukee Braves made it to the World Series in both 1957 and '58. Yet, after what was an unacceptable second place finish for Milwaukee's front office in 1959, Fred was fired. But he had an abundance of friends and connections throughout professional baseball and would not be away from the game for long. With his unique insight into the game and his congenial personality, it is easy to see why Fred was hired by NBC Sports in 1960 to work with legendary sports broadcaster, Lindsay Nelson, on their weekly televised baseball games. Following the one season in the booth for NBC, he was ready to get back to the nuts and bolts of baseball and was happy to accept Autry's offer to be the general manager of the Angels. On the other hand, the process of hiring the club's first field manager was a little more complicated.

Gene Autry was a fine gentleman who knew that the key to running a successful team was to surround himself with knowledgeable people.

After being dismissed by the Yankees, Casey Stengel moved west with his wife, Edna, to the Glendale neighborhood in the northern section of Los Angeles County. It had been Casey's idea to get as far away from

New York as possible and clear his head of all that had gone on with the Yankees and the '60 World Series. But for Fred Haney, Casey was the ideal candidate for the manager's job. They had been good friends for a long time and Haney wanted to use that relationship to coax Stengel out of retirement. He told Casey that he wanted his help with player selection and assured him that as manager, he could utilize the players any way he wanted, with no interference from the front office.

Stengel wanted to help his old friend, but he insisted on taking more time before going back on the field. However, he did offer his services to the Angels as an unofficial advisor. He was interested and willing to help Haney evaluate available players, feeling like he had something to offer. Casey was confident that the Yankees, in particular, may have some highly talented players who would be left unprotected in the upcoming player draft, and there was no team he wanted to undermine more than his former employer, the New York Yankees. Still, there was no one more interested in becoming the Angels' first manager than baseball's notorious bad boy, Leo "The Lip" Durocher, an outspoken self-promoter, who loved being in the public eye.

He had been in baseball since the 1920s, and by this time Leo had already made quite a fiery reputation for himself, first as a testy infielder with several big league clubs and later as manager of both the Dodgers and Giants. Not only did he want the job, but he was confident to the extent of speculating to friends in the Hollywood social circles that the position was his for the taking. Meanwhile, Leo was continuing to do everything possible to find his niche among the rich and famous of Tinseltown. He mingled at celebrity parties, frequented horse tracks and hung around with some of the most well known gamblers on the West Coast. And it was his open association with people of questionable character that had landed him in hot water with the officials of baseball on several different occasions. Commissioner A. B. "Happy" Chandler went as far as to suspend Durocher for the entire 1947 season for what was ruled "conduct detrimental to baseball." And even though the details of Leo's conduct were never clearly specified, his tendency to grab headlines for all the wrong reasons was not characteristic of the type of individual Autry and Haney had in mind to be the field boss of the new team. Still, Fred Haney was not out of ideas. He had lots of West Coast friends in baseball and planned to use his connections to benefit his new employer.

And after getting Autry's approval, he approached the Dodgers' first baseman, Gil Hodges, and offered the eight-time NL All-Star a sizable sum to retire as an active player and join the Angels as a player-manager. But realizing the rivalry which was already building between the two teams in Los Angeles, Hodges elected to stick with the Dodgers for a while longer. Haney was disappointed when his offer was declined, and with time being short, his search for the right man for the job continued.

Fortunately, the one candidate who did fit nicely with the ideals and plans of Autry and Haney was Bill Rigney, an easy-going Californian who lived in the Bay Area. Succeeding Durocher as manager the Giants in New York, Rigney had taken over the helm of the Giants in 1956 and stayed on as their skipper, even after the team moved to San Francisco. As a player, Bill played every position in the Giants infield in the late 1940s and early 50s, earning a spot on the National League All-Star team in 1948. As a person, he was admired and regarded as a true baseball man who worked hard to establish himself in the game. In turn, he respected the game, and as a manager, handled his players fairly. On the field, the usually even-tempered Rigney was never one to shy away from controversy. He was the tenacious type of manager who would spring from the bench at the drop of a hat and vehemently defend his players, a tendency which resulted in his being ejected from more than 50 games during his managerial career. Bill Rigney became the first field manager ever hired by the Los Angeles Angels, a position he would hold from 1961 until early in the 1969 season. Over that time he endeared himself to Angel fans, to whom he will always be remembered as someone who played an integral role in their team's history.

With the Christmas holidays quickly approaching, Cronin summoned the officials of the new expansion clubs to a meeting at his Boston office. It was urgent that players for these teams be selected as soon as possible, yet he wanted to keep as much under wraps as he could. Only the managers, general managers and owners would be permitted to attend, and to this point, Cronin had ordered all existing AL clubs not to reveal who among their players would be protected and who would be draft-eligible. He had rosters of unprotected players from each of his teams, but was adamant that the names remain secret. He didn't want players knowing who was available and who wasn't, especially during the time of year when new contracts were about to be mailed out.

There was nothing simple about the selection process. The rules and guidelines imposed by the expansion committee were complex and difficult to follow which led to instances where improper selections were made. But there was not enough time for the teams to backtrack and realign their picks, so the order of draft selections already made was allowed to stand.

The rules called for each of the eight existing teams to place seven players into the pool of draft-eligible players who had been on their active roster as of August 31, 1960. In addition, each of those teams was required to supply the pool with eight other players from their 40-man roster. The expansion clubs were then limited to no more than four picks from any one team, and no existing team would be forced to give up more than seven players all told, and to complicate the process even further, only a certain number of players of each position could be taken. It was a costly operation for these new organizations, as the Senators and Angels were required to pay $75,000 for each player drafted, with a lesser fee charged for selecting a minor league player.

It was draft day, December 14, 1960, the day of baseball's first-ever expansion draft. Together in the American League's headquarters in Boston, Joe Cronin met the officials of the new expansion clubs. It was Cronin's responsibility to oversee the draft, see that both sides were aware of the guidelines and ensure all rules would be followed. His job was basic and clear-cut. But still, confusion set in and the proceedings ran off course when Joe either failed to explain the provisions clearly or simply allowed some of the rules to be ignored. The Senators, with their ownership and staff in place weeks ahead of the Angels, had already set to work, ironing out an agreement to use Griffith Stadium as their home park and speaking "off the record" with a few players they knew would be available in the draft. Meanwhile, the Angels, flying by the seat of their pants, were frantically trying to form a draft strategy and evaluate the talent in the player pool, while still having to work out an arrangement to play their home games at Wrigley Field in Los Angeles, a cozy 20,000 seat stadium which had been used as a minor league ballpark for years.

Just a day or so before the draft, I received notification from the Yankees that they would not be protecting me, and that my name would be among those players available to be selected by the expansion clubs. None of this came as a surprise, especially after the way they had put me on the shelf at the end of the 1960 season, and in spite of having pitched well at both Richmond and New York, I knew there was no future for me in the Yankee organization. I just had no idea what the Yankees would do with me, and I truly had no clue that another team would have such interest in me.

To some, it may have come as a big surprise, while to others, it was just another frantic choice made by team officials under pressure to move quickly. But for me, it was the last thing on earth I expected. I was floored when I heard the news. Having the first pick of the 1960 American League expansion draft, the Los Angeles Angels made me their first choice. The whole matter was made even more exciting when Gene Autry and Fred Haney phoned the house and spoke with me personally to give me the news. They selected me to be the first player in the team's history! I was the first Angel to sign his name on a major league contract! It was such a thrill to be chosen to be the first Angel. The phone was ringing off the hook with reporters wanting interviews. My picture was in the sports pages across the country, with writers referring to me as the first building block for a new major league franchise.

CHAPTER 26

MY FIRST SEASON WITH A BRAND NEW BALL CLUB

fter the unexpected hoopla of the winter finally slowed down, my first order of business with the Angels was to report to spring training in Palm Springs, California. Of course, I was familiar with Southern California, having been there for training camp a few years earlier, so getting a chance to go back to that area suited me just fine. St. Petersburg, Florida, which was spring training headquarters for the Yankees, was a great spot for training camp, yet it was a seasonal town, a winter home for retirees and a tourist spot for families on summer vacation. There was no way to compare the humid Tampa-Saint Pete area to the trendy California scene, with its balmy weather, golf courses, TV and movie stars and girls in bikinis. What's more, once the baseball season started, our ballclub would move even closer to the Pacific Coast and play all our home games in downtown Los Angeles.

As the time to leave home drew nearer, I began to feel a lot better about being an Angel and a lot less bitter towards my former team, the Yankees. Because of my respect and close relationship with Ralph Houk, I chalked it up to bad timing when I heard the news that he had been selected to replace Stengel as manager for New York. I admired Ralph for all he tried to do for me years earlier when the army snatched me out of spring training and sent me straight to boot camp. For the short time we were together, he had been a father figure to me and I was certain things in New York would have been quite different if Ralph had been running the club in 1960. However, at the same time, I was relieved to hear that Casey had no interest in managing the Angels, and that Bill Rigney, a man about whom I had heard only good things, had accepted the job. Besides, there were several other ex-Yankees who were left unprotected from the expansion draft and were subsequently selected by either Los Angeles or Washington, and they were all outstanding ball players. To me, this indicated that perhaps I had not been the only guy in the Yankees' doghouse who didn't fit into their plans for the future. I was heading west to make a new start in my baseball career. And to make the long trip a more memorable one, I traveled with a couple of my former Yankee teammates, guys who had also been drafted by the Angels.

Kenny Hunt, with whom I had become good friends with when we were teammates in the Yankees' farm system at Richmond, and Michigan native, Duane "Duke Maas, a right-handed pitcher who, like me, spent the 1960 World Series in Stengel's doghouse, made it a point to stay in contact with me during the off-season. Once we discovered that all three of us would be going to spring training with the Angels, we decided to form a caravan and drive to Southern California together. Embarking on a new experience is always better when there are friends who can be part of it. The three of us met in Chicago and took off on a 2000 mile journey across the country, to be part of the first ever assembly of a brand new baseball team. It was quite a historical moment, even if we didn't recognize it as that.

By that time, the new car I ordered had arrived: a 1961 robin egg blue Ford Thunderbird, with the big 390-cubic inch motor, making it one of the fastest cars on the road at the time. I couldn't wait to get it on a straight stretch of open highway and try it out. Kenny, being the conservative type, was never one to stretch the rules. As a driver, he was always sure to give the proper signals and stay within the speed limit. Duke, the oldest of the group, was married. His car was crammed with extra luggage and small items of furniture, as his wife and children would be coming to California to live with him, once the schools in Michigan were closed for the summer. Duke was in no hurry and wanted nothing more than to arrive in Palm Springs safe and sound. Of the group, I was the only one in a hurry. I was impatient and ready to set a new land speed record. I wanted to get behind the wheel of that T-Bird and burn up the highway. But Kenny and Duke gave me strict orders to stay behind them. The rear position was the best one for me, they figured. That way, there was no chance of me driving fast, leaving them behind and us being separated.

We had driven only a couple hundred miles when we decided to stop for our first night, and after just a few hours of sleep, we got up and were back on the road early the next morning. We had driven no more than about 30 miles, when I realized I didn't have my wallet. My hands tightened on the steering wheel as I remembered leaving it in my motel room, recalling that I slipped it under my pillow for safe keeping, just before I fell asleep. Feeling panicky, I flashed my headlights at Duke and Ken, signaling for them to pull off the highway. As soon as our vehicle convoy rolled to a stop, I frantically told the others what had happened and explained that I would be driving back to the motel to retrieve my billfold. Without saying anything, Duke simply looked toward the sky and shook his head, as if he couldn't imagine someone being so careless. On the other hand, Ken was not as subtle when it came to expressing his displeasure.

"How could you be so thoughtless?" he questioned me. "That's about the dumbest thing I've ever heard of!" Not wanting to waste time arguing, I turned to go back to my car.

"Don't worry about it!" I snapped. "Just get back on the damn road and keep going. I'll catch up with you before you know it!"

The rear tires of that new Thunderbird squealed across the pavement as I burned out, making a U-turn to head back east. Fighting the steering wheel to maintained control, I left them in a cloud of smoke, standing on the roadside. Luckily there were no speed traps along the way, and I made it back to the motel in about half the time of a normal driver. After getting the key and unlocking the room, I found my wallet exactly where I had placed it the night before. I paused only long enough to take in a big sigh of relief; in a matter of seconds, I was back in my car, barreling down the road, retracing the same route I had covered just minutes earlier. And knowing the way Duke and Kenny drove, I figured it would take no more than an hour or two to catch them. It was a highway chase, much like the legendary race between the slow, laid-back tortoise and the highly favored, but overconfident hare.

I had both the nerve and the horsepower to overtake them in time for us to have lunch together, still neither of them were impressed. After all, my thoughtless mistake had done nothing to slow the progress of our trip, but neither Duke nor Ken thought much of my daring driving or the fast sleek automobile that made it possible.

"You should've gotten a ticket," quipped Ken. "You would have deserved it!"

"You may be right," I asserted. "But ya' know, this new car of mine was built to put the open road behind me, not for taking in the scenery!"

Our trip took us across the state of Missouri and into Joplin, one of the loveliest little towns in the Midwest. As a business venture, Mickey Mantle, who had played a season of minor league baseball there with the Joplin Miners, had become part-owner of a recently opened Holiday Inn, located at the southern tip of the town. On our way through, we decided to stop at the new hotel to have a look around, and depending on the prices, we were considering staying there for the night. We were impressed the moment we drove into the parking lot, seeing the giant-size Holiday Inn sign, with the words, "Operated by Mickey Mantle" written boldly across the bottom.

We paraded into lobby and to the front desk, where our unofficial spokesman, Ken Hunt, did all the talking. He explained to the clerk that we were all ex-teammates of Mickey's and that we were on our way to spring training. The clerk stepped away into a tiny office and began dialing the phone. Moments later, after hanging up, he returned to the front and summoned Ken back to the desk for short conversation. While Duke and I were too far away to hear any of the details, we watched as Ken gave the gentleman a hearty handshake and then turned to walk toward us. His chest puffed out, as if he had just run a four-minute mile.

"Okay, boys, let's go get our bags!" he offered. "Here's the deal. I explained to the clerk that we're good friends of Mickey's and we're on our way to spring training. He just made a phone call and set it all up; we each have a complimentary room for the night!"

Unprepared for such good news, Duke and I looked at each other in disbelief. "Is this some sort of joke?" Duke asked. "Are you kidding us?"

"Not at all!" Kenny answered sternly. "Mickey told 'em to cut us a break, so we're staying here free of charge."

I followed my teammates back outside to park our vehicles and grab our luggage. "We really got lucky tonight, thanks to Mick," one of them remarked. "Yeah, that Mickey's quite a guy," the other agreed.

I listened quietly to the comments being made about the man I consider to be the greatest ballplayer of my era. He was not there with us, yet he was still referred to in tones of admiration and respect. Those who knew Mickey describe him as a great player and teammate who gave the game of baseball his best. Shy, kind and generous, he was a friend to everyone who ever had the good fortune of being around him. However, in spite of any weaknesses he may have had, he was still a human being, remembered for accomplishing superhuman feats on the baseball field. There will never be another Mickey Mantle, which is unfortunate, not only for baseball, but for the rest of the world as well. I am lucky to have had him as a teammate and proud to say he was my friend.

Once I arrived at training camp, I soon discovered that the dry air of Southern California made it difficult for me to get into good physical shape. In the past I had grown accustomed to working out in the muggy, humid conditions of Florida, where I shed any extra pounds I had put on during the offseason, while strengthening my legs and building up my wind simultaneously; and to make matters worse, I was drinking more than ever. I had often heard that alcohol can slow down the metabolism and be a problem for anyone on any type of fitness program. But once again, I failed to recognize another unmistakable warning sign directly before me. There were other guys in camp who were also struggling to get into shape, but they were some of the veteran players who were nearing the end of their careers, and it was expected that they might need to work harder in training camp than the younger guys. However, at 26 years-old, I was about to enter what should have been the prime seasons of my career. I should have been honest with myself and acknowledged the true cause of my problem. Nonetheless, my attention was focused on the fact that I was the Angels' number one draft pick, and I still needed to prove myself.

We had a solid nucleus of capable veterans in our camp who, while having their best years behind them, were still willing to work extra hard to get in shape for one or two more seasons. These fellows had worked hard their entire careers, respected the game of baseball and willingly stepped forward to assume positions of leadership on this new ball club. Ted Kluszewski, a power-hitting first baseman, who came to us from the Chicago White Sox; Steve Bilko, a pick from the Detroit Tigers' minor league system; right-hand pitcher, Ned Garver, from the Kansas City Athletics, who had more than 120 major league wins to his credit; and "The Walkin' Man," Eddie Yost, also from the Tigers, who led the American League in walks six times, all became mentors, advisors and part-time coaches, on a team otherwise stocked with young players who were on the upstart of their baseball careers.

The Angels' roster had been carefully designed to include some of the finest young prospects in all of baseball. According to Fred Haney's strategic plan, obtaining the proper mixture of experienced veterans and talented young players would be the key to having a competitive club from the very start. To prove the Angels were on track to becoming the most successful first-year team in baseball history, Haney selected future stars such as shortstop, Jim Fregosi from the Boston Red Sox; right-hand pitcher, Ken McBride from the White Sox; catcher, Bob "Buck" Rodgers from Detroit; and outfielder, Albie Pearson, a minor league pick from the Orioles.

Manager Bill Rigney ran a tight ship, yet he still maintained an easy-going style of leadership. His fatherly manner permitted the younger players, most of whom were getting their first shot at a starting job in the big leagues, to go about their work without unneeded pressure. However, my dealings with Bill got off to a bad start when I allowed my bull-headed ego to get in the way of what probably would have been a good relationship.

In one of our first spring exhibition games, I was getting beat like a dirty rug. Several runs had already scored and the bases were still loaded. Rigney asked for time, made his signal to the bullpen, and slowly made his way out to the mound to give me the hook. Just as he made his final steps to the top of the hill, he reached forward with his open hand, expecting me to hand him the baseball. "Let's have the ball," he demanded in a calm tone.

I slapped the ball into the pocket of my glove, squeezed it tightly and defiantly placed my hands on my hips. Of course I was angry and disgusted with myself, but I should have never let my immature arrogance overtake me and cause me to show up my manager. Continuing to ignore his order, I stared upward at the sky. Bill finally pulled his hand back and glared at me.

"I'll give it to the new pitcher when he gets here," I murmured contentiously, "just like Casey had me do it in New York."

While it's difficult to say for sure, I believe that it was with that one incident that I sealed my fate with Bill Rigney. The season had not started. I had yet to pitch my first game for the Angels and I had already put myself in a bad position. I had alienated myself from the man who had as much control as anyone of my future with the team.

Nonetheless, when the regular season opened on Tuesday, April 11, we arrived in Baltimore for a windy, chilly afternoon game against the Orioles, who a year earlier had surprised the oddsmakers of baseball by finishing second in the American League, just eight games behind my former club, the Yankees. Reporters were swarming the city, pushing their way into the clubhouse, the dugout and even onto the playing field at Memorial Stadium, to cover the first-ever game of the Los Angeles Angels. It seemed as if everyone was wanting to talk with me, the first pick in the draft and the starting pitcher for opening day. That is, everyone except for Bill Rigney. In fact, my manager had had very little to say to me over the final few weeks of spring training.

I took the mound against the Orioles that afternoon with all the confidence of an experienced plumber about to repair another leaky faucet. Getting homerun support from teammates, Ted Kluszewski and Bob Cerv in the top of the first inning off Baltimore starter, Milt Pappas and another from "Klu" in the second, staked us to a comfortable 7-0 lead after just an inning and a half of play; an insurmountable deficit for the Birds on a day when I possessed good command of my pitches, and my battery mate, Del Rice, a seasoned catcher who had been around the big leagues since World War II, called a masterful game.

However, Baltimore got on the scoreboard with a single run in the second inning, which scored on an infield throwing error and another run in the third, when Brooks Robinson bounced into a force play at second base and an errant throw to the plate allowed another Oriole run to come home. The 7-2 score held for the rest of the day, as I went the distance for the complete-game win, allowing just six hits.

Our stay at the top of the American League standings would last only one day, as the Angels, after our Opening Day win, would go on to drop their next eight games in a row. Sadly, our team record would sink to a dismal 1 win and 7 losses before we ever got back to L.A. to play our first home game. As a franchise, the Angels would struggle through their early years, until achieving prominence with a World Series win in 2002 and six A.L. Western Division titles between 2004 and 2014. But after our opening day win in 1961, it would take more than 50 years before the team's composite record would reach the .500 plateau once again. In July 2014 the franchise's historical record would finally be balanced at 4,272 wins and 4,272 losses, a milestone indicator of organizational success.

The weather up and down the Eastern Seaboard was rainy and cold and although the 1961 season had open ten days earlier, the Angels had managed to squeeze in only three games. With a record of one win and two losses we arrived in New York to play the Yankees and were forced to hang around town for two days, because games scheduled for Tuesday and Wednesday were washed out. As the lingering storm system moved out late Wednesday and the weather improved, a few of us went out on the town for dinner and a few drinks. Being ex-Yankees, there were several of us on the Angels' ballclub who were familiar with the city and knew the best places to go. So it was no surprise when we ran into Mickey Mantle and some of his Yankee buddies while we were out making the rounds.

Mickey was as personable and friendly toward us as ever. Judging by his warm-hearted manner no one would have ever thought we were no longer teammates. As usual, he was the central figure, the life of the party, the guy telling jokes and buying everyone drinks. "Why, this is like old times, having you boys back in town," he remarked. "Why don't all y'all come on up to my place before you call it a night?" he offered in his Oklahoma drawl. "We'll have us an all-night party!" An invitation from Mickey Mantle is not something that's easy to turn down. The night was still young, so we took him up on his offer and caught a cab over to his place, the St. Moritz Hotel on Central Park South.

Inside his suite, the party was in full swing. The place was crawling with some of the most beautiful women I had ever seen! And the liquor was flowing like a river! There was no reason to think that Mickey was kidding when he suggested "an all-night party." But I needed to take it easy and get out of there at a sensible hour. After all, I was scheduled to start the next day, pitching the first game of an afternoon double header.

As it was customary for starting pitchers, I arrived at the stadium early, allowing myself time to prepare myself both mentally and physically for the game. I put on my nylon windbreaker and a pair of sweatpants and went outside to the playing field. Taking a moment to stretch my shoulders and legs, I followed up with some light calisthenics on the grass along the left-field line. Finishing up and preparing to jog across the outfield, I noticed Yogi Berra walking toward me. "What's up, Yogi?" I greeted him. "You're out here early today."

"I want to find out what you guys did to Mickey last night!" he replied sternly. "He's in pretty bad shape this morning. Matter of fact, he's in the clubhouse right now. His head is killing him and he's still throwing up! There's no way he'll be in the lineup today, not in his condition." Without giving me time to answer, he turned his back and headed in the direction of the Yankee's bench.

"I don't know what you're talking about, Yogi," I yelled as he walked away. "He was doing fine when I left his place. So, if he's sick today, don't blame me!"

"Today is my lucky day!" I muttered to myself. I stepped over the foul line, took a couple of steps and broke into a slow jog. *If Mickey is not playing today, my work will be a lot easier. He's the best hitter in the league and the last one I want to face.* The first pitch had yet to be thrown, and it looked like the Angels already had the upper hand.

With dark gray clouds breaking overhead, the Yankees sprinted from their dugout for the start of the game. I was surprised to see Mickey, sporting his familiar number 7 on the back of his shirt, hobbling across the diamond, making his way to his regular position in centerfield. *Maybe I shouldn't be so surprised*, I reminded myself. I knew Mickey well enough to know that because of his bad knees, he played every game in excruciating pain. And unless he was on his deathbed, he would be on the ball field giving it his best.

The game was still scoreless after I retired the first two hitters in the bottom of the first inning. The third hitter in Ralph Houk's lineup was Yogi, who quickly slapped a line drive which dropped in front of right-fielder, Leon Wagner, for New York's first base hit of the day. With Mantle, the clean-up batter advancing to the plate, I was ready to put the inside knowledge I had received to good use. I was all set to take full advantage of his weakened condition. Hangover or not, I was moving in for the kill.

The muscles in his forearms rippled with power as he took a couple of practice swings before stepping into the batter's box. A switch-hitter, Mickey was hitting from the left side against me and like every other pitch in the league, I knew he would be aiming for the short fence in the rightfield corner. He scratched at the dirt with the spikes and stared toward the mound. He looked upward and squinted painfully at the overcast sky, a sure indication that his pounding headache was bearing down hard.

He swung half-heartedly at a fastball over the inside corner of the plate, getting just a piece of the baseball, which bounced slowly passed the third base coach's box. *This guy's in bad shape. His bat isn't fast enough to get around on any of my pitches. I'll try a hard slider and keep it inside on his hands. He's in no condition to pull anything to rightfield.* I would never be more wrong in my life.

I threw Mickey my best slider toward the middle of the plate. At the last split second, it broke suddenly to the inside corner, almost on his fists. In a demonstration of strength and a keen batting eye, he hit a low line drive that took off like a rocket, flying through the chilly spring air. It sailed just out of the reach of Wagner's outstretched glove and over the wall in the right-field corner for a two-run homer! I was enraged. Mickey circled the bases sheepishly with his head down. Yogi waited at home and congratulated him as he stepped on the plate. Together they trotted to the dugout, grinning like a couple of thieves who had just cleaned out a bank vault. The Yanks had taken a 2 to 0 lead, and I couldn't believe what had just happened!

After the Angels pushed across runs in the second and fifth innings, we entered the home half of the fifth tied at two. Other than Berra's single and Mantle's cheap homer in the first, I had held the Yankees hitless. Nevertheless, the very idea of Mickey pulling my inside slider for a homerun was gnawing at my thoughts. Had it not been hit to the shortest portion of the field, and barely cleared the wall, perhaps I would not have been so frustrated with myself.

I continued to cruise along into the fifth, quickly retiring the first two New York batters. Suddenly, with the heart of the Yankee batting order due up, I surrendered back-to-back singles, the first to Hector

Lopez and another to that conniving Yogi Berra. With two outs and two runners on base, Mickey again, strode to the plate, receiving a thunderous ovation from the hometown fans who recalled his first-inning clout. "He won't do that to me a second time," I convinced myself, as I rubbed up a new baseball. I don't care if he is Mickey Mantle, he's going to have to hit my best pitch.

I toed the pitching rubber, assumed the set position and peered in at my catcher, Eddie Sadowski, who had just entered the game, replacing Del Rice. With his fingers hidden in his crotch, he gave the sign for an outside fastball. The runners, neither of them being fleet of foot, took only modest leads. I shook my head in disagreement with Eddie's sign and waited for him to offer another one. He put down the sign for a slider. I wanted to issue a challenge to Mickey. I would tempt him to go for another pitch, just like the one he lost in the seats a few innings earlier. I nodded to my catcher with approval. My stubborn ego was my biggest advocate and my best pitch, the slider, was on its way.

Again, the velocity and location looked good. I had hit my spot. Again, with sizzling speed, the baseball curved abruptly in on the batter's hands. Yet, as though he was reading my mind and knew precisely what was coming, Mickey made an inside-out swing, making solid contact. His body recoiled, and with the tremendous power in his wrists and forearms, he made it look too easy. The ball ripped through the air like a fiery comet. And like walking a tightrope, it followed the rightfield line, until it approached the corner wall. At the last instant, it began to slice, ever so slightly, back toward fair territory. Leon Wagner waited, timed his jump perfectly and made another gallant leap for the ball. But once again, he came up empty-handed. The moment I saw the fans in bleachers jump to their feet, their arms extending upward, reaching for the ball, my heart sank into the pit of my stomach. He had done it to me again! This time it was even worse. This was a three-run blast, which landed in the outfield seats only a few feet from the very spot where the first one had come to rest.

I should have seen this dirty trick coming a mile away! It was all a big set-up. Everything from Mickey's party invitation to Yogi's little pre-game chat. It was all part of the plan to cause me to go easy on Mickey. I was furious! I grabbed the rosin bag, squeezed it in my fist and slammed it to the ground. I stomped off the mound and down onto the grass of the infield. In a fit of rage, I charged a few paces toward Mickey as he rambled slowly from first to second. Thinking the better of it, I decided not to get any closer. I stopped in my tracks and yelled at him.

"You lousy SOB!" I fumed. "You should be real proud of yourself!"

Refusing to acknowledge me, he rounded second base and headed for third. I moved a step or two closer and resumed my rant. "You won't even look at me will you? You no-good dirty hillbilly! You'll never get away with that trick again!"

Surprisingly enough, I managed to regain my composure. I fanned the next hitter, Roger Maris, and sat the Yankees down in order in the sixth inning. But it was too late, the damage had already been done. We lost that first game of the twin-bill 7 to 5, and dropped the nightcap game 4 to 2. Our team record had suddenly plummeted to 1 and 4. My triumphant return to New York had been spoiled by a couple of sly veterans who knew all the tricks. Yogi and Mickey had played me like a banjo. But after that game, I promised myself I would never lose another game because of being overly confident. I would be sure to leave my ego in the locker room. A guy can't pitch well when he's angry.

Shown is a starting lineup often used by manager Bill Rigney during the early weeks of 1961. (left to right): Rigney, manager; Eli Grba, pitcher; Earl Averill, catcher; Gene Leek, third base; Ken Aspromonte, second base; Bob Cerv, leftfield; Ted Kluszewski, firstbase; Steve Bilko, rightfield; Albie Pearson, centerfield and Ken Hamlin shortstop. The club was a mixture of experienced veterans and talented young players.

I would fail to register my second win until early May, when at home in Los Angeles, I avenged my earlier loss to the Yankees, defeating them 5 to 3. My personal record would reach a low point later in the year, dropping to a disappointing 5-11 in August. And while I may have had a few good outings during that span, low run support contributed to a couple of my losses. Fortunately, I rebounded before the season ended and picked up six wins in my final eight decisions.

By winning 70 games and losing 91, the Los Angeles Angels of 1961 established a record for the best winning percentage (.435) ever recorded by an expansion team in its first season. The American League's new West Coast franchise was off to an exciting start. Outfielders, Ken Hunt and Leon Wagner, set the pace offensively, smashing 25 and 28 homers respectively. Ken McBride led our young pitching staff, winning 13 ballgames, while Ted Bowsfield and I chipped in with 11 victories each. There were many reasons for Angels fans to be encouraged and hopeful for the future. Better days were right around the corner.

Still, even as the season wound down, I remained in a delicate, precarious relationship with my manager. Rigney seemed to want little to do with me and the same could be said for pitching coach, Marv Grissom. Sure, as a pitcher, I had turned a decent year, but I began to doubt my future with the Angels. *Was the writing on the wall?* The more time I spent contemplating my unsettled situation, the more reasons I gave myself to worry. And again, alcohol was the crutch I used for short, temporary escapes from the problems in my life.

Still, the problems never went away; they only seemed to get worse. I had reached the undeniable point of abuse, where alcohol had taken control of my life. My personality hardened. I had become a sullen and angry young man, who often placed blame on others and gave flimsy excuses for everything that went wrong. I was in full denial and refused to acknowledge that I was on the path of self-destruction. I enjoyed living in L.A. and wanted so much to be part of the Angels future. However, based on the direction in which my life was headed, I should have realized that my time with them would be short.

I wanted so much to be part of the Angels future. However, based on the direction in which my life was headed, I should have realized that my time with them would be short.

332

CHAPTER 27
LOSING CONTROL

J ust as professor, Randy Pausch, suggested in his best-selling book, *The Last Lecture*, "No matter how bad things are, you can always make things worse," the way in which I mishandled my personal life while playing for the Angels makes a great case in point. During that time, I somehow managed to continue to pitch well, but my life of drinking, carousing and chasing young ladies was starting to catch up with me. My relationship with Bill Rigney was indifferent, to say the least. And like any baseball manager worth his salt, he was quick to notice whenever one of his players was burning the candle at both ends. There was no doubt that Bill knew what was going on, and I'm certain my behavior did nothing to endear me to him.

After getting knocked all over the park in a night game at Wrigley Field, I left my apartment early the next day and stopped in a local cocktail lounge before going to the ballpark. I had started the game, but pitched only a couple of innings before my control abandoned me for the night. It was embarrassing to get pulled from the game so early in front of the home crowd. I knew I would not pitch in this next game, so I decided to stop for a beer to help take the edge off such a disappointing performance.

This friendly gathering place had become a watering hole for some ballplayers who needed a dimly lit, out-of-the-way place to hook up with their stashes, their girlfriends who they would prefer not to be seen with in public. I would drop in from time to time for drinks and to chat with the owners after learning that the operating partners of the business were a couple of friendly, outgoing brothers of Croatian decent, John and George Metkovich. Of course, I had an instant ethnic connection with these fellows, who still had family in Yugoslavia, but an even closer tie with George, the older of the pair, who had played outfield for several big league clubs in the 1940s and 50s.

Having some extra time on my hands that afternoon, I was delighted to find that the club was hosting an afternoon fashion show that very day, featuring a lineup of leggy young girls modeling some of the newest styles of West Coast bikinis. I had nowhere to go and nothing better to do, so I pushed my chair away from the table, took another sip of beer from my frosty mug and got myself ready to enjoy the show. Soft music began to play from the speakers of the sound system and a stage curtain opened at the back of the room. The emcee introduced each of the scantily covered models as they seductively stepped out from the opening. One by one, he assisted them as they stepped down onto the floor, wearing spiked high heels. Each of the models took a turn, sashaying down the short walkway between the rows of tables.

She was probably the second or third girl in the procession, a shapely, short-haired strawberry blonde with a striking resemblance to my favorite movie star, Mitzi Gaynor. My jaw dropped open at the sight of her. "Wow!" I blurted, impulsively."She's gorgeous!" She passed my table, gave me the most inviting smile I had ever seen, turned slowly and deliberately, and headed back toward the stage. Without my knowing it, one of the Metkovich brothers had been standing quietly behind me enjoying the show. And while this may have been just another day on the job for him, he obviously was just as enthralled by the lineup of lovely young females as I was.

"You sure got that right!" he agreed. "That's Bonnie, and she's a real sweetheart! She's an airline stewardess, who helps us with our fashion shows whenever she's home. Would you like to meet her after the show?"

"You bet I would!" I replied, not believing my good fortune. "I'd be happy to meet her anytime, anyplace!"

From that point on, I don't recall even noticing any of the other models, even though the continuous parade of beautiful beach babes went on for another 20 or 30 minutes. To help pass the time, I grabbed another bowl of pretzels and ordered another beer. I couldn't wait for the show to be over. Eventually, the music stopped and there was a final applause for the entire cast of girls. The all-male audience filed out the door and headed back to their jobs, while the club owner, along with Bonnie, who had changed into an attractive blouse and skirt outfit, approached my table.

"Eli, meet Bonnie," he said. I quickly rose from my seat and offered my hand. "And Bonnie, this is Eli." Her hand was soft and her nails were perfectly manicured. A gold charm bracelet dangled from her wrist. "Now, Bonnie is a busy lady," he continued. "She's always on the go, but she agreed to hang around here long enough to have a drink with you," he joked. "Especially after I went out on a limb and told her what a great guy you are!"

The three of us enjoyed a good laugh before our congenial host excused himself and joined other customers. Suddenly, Bonnie and I were on our own. I stepped to the other side of the table, grabbed a chair and offered her a seat.

Considering we were complete strangers, our conversation flowed amazingly well. There were no awkward exchanges or uncomfortable pauses. Her soft voice and friendly manner put me at ease from the very start. We engaged in small talk, which covered a wide range of topics, including our families, hometowns and our jobs, the usual but essential elements of a proper first meeting. Her alluring smile and charming personality combined to captivate me, while her drop-dead, Hollywood good looks were nothing short of mesmerizing. She was physically fit, enjoyed cooking at home and like me, was a lover of dogs of all breeds. No doubt, we were enjoying each other's company, as our time together disappeared as quickly as a homerun heading for the upper deck. Before leaving, we exchanged phone numbers and agreed to get together again, as soon as she could return home from her next transatlantic flight, and as soon as I could get back from the Angels upcoming road trip.

Bonnie was the most extraordinary girl I had ever met. My heart was telling me to play it safe, to take it slow. But I was falling fast, perhaps too fast. Naturally, neither of us was capable of predicting the future and neither of us had any idea as to where this first meeting would lead. Yet, we grew closer and things between us progressed.

A few months later, Bonnie and I were be married. Later, she would become the mother of my two beautiful children. And as the old saying goes; "You don't know what you've got till it's gone," I would one day know the pain of realizing how much I could have had in life. I would suffer the sad reality of how much I lost. And without assigning blame to anyone other than myself, I can truthfully say that at that time, I was losing control of myself and what was happening to me. I had unknowingly entered a deadly partnership with an evil entity named alcohol. And I would soon learn the hard way that this cruel demon would be the controlling partner, the one who would dominate my life for many years to come.

About the same time that I met Bonnie, I was also introduced to an element of major league baseball of which I had heard, but knew very little about. It became part of the professional game long before I arrived and became more widespread over the course of my career. I am referring to the use of "greenies," tiny green pills, which were the popular PED (performance enhancing drug) of the time. Commonly known as speed or amphetamines, this drug was given to military personnel during World War II to help them work efficiently and stay alert. However, they later showed up in baseball clubhouses and were taken by players to sharpen reflexes and boost energy levels. There were ballplayers who claimed that greenies were good for everything from muscle strains to hangovers, and without question, the drug helped countless players each year make it through the rigors of a long demanding schedule. However, along with the measures taken by Major League Baseball to purge itself of anabolic steroids and other illegal substances, amphetamines (greenies) were banned in 2006.

No doubt, greenies were available within the Yankee organization, but during my stay with the club, they were never openly discussed and the sources for getting them were known only to a certain few. However, in Southern California, things seemed to be much more in the open and attitudes were very different. Those little pills seemed to show up everywhere I went. The use of greenies was commonplace among pilots and flight attendants making long trips with little rest in between. As for the Angel ballclub, players used them openly in the clubhouse, as they were readily available from the team trainer, who handed them out like candy mints to anyone who asked for them. I first used greenies while in the army and found they gave me an extra boost when I wasn't getting enough rest but still needed to be sharp and on my toes, so I saw no harm in resorting to them to help me maintain my crazy, nonstop lifestyle. But by the time I had finished my first season in Los Angeles, I was drinking more than ever before, with a significant increase in the frequency and amount I drank during the daytime. With no regard for the serious health risks involved when speed and alcohol are used together, I was carelessly walking a deadly tightrope.

Whenever amphetamines, such as greenies, are taken into the body, activity of the central nervous system is increased, resulting in energetic anxiety and nervousness. On the other hand, alcohol, a depressant, works in a totally opposite manner, slowing the nervous system, affecting heart rhythm, causing migraines and diminishing motor skills. When used together, the two drugs can be a lethal combination. Nevertheless, with no regard for consequences, I stumbled aimlessly into a self-destructive lifestyle, during a time when terms such as "recreational drugs" and "substance abuse" were unheard of. It was the early 1960s, and there were no organized programs to promote public awareness of the dangers and long-term effects of drug abuse. However, with my reckless, devil-may-care attitude, it is doubtful that I would have heeded anyone's warnings or advice. I was young, invincible and a professional athlete. I had the world by the tail!

Since the beginning of my professional baseball career, I had spent each off-season at home in Chicago, where the winters were so cold it was almost impossible to do anything outdoors. Yet I managed to keep myself in good physical shape by playing basketball. I played several times a week, enjoying the fierce competition, while building up my endurance and keeping my legs strong. After a winter of basketball at the Y, my body would be in top form when it was time to report to spring training. But following the 1961 season, I wasn't willing to give up the leisurely Southern California lifestyle of sand and sun in exchange for the sub-freezing temperatures and snowstorms of Illinois.

It was about that time, the winter of '62, that my life started to slip into a dark mysterious abyss. My mere existence seemed to take the form of a bad dream, awash with fear and uncertainty. I became indifferent and apathetic. I could tell that my life was in a downward spiral, yet I was powerless to do anything to correct it, or maybe it was that I didn't care enough to try. I was refusing to take responsibility for anything and began seeing my life as if it were a never-ending vacation from the real world.

I remained in California during the winter and spent time with Bonnie as often as I could. She shared an apartment with a couple of other flight attendants on beautiful Hermosa Beach, where we stayed when she was home between flights. The rest of my time was spent playing on the beaches, hanging out with friends and drinking. I even turned down an offer to play winter baseball in Puerto Rico for $1,500 per month because I was having too much fun!

After establishing themselves as a competitive team in their first year of operation, the Angels in 1962 raised expectations. Four of the hottest young prospects in all of baseball were just a few of the reasons behind the optimism: shortstop, Jim Fregosi; outfielder, Lee Thomas; and pitchers, Dean Chance and Bo Belinsky. Starters, Ken McBride and Ted Bowsfield, who won 11 and 12 games respectively in '61, would be returning to Bill Rigney's rotation and were being counted on to play key roles. And like McBride, I also finished the season with 11 wins, however, my spot on the pitching staff was not nailed down. I pitched very well in spring training, but even as the 1962 season started, my place on the club still wasn't defined. The only thing that seemed certain was that I was destined to stay in Rigney's doghouse for a long time.

In the spring of 1962 Rigney had his pitching rotation in place except for his fourth starter. (left to right) Ken McBride, Ted Bowsfield and I had already been placed in the order, while George Witt, Jim Donohue and Dean Chance competed for the final spot.

Surprisingly, I got the call to start on Opening Day in Chicago and pitched fairly well, getting pulled in the middle innings of a 1 to 1 game. We went on to lose 2 to 1 in the ninth, but I didn't get a decision. This would be typical of the way Rigney used me for much of the season. He would often take me out of close, low-scoring games, even if I were pitching effectively and showed no signs of tiring. In one particular situation, while holding a commanding six- or seven-run lead, I was suspiciously pulled from the game after the fourth inning. As expected, the Angels went on to take the game, but as the starting pitcher, I was ineligible to receive credit for the win, having failed to make the required five-inning minimum. Today, I find it revealing when I check the record books and see that I pitched in 40 games in 1962, starting 29 of them and finishing with a record of 8 wins and 9 losses. For the year, I worked 176 innings, which was the third highest total on Rigney's pitching staff. Yet, I was allowed to pitch only one complete game the entire season, dubious numbers for a guy who was the number one starter in his rotation.

It was eerie how neither Rigney nor pitching coach, Marv Grissom, hardly spoke to me and neither of them ever gave me an explanation for the way I was treated. Yet they kept me in the starting rotation through the first few weeks of the season. However, by Memorial Day, my diminishing role on the team was made more apparent when Rigney assigned me to the bullpen, where I pitched primarily in relief and got only an occasional spot start.

Nevertheless, our team continued to win consistently. Starters, Dean Chance, Bo Belinsky and Ken McBride, who struggled with nagging arm and back injuries, all stepped up and pitched masterfully. And not only did the flamboyant Belinsky, who had a knack for making headlines, win his first three decisions of the season, but he also threw the pitching gem of the season in early May when he spun a no-hitter against the Baltimore Orioles and ran his personal record to 4 and 0. But in addition to the superb pitching, our club also benefitted from clutch hitting from sluggers, Leon Wagner and Lee Thomas and from our speedy 145-pound outfielder, Albie Pearson, who was swatting the ball at a lofty .300 clip. However, it was on July Fourth that the surging Angels surprised the baseball world by grabbing the top spot in the American League, taking both ends of a doubleheader in Washington, while the powerful Yankees and the streaking Cleveland Indians fell into a tie for second. Unfortunately, our time at the top was short-lived.

However, on a personal level, my life continued to spin out of control. From the midpoint of the summer to the end of the season, I recall very little of what was happening to me. I do know that I was drinking heavily and caring less and less about my life and the direction I was headed. I had hardly any communication with my manager, and my pitching coach spoke to me only when it was absolutely necessary. I realized just how much of an outcast I really was when I got word through some of my teammates that the Angels wanted to trade me and were working to cut a deal with the Kansas City Athletics. Upon hearing that bit of scuttlebutt, I was ready to go. My troubles were mounting and I had had all I could take of Rigney and his silent treatment. I would have welcomed a fresh start with a new club. And needless to say, I was quite disappointed when I found out that Kansas City had refused the proposed trade and declined to take me. I only hoped that the Angels would continue to shop me around and not give up too soon.

Fighting to hang on to second place in the A.L. standings, we flew into Chicago in early August for a short series against the White Sox. I had finished my pregame work on the field and headed for the White Sox bench, which gave me the shortest route to the Angels' clubhouse. As I stepped into the dugout, Luis Aparicio, Chicago's star shortstop, reached out and snatched my cap from head; at the same time, he replaced it with his. "What the hell are you doing, Louie?" I snapped. "Are you crazy?"

"Oh, you'll find out soon enough," he responded, jokingly. "I just want to see how you'll look in a White Sox cap! We're trading for you, you know, and you'll be staying here in Chicago with us!"

I was dumbfounded by what Louie had told me. For me, a trade to the White Sox would be perfect. The fact that the Chicago club's record was below .500, and that they had all but been eliminated from the pennant race made no difference to me. I had been a White Sox fan since my boyhood and I would relish the chance to play for my hometown team. Besides, their pitching coach was one of the most respected in the business. Ray Berres, an ex-catcher who had played for several National League clubs, beginning during the Great Depression, had coached the White Sox pitchers since the late 1940s. He had been instrumental in the development and success of pitchers, Bob Shaw, Juan Pizarro and Frank Baumann, and was given credit for extending the careers of veterans, Billy Pierce and Early Wynn. I had often thought about how great it would be to get back to Chicago and work with Berres. With him as my coach and mentor, I felt it was possible that I could get my career back on the right track. But once again, things didn't work out the way I had hoped.

It seems that the whole trade fell apart once the Angels insisted on getting a left-handed pitcher in the deal. Instead, the White Sox offered infielder, Sammy Esposito, a long-time friend of mine from Chicago, who I played basketball with during the off season. Sammy was getting only limited playing time with the White Sox, and was ready to go to a club where he could have been in the everyday lineup. Nonetheless, by the time we left Chicago, the trade talks between the Angels and White Sox had collapsed and my fate was sealed. And no matter how strained my relationship with my manager was, I would need to make the best of it because I wasn't going anywhere.

When we finally returned from the tiresome, five-city road trip, I was hoping to come home to a friendly and more peaceful environment. I was expecting to spend time with Bonnie and have fun hanging out at the bars and beaches when I wasn't at the ballpark. Instead, I returned to LA to find that there were other aspects of my life which were about unravel.

Searching for some form of meaning and stability, I developed an interest in Freemasonry and decided to petition one of the local lodges for membership. I believed the moral and spiritual values of the fraternity would give me a positive influence in my life, which seemed to be crumbling beneath me. Even then, I found my decision to become a Mason to be a controversial one. I soon found that it did not sit well with some friends who had preconceived opinions about the organization, and with others who were staunch Catholics, who disapproved because of their religious views.

At the same time, my roommate, Kenny Hunt, and I started to drift apart. We had once been close friends, but suddenly small disagreements began to turn into bitter arguments and the distance between us widened. There was no way the two of us could stay in the same apartment.

I was becoming difficult to live with and I could tell that I was no longer the jovial, easy-going person I had been before. And just when I thought things could not get any worse, the turmoil in my life began to snowball.

While Kenny and I remained at odds, I was unexpectedly blindsided by an old girlfriend who I hadn't heard from in almost two years. She was the type I had been warned about, the type who wanted nothing to do with me, but only wanted my money. This girl had no intentions of dating me again or rekindling an old romantic flame, but rather, she was part of a well devised blackmail scheme that, by design, ruined the personal lives of many men. This ruthless woman was part of a well-planned plot and she was out for all she could get.

There were unscrupulous airline stewardesses who stayed at the Flamingo Hotel in Chicago, who along with a shameless doctor practicing there in the nearby Hyde Park neighborhood, devised a plan to dupe unsuspecting ballplayers out of thousands of dollars by accusing them of fathering their illegitimate babies. Months, and sometimes years after they were together, the girl would contact the player, claiming to have had an abortion, for which he would have to pay; otherwise, his name would be dragged through the mud and his family life would be ruined. All the while, the doctor, who also got a cut of the money, only had to provide signed paperwork attesting to an abortion, which was never performed, and demanding outlandish fees for his services. Many a poor baseball player had fallen victim to this scam and paid extreme sums of money to hide affairs from their wives, families and girlfriends. And even before I had learned much about how to deal with extortion artists of this sort, I came to the aid of an Angel teammate on the '61 team, who was on the verge of becoming a blackmail victim. Wanting to help, I loaned him enough money to make the payoff and avoid wrecking his marriage, only to have the same trick played on me a year later. But fortunately, by that time, I had received some good advice which helped save me from enormous grief. "Call their bluff," I was told. "If you stand your ground, they'll back off and go into hiding every time." Still, it would take a lot of courage for me to challenge them.

I had met this girl near the end of the '60 season, just before the World Series, and hadn't seen or heard from her since. The whole chain of events fit well with the pattern of threats and accusations other players had faced. Yet even knowing it was all a set-up by these low-life con artists, it still took a lot of courage for me to face the challenge. I stood firm, defying her to take me to court. After a few weeks, I was relieved when her letters and phone calls finally stopped. At least I had gotten rid of one big worrisome problem in my still tumultuous life.

I was a major league baseball player, closing in on my 28th birthday. I was lonely, my spirit was low and my drinking was evolving to the more sophisticated stuff. I was downing martinis instead of beer and cheap whiskey. The alcohol would help me escape from my uncertainty and confusion, but only for short periods of time. No one could have been more afraid and disconnected from life than me.

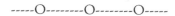

Meanwhile, the Angels were fighting desperately to hang on to second place, while the Yankees continued to win, extending their lead over the rest of the league. And equally as surprising as the Angels' showing, was the Twins, who had found new life since relocating from Washington to Minnesota. They were gaining ground fast. Led by a young, muscle-bound slugger from Idaho, Harmon Killebrew, the Twins had become the new powerhouse club of baseball, and with just one month to go in the 1962 season, the run for the American League title had turned into a three-club race.

However, the Angels were slowly running out of steam. In spite of outstanding pitching down the stretch from Dean Chance, who went on to win 14 games on the season, and Dan Osinski, a right-hander we acquired through a midseason trade with Kansas City, the Twins leap-frogged over us into the second spot, while New York went on their usual late-season winning streak and grabbed the pennant. With a total of 86 wins for the year, we had to settle for third place, which was still an impressive record for a second-year club. But that finish was still far short of the high expectations we held for ourselves at the beginning of the season.

Having not contributed much over the second half of the season, I was really down on myself. It wasn't that I pitched poorly during that time, but I was used infrequently and pulled out of games once we had established a lead. I was angry and frustrated with Rigney and the whole Angel organization. Mentally, my head was in the clouds. My attitude was one of strong will and stubbornness, while my mindset was defensive and volatile. I was ready to lash out at anyone over almost anything. There were other times when I was skittish and high-strung and I had a difficult time with concentration. My memory was "hit and miss." And still today, after so many years, I have trouble recalling much of what I did during this particular time of my life and why.

Without considering where our relationship was heading, Bonnie and I continued to see each other, spending all of our time together whenever she was home. We lived together at her place in an arrangement which for both of us, was one of comfort and convenience. Neither of us had any idea of how to responsibly plan for the future. We were clueless when it came to managing finances, buying a home, raising a family and making a long-term commitment. We were both guilty of pushing aside differences and ignoring signs that should have told us that we were opposite personalities, with no chance for a future together. Instead, we inattentively stood by and allowed our relationship to move forward. And as expected, we began talking about marriage!

During my time with the Angels, I had the good fortune of working with Bud Furillo, one of the most respected sportswriters in the Los Angeles area. Bud had a good relationship with all the ballplayers and was known for his candid reporting, and for respecting the players' privacy. He had a knack for making players comfortable whenever he talked with them, and in return, they trusted him, knowing that whatever appeared in his daily column in the Herald-Examiner would be truthful and fair.

In one of our pregame chats, I casually mentioned to Bud that Bonnie and I had talked about getting married. I explained that we had no firm plans, but that it could happen at any time. Bud was elated with the news and was very encouraging and supportive. For a few days his column was devoted to the up-and-down season I was having and how getting married would be exactly what was needed to help get my career back on course. As a pitcher, Bud described me as having all the necessary tools to be an exceptional pitcher. "Once he gets his personal life squared away, Grba will be one of the most versatile right-handers in the league," he predicted. "Getting married and settling down will give him the stability he needs."

Sitting on the fence as I was, it took very little to convince me to make a move. I was young and uncertain, and with such a confused and detached state of mind, I was very vulnerable. I will never say that Bud's column was the deciding factor, but I admired him and I took what he had to say to heart. Within a few days after reading his article, I was ready and willing to take the plunge. I wanted Bud to be right, but I also recognized the need to point my life in a different direction. Arrangements were made for a beautiful ceremony at Wayfarers Chapel in Palos Verdes, our friends and families were invited. And on Saturday, October 6, 1962, Bonnie and I were married. It was a crazy time for both of us. And who knows what we were thinking, or if we were even thinking at all!

It didn't take long for me to find out just how far off-base Bud Furillo had been with his prediction. It was soon clear for both Bonnie and me that marriage was not the way for either of us to find a happy, settled life. I wasn't ready to settle down and I was too immature and irresponsible to be a husband to any woman. With the way my life was going, I was incapable of taking care of myself, much less the needs of another person.

We got a place of our own, a lovely place near the ocean at Manhattan Beach. It was a great location, only a short drive from the L.A. Airport, making it ideal for Bonnie and not too far from Dodger Stadium, where at the time, the Angels were playing their home games. Yet as close as we were to our jobs, there was still no guarantee that I would always be able to get myself to work on time.

It was mid-August, and I was scheduled to pitch the second game of a weekday doubleheader in L.A. against the Boston Red Sox. Bonnie had just arrived home the previous night from a long overseas flight, so we had a lot of catching up to do to make up for lost time. I was sure I had plenty of time to spare when I hopped into the car to leave the house, and that I would arrive at the ballpark by the fifth inning of the first game, which was one of Rigney's strict rules for game-two starters. I flipped on the radio and dialed in the game, only to find out that I was already behind schedule. They were playing the bottom of the sixth inning; the Angels held a 1 to 0 lead and Dean Chance was pitching a brilliant game. To this point he had handcuffed the Boston batting order, facing only one batter more than the minimum. "My gosh, I'm gonna be late!" I grumbled, as I floored the accelerator. "Rigney's gonna jump my ass again!"

I raced up the entrance ramp and onto the freeway. I turned down the volume on the game to concentrate on my driving. Ignoring the speed limit, I zigzagged in and out of traffic and had only a couple miles left before my exit when I hit my brakes. All at once, the vehicles in front of me came to a screeching halt. I had run upon the traffic jam from hell! Not a car was moving and there was no place to go. I was fuming! Every minute that I sat, waiting for the traffic to move, seemed like an eternity. But police finally arrived on the scene and cleared the impasse. At breakneck speed I made it to my exit, drove several blocks to the stadium and pulled up to the gate of players' parking lot.

"You can't park here!" A loud, shaggy-haired teenager barked at me as I rolled to a stop. "This lot, it's for players only."

"Look, buddy," I pleaded calmly, trying to keep my cool. "I'm the Angels' starter for the second game. I'm Grba. I don't have my pass, it's in my other pants at home." He wasn't impressed in the least.

"Yeah, sure you are," he responded smugly. The kid wouldn't budge. He strutted around to the front of my car and stood with his arms folded. Squealing tires, I backed away from the players' lot and drove straight for the public parking area, paid two dollars to park my car and stormed across the pavement and into the Angels' clubhouse without a minute to spare.

Without unfastening the buttons on my flowery sport shirt, I yanked it over my head and tossed it on the floor. I frantically kicked off my shoes and turned away from my locker only long enough to get the attention of our team trainer. "Pop!" I yelled to him. "Pop" was our code word for "greenie." He gave me a quick nod to let me know one was on the way.

In spite of Dean's outstanding pitching, Boston pushed across a couple of runs in the ninth inning to win the first game 2 to 1, and as was typical after a disappointing loss, the atmosphere in the clubhouse was quiet and glum. There were a few guys grumbling and cursing, but no one spoke to me. With only a few minutes to get ready for the game, I got dressed and was out on the field in record time. I got a cold stare from Rigney as I passed him on my way out the door. By the time I finished stretching and throwing about a dozen pitches in the bullpen, it was time to grab my jacket and head to the dugout. It was time for the game to start and I was in no shape to pitch. I had had several drinks earlier at the house and had just topped things off with a greenie in the clubhouse. Plus the traffic jam on the freeway and the parking situation at the stadium still had me steaming mad. I was as agitated as a bull in a house with red curtains!

I walked the first Boston batter and before I could work up a sweat, I gave up line-drive singles to the next two. With one run already having crossed the plate, the Red Sox clean-up hitter, Lou Clinton, worked me to a full count before swinging at a high fastball, which sailed inward about shoulder-high. With the handle portion of his bat, he chopped the ball downward onto the grass in front of the plate, causing it to roll slowly out toward the pitcher's mound. Instinctively, I charged in to field the ball. It had stopped rolling and was lying on the grass, only a few feet in front of me. I planted my feet and with my right hand, reached down to grab it. Suddenly, with the tips of my fingers, I clawed desperately at the grass, but the ball wasn't there. It was like it had vanished before my eyes! Dumbfounded and dazed, I searched frantically all around before I spotted it in the grass, a short distance away. By the time I retrieved it, it was too late to make a play. Everyone was safe and Boston had loaded the bases. The crowd booed furiously as I turned to walk back to the mound. It was the top of the first inning with no outs, and the fans had already seen enough of me.

Without coming close to the strike zone, I walked the next hitter on four pitches. Another round of boos erupted in the stands just before Rigney shot out of the Angels' dugout and headed to the mound. He signaled to the bullpen for a new pitcher before stepping across the baseline. His face was rigid with anger and as red as the bill of his cap. Avoiding eye contact, we stood on the mound, waiting for the new pitcher, neither of us uttering a word. The very instant that Rigney handed the baseball to the reliever, I walked off the field to another chorus of catcalls and boos from the disappointed hometown crowd.

Nevertheless, I couldn't blame the fans. They had paid to see a well-played major league baseball game and they deserved a lot better. It was the most dreadful performance of my career. I pitched to five Red Sox batters and retired none of them, allowing four runs. Perhaps the Angels, who at the time, were still in contention for the American League title, could have tightened the race and moved a game closer to the Yankees, had they not called on a starting pitcher whose mind was clouded by a mixture of alcohol and amphetamines.

I had let down my ballclub and disappointed the fans. Yet more importantly, while I was deep into the process of throwing away my baseball career, I was also quickly and carelessly destroying my life. Often, it seemed as if I were watching from a distance as someone else's life was coming apart, but it was mine and I was responsible for my own undoing. I was alone, spellbound by addiction, with no one to turn to for help.

Alcohol and drug abuse are two dangerously destructive paths which are open to people of all races, levels of income and all walks of life, and they lead to the same horrific destination. And make no mistake about it, using them together will only hasten the journey.

CHAPTER 28
BACKED INTO A CORNER, WITH NO WAY OUT

For Bonnie and me, our first winter after getting married was a crazy one. As naive newlyweds, we made it our first priority to search for a new house. We drove around the Los Angeles area looking at available real estate when we came upon a house in the most recently developed section of the Woodland Hills neighborhood. It was a lovely place, nestled in the beautiful San Fernando Valley and located about 25 miles northwest of the city. At $36,000, it was way out of our price range, but what did we know? We were young and foolish, with a lot of big ideas and very little money.

A few days later, we stopped to gas up the car at the corner filling station near our place at Manhattan Beach. As regular customers, we had become friends with the station owner, Branko, a courteous Serbian gentleman, who seemed to be on a first-name basis with all of his customers. He knew Bonnie and all the other stewardesses who lived in the neighborhood and was always willing to sell them gas on credit whenever they got in a pinch. We stopped in to say hi and get a fill-up, and as he pumped the gasoline and cleaned the windshield, we enjoyed another of our friendly conversations with him.

"If you folks like that new house up in Woodland Hills, I think you should go ahead and buy it," he suggested. "Nothing can be more exciting for a young couple than to buy a new home they both like." He pulled a rag from his back pocket and wiped his hands. I took a five dollar bill from my wallet and handed it to him.

"You're right about that," I agreed. "But ballplayers don't earn very much, and right now, Bonnie and I can't even afford a down payment on a place like that."

"Yeah, but I sure wish you kids could buy that house," he said wistfully. He paused for a few seconds and smiled quietly to himself as he turned to go back to the station. "I'll be right back with your change," he offered. "Don't go anywhere."

Bonnie and I waited in the car, while it seemed to take a little longer than usual for him to return. "Maybe he can't open the cash register," I said jokingly. "Maybe he lost the key."

About that time, Branko walked around to the driver's side of the automobile and handed me the change. He was also carrying a small paper bag, which he held up outside the window.

"Here's a little something I have for the two of you," he explained. "You're a great couple, and I hope this will help." He passed the crumpled sack to me and turned to walk away. I unrolled the top of the bag to have a peek, when suddenly, my jaw dropped open in disbelief. The bag was filled with cash! "Hey, wait just a minute!" I gasped. "What the hell is this for?" He stopped in mid-stride and walked back towards the car to answer my question.

"It's a down payment for that house you picked out," he replied sharply. "It's five thousand dollars. You can pay me back when you get the chance." To make it clear that the matter was not open for further discussion, he pushed his hands deep into his pockets, spun on his heel and headed back inside.

Totally speechless, I looked over at Bonnie and handed her the bag. I started the motor and began to drive away from the pump. For a moment I paused and watched in the mirror as he walked into the building and closed the plate glass door behind him. Obviously Branko was the type of man who wanted no part in being mushy or sentimental and gave us no chance to express our gratitude. We honked the horn and waved as we drove back onto the highway. But by this time, he was already back at work and too busy to notice us.

Of course, Bonnie and I continued to stop by Branko's service station, even after we made the down payment and moved in to that beautiful house in Woodland Hills. And although his gesture of kindness was totally unexpected, it was the most special thing anyone ever did for us. He was a modest, humble man who seemed uncomfortable whenever we brought the subject up, yet we continued to thank him for his generosity whenever we saw him.

However, even after getting the mortgage and moving in to such an affluent neighborhood, monthly payments still had to be made. We were too naive to know that the down payment was only the first step to becoming homeowners. We had no idea that the financial burden of that house would be more than the two of us could afford. We were so far in over our heads that we couldn't even make our mortgage payments on time, much less pay back the loan from Branko.

Unfortunately, buying that house would be just one of the many blunders we would make during our years together. We seemed to have had a long list of things that we could not agree on or manage together. Bonnie and I would soon discover for ourselves that a beautiful house does not make a happy home and marriage license cannot make anyone a husband or wife.

Dating back to the infamous Black Sox scandal, when eight members of the Chicago White Sox agreed to take gamblers' money to throw the 1919 World Series, every baseball player who has ever signed a contract to play professionally has been made well aware of the game's cardinal sin, gambling. For almost a century, gambling has been the one offense for which the rulers of baseball have refused to tolerate and have shown no leniency towards the convicted. Yet, there are well documented cases where drug users, wife beaters, assaulters of umpires and even one player who claimed to have been murderer, were each punished with a temporary suspension from the game, but were eventually awarded baseball's most coveted honor, induction into the Baseball Hall of Fame.

Nevertheless, players known to have bet on games, accepted money to fix games or had associations with known gamblers have all been banned from baseball for life. Gambling is seen as the sole transgression that can damage the integrity of the game more than any other. It was the opinion of baseball's first commissioner, Judge Kennesaw M. Landis, that if the honesty and integrity of the game are ever suspect or in doubt, then all is lost.

As rookies in the lower classifications of professional baseball, we are all advised to be careful of the friends we make, the strangers we talk with and the favors we accept. Young players are instructed to avoid offers for free drinks, meals, hotel rooms and invitations to attend parties and meet women. These situations can all lead to a ballplayer becoming indebted to someone, who at first, seemed to be a well-meaning fan asking innocent questions, but in reality was a gambler looking for the inside scoop on an upcoming game or the condition of a teammate.

I had met Nick Colich in New York back in 1960. A little older than me and a sharp dresser, he introduced himself to me as a Serbian businessman, who had established himself in the Minneapolis-Saint Paul area. He was the owner of both a restaurant and a nightclub there and was an avid baseball fan, who often had some of the other players visit his places as his special guests. He invited me to drop by whenever I could make it to Minnesota and enjoy dinner and a few drinks while I was in town. He assured me that the food and drinks would be the best and that he would introduce me to some of the beautiful ladies who frequented his clubs. We had dinner together while he was in New York, and during the evening conversation he explained how he heard about me through mutual friends, who worked with the Ironworkers Local back in Chicago. We enjoyed our time together that night, discussing nearly every topic imaginable, while only touching lightly on the subject of baseball. He was generous enough to offer to pick up our tab, but to keep things simple, I was careful to decline. It had been a great evening, and before we parted company, we agreed to meet again sometime in the future, when our schedules would allow.

I was totally out of shape when I reported to training camp in the spring of '63. I had abused myself over the winter months, eating, drinking, partying and completely ignoring all the rules of good health and fitness. By the time I went to Palm Springs to start spring training I was ten pounds overweight and in no shape mentally to play baseball. I was carrying a negative attitude and I could see for myself that I wasn't the talkative, fun-loving guy I once was. I could tell that I was not as outgoing and had become a lot more moody and sullen. I didn't pitch very often and when Rigney called on me, I struggled with my control. I had fallen from the number one spot in the pitching rotation to being the last guy in the back of the bullpen, all in the span of two seasons.

The regular season had just gotten underway when the Angels traveled to Minnesota to begin our first road trip of the year. We had already played the first handful of games at home in Dodger Stadium but I had seen no action at all. Rigney had me warm up in the bullpen on a couple of occasions, but never called me into a game. It was a cold, blustery weekday afternoon in Bloomington when the series opened, with only a sparse gathering of dedicated Twins fans on hand to watch. Having just left the warmth of LA, the biting cold at Metropolitan Stadium was especially hard for our guys to take. Nevertheless, an old-fashioned pitching duel was expected for the first game, with Dean Chance getting the nod to start for us and lefty, Jim Kaat going for the Twins. But like an insightful baseball fan once told an unconvinced friend while they watched a close game from the bleachers: "Baseball is the most unpredictable of all sports, and that's what makes it great!"

In a game which featured nearly every aspect of baseball except good pitching, base hits were easy to come by for batters from both clubs. Having to contend with cold temperatures and gusty winds, neither of the starting pitchers could find their groove and were out of the game by the middle innings. Of course, the relief pitchers were forced to deal with the same brutal conditions and didn't fare much better. The Angels pushed across two runs just before the seventh inning stretch to take the lead at 7 to 5. But it was a margin that our bullpen would be unable to hold, as the Twins' power-hitting rightfielder, Bob Allison, blasted a dramatic two-run homerun with two out in the bottom of the ninth, to send the game into extra innings.

The parade of pitchers continued through 12 innings with the score knotted at 9 to 9. Then, to the dismay of the freezing few Minnesota fans who remained, we managed to break the tie, scoring once in the top of the 13th. And although I had warmed up several times throughout the course of the game, I was the only pitcher remaining in the bullpen once Ron Moeller, a left-hander was summoned to the mound with two runners aboard and only one out. At this point, our 10 to 9 advantage seemed negligible. The momentum had swung back to the Twins and the game had reached the most pivotal point of the day. And once again, I was told to begin warming up, not that Rigney wanted me in the game, but by the process of elimination, I was the only pitcher left.

Moeller entered the game and promptly surrendered an RBI single tying the score. No sooner had the runner stepped on the plate and the baseball thrown back to the infield, than Rigney rushed from the dugout, giving the signal for a new pitcher. I grabbed my jacket and took off across the outfield to meet Rigney and catcher, Bob Rodgers on the mound. The conditions were far from ideal, but I was pleased to finally get my first pitching assignment of the season.

Rigney slapped the ball into my glove as I stepped up onto the hill. "We're not pitching to this guy," he ordered bluntly. "We're going to load the bases and then we're going to take our chances with the next one. Understand me?" I nodded in agreement and blew my warm breath into my clinched right hand.

"You got it, Rig," I answered. He turned to go back to the dugout, while Rodgers gave me an encouraging slap on the hip with his mitt and jogged back behind the plate to take his position.

Standing erect in the catcher's box, Rodgers extended his right arm to his side and used his fist as a high and outside target, typical form for issuing an intentional walk. To the Twins' batter, veteran Bill Tuttle, who had just been announced into the game as a pinch hitter for the pitcher, I delivered four consecutive slow pitches, high and wide of the strike zone. Without lifting his bat from his shoulder, he watched each of them sail by. He flipped his bat aside, and headed for first base. To a rousing ovation offered by the scant crowd still left in the stands, the next hitter, George Banks, a young utility player stepped to the plate with the game on the line. The bases were loaded with still only one out. And with each of the Twins' runners straying from their bases with modest leads, I took advantage of the chance to work from a full windup.

My first two offerings to Banks were borderline pitches, over the outside corner of the plate, but strangely enough, plate umpire, Ed Runge called them both balls. Behind in the count, I lobbed an off-speed pitch down the middle which caught Banks offguard, inducing him to swing awkwardly at the last split second, making only enough contact to foul the ball straight back against the screen. With my next delivery I served up a hard, nasty slider, which broke away from the right hand hitting Banks and again caught the outside edge of the plate.

"Ball!" Runge barked, raising his fingers to indicate a count of three balls and one strike.

"Oh, come on, Ed! I snapped. "You know better than that!"

I turned my back to homeplate and looked up at the cold Minnesota sky. "He's not giving me anything," I mumbled. "I'll have to put it right down the middle to get a call from this guy."

Seeing that I was getting riled, Bob Rodgers asked the ump for time and walked out the mound to offer some encouragement. "Keep it down and over the plate, Gerbie," he reminded me. "Just take it easy and we'll be okay." He trotted back to his position, squatted down and pulled his mask down over his face. Between his legs, he put down the signal calling for another slider. With his mitt, he gave me a target directly over the heart of the plate. It was obvious that the batter was edgy and hesitant and wanted no part of my slider. All I needed to do was throw a strike.

My sights were fixed on Rodgers's mitt. An eerie hush swept over the stadium as I started my windup. At the height of my delivery, I released what seemed like the ideal pitch. With perfect velocity and rotation, the baseball sailed inward toward the batters hands at a height just below his belt. In an instant it broke away and dropped to a level above the knees. Banks was frozen with indecision. The pitch had hit its target. Bob hardly moved his mitt to catch it. Satisfied that I had run the count full to three and two, I pounded my fist into the palm of my glove. I knew I had gained the upper hand on this young, inexperienced hitter.

"Ball four!" the umpire shouted. "Game's over!" I stormed down from the mound and stopped about halfway to the plate. I was furious. I kicked at the grass and yelled back at Runge.

"You gotta be kidding! What the hell was wrong with that one? I had the outside corner!"

Ignoring my protest, he stayed on the field only long enough to watch the runner, forced from third base, step on the plate to score the winning run. He sheepishly ducked away and headed for his dressing room. "That's right, Ed!" I shouted. "Blow the call and go into hiding, you no-good coward!"

With that controversial base on balls, I had walked in the deciding run in a 11 to 10 loss to the Twins. It was one of the most humiliating moments of my career. Sure, it was the umpire who missed pitches that could have been called either way, but it was my manager who hung me out to dry. It was Rigney who had me warm up multiple times on such a frigid afternoon, only to shut me down and bring another pitcher into the game. And it was Rigney who made no effort to argue or protest on my behalf, while an umpire was stealing the game. At this point, I was only wondering if my career was being purposely derailed. However, I would soon learn that, in fact, that was the case.

Following that bizarre 13-inning series opener, we still had a couple of games left to play in Minnesota before moving on to the other scheduled stops on the road trip. All the while, I was growing more doubtful about my future with the ballclub. The very idea that neither my manager or pitching coach were talking to me, only fueled my insecurity. I could sense that my job was hanging by a thread, and I was learning not to trust anyone who was part of the Angels' management.

Considering all that was happening to me, both on and off the field, I was pleased to hear from Nick Colich, who gave me a phone call while we were still in Minnesota. I hadn't heard from Nick since we met in New York a few years earlier, and I was quick to take him up on his offer to join him at his house for dinner. For me, the invitation came at a good time and gave me a break from the usual road trip routine of staying out late at restaurants and bars. It was good to see him again and catch up on what was going on with our friends. He mentioned that he planned to have a cocktail party there at his place for all the ballplayers before the Angels left town. "Good idea, Nick!" I agreed, making no commitment. "I'm sure all the guys will go for it."

I had enjoyed another pleasant evening with Nick. He was the sort of man who was comfortable being himself. He seemed to have everything he wanted and was satisfied with his life. I just had no idea that having a quiet dinner at a friend's house could bring about so much trouble.

Several days later we arrived back home in Los Angeles. After such a long tiresome trip, everyone on the club was happy to be starting a homestand at Dodger Stadium and settling into a less hectic routine. For professional baseball players, getting home means not having to deal with hotels, luggage, flights and curfews for a while, but only until it's time to pack up and hit the road again. However, this return home for the Angels was not like any of the others I had experienced. This time, before we played our first game, a special team meeting was called. The urgency and short notice surprised everyone. It was our traveling secretary, Tommie Ferguson, who walked through the clubhouse giving us our orders. Announcing a meeting for players only, he said no one was to leave; instead, we were all to report immediately to the football meeting room, just down the hall.

The room was buzzing with speculation. At the very front of the room stood team owners, Gene Autry and Bob Reynolds, along with general manager, Fred Haney and, of course, Bill Rigney. Once the room quieted, Rigney was the first to speak.

"As all of you guys know by now, a couple of pro football players have just been suspended for betting on games. Both Paul Hornung and Alex Karras were tailed by FBI agents for weeks while they were gambling, and now each of them has received a one-year suspension from the NFL Commissioner." A nervous murmur suddenly vibrated the meeting room, prompting Rigney to call for quiet. "Now before we proceed," he continued, "we want everyone to know that we are not here to point fingers at any of you fellows, but we are asking you to be extra careful about who you associate with, once you leave the ballpark." Again, chattering and whispering broke out all around. Rigney paused and raised his hand in the air, appealing for silence. "There is one guy in particular, who you all need to be aware of," he warned, "his name is Nick Colich." He paused again to allow the seriousness of the situation to sink in. "This man is a big-time gambler and is known for being involved in a long list of illegal activities. We were given reports which indicate that some of you were spotted at a wild party, which took place last week at this man's house in Minnesota, and with that being said, some of you may already be in big trouble."

I felt the blood rush from my face the moment I heard the name "Nick Colich" specifically called out. *This was my friend Rigney was referring to. Surely, they can't tie me into any wrongdoing. I didn't attend the party. As a matter of fact, I turned in unusually early that night.*

Nevertheless, I could sense that Rigney was deriving some amount of satisfaction by delivering such serious accusations. He had the smug look of a farmer who had just cornered a fox in his hen house. Suddenly,

I felt like I was the only one in the room. "And what's all this leading to?" I blurted impulsively. "I know Nick, he's a friend of mine!" The room suddenly fell deathly silent in reaction to my challenging question. Rigney, on the spot, moved quickly to close the meeting.

Okay, boys," he announced, dismissing the group. "That's all for now. We just wanted to help keep you guys stay out of trouble." Everyone began to file out of the room, but as infuriated as I was, I decided to hang around and press Rigney for answers. With the exception of Haney, Rigney and me, the room was cleared. I walked toward the front, ready to confront the two of them face to face.

"I told you that Nick Colich is a friend of mine! And who in the hell are you to tell me who I can be friends with?"

"We know all about that." Rigney responded indignantly, using the tone of a prosecuting attorney. "And that's precisely why you are being followed by the FBI."

"What in the hell are you talking about?" I fired back angrily.

"Well, you were spotted at the party at Nick Colich's house by one of the FBI agents, so naturally, you are suspected of being an associate of his."

Feeling an urge to put his own two cents worth in, Fred Haney chimed in. "Eli, you were seen at the party, and you might as well own up to it. It's all here in the reports."

"To hell with your reports, Fred, I wasn't there!" I took a quick glance over at Rigney, but only long enough to notice how satisfied he was to see me on the defensive. And with Haney being the more reasonable and credible of the pair, I turned to him to plead my case.

"I'm telling you the truth, Fred," I offered, trying to stay calm. "Rather than go to Nick's party that night, I went out with Billy Moran for a quiet dinner. We each had a steak dinner at a restaurant close to our hotel, and I was back in my room in time to call my wife at home in California, well before curfew." Neither of them seemed interested in my story, but I wasn't about to back down.

"Why don't you check with Billy?" I argued. "I'm sure you'd believe him; he's never been in trouble his whole life!"

"Never mind about Moran," Rigney responded bluntly. "He has nothing to do with this."

I took a step back and shook my head in frustration. I could sense that I was fighting a losing battle. It was quite clear that their minds were made up, and in this case, the truth was not what was important. There was no interest in hearing the input of anyone else. It was me that Rigney wanted to hang.

Without having enough nerve to even look at me, Rigney started talking in a solemn voice, like he was eulogizing a close friend.

"And there's one other thing you need to know about: I got a call from the commissioner's office, and Ford Frick wants to see you next Thursday in his office in New York. I believe he has a few questions of his own for you."

Fred Haney, being more considerate, stood by quietly, neither charging me nor defending me. He may even have been bothered by the idea that one of his players could be involved in such a ugly situation. Rigney, on the other hand, was satisfied, and seemed to relish the opportunity to bring such serious accusations against me.

Over the next few days my head was filled with all sorts of thoughts about why I was called out in front of the whole team, falsely and purposely framed, and forced to respond to such serious accusations. Needless to say, I was anxious and frightened to the point that I might not have been thinking rationally. Consequently, some of my notions may have come from fear and paranoia. For days, my head was spinning as I tried to figure out why this was happening to me.

The game in Minnesota, when I walked in the winning run, could they be thinking that I was on the take? Would they suspect me of giving in to gamblers and losing that game, or any other games on purpose? And what about the huge luxurious home that Bonnie and I had just bought? These guys knew my salary, and they knew that we couldn't have gotten a mortgage on a place like that on our own. And to further complicate matters, I learned later that Jack Paepke, a member of the Angels' coaching staff, had actually attended Nick's party, a matter that Rigney or Haney never talked about. According to teammates, Paepke, well-known for his boorish horseplay, was in fact there, and as part of his shenanigans, introduced himself to unsuspecting party guests as Eli Grba!

More frustrating was the fact that I knew nothing about Nick Colich's business dealings, other than he owned a restaurant and a couple of nightclubs in Minneapolis. He had been nothing more than a good friend, who never tried to take advantage of me or pump me for inside information which could have been used for gambling. There had been only one instance when he asked me anything about baseball, and that was in 1960, when we first met in New York. As I remember, Whitey Ford had struggled early in the year with an inflamed shoulder, but recovered by midseason, in time to be named the starting pitcher for the American League All-Star team. Being a close follower of baseball, Nick casually asked me, over the course of the evening, about the condition of Whitey's pitching arm. "Oh, he's fine," I replied off the cuff. "Whitey's in good shape." Hardly any revealing information in that response!

Was I suffering from an overactive imagination or were Rigney and his henchmen truly willing to go to any extreme to ruin my career and railroad me right out of baseball?

With only two days remaining until my meeting with Ford Frick in New York, my story took still another unexpected turn, which served to remind me, never expect things to go according to plans, whenever baseball management is involved. We were at the stadium in L.A. and I was half-heartedly going about my running and bullpen work, when Tommie Ferguson came rushing onto the field, hurrying straight for me. "What's up Tommie?" I asked. "You look like you have something important on your mind."

"Perhaps I do, Gerb," he hinted, pausing to catch his breath. "Number 18 wants to see you in his office right away."

"Well, I'm sure it's important, alright," I sneered. "Why would Rigney want to see me? Has he found another knife to stick in my back?"

"Now just wait a minute here, Eli!" he snapped. "There's no call for you to bite my head off. I'm just the messenger, okay?" With that, Tommie turned and walked away. He had just seen for himself the bitter, contentious person I had become. He had been a good friend to me since I first joined the club, and I was wrong to make him a target of my frustration. I wanted to squeeze in an apology before he left me, but he hurried on his way. And like a lot of others at that time, Tommie had grown wary of me.

Without saying a word, I walked into the manager's office and closed the door behind me. Rigney was seated at his desk, but it wasn't until I had grabbed a chair that I noticed Fred Haney, sitting quietly off to the side. "What do you guys have for me today?" I scoffed. "More good news?"

Refusing to react to my sarcasm, Rigney scooted his chair against the wall, while Haney opened the meeting in his usual calm tone. "Well, Eli, we need to send somebody out to the minors. We need to send a pitcher to the Hawaii club." I sat perfectly still, gripping the sides of my chair to help me suppress my emotions. Haney, who was always careful to use the right words, paused for a moment to collect his thoughts. That's when Rigney butted in and took control.

"You know, Fred and I have given this a lot of consideration," he began, using his usual pompous tone, "and we thought we would send Tom Morgan down. His days in this league are just about over. He's been pitching like a bush leaguer, and I actually don't know why we should keep somebody like him on the payroll. But the truth is, he's got more than ten years in the big leagues and he doesn't have any options left on his contract, so we need to take another course." He stopped long enough look at Haney for approval. "And since we still have available options on you, we're sending you out to Hawaii."

My jaw tightened as a burning wave of rage swept across my back and shoulders. "Of all the dirty, no-good tricks!" I snarled angrily. "You have a lot of nerve! You're sitting here, bad-mouthing Tom Morgan, a man who has given you his best and done so much for this stinking organization. You are unbelievable! And you've had me on the shelf since the start of the season, and now, you're sending me out!" I took a deep breath and pointed my finger, first at Haney and then, directly at Rigney. I sensed that I was on the verge of losing my composure, so I consciously switched to a calmer, more restrained voice. "I know what you're trying to do to me," I said accusingly. "And I won't let you two sons of bitches get away with it! I won't let the two of you destroy my confidence."

Little did I know, but it was already too late. Haney and Rigney, together had already accomplished that. My self-confidence was in ruins. I questioned my ability as a major league pitcher. I even asked myself if I still deserved to be in professional baseball. My spirit was crushed.

I stormed out of the office and headed straight for my car. Speeding down the freeway, I was so enraged I could have crashed. I stopped by a beer joint along the way, Ernie's Bar, and spent the next few hours getting snockered before driving home to Bonnie. I wasn't sure how to break the news to her. Since I was so disappointed in myself, I thought she would feel the same way.

The red California sun had already dropped below the crest of the hills by the time I drove into our driveway. I noticed that our outdoor patio lights were on, so I walked to the back of the house and found Bonnie, having a drink by the pool. I was surprised to find that she knew a lot more than I thought.

"So, we're going to Hawaii!" she greeted me, getting up from her lounge. "I heard all about it on the radio and I think it's wonderful! Maybe I can get away from work and join you for a nice, long summer vacation. How do you feel about that?" I stopped dead in my tracks. Now, I had always known that Bonnie was one who couldn't care less about baseball and had no interest in knowing about my profession. But how could she miss the impact of such a humiliating situation? Suddenly, it became clear that our thoughts were traveling in completely opposite directions.

"Don't you realize what just happened?" I asked. "I was just given a demotion. I am being sent down to the minor leagues, for God's sake! This may turn into a vacation for you, but it certainly won't be one for me." My lip began to tremble. Tears welled up in my eyes and began to trickle down my cheeks. For the first time since I was a small child, I cried openly in the presence of a woman. There was nothing Bonnie could do to console me. "Why didn't you come home?" she questioned me. "We could have talked things over."

"I just couldn't make myself do it," I sobbed. "I was too embarrassed and too ashamed to let anyone see me. It hurts too much!"

It was a long, agonizing night and it was well past midnight before I finally closed my eyes. Even after falling asleep, I couldn't escape the painful reality of all that had happened. Nevertheless, Bonnie had me up and ready the following morning in time to make my seven-hour flight to Hawaii. Had it not been for her, I probably would have spent the day in bed.

The weeks and months that followed were like a blur to me. At first, I was full of resentment, and went about my work quietly, speaking to no one unless I had to. I had no faith in the assurance Fred Haney gave me to bring me back to L.A., since by that time, I believed nothing he or Rigney had to say. I was as angry and bitter as I had ever been, and I was willing to forgo my career to spite them.

Nonetheless, the 1963 edition of the Hawaii Islanders was a talented ballclub that played above the .500 mark most of the season. They were predicted to be among the year's top contenders for the Pacific Coast League crown. But all the while I was there, I was aware that my time in the Angels' organization was nearing an end. I made out fine with Irv Noren, the Islanders' manager, who is remembered more for slapping $50 fines on players for getting themselves sunburned, than for anything else he did while he was in Hawaii. Noren, a veteran outfielder, who played a large portion of his career with the New York Yankees, was the type of manager who worked at preventing little issues from becoming big ones and solving more problems than he created. Perhaps he knew I would only be with his club for a short time and purposely avoided having any disagreements with me. He immediately gave me opportunities to pitch, using me primarily as a starter. But none of that did anything to change my sour disposition. As expected, I reacted by drinking every day, trying to drown my miseries in alcohol, a perilous trend, which only made matters worse.

While I can't recall many of the details from that summer in Honolulu, I learned from the record books of baseball that I won nine games for the Islanders and lost only seven, which was not bad for a hard-drinking pitcher whose career, as well as his personal life, were simultaneously heading down the path to imminent ruin.

The surprise of the season occurred at the end of July, when I was recalled and told to rejoin the Angels, just as they were finishing up a long stint on the road. In spite of Haney's promise that he would bring me back to the parent club after just one month, three months had passed and the struggling Angels were fighting to hang onto seventh place, falling far short of their preseason expectations. But waiting three months to be recalled was not nearly as unexpected as the fact that he would bring me back at all. Moreover, the situation had not changed. Feelings toward me were the same as when I left, as I discovered the day I returned and was told to meet with Rigney in his office.

"Let's get one thing straight, three-three," he scowled, referring to my uniform number. "I didn't ask for you and I don't want you here." And you may as well find a comfortable seat in the corner of the bullpen and have fun, because I'm not going to pitch you!"

"That's alright with me!" I snapped. "You don't have to tell me to have fun. I'll do that on my own. You just make sure the paychecks keep coming and I'll be fine." He glared at me with disdain, took a puff from his cigarette and blew a column of smoke upward to the ceiling. His eyes burned with anger, his face was as hard as granite. I turned and walked out, slamming the door behind me, satisfied that I had spoken to him for the last time.

Making good on his threat, Rigney stuck me in the bullpen, practically ignoring me for the rest of the season. I was brought into one game for a mop-up job during the first week in August, in what would be my final appearance of the year. In the meantime, strange rumors began to surface around the league, rumors implying that I was suffering from a sore elbow. But it wasn't until mid-August, when the Washington Senators arrived in L.A. and I got a chance to talk with ex-Angel teammate, Ronnie Kline, during a pregame workout, that I was able to put it all together.

"How's your elbow doing?" he asked. "Is it getting any better, now that you aren't pitching?"

"What in the world are you talking about, Ronnie?" I chuckled. "There's nothing wrong with my elbow. Where did you hear that?"

"Well, you know how badly the Senators need good pitchers. "Gil Hodges has been trying to get you for our club, but he was told that you were dealing with a sore arm. Once Gil heard that, he dropped the whole idea."

"There's nothing wrong with my arm!" I fumed. "That's just another one of Rigney's lies!" I pounded my fist into the palm of my glove. I felt my pulse quicken with anger. "Well, that dirty son of a bitch!" I cursed. "Do you see what they're trying to do to me, Ronnie? They want to put me on waivers. They know good and well that no one will claim me, if everyone thinks I'm hurt. That way, after clearing waivers, the Angels will give me an unconditional release, and I'll be out of baseball!"

Appalled at what he had heard, Ronnie was speechless. He stared at the ground and rutted the dirt with the toe of his spikes. "What can you do, Eli?" he finally asked. "Those guys hold all the cards."

"I'll tell you what I going to do, Ronnie." I steamed. "I'm going to start throwing right now. You run over to your bench and tell Hodges to watch. I'll show everybody, once and for all that there's nothing wrong with my elbow!"

I grabbed a baseball from the bucket behind the pitcher's mound and yelled to Eddie Sadowski, our backup catcher, who agreed to warm me up on the grass, along the right field foul line. Starting with the first pitch, I began bombarding Eddie's mitt with a continuous stream of hard fastballs and sliders, sliders that broke the air with an audible hissing sound, just before popping into his glove. I was throwing as hard as ever, locating the ball perfectly. I glanced over at the Senators' dugout and saw Hodges standing on the top step, studying me and watching my every move.

Suddenly, out of nowhere, my pitching coach, Marv Grissom, came storming up to me, shouting as if like his pants were on fire. "Put that ball down, right now!" he ordered. "You're not supposed to be throwing!"

I squeezed the baseball firmly in my right hand and held it defiantly, only inches away from his face. "Why don't you try to stop me?" I challenged him. "Just try, and I'll knock you on your ass!" His eyes widened as he took a step back. My reaction was a lot more violent than he expected. Physically, he was a big man, my size, or even bigger, but it made no difference. I had been backed into corner with no way out. Emotionally, I was demoralized and teetering on the edge of despair. Yet, I was willing to fight for what little self-esteem I still had.

CHAPTER 29
"THERE'S NO INTEGRITY IN BASEBALL!"

When the 1963 season finally ended, I felt like a heavy weight had been lifted from my shoulders. It had been the most demoralizing year I had ever experienced. For the whole season, I worked in only 12 games with the Angels, all of them as a reliever, except for one ineffective start in Cleveland, where we fell behind early and I was lifted in the early innings. I had pitched regularly in Hawaii, which was good for keeping my control sharp and my arm in good shape. But like it would have been for any other pitcher, inactivity began to take a toll on me, both physically and mentally. I knew I would need to pitch in the offseason to stay in shape, otherwise I would be saying goodbye to baseball.

After returning home to Woodland Hills and spending a few days relaxing around our newly installed in-ground swimming pool, I got on the phone and began calling around to some of my contacts, asking about the possibilities of playing baseball over the winter. Physically, I needed the work. Financially, we needed the money, as Bonnie and I finally came to our senses and suddenly realized that we were up to our eyeballs in debt.

Luckily, I found an opening and arranged to play winter ball in Venezuela. I had enjoyed playing there in 1959 in the winter league which Luis Aparicio helped organize in his native country, and I welcomed the idea of going back. The league would last a couple of months and the salary was great. I also wanted to use the time to disprove the false rumors about my having a sore elbow and convince any scouts, who may be watching, that I was far from being washed up. And to make the job more pleasurable, Bonnie was able to take time off from her job and join me, for what would be her first chance to visit Venezuela and the city of Caracas.

I pitched very well and got myself back into top form. All the while, Bonnie and I enjoyed our time together. We toured the countryside, spent time on the beaches and visited many of the clubs and restaurants. It turned into a much-needed vacation, which helped take our minds off our exorbitant mortgage, our mounting debt and most of all, the Los Angeles Angels. It would be the best of times for us over the course of our otherwise stormy, unstable marriage. And like all good things, our time in Venezuela came to an end. However, in this case, the end of our good time came unexpected and much sooner than we could have ever anticipated.

By the fall of 1963, the democratic government of Venezuelan President Romulo Betancourt, was subjected to serious threats and violent attacks from the communist underground, backed by the new communist government of Cuba and Prime Minister Fidel Castro. Anti-American sentiment was quickly taking hold, prompting officials to advise all visitors and foreign nationals of the dangerous situation. Venezuela, and especially the city of Caracas, were close to a point of violent political upheaval.

It was Friday afternoon, November 22nd, Bonnie and I were relaxing in our hotel room. She had been flipping through the channels on the old-styled, black and white television set, when she stopped on what appeared to be a special news alert. A rattled Spanish-speaking reporter was clamoring nervously in a high-pitch voice. "What's going on?" I asked. "Whatever it is, it sure has this guy excited." Ignoring me, Bonnie sprung to her feet and stood in front of the TV and stared intently at the screen. She knew the native language a lot better than I did, so I waited quietly for a few seconds for her to make sense of the report.

"Oh, my dear God!" she gasped, covering her mouth with her hand. "President Kennedy has been assassinated! He died just minutes ago in a hospital in Dallas!" Tears filled her eyes as she turned to watch more of the broadcast. "This can't be happening!' she blurted. "It just can't be true!" She grabbed a handful of tissues from the box on the dresser and rushed into the bathroom. "Turn that off!" she pleaded. "I can't bear to hear any more."

It was only minutes later that our phone was ringing. It was the ballclub calling all American players on the roster, urging them to leave Venezuela as soon as possible. Rumors were already circulating that Castro's government was behind the horrible assassination and more trouble was expected. Suddenly, Caracas was no longer a vacation spot. It had suddenly turned into a political powder keg about to explode. It had become a very dangerous place for any Americans.

Soon after returning home, I received a contract from the Angels for the 1964 season and as expected, the offer was nothing short of insulting. The proposed annual salary of $7,000 represented a cut of more than 50% from the $16,500 I had earned the year before. The contempt they had for me had never been more obvious. Playing along in their silly game of cat and mouse was the only choice I had, but their motive was clear, they were determined to get rid of me.

Refusing to accept such a measly pittance, I mailed the unsigned contract back to the Angels and decided to wait for a more suitable offer to be made. The holiday season came and went and so did the months of January and February, and still no new contract arrived. In the meantime, the stress and worry continued to mount. "Don't let them off the hook so easily," I reminded myself. "These guys cannot be trusted." I could see that I was growing more stubborn and bitter as I continued to hold out. Nonetheless, I was determined to wait for as long as it would take.

In early March, I went as far as to report to spring training without a contract. I threw the ball well and proved to everyone that my arm was fine and I hadn't lost a step over the winter. After about two weeks in camp, I was offered another contract, this one for $12,500, an amount still well below my previous salary, but enough to coax me to agree. I signed reluctantly and still had the feeling that all was not settled. Even at this point, I wasn't aware of the trick the Angels were about to pull. However, it wouldn't take long before their underlying motive would be as clear as crystal.

As spring training went into its final weeks, I began to notice how little I had pitched since signing the new agreement. The same eerie silence which existed between myself and my manager and coaches the year before was back again and only time would tell where it would all lead.

Once again, I was called to Fred Haney's office, a sure sign that more trouble was on the way. Before stepping inside the room, I had decided I would not even speak to him unless he asked a question.

"You're now property of our triple-A club in Hawaii," he announced sternly, skipping over any pleasantries. "Your contract has been sold to the Islanders, and you're to go to their training camp in Indio immediately." The smirky look on his face told me he was very pleased with himself, having completed a job he started more than two years earlier. "When you arrive," he continued, "you are to report to their manager, Bob Lemon. Do you have any questions?"

I left the office without saying a word and headed straight to my locker and to begin packing. "My next stop has to be better," I told myself. I had just walked away from the coldest, most vindictive man I had ever met, so I wanted to believe that better days lay ahead.

Happy to get away from Haney, Rigney and the whole ugly situation, I pitched effectively for the Islanders. I had no trouble with first-year skipper, Bob Lemon, a former pitching great with the Cleveland Indians, who used me in several games before the end of the exhibition schedule. Being somewhat encouraged, I had good reasons to believe that I might begin the year as a member of Lemon's starting staff. So positive I was, that I phoned Bonnie, who had no interest at all in baseball, just to share my expectations.

"There are reasons to be hopeful," I tried to explain."Surely, there are major league clubs out there who need extra pitching, and the Pacific Coast League is a great league. There's no telling which teams will send scouts to watch me and what kind of offers they'll make!" Next, there was a long pause in our conversation.

"Just be careful," she responded. "I don't want to burst your bubble, but you should know better than trust anyone in this business. There's no integrity in baseball!" After hearing Bonnie's short bit of advice, there was another period of silence on the phone. I knew deep inside she was right. I only wish I had taken time to remind myself of an old proverb which says: "The only way to suffer deep disappointments is to have high expectations." Nonetheless, I felt like it had been a long time since I had caught a break and I was desperate for something positive to happen.

A day or two later we broke training camp in time to start the regular season. Regrettably, I remember this as the time I lost my last hopes of ever making it back to the major leagues. Over the next few years, there would be other situations with other clubs, but they would all be nothing more than low-salary, minor league offers for an over-the-hill, alcoholic pitcher who wanted to hang on for one more season.

After so many years in professional baseball, I should have learned two basic rules which come with the business: never get comfortable, and never take things for granted. Yet, in the spring of 1964 I dropped my guard and started believing I would have time enough with the Hawaii club to begin working my way back to the majors. But being in the unprincipled world of professional baseball, I should have suspected that something was up when almost two weeks of the regular season had passed and I had not yet been called to pitch my first game. The Islanders were hardly a dozen games into their 1964 schedule when they cut me from the team and gave me an outright release.

After having a successful spring training, getting released shattered my confidence and left me emotionally crushed, and for Bonnie and me, it was more than just another disappointing setback in my baseball career. Our irresponsible spending had landed us in heavy debt, and though I had no means of income, the stack of bills on our kitchen counter continued to grow higher and higher. We were on the brink of losing our cars, our house and everything else we owned. We were desperate for something to come along that would change the course of our lives, and we got it. Bonnie soon got word from her doctor that she was pregnant with our first, and our beautiful baby girl, Stacy, would be arriving soon! And in the midst of all of this, an assuring voice told me that all of us would be okay. But sadly, there was never a chance that I would be the sort of dedicated husband and father that my family needed me to be.

Thankfully, when we had reached a point where we didn't have another dollar left to spend, I received a call from the Washington Senators, a ballclub that had languished at the bottom of the American League since its inception, and was known for having one of the tightest operating budgets in all of baseball. They offered me a minor league contract to play for their AAA affiliate of the International League, the Toronto Maple Leafs. And while their proposal would pay me a salary of $1,500 per month to play in a city located some 3,500 miles from my home, it was the only offer I had received. I had no other choice, but to jump at the chance.

The Toronto club was under a working agreement with both the Washington Senators and the Milwaukee Braves, meaning it served as a farm team for both franchises. The team's owner was the legendary Jack Kent Cooke, a shrewd Canadian entrepreneur, who would later find fame as the owner of several successful sports franchises, such as the Los Angeles Lakers and Washington Redskins. And it was Cooke who hired George "Sparky" Anderson, a thirty-year-old ex-infielder to be the manager of the Maple Leafs in 1964.

After playing just one season in the major leagues for the Philadelphia Phillies, Anderson returned to the minors and played four consecutive years for Toronto before taking over as the team's manager. He had played professionally since the early 1950s and had, no doubt, acquired a strong background in baseball fundamentals and strategy. But this was his first managerial job at any level, and it was quickly evident that he had a lot to learn in the areas dealing with his players, respecting them as individuals and treating them as adults. Of course, Sparky would go on to become one of the most respected managers in baseball history, leading his clubs to three World Series titles, while carving out a long career which earned him a spot in the National Baseball Hall of Fame. However, this was back in the early days of his managerial career, when things didn't always run so smoothly, and in many cases, it was his own fault.

I became a part of a very talented team when I joined the Toronto Maple Leafs. The club was stocked with both position players and pitchers who were well on their way to the major leagues, as well as an assortment of veterans who were working their way back. Former Yankee, Jim Bronstad, and Ron Piche, who had put in several seasons with the Braves, were the leaders of the pitching corps. The team also had its share of longball hitters, including outfielders, Bobby Del Greco and Jim McKnight, and a jovial, left-hand hitting catcher from Illinois, Ken Retzer. And it was because of the exceptional level of skill and experience up and down the roster that the Maple Leafs managed to pull off a winning season, in spite of manager, Sparky Anderson who was continually breathing down the necks of his players, openly criticizing them and igniting volatile situations which would turn teammates against each another.

During all of this, I was carelessly allowing my off-the-field behavior to drop to new depths. I was on the run every night, usually with my drinking buddy, Jim Bronstad, whose hankering for alcohol was equal to mine, drinking, chasing women and cavorting all over town. Sadly, my moral values became nearly non-existent, which I have since learned is common characteristic of alcoholics seeking to escape commitments and responsibilities. I had sunk to a point where nothing seemed to matter, not even life itself.

How I did it, I'll never know. I somehow managed to win nine games for Toronto that season, while losing eight. I kept my earned run average around 2.50, and was awarded with a selection to the International League all-star team. Yet, after what I saw as a successful season, it was a stinging disappointment to get passed over for a promotion to the parent club when Bronstad was recalled by the Senators near the end of the year.

But for much of what happened in between, I can recall very little. So much of that period is lost from my memory and I place blame on no one but myself. The combination of alcohol and amphetamines had already taken hold of my mental state, clouding my thoughts and poisoning my spirit.

I can see now how the years of reckless abuse have taken many of my memories, ruined my career and cost me precious time with my family. I see how it turned me into a person I couldn't recognize and did not like. I wanted to believe I was strong, that I could solve my own problems and do whatever I wanted to do with my life. But while in the clutches of alcohol, I found I was totally helpless, and had no means of escape until I finally acknowledged the disease for what it was and sought professional help.

Because of alcoholism, I paid a tremendous price. And while it was never my intent or purpose, my friends and family members, who were never given a choice, were forced to suffer immeasurable pain and heartache. For this, I humbly and sincerely apologize to each of you, and ask for your forgiveness.

I know in my heart that I have already received God's forgiveness. For it is through His infinite power and boundless love that I am alive today, sharing my life story, so it may give hope to others who are facing some of the same traps and pitfalls I encountered, and that it may point out some of the warning signs that I failed to notice.

But if by my story, one person is redirected from the hopelessness of alcohol abuse to a recovery program, then my work is a success. For in addition to giving the reader a close-up and personal view of what professional baseball was really like in a bygone era, this cause is the primary purpose for writing this book. It will be my ongoing objective to wage war against alcohol abuse and inform others of its dangers. And just like in the old days, when any other opponent dared to step into the batter's box to face me, I'm sure to deliver my best pitch!

I am grateful to have made it back to professional baseball in 1982 as a minor league coach with the Milwaukee Brewers organization. It was even more rewarding to land a job working in the Angels' farm system. In 1984, I was a pitching coach in the AA Eastern League with the Waterbury Angels. (above)

80765345R00209

Made in the USA
Lexington, KY
07 February 2018